Ultimate T-SQL for SQL Server Professionals

Master Query Optimization, Advanced Programming, and Enterprise Database Solutions in Microsoft SQL Server

Alula Mekonnen Kassa

www.orangeava.com

First Published: April 2026

Published By: Orange Education Pvt Ltd, AVA®

Address: 9, Daryaganj, Delhi, 110002, India

275 New North Road Islington Suite 1314 London,
N1 7AA, United Kingdom

ISBN (PBK): 978-93-49887-89-3
ISBN (E-BOOK): 978-93-49887-05-3

www.orangeava.com

Get a Free eBook

We hope you're enjoying your recent book purchase! Your feedback is incredibly valuable to us and helps other readers discover books that truly make a difference.

If you found this book useful or enjoyable, we'd greatly appreciate it if you could leave a short review with a 5-star rating on Amazon. Your review supports our work and allows us to reach more learners worldwide.

As a thank-you, we're happy to offer you a **free digital copy of this book** plus a **30% discount code** for your next purchase on our official websites:

www.orangeava.com

www.orangeava.in (For the Indian Subcontinent).

☑**How it works:**

Leave your review on Amazon, take a screenshot of the confirmation or use the following link to submit the claim and email it to **info@orangeava.com.** Once received the required detail, we will send your rewards within 24 hours, **along with one month free subcription to the book on AVA SkillShelf!**

Claim Form
https://rebrand.ly/4d2477

Thank you for your support—it truly means a lot to us.

Enjoy 1 Month of Free Access to AVA SkillShelf!

The future belongs to lifelong learners. With AVA SkillShelf, you go beyond reading books and start building real, job-ready skills curated by industry experts.

Your membership unlocks **200+ learning products** covering AI, Cloud, Python, Cybersecurity, Data Science, DevOps, and more—all in one platform. Our bestselling technical books are transformed into structured courses designed for practical, real-world application.

Learn directly from experienced professionals and published authors, with no filler—just actionable insights. Earn **verified digital certifications** to strengthen your CV, LinkedIn profile, and professional credibility.

Learn anytime, anywhere, on any device, at your own pace. Ideal for students, professionals, career switchers, and tech leaders.

For full access to all current and future courses, choose our **Annual Membership**. Simply scan the QR to get started!

For 1 month Free access, simply refer to the steps on the previous page titled: Get a Free ebook!

https://www.avaskillshelf.com/

Downloading the code bundles and colored images

Please follow the links or scan the QR codes to download the
Code Bundles and Images of the book:

https://github.com/ava-orange-education/Ultimate-T-SQL-for-Modern-Database-Development

The code bundles and images of the book are also hosted on
https://rebrand.ly/129ldzr

In case there's an update to the code, it will be updated on the existing GitHub repository.

Errata

We take immense pride in our work at **Orange Education Pvt Ltd**, and follow best practices to ensure the accuracy of our content to provide an indulging reading experience to our subscribers. Our readers are our mirrors, and we use their inputs to reflect and improve upon human errors, if any, that may have occurred during the publishing processes involved. To let us maintain the quality and help us reach out to any readers who might be having difficulties due to any unforeseen errors, please write to us at :

errata@orangeava.com

Your support, suggestions, and feedback are highly appreciated.

Dedicated to

My Beloved Children, Saizana and Kirubel, Whose Love, Laughter, and Boundless Joy Inspire Every Dream I Pursue.

My Dear Parents, Mekonnen Kassa and Mihret Asgele, Whose Strength, Faith, and

Unconditional Love has Shaped the Person I am Today.

In the Loving Memory of My Beloved Sister, Zuryashwork Amare Kassa, Whose Courage, Graces, and Enduring Spirit Continues to Live on in Our Hearts. Her Selfless, Love, Kindness, and Light Remain with Me Always. This Book Stands as a Tribute to Her Life, Strength, and Her Everlasting Presence in My Soul.

To Eleni, Asefu, Amanuel, Mieraf, and Mahlet, for Your Constant Encouragement, Unwavering Support, and the Cherished Memories that Keep Me Grounded.

And to My Forever Best Friend, Meron Abera, Whose Kindness, Hope, and Unwavering Friendship Continue to Bring Light to My Journey.

In the Honor of My Children, the Memory of My Sister, and the Tigray Community in Colorado, I am Donating 100% of My Author Proceeds from This Book to St. Jude Children's Research Hospital, in the Hope of Bringing Comfort, Healing, and Hope to Children and Families in Need.

About the Author

Alula Mekonnen Kassa is an accomplished data and database professional, author, and technology enthusiast with extensive experience in healthcare, finance, airline, and aerospace industries. Based in Denver, Colorado, Alula has spent over a decade mastering SQL Server, T-SQL, and database management, helping organizations optimize their data workflows, and make informed business decisions.

Alula's professional journey reflects a passion for problem-solving, efficiency, and continuous learning. He has led and contributed to critical projects spanning database design, business intelligence, analytics, and automation, combining technical expertise with practical solutions for real-world challenges. His experience across multiple industries has provided him with a unique perspective on data management, performance optimization, and the application of T-SQL in diverse scenarios.

As an author, Alula is committed to sharing his knowledge with both aspiring and seasoned database professionals. This book embodies his practical approach to learning, blending theory with hands-on examples, advanced techniques, and real-world applications.

Besides his professional life, Alula is deeply engaged in community service, particularly supporting children and families. He is the president of Agazi Alumni, a non-profit organization that has been supporting schools and students in Tigray, Ethiopia, for more than 30 years. He is also a proud father, dedicating many of his efforts to creating a positive and supportive environment for his children.

About the Technical Reviewer

Bhushan Nikhar is a technology leader and enterprise architect with over 14 years of experience in software development and architecture. His experience and expertise spans over cloud-native systems, distributed computing, and emerging technologies. Bhushan's core skills lie in technical solution, and enterprise architecture—applied across AWS, Azure, and Google Cloud platforms.

He has designed and led large-scale systems in banking and financial services, healthcare, retail, and e-commerce, with a particular focus on scalable data platforms and intelligent automation. Bhushan has also delivered impactful AI/ML solutions, and currently contributes as an Enterprise Architect for a leading U.S. Bank's credit card business, while mentoring internal teams in AI and cloud transformation.

As a recognized reviewer for industry publications, Bhushan has reviewed multiple technical books, reflecting his commitment to advancing the global developer and architecture community. He is deeply passionate about cultivating deep technical expertise within teams, and envisions India emerging as a hub for next-generation deep tech innovation.

Acknowledgments

There are several people I wish to thank for their ongoing support and encouragement during the writing of this book. First and foremost, I want to express my deepest gratitude to my beloved children, Saizana and Kirubel, whose curiosity, laughter, and love inspire me every day. Their presence has been a constant source of motivation throughout this journey.

I am profoundly thankful to my parents, Mekonnen Kassa and Mihret Asgele, for their unwavering support, guidance, and encouragement. I could not have completed this book without their inspiration and belief in me.

I am especially grateful to my friend and confidant, Meron Abera, for her unconditional support, encouragement, and for always being a source of wisdom and positivity.

I also wish to acknowledge my professional mentors, colleagues, and the various resources that allowed me to develop the knowledge and skills necessary to write this book. Their guidance and expertise have been invaluable in shaping the content, and ensuring its quality.

Finally, I extend my heartfelt gratitude to the broader Tigray community, and everyone who has supported me along the way, providing motivation, feedback, and encouragement. "This book is as much a reflection of your support as it is of my efforts."

Preface

The book, *Ultimate T-SQL for SQL Server Professionals*, is your comprehensive guide to mastering T-SQL and SQL Server for real-world data challenges. So, whether you are a professional, student, or database enthusiast, this book provides a practical, example-driven approach to querying, managing, and optimizing data in SQL Server.

From foundational concepts to advanced techniques, Ultimate T-SQL empowers readers to write efficient queries, automate tasks, and develop robust database solutions. Each chapter builds logically on the previous one, ensuring that you gain confidence, while applying T-SQL skills in real scenarios across industries such as healthcare, finance, and technology.

Why This Book is Different:

- Real-world examples and exercises for hands-on learning.
- Step-by-step guidance from basic queries to advanced topics.
- Covers T-SQL in a professional, practical, and industry-ready context.
- Provides insights on the best practices, optimization, and troubleshooting.

Chapter Highlights:

- **Chapter 1 – Getting Started with T-SQL:**

  Get introduced to the SQL Server ecosystem, core database objects, and the fundamentals of writing SELECT statements. This chapter lays the groundwork for understanding how T-SQL interacts with relational data.

- **Chapter 2 – Data Types, NULLs, and Conversions:**

  Learn how SQL Server stores data, and how to choose the correct data types for accuracy and performance. This chapter explains NULL handling and type conversions to prevent logic errors and data inconsistencies.

- **Chapter 3 – SELECT Statements and Filtering Logic:**

  Master data retrieval using filtering, sorting, conditional logic, and query execution order.

  This chapter focuses on writing precise, readable SELECT queries that reflect real-world business rules.

- **Chapter 4 – Joins, Set Operations, and Subqueries:**

  Understand how to combine data across multiple tables using joins, unions, and subqueries. This chapter teaches you how to model relationships and solve complex data problems efficiently.

- **Chapter 5 – Views, Functions, and Stored Procedures:**

  Encapsulate logic into reusable database objects for cleaner code and better maintainability. This chapter covers how to design, manage, and optimize programmable database objects.

- **Chapter 6 – CTEs, MERGE, Pivoting, JSON, and XML:**

  Explore advanced querying techniques for transforming and reshaping data. This chapter demonstrates how SQL Server handles hierarchical data and modern data formats.

- **Chapter 7 – Dynamic SQL, Triggers, and Table-Valued Functions (TVFs):**

  Implement flexible and automated database logic using dynamic SQL and event-driven programming. This chapter highlights performance considerations and best practices for advanced database automation.

- **Chapter 8 – Query Optimization and Performance Tuning:**

  Learn how SQL Server executes queries, and identify performance bottlenecks using indexing strategies, statistics, and query rewrites. This chapter focuses on writing efficient T-SQL that scales well under real-world workloads.

- **Chapter 9 – Execution Plans and Query Store:**

  Understand how to read and interpret execution plans to diagnose slow queries and resource-intensive operations. Explore Query Store to track performance changes, compare plans, and stabilize query behavior over time.

- **Chapter 10 – Transactions, Concurrency, and Isolation Levels:**

  Master transaction control and concurrency management to maintain data consistency in multi-user environments. This chapter explains isolation levels, locking, blocking, and deadlocks with practical examples.

- **Chapter 11 – Automation with SSIS, SQL Agent, and PowerShell:**

  Automate database workflows using SQL Server Integration Services, SQL Server Agent jobs, and PowerShell scripting. Learn how to schedule, monitor, and maintain repeatable database operations efficiently.

- **Chapter 12 – Azure SQL and Synapse Integration:**

  Discover how T-SQL extends into the cloud with Azure SQL Database and Azure Synapse Analytics. This chapter covers cloud readiness, performance considerations, and hybrid integration scenarios.

- **Chapter 13 – Security, Permissions, and Auditing**

  Protect the sensitive data using SQL Server security features such as roles, permissions, and encryption. Also, learn how to implement auditing and access controls that align with enterprise and compliance requirements.

- **Chapter 14 – Unit Testing T-SQL with tSQLt:**

  Introduce test-driven development principles to the database layer using the tSQLt framework. This chapter demonstrates how to validate logic, prevent regressions, and improve code reliability.

- **Chapter 15 – Case Studies and the Future of T-SQL:**

  Apply T-SQL concepts through real-world case studies that reflect common enterprise challenges. Explore the emerging features and evolving best practices shaping the future of T-SQL development.

- **Chapter 16 – Best Practices for T-SQL Development and Database Design:**

  Consolidate the proven patterns for writing clean, maintainable, and high-performance T-SQL codes. In fact, this chapter provides practical guidelines for schema design, coding standards, and long-term maintainability.

Thus, this book equips you with the knowledge and confidence to tackle SQL Server challenges effectively, helping you to become a proficient, industry-ready T-SQL professional!

DID YOU KNOW

Did you know that Orange Education Pvt Ltd offers eBook versions of every book published, with PDF and ePub files available? You can upgrade to the eBook version at **www.orangeava.com** and as a print book customer, you are entitled to a discount on the eBook copy. Get in touch with us at: **info@orangeava.com** for more details.

At **www.orangeava.com**, you can also read a collection of free technical articles, sign up for a range of free newsletters, and receive exclusive discounts and offers on Print Books and eBooks.

PIRACY

If you come across any illegal copies of our works in any form on the internet, we would be grateful if you would provide us with the location address or website name. Please contact us at **info@orangeava.com** with a link to the material.

ARE YOU INTERESTED IN AUTHORING WITH US?

If there is a topic that you have expertise in, and you are interested in either writing or contributing to a book, please write to us at **business@orangeava.com**. We are on a journey to help developers and tech professionals to gain insights on the present technological advancements and innovations happening across the globe and build a community that believes Knowledge is best acquired by sharing and learning with others. Please reach out to us to learn what our audience demands and how you can be part of this educational reform. We also welcome ideas from tech experts and help them build learning and development content for their domains.

REVIEWS

Please leave a review. Once you have read and used this book, why not leave a review on the site that you purchased it from? Potential readers can then see and use your unbiased opinion to make purchase decisions. We at Orange Education would love to know what you think about our products, and our authors can learn from your feedback. Thank you!

For more information about Orange Education, please visit **www.orangeava.com**.

Table of Contents

CHAPTER 1
Getting Started with T-SQL

Introduction

Welcome to the world of T-SQL, which is the powerful extension of SQL designed to unlock the full potential of Microsoft SQL Server. Whether you are new to database programming, or are transitioning from other SQL dialects, this chapter will provide you with a solid foundation to begin writing efficient, clear, and maintainable T-SQL code.

We will start by exploring the fundamental concepts, syntax rules, and execution flow that form the backbone of T-SQL programming. You will learn how to write basic queries, understand batch processing, and discover the best practices that will prepare you for more advanced topics. Hence, by the end of this chapter, you will have the confidence and tools necessary to interact with SQL Server effectively, and build a strong base for mastering data manipulation and retrieval.

Transact-SQL (T-SQL) is Microsoft's proprietary extension of SQL, designed specifically for SQL Server and Azure SQL Database. While ANSI SQL provides the foundational language for interacting with relational databases, T-SQL adds programming capabilities such as variables, loops, conditionals, error handling, and system functions.

Why T-SQL is Critical

T-SQL is not merely a query language in real-world enterprise environments; it serves as the backbone of critical operations across multiple domains. It powers reporting and analytics by enabling efficient data extraction for dashboards, business intelligence tools, and ad-hoc reporting. It also supports transactional systems by managing everyday operations such as inserts, updates, and deletes within business applications. In addition, T-SQL plays a key role in database automation through scheduled jobs, triggers, and stored procedures, and it is essential for data migration and ETL processes by facilitating the movement and transformation of data between systems. By mastering T-SQL, you gain the ability to work closer to the data layer while ensuring strong performance, maintaining data integrity, and enforcing business rules effectively at scale.

Hence, by the end of this chapter, you will be able to write clean queries, manipulate data confidently, and adopt best practices that can scale into professional database development.

Structure

In this chapter, we will cover the following topics:

- Setting up Your Environment
- T-SQL vs. ANSI SQL

- Batch Processing and the GO Command
- Data Definition Language (DDL)
- CRUD Operations
- Variables, Expressions and Operator Precedence
- Writing Clean, Maintainable, and Well-Documented T-SQL Code
- Debugging and Best Practices

Setting up Your Environment

Before writing T-SQL, you need to install and configure SQL Server and its tools.

Apart from SSMS, users may prefer alternative SQL clients such as Azure Data Studio, DBeaver, or SQLCMD for running scripts. These tools provide similar functionalities like query execution, viewing tables, and debugging, which eventually gives us flexibility to choose a preferred interface.

Installing the SQL Server

Microsoft offers several editions such as:

- **Express Edition (Free)**: Ideal for learning and small apps
- **Developer Edition (Free)**: Full feature set for development only
- **Standard/Enterprise Edition**: Offers production-level licenses

Installing SQL Server Management Studio (SSMS)

SSMS is the GUI for managing SQL Server, and performs the following functions:

- It writes and executes T-SQL scripts.
- It helps us view tables, indexes, and query plans.
- It helps us administer security and backups.

Exercise 1.1: Connecting to SQL Server

1. Open SSMS.
2. Choose "`Database Engine`" as the server type.
3. Enter the server name (for example, localhost for local installations).
4. Click on '`Connect`'.

☑ Once you have connected, expand the Databases node to explore system and user databases.

T-SQL vs. ANSI SQL

T-SQL and ANSI SQL both serve as languages for managing and querying relational databases, but they differ in scope and functionality. ANSI SQL is a standardized language defined by the American National Standards Institute, designed to provide a consistent way to interact with relational databases across different systems. It focuses on core operations such as SELECT, INSERT, UPDATE, DELETE, and basic schema definitions, ensuring portability between database platforms. In contrast, T-SQL (Transact-SQL), used primarily in Microsoft SQL Server, extends ANSI SQL by adding powerful procedural programming features such as variables, control-of-flow statements (IF, WHILE), error handling, and advanced functions. It also includes enhancements for performance tuning, transaction control, and system-level operations. As a result, while ANSI SQL emphasizes portability and standardization, T-SQL provides greater flexibility and control, making it more suitable for complex, enterprise-level database solutions.

Now, as we have understood the differences between ANSI SQL and T-SQL, let us see how batch processing works, and how the GO command affects execution.

For beginners, understanding the difference between T-SQL and standard SQL can be confusing. In short, ANSI SQL provides the basic language for querying relational databases, while T-SQL adds procedural programming, system functions, batch processing, and advanced error handling to enable more powerful and flexible database operations.

With this foundational understanding of T-SQL and SQL, let us explore batch processing and how the GO command affects execution.

```
-- Single-line comment
/*
   Multi-line comment
   Demonstrating basic T-SQL structure
*/

USE tempdb;
GO

SELECT
    name,
    database_id
FROM sys.databases;
GO
```

Figure 1.1: *Basic T-SQL Script Structure, Comments, and Batch Separation Using GO*

ANSI SQL: The Foundation

ANSI SQL defines the following:

- Data Query Operations (**SELECT**)
- Data Modification (**INSERT**, **UPDATE**, **DELETE**)
- Schema Definition (**CREATE**, **ALTER**, **DROP**)

Example ANSI SQL query:

```
SELECT customer_name
FROM customers
WHERE customer_id = 101;
```

T-SQL Extensions

T-SQL adds:

1. **Procedural Programming**:

```
DECLARE @Counter INT = 1;
WHILE @Counter <= 5
BEGIN
  PRINT 'Count: ' + CAST(@Counter AS VARCHAR);
  SET @Counter += 1;
END;
```

2. **System Functions**: `GETDATE()`, `ISNULL()`, `SCOPE_IDENTITY()`
3. **Batch Processing**: The `GO` keyword to segment scripts
4. **Error Handling**: `TRY...CATCH` blocks for runtime errors

Comparison Table

Feature	ANSI SQL	T-SQL (SQL Server)
Portability	High	SQL Server only
Variables	✗	☑
Loops and Conditionals	✗	☑
Functions (Date, and so on)	Limited	Extensive built-ins
Proprietary Keywords	✗	`TOP`, `OUTPUT`, `MERGE`

Table 1.1: *Comparison of ANSI SQL and T-SQL (SQL Server)*

Exercise 1.2: ANSI vs. T-SQL

1. Write an ANSI SQL query to select top 10 customers.
2. Rewrite it in T-SQL using TOP, in the following way:

```
SELECT TOP 10 customer_name FROM customers;
```

Batch Processing and the GO Command

A batch is a group of one or more T-SQL statements that are sent to SQL Server as a single unit.

With batch processing understood, we can now explorc how Data Definition Language (DDL) commands help structure your database objects.

With batch processing understood, we can now explore how Data Definition Language (DDL) commands help structure your database objects. The following example demonstrates how batches are used to create a table, insert data, and then retrieve that data step by step. In this example, a table named TestBatch is created using the CREATE TABLE statement, followed by separate execution batches defined by the GO command. A value is then inserted into the table using an INSERT statement, and finally, the data is retrieved with a SELECT query. Each GO keyword signals the end of a batch, ensuring that each set of commands is compiled and executed independently within SQL Server.

```
CREATE TABLE TestBatch (ID INT);
GO
INSERT INTO TestBatch (ID) VALUES (1);
GO
SELECT * FROM TestBatch;
```

Each GO signals SSMS to send a new batch. Without it, SQL Server might show dependency errors.

Variable Scope across Batches

Variables reset between batches looks like:

```
DECLARE @Test INT = 10;
GO
PRINT @Test; -- Error: Must declare the scalar variable "@Test"
```

Exercise 1.3: Batch Experimentation

1. Declare a variable @Name in one batch, and try using it after a GO.
2. Observe the scope error.
3. Fix it by removing GO.

[Diagram Placeholder: SQL Script → Parser → Execution Engine → Batch Execution]

Data Definition Language (DDL)

Data Definition Language (DDL) is a subset of SQL commands used to define, modify, and manage the structure of database objects such as tables, schemas, indexes, and constraints. Unlike DML (Data Manipulation Language), which deals with data itself, DDL focuses on how the data is stored by creating, or modifying database objects.

DDL commands automatically commit changes, meaning once executed, they are permanent, and thus cannot be rolled back (except in some database systems with transactional DDL support).

Now that you have hands-on experience with creating, altering, truncating, and renaming tables, let us move on to CRUD operations to manipulate data within those tables.

Key DDL Commands:

The primary DDL commands are:

- **`CREATE`**: Define new database objects.
- **`ALTER`**: Modify existing structures.
- **`DROP`**: Remove database objects permanently.
- **`TRUNCATE`**: Delete all data from a table while retaining its structure.
- **`RENAME`**: Change the name of existing objects.

CREATE

The **`CREATE`** command is used to create database objects such as tables, views, indexes, or schemas.

Syntax:

```
CREATE TABLE TableName (
        Column1 DataType Constraints,
        Column2 DataType Constraints,
        ...
);
```

Example of Creating a Table:

```
CREATE TABLE Employees (
        EmployeeID INT PRIMARY KEY,
        FirstName NVARCHAR(50),
        LastName NVARCHAR(50),
        HireDate DATE NOT NULL,
        Salary DECIMAL(10,2) DEFAULT 50000.00
);
```

Explanation:

- **`EmployeeID INT PRIMARY KEY`**: It is a unique identifier for each employee.
- **`FirstName`**, **`LastName NVARCHAR(50)`**: It supports variable-length strings up to 50 characters.

- **HireDate DATE NOT NULL**: It notifies the mandatory date of hire.
- **Salary DECIMAL(10,2)**: It stores monetary values (10 digits, 2 decimal places) with a default of 50,000.00.

Other **CREATE** Examples:

- **CREATE DATABASE**: Define a new database.
- **CREATE INDEX**: Improve query performance by indexing columns.
- **CREATE VIEW**: Save complex queries as virtual tables.

ALTER

The **ALTER** command modifies the structure of an existing table or object, without needing you to drop it.

Common **ALTER** Operations are:

1. **Add a Column.**

   ```
   ALTER TABLE Employees ADD Email NVARCHAR(100);
   ```

   - This adds a new Email column to the Employees table.

2. **Modify a Column.**

   ```
   ALTER TABLE Employees ALTER COLUMN Salary DECIMAL(12,2);
   ```

   - It changes the Salary column from **DECIMAL(10,2)** to **DECIMAL(12,2)** to store larger salary values.

3. **Drop a Column.**

   ```
   ALTER TABLE Employees DROP COLUMN Email;
   ```

   - It removes a column from the table.

4. **Add Constraints.**

   ```
   ALTER TABLE Employees ADD CONSTRAINT UQ_Email UNIQUE (Email);
   ```

   - It adds a unique constraint on the Email column.

Thus, the best practice is to verify structural changes in a development environment before altering production tables.

DROP

The **DROP** command permanently removes a database object. Once dropped, the object and its data are lost.

Syntax:

```
DROP TABLE TableName;
```

Example:

```
DROP TABLE Employees;
```

This removes the Employees table entirely, including its structure, data, indexes, and constraints.

Other DROP Examples:

·`DROP DATABASE HRDB;` → Deletes the entire database

·`DROP INDEX idx_salary;` → Removes an index

⚠ However, you must be careful and always backup or verify dependencies before using DROP.

TRUNCATE

TRUNCATE quickly removes all rows from a table, and retains its structure for future use.

Syntax:

```
TRUNCATE TABLE TableName;
```

Example:

```
TRUNCATE TABLE Employees;
```

- All data in the Employees table is deleted, but the table structure (columns, constraints) remains.
- It is faster than **DELETE** because it does not log individual row deletions.

Key Differences from **DELETE**:

- **DELETE** logs each row deletion, while **TRUNCATE** does not.
- **TRUNCATE** cannot be used if a table is referenced by a foreign key constraint.

RENAME

The **RENAME** operation changes the name of a database object.

SQL Server Syntax (Using Stored Procedure):

```
EXEC sp_rename 'Employees', 'Staff';
```

This renames the Employees table to Staff.

Other Examples:

- Renaming a column:
  ```
  EXEC sp_rename 'Staff.Salary', 'BaseSalary', 'COLUMN';
  ```
- Renaming indexes or constraints similarly uses sp_rename.

DDL Command Properties

- **Auto-Commit**: Once they are executed, the changes are permanent.
- **Affect Structure, and Not Data**: Unlike DML, DDL commands modify schema-level definitions.
- **Dependency Impact**: Dropping or renaming tables may break dependent views, stored procedures, or foreign keys.
- **Security Control**: DDL operations require higher privileges (for example, **ALTER**, **DROP** permissions).

Exercise 1.4: Build a Schema.

1. Create Departments and Employees tables with foreign keys.
   ```
   CREATE TABLE Departments (
     DeptID INT PRIMARY KEY,
     DeptName NVARCHAR(100) NOT NULL
   );

   CREATE TABLE Employees (
     EmployeeID INT PRIMARY KEY,
     FirstName NVARCHAR(50),
     LastName NVARCHAR(50),
     HireDate DATE NOT NULL,
     Salary DECIMAL(10,2),
   ```

```
    DeptID INT,
    CONSTRAINT FK_Employees_Departments FOREIGN KEY (DeptID)
            REFERENCES Departments (DeptID)
);
```

2. **Add an Email Column to the Employees table**.

   ```
   ALTER TABLE Employees ADD Email NVARCHAR(100);
   ```

3. **Truncate all the Employees**.

   ```
   TRUNCATE TABLE Employees;
   ```

4. Rename Employees to Staff.

   ```
   EXEC sp_rename 'Employees', 'Staff';
   ```

Key Takeaways:

- DDL commands manage database structure (tables, constraints, schemas).
- **CREATE** defines new objects, while **ALTER** modifies existing ones.
- **DROP** and **TRUNCATE** remove data/objects but differ in scope.
- **RENAME** updates object names without losing data.
- DDL commands are auto-committed; therefore, you should test them in staging before production use.

CRUD Operations

CRUD stands for Create, Read, Update, and Delete, and represents the four basic operations used to manage data in a database. These operations form the foundation of interacting with relational databases using SQL. Create refers to inserting new records into a table, typically using the INSERT statement. Read involves retrieving data from the database using SELECT queries. Update is used to modify existing records with the UPDATE statement, allowing changes to specific columns based on defined conditions. Delete removes records from a table using the DELETE statement, either selectively with conditions or entirely when needed.

Now, as we have learned about each CRUD operation individually, let us see how they come together in a combined workflow to efficiently maintain data.

CREATE (INSERT)

The CREATE operation is performed using the INSERT statement. It adds new records to a table. Each record inserted must match the table's structure, and also respect data types and constraints (for example, primary keys, **NOT NULL**, unique constraints).

Syntax:

```
INSERT INTO TableName (Column1, Column2, ..., ColumnN)
VALUES (Value1, Value2, ..., ValueN);
```

- **TableName**: The table where the data will be inserted
- **Columns**: List of columns receiving data
- **Values**: The values to insert, matching the column order

Example:

```
INSERT INTO Employees (EmployeeID, FirstName, LastName, HireDate, Salary)
VALUES (101, 'Alice', 'Johnson', '2022-05-01', 70000);
```

Here, we will add a new employee record with details like ID, name, hire date, and salary.

Best Practices for `INSERT`:

- Always specify the column names to avoid dependency on column order.
- Validate data types to prevent insertion errors.
- Use transactions for bulk inserts to ensure atomicity.

READ (SELECT)

The **`READ`** operation retrieves data using the **`SELECT`** statement. It allows you to filter, sort, join tables, and project specific columns.

Syntax:

```
SELECT Column1, Column2, ...
FROM TableName
[WHERE condition]
[ORDER BY column ASC|DESC];
```

- **`WHERE`** filters records based on conditions.
- **`ORDER BY`** sorts results in ascending (ASC) or descending (DESC) order.

Example:

```
SELECT FirstName, LastName
FROM Employees
WHERE HireDate > '2020-01-01'
ORDER BY Salary DESC;
```

This query retrieves employees hired after January 1, 2020, while displaying their first and last names sorted by salary in descending order.

Advanced **`SELECT`**:

- Aggregations: **`COUNT`**, **`AVG`**, **`SUM`**, **`MIN`**, **`MAX`**
- Joins: They combine data from multiple tables.
- Aliases: They are used to rename columns or tables for readability.

UPDATE

The **`UPDATE`** operation modifies existing records in a table. It uses **`SET`** to change column values, and **`WHERE`** to limit the records that are updated.

Syntax:

```
UPDATE TableName
SET Column1 = Value1, Column2 = Value2
WHERE condition;
```

- Always include a **`WHERE`** clause to avoid updating all rows unintentionally.

Example:

```
UPDATE Employees
SET Salary = Salary * 1.05
WHERE HireDate < '2020-01-01';
```

This increases the salary by 5% for employees hired before January 1, 2020.

Best Practices for UPDATE:

- Test the condition with a **SELECT** first to confirm affected rows.
- Use transactions for critical updates.
- Backup data before mass updates.

DELETE

The **DELETE** operation removes records from a table.

Syntax:

```
DELETE FROM TableName
WHERE condition;
```

- Without **WHERE**, all records are deleted, but the table structure remains intact.

Example:

```
DELETE FROM Employees
WHERE EmployeeID = 101;
```

This removes the employee with ID 101.

Safe **DELETE** Practices:

- Always confirm the condition with **SELECT**.
- Use transactions to allow rollbacks.
- For archiving, consider marking records inactive, instead of deleting them.

CRUD in Action (Combined Workflow)

Now that CRUD operations are clear, we will explore variables, expressions, and operator precedence, which are essential for creating dynamic and flexible T-SQL scripts.

A typical database workflow involves:

1. **INSERT** new data (for example, new hires).
2. **SELECT** data for viewing or reporting.
3. **UPDATE** records when information changes (for example, salary raise).
4. **DELETE** obsolete or incorrect data.

These operations ensure data integrity and consistent access for business processes.

```
DECLARE @BaseSalary INT = 50000;
DECLARE @Bonus INT = 5000;
DECLARE @TaxRate DECIMAL(5,2) = 0.20;

SELECT
    @BaseSalary + @Bonus AS GrossPay,
    (@BaseSalary + @Bonus) * (1 - @TaxRate) AS NetPay;
```

***Figure 1.2**: Variables, Expressions, and Operator Precedence in T-SQL*

Exercise 1.5: CRUD Hands-On

Practice CRUD with the following exercises:

1. **Insert 5 Employees.**

```
INSERT INTO Employees (EmployeeID, FirstName, LastName, HireDate, Salary)
VALUES
(102, 'Bob', 'Smith', '2023-02-10', 65000),
(103, 'Clara', 'Lopez', '2024-04-15', 72000),
(104, 'David', 'Kim', '2021-11-20', 80000),
(105, 'Eva', 'Brown', '2022-09-05', 69000),
(106, 'Frank', 'Wright', '2024-01-18', 71000);
```

2. **Select Employees Hired in the Last Year.**

```
SELECT EmployeeID, FirstName, LastName, HireDate
FROM Employees
WHERE HireDate >= DATEADD(YEAR, -1, GETDATE());
```

3. **Update Salaries for Long-Term Employees.**

```
UPDATE Employees
SET Salary = Salary * 1.10
WHERE HireDate < '2020-01-01';
```

4. **Delete an Employee Record Safely.**

```
-- Verify before deleting.
SELECT * FROM Employees WHERE EmployeeID = 106;
 -- Delete if it is correct.
DELETE FROM Employees WHERE EmployeeID = 106;
```

Key Takeaways

- CRUD is fundamental for database interaction.
- Always use **WHERE** in **UPDATE** and **DELETE** to prevent unintentional changes.
- Combine CRUD with transactions and constraints for data safety.
- Practice CRUD queries regularly to build proficiency.

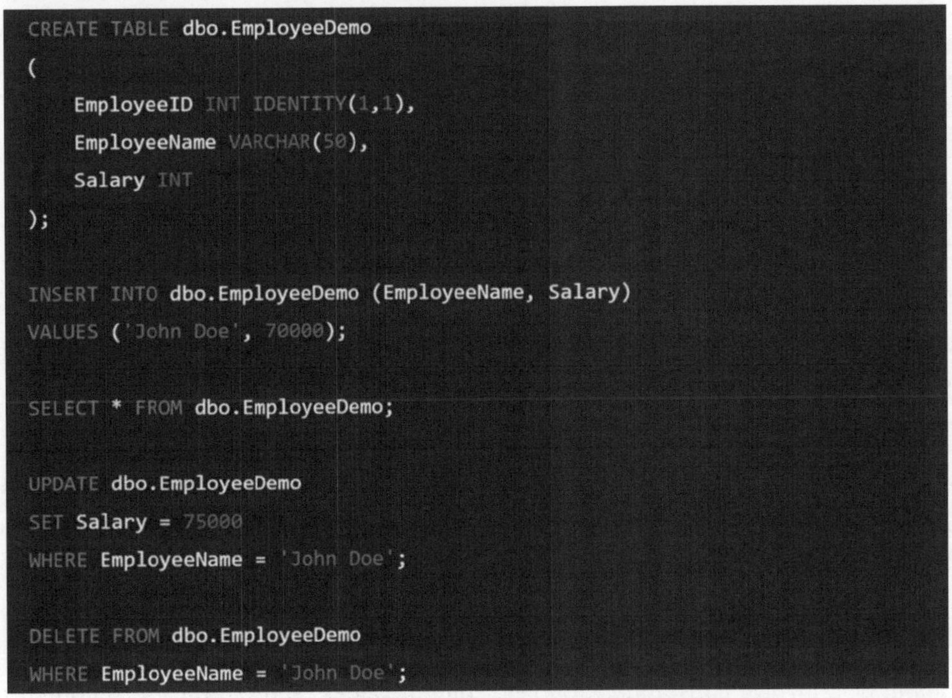

```
CREATE TABLE dbo.EmployeeDemo
(
    EmployeeID INT IDENTITY(1,1),
    EmployeeName VARCHAR(50),
    Salary INT
);

INSERT INTO dbo.EmployeeDemo (EmployeeName, Salary)
VALUES ('John Doe', 70000);

SELECT * FROM dbo.EmployeeDemo;

UPDATE dbo.EmployeeDemo
SET Salary = 75000
WHERE EmployeeName = 'John Doe';

DELETE FROM dbo.EmployeeDemo
WHERE EmployeeName = 'John Doe';
```

Figure 1.3: *Example of CRUD Operations Executed in T-SQL*

Variables, Expressions and Operator Precedence

In T-SQL, variables and expressions are fundamental for controlling logic, storing temporary data, and performing calculations within scripts or stored procedures. Therefore, operator precedence determines how complex expressions are evaluated in SQL.

Hence, with a solid understanding of variables and expressions, we can now focus on writing clean, maintainable T-SQL that your team can understand and work with efficiently.

Declaring Variables

Variables in T-SQL are used to store temporary data during the execution of queries, batches, or stored procedures. They help make SQL scripts dynamic and reusable.

Syntax:

```
DECLARE @VariableName DataType [= InitialValue];
```

- **`DECLARE`** initializes a variable.
- **`@`** prefix denotes a variable.
- Optionally, you can assign a value during declaration.

Example:

```
DECLARE @Today DATE = GETDATE();
PRINT @Today;
```

- Here, **`@Today`** stores the current date retrieved by **`GETDATE()`**.
- The **`PRINT`** statement outputs its value.

Assigning Values: Variables can be assigned values using **`SET`** or **`SELECT`**.

Using **`SET`**:

```
DECLARE @Name NVARCHAR(50);
SET @Name = 'Alice';
PRINT @Name;
```

Using `SELECT`:

```
DECLARE @Salary DECIMAL(10,2);
SELECT @Salary = Salary FROM Employees WHERE EmployeeID = 101;
PRINT @Salary;
```

- **`SET`** assigns a single value explicitly.
- **`SELECT`** can retrieve and assign directly from a query (this applies if multiple rows return, and only the last row value is stored).

Scope of Variables:

- **Local Variables**: They exist only within the batch, procedure, or function where defined.
- **Global Variables**: They are prefixed with @@ and predefined by the SQL Server (for example, **`@@VERSION`**, **`@@ROWCOUNT`**).

Arithmetic and Logical Expressions

Expressions in SQL involve constants, variables, column values, and operators to compute results. They are of two types, which are discussed as follows:

Arithmetic Expressions

Arithmetic operators perform mathematical operations.

Operator	Description	Example	Result
+	Addition	SELECT 10 + 5;	15
-	Subtraction	SELECT 10 - 3;	7
*	Multiplication	SELECT 6 * 4;	24
/	Division	SELECT 20 / 4;	5
%	Modulus (Remainder)	SELECT 22 % 5;	2

Table 1.2: *Common Arithmetic Operators in T-SQL*

Example:

```
SELECT (100 + 20) * 0.1 AS Bonus;
```

- First (100 + 20) is evaluated, and is then multiplied by 0.1.

Logical Expressions

Logical operators control filtering and conditions.

Operator	Description	Example
AND	It is true, if both conditions are true.	`WHERE Salary > 50000 AND DeptID=2`
OR	It is true, if any condition is true.	`WHERE DeptID=2 OR DeptID=3`
NOT	It reverses the condition itself.	`WHERE NOT DeptID=2`

Table 1.3: *Logical Operators in T-SQL*

Operator Precedence

SQL evaluates expressions based on operator precedence. Operators with higher precedence execute first.

Order of Precedence:

1. Parentheses `()`: Highest priority
2. Arithmetic Operators: Multiplication/division before addition/subtraction.
3. Comparison Operators (for example, =, <, >)
4. Logical Operators: **`NOT`** before **`AND`**, and before **`OR`**.

Example: Operator Precedence

```
SELECT 10 + 5 * 2 AS Result;
Result = 20
```

(Multiplication executes before addition → 10 + (5 * 2))

To override precedence:

```
SELECT (10 + 5) * 2 AS Result;
Result = 30
```

(Parentheses force addition first.)

Logical Precedence (**AND** vs. **OR**):

AND is evaluated before OR.

Example:

```
SELECT * FROM Employees
WHERE DeptID = 2 OR DeptID = 3 AND Salary > 60000;
```

- Here, **AND** is evaluated first:

  ```
  DeptID = 2 OR (DeptID = 3 AND Salary > 60000)
  ```

- To change order:

  ```
  SELECT * FROM Employees
  WHERE (DeptID = 2 OR DeptID = 3) AND Salary > 60000;
  ```

Practical Usage in Queries

Variables and expressions are often combined for dynamic filtering:

```
DECLARE @MinSalary DECIMAL(10,2) = 60000;
SELECT FirstName, Salary
FROM Employees
WHERE Salary > @MinSalary AND DeptID = 2;
```

Common Use Cases

- Storing dynamic parameters in stored procedures
- Performing calculations (for example, bonuses, tax deductions)
- Building conditional logic with **IF...ELSE** using variables
- Testing precedence in complex WHERE clauses

Exercise 1.6: Precedence Testing

1. **Test AND vs. OR Precedence**

   ```
   -- Query 1: Without Parentheses
   SELECT * FROM Employees
   WHERE DeptID = 2 OR DeptID = 3 AND Salary > 60000;

   -- Query 2: With Parentheses (Altered Logic)
   SELECT * FROM Employees
   WHERE (DeptID = 2 OR DeptID = 3) AND Salary > 60000;
   ```

   Now, you can compare how the results differ.

2. **Variable Assignment with Arithmetic**

   ```
   DECLARE @BaseSalary DECIMAL(10,2) = 50000;
   DECLARE @BonusRate DECIMAL(5,2) = 0.10;
   DECLARE @FinalSalary DECIMAL(10,2);

   SET @FinalSalary = @BaseSalary + (@BaseSalary * @BonusRate);
   PRINT @FinalSalary;
   ```

3. **Logical Testing**

   ```
   DECLARE @Check INT = 1;
   IF (@Check = 1 AND NOT @Check = 0)
     PRINT 'Condition True';
   ```

```
ELSE
  PRINT 'Condition False';
```

Key Takeaways

- Variables store temporary values and improve script flexibility.
- Arithmetic operators follow math rules, while parentheses override defaults.
- Logical **AND** executes before OR, unless parentheses change it.
- Test precedence carefully in complex **WHERE** clauses.

Writing Clean, Maintainable, and Well-Documented T-SQL Code

Clean, well-structured, and maintainable T-SQL code is crucial for collaboration, debugging, and long-term support. It is because readable SQL ensures that developers, DBAs, and analysts can easily understand and modify code. Therefore, following consistent formatting and commenting standards results in fewer errors and better performance tuning.

Now that you know how to document your T-SQL code clearly with comments, it is important to understand that proper documentation not only explains what each part of your code does but also makes it easier for others (and your future self) to read, debug, and maintain. With this foundation, we can now explore broader best practices that help ensure your queries are both maintainable and efficient, including consistent formatting, meaningful naming conventions, and thoughtful structuring of complex operations.

Formatting Conventions

Proper formatting enhances readability and reduces ambiguity in complex queries. Here are the essential guidelines:

1. **Use Uppercase Keywords.**

   SQL keywords such as **SELECT**, **FROM**, **WHERE**, and **JOIN** should always be written in uppercase, while table and column names remain lowercase or PascalCase.
   This improves visual distinction between SQL syntax and identifiers.

   Example:

   ```
   SELECT EmployeeID,
          FirstName,
       LastName
   FROM Employees
   WHERE HireDate > '2020-01-01';
   ```

2. **Align Columns Vertically.**

   For multi-column queries, aligning columns vertically makes it easier to scan and modify later.

   Good Formatting:

   ```
   SELECT EmployeeID,
          FirstName,
          LastName,
          HireDate,
          Salary
   FROM Employees;
   ```

Poor Formatting:

```
SELECT EmployeeID, FirstName, LastName, HireDate, Salary FROM Employees;
```

- The compact single-line query is harder to read and maintain.

3. **Break Long Queries into Logical Parts.**

   For better readability:

   - Place each clause (**SELECT**, **FROM**, **JOIN**, **WHERE**, and **ORDER BY**) on a new line.
   - Indent subsequent lines for nested queries.

   Example:

```
SELECT e.EmployeeID,
           e.FirstName,
           e.LastName,
           d.DeptName
FROM Employees AS e
JOIN Departments AS d
  ON e.DeptID = d.DeptID
WHERE e.HireDate > '2020-01-01'
ORDER BY e.Salary DESC;
```

4. **Use Aliases Wisely.**

   - Use short and meaningful aliases to simplify code.
   - Always include AS for clarity.

   Example:

```
SELECT e.FirstName,
           e.LastName,
           d.DeptName
FROM Employees AS e
JOIN Departments AS d ON e.DeptID = d.DeptID;
```

5. **Ensure Consistent Indentation.**

   Indent nested queries or CASE expressions, as shown here:

```
SELECT FirstName,
           LastName,
           CASE
             WHEN Salary > 80000 THEN 'High'
           WHEN Salary BETWEEN 50000 AND 80000 THEN 'Medium'
           ELSE 'Low'
           END AS SalaryRange
FROM Employees;
```

Commenting Code

Comments explain logic, which makes T-SQL easier to maintain. Without comments, future developers (or even you) may struggle to understand query intent. You may refer to the following comment categories to know more about them.

Single-Line Comments

Use `--` for quick notes or inline comments.

Example:

```
-- Select employees hired after 2020
SELECT EmployeeID,
        FirstName,
        HireDate
FROM Employees
WHERE HireDate > '2020-01-01';
```

Multi-Line Comments

Use `/* ... */` for detailed explanations, or to temporarily disable blocks of code.

Example:

```
/* Increase salary by 5%
   for employees hired before 2020 */
UPDATE Employees
SET Salary = Salary * 1.05
WHERE HireDate < '2020-01-01';
Commenting for Code Blocks (Disabled Code):
/* The following query is disabled during testing:
SELECT * FROM Employees WHERE Salary > 100000;
*/
```

Explain Complex Logic

Always explain business rules or unusual joins/conditions, such as shown in the example here:

```
-- Use LEFT JOIN to include employees without assigned departments.
SELECT e.EmployeeID, e.FirstName, d.DeptName
FROM Employees AS e
LEFT JOIN Departments AS d ON e.DeptID = d.DeptID;
```

Best Practices for Maintainable T-SQL

****Avoid `SELECT *`.**

Explicitly specify the required columns:

```
SELECT FirstName, LastName FROM Employees; -- Better than SELECT *
```

Use Meaningful Names.

Choose clear table, column, and variable names (**`EmpSalary`** vs. **`ESal`**).

Break Down Complex Queries.

- Use Common Table Expressions (CTEs) to simplify nested subqueries.

```
WITH RecentHires AS (
        SELECT EmployeeID, FirstName, HireDate
        FROM Employees
```

```
        WHERE HireDate > '2020-01-01'
)
SELECT * FROM RecentHires;
```

Ensure Consistent Case Usage

Pick a case style for identifiers (**PascalCase**, **snake_case**), and make sure that you stick with it.

Avoid Deep Nesting

Excessive nested queries or **CASE** statements reduce readability. Therefore, you can break it into smaller queries.

Document Stored Procedures and Functions

Include header comments, such as:

```
/* Procedure: usp_GetRecentHires
   Purpose: Fetch employees hired last year.
   Author: John Doe
   Date: 2025-08-01
*/
```

Separate Logic from Presentation.

Use views or stored procedures to encapsulate logic, instead of embedding complex queries in reports or applications.

Example: Poor vs. Clean SQL

Here is how a poorly written query looks like:

```
select * from employees e join departments d on e.deptid=d.deptid where salary>50000
or hiredate>'2020-01-01' order by salary desc;
```

Now, look at a well-written query:

```
-- Fetch employees earning above $50K or hired after 2020
SELECT e.EmployeeID,
        e.FirstName,
        e.LastName,
        d.DeptName,
        e.Salary
FROM Employees AS e
JOIN Departments AS d
        ON e.DeptID = d.DeptID
WHERE e.Salary > 50000
   OR e.HireDate > '2020-01-01'
ORDER BY e.Salary DESC;
```

Key Takeaways

- Readable code saves time for debugging and teamwork.
- Use uppercase keywords, aligned columns, and proper indentation.
- Always comment on complex logic to explain reasoning.
- Break down complex queries into manageable parts by using CTEs or views.
- Maintain consistency in formatting and naming, as it is essential for maintainability.

Debugging and Best Practices

Efficient debugging and adherence to best practices are critical to ensure that T-SQL code is reliable, performant, and safe for production environments. Debugging helps identify errors early, while best practices prevent common mistakes and performance issues.

Finally, after exploring debugging techniques and best practices, let us summarize the key takeaways from this chapter, and test your knowledge with a quiz.

Debugging T-SQL Code

Debugging involves testing queries step-by-step to validate their correctness before applying them in a live database. Hence, you must consider the following tips while debugging:

Always Test in Development

- Never execute untested queries directly on production databases.
- Use a development or staging environment with a copy of production data.
- Validate:
    - Query Correctness
    - Data Accuracy
    - The Impact of Updates or Deletions

Example:

Test a delete query safely, as shown in the following way:

```
-- Test using SELECT first
SELECT * FROM Employees WHERE EmployeeID = 999;
 -- Then run DELETE only if correct
DELETE FROM Employees WHERE EmployeeID = 999;
```

Use Transactions for Safe Changes

Transactions allow you to group operations, and either commit them permanently, or roll them back if issues occur.

Syntax:

```
BEGIN TRAN;      -- Start transaction.
DELETE FROM Employees WHERE EmployeeID = 999;

ROLLBACK TRAN;   -- Undo changes (Testing Phase).
-- COMMIT TRAN;   -- Finalize only when it is verified.
```

- Use **`ROLLBACK TRAN`** to undo mistakes during debugging.
- In production, confirm the results first, and then use **`COMMIT TRAN`**.

Use `PRINT` or `SELECT` for Debugging

- Use **`PRINT`** to display variable values or debugging messages.
- Use **`SELECT`** statements to preview affected rows before running updates/deletes.

Example:

```
DECLARE @Count INT;
SELECT @Count = COUNT(*) FROM Employees WHERE Salary > 80000;
PRINT 'Employees above 80K: ' + CAST(@Count AS NVARCHAR(10));
```

Use TRY...CATCH for Error Handling

Handle runtime errors gracefully, as shown here:

```
BEGIN TRY
        UPDATE Employees SET Salary = Salary / 0; -- Error
END TRY
BEGIN CATCH
        PRINT 'Error: ' + ERROR_MESSAGE();
END CATCH;
```

Best Practices for T-SQL

Adopting best practices improves code quality, prevents mistakes, and enhances performance. Therefore, here are a few of them:

Avoid SELECT * in Production

Fetch only the necessary columns to reduce overhead, as shown here:

```
-- Avoid
SELECT * FROM Employees;

-- Use
SELECT EmployeeID, FirstName, LastName FROM Employees;
```

Use Execution Plans to Optimize Performance

Execution plans visualize how SQL Server executes your queries, while showing index usage, joins, and scans. To view them in SSMS, press *Ctrl+M* before running a query to display the estimated execution plan. This should be done because reading execution plans helps identify bottlenecks, besides allowing us to optimize query performance.

Example:

```
SELECT e.EmployeeID, e.FirstName, d.DeptName
FROM Employees e
JOIN Departments d ON e.DeptID = d.DeptID
WHERE e.Salary > 50000;
```

Execution plans in SQL Server Management Studio (SSMS) help identify:

- Index Usage
- Table Scans vs. Index Seeks
- Bottlenecks in Queries

Shortcut: Press *Ctrl* + M in SSMS before executing to view the estimated plan.

Use Proper Indexing

Create indexes on frequently queried columns (for example, **WHERE**, **JOIN**, **ORDER** BY).

Example: `CREATE INDEX idx_Employees_HireDate ON Employees(HireDate);`

Parameterize Queries

Avoid hardcoding values in production queries, as shown here:

```
DECLARE @MinSalary DECIMAL(10,2) = 60000;
SELECT FirstName, Salary FROM Employees WHERE Salary > @MinSalary;
```

Comment Critical Logic

Always explain complex conditions, joins, or business rules:

```
-- Filtering employees in the Sales department who earn above $70,000.
SELECT FirstName, Salary FROM Employees WHERE DeptID = 3 AND Salary > 70000;
```

Validate Row Counts before DML

Use `SELECT COUNT(*)` to confirm the affected rows before `UPDATE` or `DELETE`.

Key Takeaways

- Debug in development, and not during production.
- Use transactions and rollbacks for safe testing.
- Avoid `SELECT *`, and retrieve only needed columns.
- Use execution plans and indexing to improve performance.
- Comment and parameterize code for maintainability.

Conclusion

In this chapter, we have built a solid foundation for working with T-SQL by covering the essential concepts and practices that every database professional should know. You learned how to set up your environment, understood the differences between T-SQL and ANSI SQL, and explored batch processing with the GO command. We examined how Data Definition Language (DDL) commands help structure your database objects, and delved into the core CRUD operations for managing data. Additionally, you became familiar with variables, expressions, and operator precedence, and learned the importance of writing clean, maintainable, and well-documented T-SQL code. Finally, we discussed debugging techniques and best practices to ensure your queries are efficient and reliable. With these tools and knowledge, you are now equipped to write T-SQL code that is both powerful and professional, setting the stage for more advanced topics in database development and management.

Key Takeaways

- **T-SQL Extends ANSI SQL with Procedural Logic**: T-SQL includes variables, loops, conditions, and error handling, which makes it more powerful than standard SQL for complex database operations.
- **Batches and GO Define Execution Boundaries**: A batch is a group of SQL statements sent to SQL Server for execution together. The GO command separates batches, and then resets variable scope.
- **CRUD and DDL Form the Foundation of T-SQL**: CRUD (Create, Read, Update, Delete) handles data manipulation, while DDL (Data Definition Language) manages database structures.
- **Clean Formatting and Comments Facilitate Maintainability**: Consistent indentation, clear naming conventions, and proper commenting improve readability and teamwork, which eventually reduces errors in large projects.

```
-- Create table
CREATE TABLE dbo.ProductDemo
(
    ProductID INT PRIMARY KEY,
    ProductName VARCHAR(100),
    Price DECIMAL(10,2)
);

-- Alter table
ALTER TABLE dbo.ProductDemo
ADD CreatedDate DATETIME DEFAULT GETDATE();

-- Drop table (demo cleanup)
DROP TABLE dbo.ProductDemo;
```

***Figure 1.4**: DL Operations with Clean Formatting and Comments*

Quiz

1. What is the difference between **DELETE** and **TRUNCATE**?
    - **DELETE** removes rows one by one, logs each deletion, and can include a **WHERE** clause.
    - **TRUNCATE** quickly removes all rows, resets identity columns, and cannot include **WHERE**.
2. How does GO affect variable scope?
    - Variables declared in one batch are not accessible after a GO statement because GO ends the batch, and also resets the scope.
3. Which has higher precedence: **AND** or **OR**?
    - **AND** has higher precedence than OR. Moreover, parentheses should be used to enforce the intended logical grouping.
4. Write a query to list the top 3 highest-paid employees.

```
SELECT TOP 3 EmployeeID,
         FirstName,
             LastName,
         Salary
FROM Employees
ORDER BY Salary DESC;
```

CHAPTER 2

Data Types, NULLs and Conversions

Introduction

Data types are the foundation of every SQL Server database. They define how information is stored, processed, compared, and retrieved. Therefore, choosing the right data type goes beyond syntax preference; it directly impacts storage efficiency, query performance, accuracy, and scalability. Poor choices can lead to wasted disk space, slow queries, unexpected type conversion errors, and even incorrect results such as rounding errors when storing monetary values in floating-point columns, or performance degradation from overly large character types. Therefore, this chapter provides a comprehensive exploration of SQL Server data types and related concepts, while covering numeric, character, binary, and date/time types, as well as the behavior of `NULL` values and specialized functions like `ISNULL`, `COALESCE`, and `NULLIF`. It also explains data type conversions like implicit and explicit using core functions like `CAST` and `CONVERT`, offers guidelines for selecting optimal types, and examines how identity columns and sequence objects automate key generation. Throughout the chapter, detailed examples, practical pitfalls, performance considerations, and real-world case studies are provided, along with exercises to reinforce your understanding of each concept.

Structure

In this chapter, we will cover the following topics:

- Numeric Data Types
- Character Data Types
- Binary Data Types
- Handling `NULL`s in Expressions and Queries
- Using `ISNULL`, `COALESCE`, and `NULLIF` Functions
- Implicit vs. Explicit Type Conversions
- `CAST` and `CONVERT` Functions
- Choosing Optimal Data Types for Storage and Performance
- Identity and Sequence Objects

Numeric Data Types

Numeric data types represent numbers, which are both exact and approximate. Hence, choosing the right one depends on range, precision, and storage requirements.

Exact Numeric Data Types

Exact types store numbers without any approximation.

The following table summarizes common SQL Server numeric data types, including their storage requirements, ranges, and common use cases.

<table>
<tr><th>Data Type</th><th>Storage</th><th>Range</th><th colspan="3">Notes</th></tr>
<tr><td>TINYINT</td><td>1 byte</td><td>0 to 255</td><td colspan="3">Good for small enumerations (for example, age groups, rating levels)</td></tr>
<tr><td>SMALLINT</td><td>2 bytes</td><td>-32,768 to 32,767</td><td colspan="3">Useful for counts, small ranges</td></tr>
<tr><td>INT</td><td>4 bytes</td><td>-2,147,483,648 to 2,147,483,647</td><td colspan="3">Default integer type for most cases</td></tr>
<tr><td>BIGINT</td><td>8 bytes</td><td>±9 quintillion</td><td colspan="3">For very large counts (social networks, IoT data)</td></tr>
<tr><td>DECIMAL(p,s) / NUMERIC(p,s)</td><td></td><td></td><td colspan="3"></td></tr>
<tr><td rowspan="2">BIT</td><td rowspan="2">1 bit (storage optimized to 1 byte)</td><td rowspan="2">0, 1, NULL</td><td colspan="3">Good for flags (yes/no, true/ false).</td></tr>
<tr><td>-17 bytes</td><td>User-defined precision and scale</td><td>Best for financial and scientific applications requiring accuracy</td></tr>
</table>

Table 2.1: *SQL Server Numeric Data Types and Their Characteristics*

Example: Choosing an Integer

```
-- Population of a small town (INT is enough)
CREATE TABLE Town (
    TownID INT PRIMARY KEY,
    Name NVARCHAR(100),
    Population INT
);

-- Population of a country (BIGINT is required)
CREATE TABLE Country (
    CountryID INT PRIMARY KEY,
    Name NVARCHAR(100),
    Population BIGINT
);
```

Tip: *Always choose the smallest integer type that fits your needs, as using BIGINT everywhere wastes space.*

Example: Using Decimal for Currency

```
-- Correct way to store money
CREATE TABLE Orders (
    OrderID INT PRIMARY KEY,
    Amount DECIMAL(18,2) NOT NULL
);

-- WRONG: Using FLOAT may cause rounding errors
CREATE TABLE BadOrders (
    OrderID INT PRIMARY KEY,
    Amount FLOAT
);
```

Approximate Numeric Data Types

Approximate types use floating-point representation, which can introduce rounding issues, but can also support very large ranges.

The following table presents the approximate numeric data types in SQL Server, and highlights their storage requirements and precision levels.

Data Type	Storage	Approximate Precision
REAL	4 bytes	~7 decimal digits
FLOAT(n)	4–8 bytes	1–15 digits depending on n

Table 2.2: *SQL Server Approximate Numeric Data Types*

Example: Scientific Data

```
CREATE TABLE TemperatureReadings (
    ReadingID INT PRIMARY KEY,
    TempCelsius FLOAT(10), -- High precision for scientific values
    RecordedAt DATETIME2
);
```

Warning: *Never use* FLOAT *for money or values that require exact accuracy.*

Character Data Types

Character data types are used to store letters, digits, symbols, and other text-based information in SQL Server. Thus, choosing the right character type is critical for storage efficiency, performance, and to ensure that international data is being handled properly. Since most business applications rely heavily on text (customer names, addresses, product descriptions, comments, log messages, and so on), understanding these types in detail is essential.

SQL Server provides two broad families of the following character types:

- Non-Unicode Types (**CHAR**, **VARCHAR**, **TEXT - legacy**): They store ASCII characters (1 byte per character).
- Unicode Types (**NCHAR**, **NVARCHAR**, **NTEXT - legacy**): They store characters using 2 bytes per character, while supporting multiple languages and special symbols.

CHAR and VARCHAR: Non-Unicode Type Characters

CHAR(n):

- It is a fixed-length string data type.
- It always reserves n bytes, regardless of the actual stored content.
- The values are shorter than n are right-padded with spaces.

The following table describes the properties of the CHAR(n) data type in SQL Server, including its storage requirements, range, and typical use cases.

Property	Details
Storage	Exactly n bytes
Range	1 to 8,000 characters
Usage	Best for values of consistent length (for example, 2-letter state codes, fixed ID formats)

Table 2.3: *SQL Server CHAR(n) Data Type Characteristics*

Example:

```
CREATE TABLE States (
    StateCode CHAR(2) PRIMARY KEY,    -- Always 2 characters
    StateName VARCHAR(50)
);
INSERT INTO States VALUES ('CO', 'Colorado'); -- Stored as 'CO'
INSERT INTO States VALUES ('N', 'Test');    -- Stored as 'N ' (note the padding)
```

Tip: *CHAR can waste storage if used for variable-length data. However, it is extremely efficient for fixed codes such as "US", "CA", "NY".*

VARCHAR(n):

- It is a variable-length string data type.
- It stores only the actual number of characters that are entered.
- It adds 2 bytes of overhead for length tracking.

The following table outlines the properties of the **VARCHAR(n)** data type in SQL Server, including storage, range, and common usage scenarios.

Property	Details
Storage	Actual length + 2 bytes
Range	1 to 8,000 characters
Usage	Best for flexible text such as names, addresses, descriptions.

Table 2.4: *SQL Server VARCHAR(n) Data Type Characteristics*

Example:

```
CREATE TABLE Customers (
    CustomerID INT PRIMARY KEY,
    FirstName VARCHAR(50),
    LastName VARCHAR(50),
    Email VARCHAR(100)
);
```

Tip: *VARCHAR saves space compared to CHAR for text that varies in length.*

Performance Considerations: CHAR vs. VARCHAR:

- CHAR performs slightly faster for fixed-length values because the SQL Server does not need to manage varying lengths.
- VARCHAR saves space in most real-world scenarios, but adds minimal overhead for tracking size.
- Rule of Thumb: Use CHAR for fixed-length fields (postal codes, gender codes, and country abbreviations), and VARCHAR for variable-length text (names, addresses, and comments).

NCHAR and NVARCHAR: Unicode Type Characters

With globalization, applications must handle multiple languages, alphabets, and symbols. Unicode types support this by storing characters in 2 bytes each. This allows them to represent characters beyond ASCII.

`NCHAR(n)`:

- These are fixed-length Unicode strings.
- These characters always use 2n bytes.
- These characters are padded with spaces for shorter values.

`NVARCHAR(n)`:

- These are variable-length Unicode strings.
- These characters use 2 times the length and 2 additional bytes as overhead.
- These characters support up to 4,000 characters (**`NVARCHAR(MAX)`** supports up to ~2GB).

The following table compares the SQL Server Unicode character data types **NCHAR** and **NVARCHAR**, as well as their storage, usage, and maximum lengths.

Property	NCHAR	NVARCHAR
Storage	Fixed (2n bytes)	Variable (2 × actual length and 2 bytes)
Best For	Fixed-length Unicode codes	Names, addresses, or multilingual text
Maximum Length	4,000 characters	4,000 characters (MAX = 2GB)

Table 2.5: *SQL Server Unicode Character Data Types*: NCHAR *vs.* NVARCHAR

Example:

```
CREATE TABLE InternationalUsers (
    UserID INT PRIMARY KEY,
    FullName NVARCHAR(200),
    CountryCode NCHAR(3)
);

-- Supports Chinese, Arabic, Hindi, Japanese, and so on
INSERT INTO InternationalUsers VALUES (1, N'李明', N'CHN');
INSERT INTO InternationalUsers VALUES (2, N'محمد علي', N'EGY');
```

However, you must note that the N prefix when inserting Unicode literals (for example, N'李明'). Without it, SQL Server assumes non-Unicode, and may cause data loss.

TEXT and NTEXT: Deprecated

The following points summarize the key information about the **TEXT** and **NTEXT** data types in the SQL Server:

- They are used in older versions of SQL Server for storing large text.
- They are replaced by **`VARCHAR(MAX)`** and **`NVARCHAR(MAX)`**.
- They are still found in legacy databases, so you may need to handle them.

The following table lists the legacy large text data types in SQL Server, as well as their modern replacements for handling large text values.

Data Type	Storage	Replacement
`TEXT`	Up to 2GB of ASCII text	`VARCHAR(MAX)`
`NTEXT`	Up to 2GB Unicode text	`NVARCHAR(MAX)`

***Table 2.6:** Legacy Large Text Data Types and Their Replacements in SQL Server*

Best Practice: *Avoid* **`TEXT/NTEXT`** *in new designs, and always use* **`MAX`** *types for modern applications.*

Collation and Sorting Rules

Collation defines:

- Character Set (ASCII versus Unicode)
- Case Sensitivity (for example, **`SQL_Latin1_General_CP1_CI_AS`** → **`CI = case-insensitive`**)
- Accent Sensitivity (Treating "é" versus "e")
- Sort Order

Example:

```
-- Case-insensitive collation
SELECT 'Hello' = 'HELLO'; -- Returns TRUE

-- Case-sensitive collation
SELECT 'Hello' = 'HELLO' COLLATE SQL_Latin1_General_CP1_CS_AS; -- Returns FALSE
```

Collation impacts performance in joins and searches. When columns involved in comparisons or joins have different collations, SQL Server may need to perform implicit conversions, which can slow down query execution. To avoid this, you must always ensure consistent collation across related columns, particularly in large tables or databases with multilingual data. Therefore, consistent collation not only improves performance, but also prevents unexpected query results.

Indexing and Storage Impact

The following recommendations describe the best practices for indexing large text fields in the SQL Server:

- Indices on large **`VARCHAR`** or **`NVARCHAR`** fields can be inefficient.
- A common practice is to index smaller fixed-length **`CHAR/NCHAR`** keys instead of large text fields.
- Use a full-text search for indexing very large text fields.

Real-World Scenarios

The following examples illustrate typical use cases for different SQL Server character data types in various industries:

- **E-Commerce System**: Product descriptions use **`NVARCHAR(MAX)`** because they vary in length and need multilingual support.
- **Banking System**: Account numbers are stored as **`CHAR(12)`** for consistency.
- **Healthcare Database**: Patient names in multiple languages require **`NVARCHAR(100)`**.
- **Government Records**: Country codes are stored as CHAR(3) using ISO standards.

Common Mistakes and Pitfalls

The following common pitfalls highlight the mistakes to avoid when you are working with SQL Server character data types:

- Do not use `CHAR(100)` for variable names, as it wastes space.
- Do not forget the `N` prefix when inserting Unicode, as it will result in data corruption.
- Do not use `TEXT` in new systems, as it is deprecated and difficult to manage.
- Do not align collation, as it causes join errors like: "*Cannot resolve collation conflict*".

Binary Data Types

Binary data types in SQL Server are used to store raw byte-oriented data rather than human-readable text or numeric values. Unlike character or numeric types, binary types do not undergo collation, sorting, or formatting transformations; they are stored and retrieved exactly as they are written, which makes them the backbone for handling files, cryptographic values, multimedia, and system-level data.

Hence, understanding binary data types is crucial for developers and DBAs working with images, PDFs, encrypted values, digital certificates, hashed passwords, and system identifiers.

Types of Binary Data in SQL Server

SQL Server provides several binary types, each with specific use cases.

Table 2.7 summarizes the SQL Server binary data types, including their storage type, size, and typical usage.

Data Type	Storage Type	Size	Description
`BINARY(n)`	Fixed-Length	1 to 8,000 bytes	It always reserves n bytes, and pads with zeros for smaller values.
`VARBINARY(n)`	Variable-Length	1 to 8,000 bytes	It stores actual data length and 2 additional bytes overhead.
`VARBINARY(MAX)`	Variable-Length	Up to ~2GB	It is used for very large binary objects (images, documents, and videos).
`IMAGE (deprecated)`	Variable-Length	Up to 2GB	It is an old type for binary large objects, and is replaced by `VARBINARY(MAX)`.
`ROWVERSION / TIMESTAMP`	Auto-Generated	8 bytes	It is a system-maintained unique binary number used for versioning.

Table 2.7: *SQL Server Binary Data Types and Their Characteristics*

BINARY vs. VARBINARY

`BINARY(n)`:

- Stores fixed-size binary values
- Always allocates the full defined size n
- Pads unused space with 0x00 (zero bytes)

Example:

```
CREATE TABLE SecurityKeys (
    KeyID INT PRIMARY KEY,
```

```
    KeyValue BINARY(16)   -- Always 16 bytes, ideal for GUID-like keys
);

INSERT INTO SecurityKeys VALUES (1, 0xAABBCCDDEEFF00112233445566778899);
```

Additionally, it is the best choice for fixed-length encrypted values, checksums, hashes (MD5, SHA-256), or keys.

`VARBINARY(n)`:

- Stores variable-length binary values
- Uses 2 extra bytes to track length
- Saves storage whenever the binary data varies in size

Example:

```
CREATE TABLE Documents (
    DocID INT PRIMARY KEY,
    DocContent VARBINARY(8000)    -- Flexible for medium-sized documents
);

INSERT INTO Documents VALUES (1, CAST('This is binary text' AS VARBINARY));
```

Hence, this type is the best choice for files, encoded values, and small media objects.

`VARBINARY(MAX)`

- Handles **very large binary objects** (LOBs)
- Supports up to **2^31-1 bytes (~2GB)**
- Stored in-row if ≤ 8,000 bytes, otherwise it is stored out-of-row in special LOB pages.

Example:

```
CREATE TABLE MediaFiles (
    FileID INT PRIMARY KEY,
    FileName NVARCHAR(200),
    FileData VARBINARY(MAX)
);

-- Insert an image
INSERT INTO MediaFiles (FileID, FileName, FileData)
SELECT 1, 'logo.png', BulkColumn
FROM OPENROWSET(BULK 'C:\Files\logo.png', SINGLE_BLOB) AS BinaryData;
```

This type is ideal for images, PDFs, audio, video, or any large files that are stored in the database.

You must also know that storing very large files in SQL Server can bloat backups, thereby reducing performance. In many systems, a hybrid approach is used, where you store the file path in SQL Server, and keep the actual file in the cloud or the filesystem storage.

IMAGE: Deprecated

The following points summarize the status of the deprecated IMAGE data type in SQL Server:

- It is supported for backwards compatibility only.
- It is replaced by **`VARBINARY(MAX)`** in SQL Server 2005 and later.
- It is still encountered in legacy systems.

Migration Tip: If you inherit an older database using IMAGE, convert it to **`VARBINARY(MAX)`** using:

```
ALTER TABLE Old.Table
ALTER COLUMN ImageColumn VARBINARY(MAX);
```

ROWVERSION (or TIMESTAMP)

The following points describe the characteristics and usage of the **`ROWVERSION`** (formerly **`TIMESTAMP`**) data type in SQL Server:

- This is an 8-byte auto-incrementing binary number maintained by SQL Server.
- This is not related to actual timestamps or dates (despite the old name **`TIMESTAMP`**).
- This is used for optimistic concurrency control.

Example:

```
CREATE TABLE Orders (
    OrderID INT PRIMARY KEY,
    OrderDate DATETIME,
    RowVer ROWVERSION
);
```

Every time a row is modified, **`RowVer`** updates automatically.

Hence, it is the best choice for detecting row changes across transactions.

Binary Literals

Binary values are expressed in hexadecimal notation that are prefixed with 0x. Some of them are:

- `0x41 = "A"`
- `0x48656C6C6F = "Hello"`

Example:

```
-- Store hexadecimal binary value
INSERT INTO SecurityKeys VALUES (2, 0xDEADBEEF);
```

Storage and Performance Considerations

The following considerations highlight the best practices and the limitations that you will encounter while working with SQL Server binary data types:

- **Fixed vs. Variable Storage**
  - Use **`BINARY(n)`** when all the values are exactly the same size.
  - Use **`VARBINARY(n)`** for variable-length data to save space.
- **In-Row vs. Out-of-Row Storage**
  - Values ≤ 8,000 bytes are stored directly in the row.
  - Larger values (**`VARBINARY(MAX)`**) are stored in LOB pages (out-of-row).
- **Backup and Restore Overhead**
  - Databases with large **`VARBINARY(MAX)`** fields (for example, storing PDFs, videos) can significantly increase backup size and restoration time.

- **Indexing Limitations**
    - You cannot directly index **VARBINARY(MAX)**.
    - Use **hashing** (for example, computed columns with SHA2), or a **full-text search** for searching large objects.

Security Implications

The following points outline the most common uses of binary data types in SQL Server and the built-in functions that are available for security-related operations:

- Binary types are often used for password hashes, encryption keys, and digital signatures.
- SQL Server provides built-in functions for hashing and encryption, as shown here.

Example:

```
-- Hashing a password
SELECT HASHBYTES('SHA2_256', 'MySecurePassword');
```

Best Practices to Follow:

- Never store raw passwords.
- Always store salted hashes in **VARBINARY**.
- Use SQL Server encryption features (**ENCRYPTBYKEY**, **DECRYPTBYKEY**) for secure storage.

Real-World Use Cases

The following examples illustrate the real-world applications of SQL Server binary data types across different industries and scenarios:

- **Banking and Security Systems:** Storing hashed PINs and digital certificates in **BINARY(32)** or **VARBINARY(64)**
- **Medical Imaging Systems:** Storing X-rays, MRI scans, and reports in **VARBINARY(MAX)** for audit compliance
- **Content Management Systems (CMS):** Documents, PDFs, and videos stored in **VARBINARY(MAX)** columns
- **IoT Systems**: Raw sensor data (byte streams) stored in **VARBINARY** for decoding later
- **Concurrency Tracking**: **ROWVERSION** used in e-commerce apps to detect conflicting updates

Common Pitfalls and Mistakes

The following pitfalls highlight the common mistakes to avoid when you are working with SQL Server binary data types:

- Using **BINARY(n)** for variable data, as it leads to wasted space
- Storing huge videos directly in SQL Server, which results in database bloat and performance issues
- Using **IMAGE** in new systems, which is deprecated and unsupported in future versions
- Forgetting that **ROWVERSION** is not a timestamp, which might lead to misinterpretation in applications

Implicit vs. Explicit Type Conversions

One of the most important aspects of working with SQL Server is to understand how it handles type conversions, as well as the process of changing data from one data type to another. This process can be implicit (SQL Server decides for you) or explicit (you instruct SQL Server using **CAST** or **CONVERT**).

Therefore, a solid understanding of conversions is crucial because they directly affect:

- **Performance**: Conversions may prevent index usage, or add unnecessary overhead.
- **Accuracy**: Data can be truncated or rounded if conversions are not handled carefully.
- **Maintainability**: Relying on implicit conversions can make queries unpredictable or inconsistent.

Implicit Type Conversion

Description:

- Implicit conversion happens automatically when SQL Server needs to reconcile two different data types in an expression or comparison.
- SQL Server chooses a "higher-precedence" data type based on its type precedence hierarchy.

For example:

```
SELECT 1 + 1.5 AS Result;
-- SQL Server automatically converts INT (1) to FLOAT
-- Result: 2.5
```

Here, 1 (**INT**) is implicitly converted to 1.0 (**FLOAT**) because **FLOAT** has higher precedence.

Type Precedence (Simplified Order)

SQL Server defines a strict data type precedence order. When two different data types are combined, the lower-precedence type is converted to the higher-precedence one.

Therefore, common precedence (high → low) looks like this:

1. `SQL_VARIANT`
2. `DATETIMEOFFSET`
3. `DATETIME2`
4. `DATETIME`
5. `FLOAT`
6. `REAL`
7. `DECIMAL/NUMERIC`
8. `MONEY/SMALLMONEY`
9. `BIGINT`
10. `INT`
11. `SMALLINT`
12. `TINYINT`
13. `BIT`
14. `NVARCHAR`
15. `NCHAR`
16. `VARCHAR`
17. `CHAR`

Implicit Conversion Examples

Example 1: Mixing INT and DECIMAL

```
SELECT 10 + 5.75 AS Result;
-- INT 10 is implicitly converted to DECIMAL
-- Result: 15.75
```

Example 2: Comparing VARCHAR with INT

```
SELECT CASE
         WHEN '123' = 123 THEN 'Equal'
         ELSE 'Not Equal'
       END AS ComparisonResult;
-- VARCHAR '123' is converted to INT
-- Result: Equal
```

Example 3: Danger with Non-Numeric Strings

```
SELECT CASE
         WHEN 'ABC' = 123 THEN 'Equal'
         ELSE 'Not Equal'
       END AS ComparisonResult;
-- SQL Server tries to convert 'ABC' to INT -> Error
```

Warning: *Implicit conversion can cause runtime errors if the conversion fails.*

Performance Issues with Implicit Conversion

Consider this table:

```
CREATE TABLE Customers (
    CustomerID INT PRIMARY KEY,
    PhoneNumber VARCHAR(20)
);
```

Now, query it via:

```
SELECT *
FROM Customers
WHERE PhoneNumber = 12345;
```

In this example:

- SQL Server implicitly converts **`12345 (INT)`** into **`'12345' (VARCHAR)`**.
- The index on **`PhoneNumber`** cannot be used efficiently because conversion must happen for each row.
- This may cause full table scans instead of index seeks.

Hence, you must always write queries using matching data types for columns and expressions. When data types do not align, SQL Server may perform implicit conversions to reconcile differences, which can prevent the use of indexes, and significantly degrade the query performance. Therefore, ensuring that data types match across joins, filters, and comparisons not only improves efficiency, but also reduces the risk of unexpected results or errors. This practice is especially important in large databases where even small inefficiencies can have a noticeable impact on overall performance.

Explicit Type Conversion

Description: Explicit conversion means that you can instruct SQL Server to perform a conversion using **CAST** or **CONVERT**.

- **CAST** is the ANSI-SQL standard, and hence more portable.
- **CONVERT** is T-SQL specific, with formatting options (which is especially useful for dates).

Examples of Explicit Conversion

Example 1: Casting a Value

```
SELECT CAST('123' AS INT) AS Result;
-- Explicitly converts string to INT -> Result: 123
```

Example 2: Converting a Float to Decimal

```
SELECT CAST(123.4567 AS DECIMAL(10,2)) AS RoundedValue;
-- Result: 123.46 (rounded to 2 decimals)
```

Example 3: Using CONVERT for Date Formatting

```
SELECT CONVERT(VARCHAR(10), GETDATE(), 101) AS USDateFormat;
-- Output: MM/DD/YYYY
```

Example 4: Preventing Errors

```
SELECT TRY_CAST('ABC' AS INT) AS Result;
-- Result: NULL (instead of error)
```

Comparing Implicit vs. Explicit Conversion

Table 2.8 highlights the key differences between implicit and explicit data type conversions in SQL Server, while comparing aspects such as control, performance, error handling, and readability.

Aspect	Implicit Conversion	Explicit Conversion
Control	SQL Server decides	Developer decides
Performance	It may cause hidden overhead.	It is usually safer and more predictable.
Errors	It may throw a runtime error unexpectedly	It is easier to handle using **TRY_CAST** / **TRY_CONVERT**.
Readability	The code looks shorter, but is also ambiguous.	The code is longer, but is clearer.

Table 2.8: *Comparison of Implicit and Explicit Conversions in SQL Server*

Case Study: The Safety of Explicit Operations

Scenario: A banking system storing amounts in **DECIMAL(18,2)**

```
-- Implicit conversion
SELECT *
FROM Transactions
WHERE Amount = 100;
```

Here, 100 (INT) is converted to DECIMAL(18,2) implicitly.

Safer Version:

```
-- Explicit conversion
SELECT *
FROM Transactions
WHERE Amount = CAST(100 AS DECIMAL(18,2));
```

The second query makes the developer's intent clear, and avoids ambiguity.

Common Pitfalls in Conversions

The following examples demonstrate common issues and risks that can occur when performing explicit conversions in SQL Server:

- **Loss of Precision**

  ```
  SELECT CAST(123.456 AS INT); -- Result: 123 (decimal truncated)
  ```

- **Silent Truncation**

  ```
  SELECT CAST('ABCDE' AS CHAR(3)); -- Result: 'ABC'
  ```

- **Rounding Differences**

  ```
  SELECT CAST(123.45 AS DECIMAL(4,1)); -- Result: 123.5
  ```

- **Date Conversion Errors**

  ```
  SELECT CAST('31-02-2024' AS DATE); -- Error: Invalid date
  ```

Conversion Best Practices

The following best practices help ensure safe and efficient use of data type conversions in SQL Server:

- Always match column types in **`WHERE`** and **`JOIN`** conditions.
- Prefer explicit conversions for clarity.
- Use **`TRY_CAST`** or **`TRY_CONVERT`** when dealing with unpredictable user input.
- Be careful when you are converting between **`CHAR/NCHAR`** and **`VARCHAR/NVARCHAR`**.
- For financial data, never use **`FLOAT`**; instead, stick to **`DECIMAL`** or **`NUMERIC`**.

Summary

The following key takeaways summarize the best practices and cautions when you are working with data type conversions in SQL Server:

- Implicit conversions are automatic, but they can be dangerous and inefficient.
- Explicit conversions (**`CAST`**, **`CONVERT`**) grant control, predictability, and safety.
- Understanding SQL Server's type precedence is essential to avoid surprises.
- Always write queries with consistent data types to ensure excellent performance and correctness.

Rule of Thumb: *If accuracy matters, then you must convert explicitly. However, if performance matters, then avoid conversions altogether by designing schemas properly.*

Handling NULLs

Working with NULL values in SQL Server is one of the most important, and sometimes, the **most misunderstood** aspects of relational database design and query development. Unlike zero, an empty string, or the word "unknown," a NULL represents the **absence of a value;** it literally means that *no data has been stored in that column for that row*. Therefore, understanding how NULL behaves in queries, conditions, and expressions is critical for writing correct and efficient SQL.

NULL

The following points explain the concept and use of NULL in SQL Server:

- `NULL` is a marker in SQL Server, and not a value itself. It represents missing or unknown information.
- For example:
  - If a customer has not provided their middle name, that field may be `NULL`.
  - If an employee's termination date has not been determined, the column may store `NULL`.

Hence, understanding `NULL` in SQL Server requires careful attention because it behaves differently from ordinary values. Unlike zero or an empty string, NULL represents the absence of a value rather than a specific value itself. This distinction is thus critical for correctly interpreting query results, performing calculations, and designing database logic. The following clarifications highlight the key points about how NULL works, and how it affects SQL operations:

Important Clarifications

- `NULL` is not zero (0).
  - Zero is an actual numeric value.
  - `NULL` means that the value does not exist.
- `NULL` is not an empty string.
  - An empty string means that the user explicitly provided a blank.
  - `NULL` means that no value was given at all.
- `NULL` is not the same as "unknown" as in plain English.
  - In SQL's three-valued logic, `NULL` introduces a third possibility in Boolean operations: `TRUE`, `FALSE`, or `UNKNOWN`.

This behavior means that any comparison or logical operation involving `NULL` does not evaluate to a simple `TRUE` or `FALSE` operation. For example, expressions like `Column = NULL` or `Column <> NULL` will return `UNKNOWN` rather than `TRUE` or `FALSE`. Hence, to properly handle `NULL` values in queries, SQL Server provides special operators such as `IS NULL` and `IS NOT NULL`, as well as functions like `COALESCE` and `ISNULL` to manage or replace missing values in expressions.

NULL and Comparisons

This is where most new SQL developers make mistakes. Comparisons involving `NULL` always return `UNKNOWN`, unless they are handled explicitly.

Example: Direct Comparison

```
SELECT *
FROM Employees
WHERE MiddleName = NULL;    -- Incorrect!
```

- This query will never return any rows because **NULL = NULL** is **UNKNOWN**, and is not **TRUE**.

The Correct Way:

```
SELECT *
FROM Employees
WHERE MiddleName IS NULL;   -- Correct
```

- SQL provides **IS NULL** and **IS NOT NULL** operators to check for missing values.

NULL in Logical Expressions

Since SQL uses three-valued logic, Boolean expressions that involve **NULL** behave differently:

Table 2.9 illustrates how **NULL** values behave in SQL Server's three-valued logic, while showing the results of various expressions involving NULL.

Expression	Result
5 > NULL	UNKNOWN
NULL = NULL	UNKNOWN
NULL <> NULL	UNKNOWN
NOT (NULL = 5)	UNKNOWN
NULL OR TRUE	TRUE
NULL AND TRUE	UNKNOWN
NULL AND FALSE	FALSE

Table 2.9: *Results of Expressions Involving NULL in SQL Server Three-Valued Logic*

Explanation: SQL uses three-valued logic: **TRUE**, **FALSE**, and **UNKNOWN**. Here, **NULL** represents "unknown/ missing" data.

- When you do **NULL AND TRUE**, SQL cannot determine the truth of the **NULL** part,; therefore, the result is **UNKNOWN**.
- **NULL** OR **TRUE** returns **TRUE** because **TRUE** dominates in the OR logic.

  This is why direct comparisons with **NULL (= NULL)** always fail. Hence, you must always use **IS NULL** / **IS NOT NULL** to check for missing values.

Reasons To Do So:

- SQL Server cannot determine whether a comparison involving **NULL** is true or false; it is *unknown*.
- This is why conditions with **NULL** may exclude rows unexpectedly.

NULL in Aggregations

Aggregate functions behave differently with **NULL** values in the following ways:

- **COUNT(column)**: It counts only non-**NULL** values.
- **COUNT(*)**: It counts all rows, including those with **NULL**.
- **SUM**, **AVG**, **MIN**, **MAX**: They ignore **NULL** values.

Example:

```
CREATE TABLE Sales (
    SaleID INT PRIMARY KEY,
```

```
    Amount DECIMAL(10,2) NULL
);

INSERT INTO Sales VALUES
(1, 100.00),
(2, NULL),
(3, 50.00);

-- Example aggregations
SELECT COUNT(*) AS TotalRows,       -- 3
       COUNT(Amount) AS NonNullRows,-- 2
       SUM(Amount) AS TotalAmount,  -- 150.00
       AVG(Amount) AS AverageAmount -- 75.00
FROM Sales;
```

Key point: *Aggregates ignore* **`NULL`** *values; therefore, you must be careful while interpreting results.*

NULL in Joins

When you are joining tables, **`NULL`** values can lead to unexpected results, as shown here:

Example:

```
CREATE TABLE Customers (
    CustomerID INT PRIMARY KEY,
    Email NVARCHAR(100) NULL
);

CREATE TABLE Orders (
    OrderID INT PRIMARY KEY,
    CustomerEmail NVARCHAR(100) NULL
);

-- Attempting a join on email
SELECT c.CustomerID, o.OrderID
FROM Customers c
JOIN Orders o
    ON c.Email = o.CustomerEmail;
```

- If either Email or **`CustomerEmail`** is NULL, those rows **will not match** because **`NULL = NULL`** is **`UNKNOWN`**.

Best Practice: Always prefer **surrogate keys** (like **`CustomerID`**) for joins instead of nullable natural keys (like email).

NULL in ORDER BY and GROUP BY

When ordering results, **`NULL`** values are treated as the lowest values, and thus appear at the very first (ascending order), or at the last (descending order).

Example:

```
SELECT *
FROM Customers
ORDER BY MiddleName ASC;  -- NULLs will appear first
```

- In **`GROUP BY`**, **`NULL`** values are grouped together.

Example:

```
SELECT MiddleName, COUNT(*)
FROM Employees
GROUP BY MiddleName;
```

- All rows with **NULL** in **MiddleName** will form a single group.

NULL in Expressions

Arithmetic or string expressions involving **NULL** also return **NULL**, as shown here:

Arithmetic Example:

```
SELECT 5 + NULL;    -- Returns NULL
```

In the SQL Server, any arithmetic operation involving **NULL** results in **NULL**. This is because **NULL** represents an unknown or missing value, and combining a known value with an unknown value produces an indeterminate result. Therefore, expressions like 5 + **NULL** do not return a numeric value but **NULL**. To handle such cases, functions like **ISNULL** or **COALESCE** can be used to provide a default value in place of **NULL**, and ensure meaningful results in calculations.

String Example:

```
SELECT 'Hello ' + NULL;    -- Returns NULL
```

Tip: *To prevent this, use functions such as **ISNULL** or **COALESCE** to substitute defaults.*

Dealing with NULLs: Strategies

Doe to the potential complications, developers often need strategies for handling NULL.

- **Prevent NULLs Whenever Possible:** Use **NOT NULL** constraints in table definitions when the column should always have a value.

```
CREATE TABLE Employees (
    EmployeeID INT PRIMARY KEY,
    FirstName NVARCHAR(50) NOT NULL,
    LastName NVARCHAR(50) NOT NULL
);
```

To maintain data integrity and simplify query logic, it is best to prevent **NULL** values whenever possible. Therefore, using **NOT NULL** constraints in table definitions ensures that critical columns always contain valid data, which reduces the need for special handling of missing values in queries and calculations. For example, defining the **FirstName** and **LastName** columns as **NOT NULL** in an Employees table guarantees that every record will include these essential pieces of information. This helps in preventing errors and inconsistencies in the database.

- **Substitute Defaults:** Use **DEFAULT** constraints to avoid **NULL** values.

```
CREATE TABLE Products (
    ProductID INT PRIMARY KEY,
    Price DECIMAL(10,2) NOT NULL DEFAULT 0.00
);
```

Using **DEFAULT** constraints is an effective way to prevent **NULL** values while still allowing flexibility in data entry. Therefore, by specifying a default value for a column, SQL Server automatically populates the field when no explicit value is provided. For instance, setting the Price column in a Products table to **DEFAULT 0.00** ensures that every product record has a valid price, while eliminating **NULL** values. It also reduces the need for additional handling in queries and calculations.

- **Handle NULLs Explicitly in Queries**
  - Replace `NULL` with fallback values using functions such as `ISNULL`, `COALESCE`.
  - Use `CASE` expressions for fine-grained control.

Hence, when you are working with `NULL` values in queries, it is often necessary to handle them explicitly to avoid unexpected results. Functions like `ISNULL` and `COALESCE` allow you to replace `NULL` with fallback values, while ensuring that calculations, aggregations, and display logic are behaving as intended. For more complex scenarios, `CASE` expressions provide fine-grained control, which facilitates the conditional handling of `NULL` values based on specific business rules or query requirements.

Example: Customer Communication

Suppose you have a customer table where some customers do not have an email:

```
CREATE TABLE Customers (
    CustomerID INT PRIMARY KEY,
    Name NVARCHAR(100),
    Email NVARCHAR(100) NULL
);

INSERT INTO Customers VALUES
(1, 'Alice', 'alice@email.com'),
(2, 'Bob', NULL),
(3, 'Charlie', 'charlie@email.com');
```

If you query it via:

```
SELECT Name, Email FROM Customers;
```

You will get `NULL` for Bob's email.

To replace it with a placeholder, use:

```
SELECT Name, ISNULL(Email, 'No Email Provided') AS ContactEmail
FROM Customers;
```

The result will look like this:

Name	ContactEmail
Alice	alice@email.com
Bob	No Email Provided
Charlie	charlie@email.com

NULL Best Practices

The following best practices guide you on how to minimize and properly handle NULL values in SQL Server databases:

- **Minimize the Use of `NULL`.**
  - Only allow `NULL` when missing data is expected and meaningful.
- **Always use `IS NULL`/`IS NOT NULL`**
  - Never compare directly with = or <>.
- **Be Cautious with Aggregates.**
  - Remember that `NULL` values are ignored.

- **Default Values are Your Friend.**
  - Prevent **NULL** proliferation by using **DEFAULT**.
- **Test Joins Carefully.**
  - Nullable join columns can lead to missing results.
- **Document the Business Meaning of NULL.**
  - Does it mean "**not applicable**," "**unknown**," or "**not provided**"?
  - Be explicit in your schema design and documentation.

Real-World Scenarios

The following examples illustrate the practical scenarios where NULL values must be carefully handled in different industries:

- **Healthcare Database**
  - A patient's **DateOfDeath** may be **NULL** if they are still alive.
  - Therefore, queries for survival rates must explicitly handle this.
- **E-Commerce Orders**
  - An order's **ShippedDate** may be **NULL** if it is not shipped yet.
  - The business logic must treat this carefully when calculating delivery times.
- **Finance Applications**
  - Missing **InterestRate** fields should not be assumed to be 0.
  - **NULL** must be differentiated from an explicit 0%.

NULL Functions

Handling **NULL** values effectively is one of the most important aspects of working with relational databases, especially in SQL Server. Since **NULL** represents "unknown", "not applicable", or "missing" data, it requires special handling in queries, calculations, and logic. SQL Server provides several specialized functions to deal with **NULL** values, namely **ISNULL**, **COALESCE**, and **NULLIF**. Each of these functions solves a particular problem, and mastering them ensures accuracy, prevents unexpected query results, and also improves application reliability.

Hence, in this section, we will explore each function in depth, compare their usage, review performance implications, and see real-world examples where they are critical.

The Need for NULL Functions

Before diving into the functions themselves, it is important to understand *the reason why* SQL Server provides them.

Consider this scenario: You are calculating the total revenue for a store. If some orders have discounts recorded and others do not (stored as **NULL**), adding them directly may produce incorrect results.

```
SELECT OrderID, Price, Discount, (Price - Discount) AS NetPrice
FROM Orders;
```

Therefore, if **Discount** is **NULL**, the entire expression (Price - Discount) evaluates to **NULL**. This is because any arithmetic operation involving **NULL** will result in **NULL**.

To prevent this, you need a way to replace **NULL** with a default value (for example, 0). This is where functions such as **ISNULL** and **COALESCE** come in. Similarly, **NULLIF** helps simplify conditions by converting equal values into **NULL**.

ISNULL Function

The ISNULL function is the simplest and the most commonly used NULL-handling function in SQL Server.

Syntax:

```
ISNULL(expression, replacement_value)
```

- **expression**: The value or column to check
- **replacement_value**: The value to return if the expression evaluates to **NULL**

Key Characteristics:

- **ISNULL** always returns **one data type**; this is the type of the first argument (expression).
- If the replacement value is of a different type, SQL Server attempts to convert it.
- It is limited to handling **only two arguments**, which are the original expression and a replacement.

Examples:

- Replacing **NULL** with zero:

  ```
  SELECT OrderID, ISNULL(Discount, 0) AS DiscountApplied
  FROM Orders;
  ```

- Returning a placeholder string when **NULL**:

  ```
  SELECT CustomerName, ISNULL(Phone, 'N/A') AS ContactNumber
  FROM Customers;
  ```

- Handling division with potential **NULL**:

  ```
  SELECT EmployeeID,
         SalesAmount / ISNULL(NumSales, 1) AS AvgSale
  FROM EmployeeSales;
  ```

Note: *Since ISNULL returns the data type of the first argument, watch out for unintended truncation or type mismatches.*

Example of Truncation:

```
SELECT ISNULL(NULL, 123.45); -- Returns INT, result = 123
```

The first argument (NULL) defaults to INT, which causes 123.45 to be truncated.

COALESCE Function

The **COALESCE** function is more flexible than **ISNULL**. It allows you to check multiple values, and returns the first non-**NULL** expression.

Syntax:

```
COALESCE(expression1, expression2, ..., expressionN)
```

Key Characteristics:

- It can take two or more arguments.
- It returns the first non-`NULL` value in the list.
- Data type determination follows data type precedence rules in SQL Server, which may lead to different behavior compared to `ISNULL`.

Examples:

- Returning the first available contact number:

```
SELECT CustomerID,
       COALESCE(HomePhone, MobilePhone, WorkPhone, 'No Contact') AS
PrimaryContact
FROM Customers;
```

- Handling multiple discount levels:

```
SELECT OrderID,
       COALESCE(SpecialDiscount, SeasonalDiscount, StandardDiscount, 0) AS
EffectiveDiscount
FROM Orders;
```

- Providing fallback for text columns:

```
SELECT EmployeeName,
       COALESCE(Nickname, PreferredName, FullName) AS DisplayName
FROM Employees;
```

Note on Type Precedence:

```
SELECT COALESCE(NULL, 123.45, 1);
```

The result is **`123.45 (DECIMAL)`**, and not 1 because **`DECIMAL`** has higher precedence than INT.

NULLIF Function

The **`NULLIF`** function is designed for a very specific purpose—it returns **`NULL`** if two expressions are equal; otherwise, it returns the first expression.

Syntax:

```
NULLIF(expression1, expression2)
```

Use Cases:

- Avoiding divide-by-zero errors
- Simplifying conditional logic
- Normalizing equal values into NULL for easier aggregation

Examples:

- Preventing divide-by-zero:

```
SELECT SalesAmount / NULLIF(NumSales, 0) AS AvgSale
FROM EmployeeSales;
```

If **`NumSales = 0`**, the division is attempted with **`NULL`**, which results in **`NULL`** instead of an error.

- Normalizing duplicate values:

  ```
  SELECT NULLIF(Gender, 'Unknown') AS NormalizedGender
  FROM Customers;
  ```

  If Gender = 'Unknown', it becomes NULL.

- Simplifying CASE expressions: Instead of writing:

  ```
  CASE WHEN A = B THEN NULL ELSE A END
  ```

You can use this instead:

```
NULLIF(A, B)
```

Comparing ISNULL, COALESCE, and NULLIF

Table 2.10 compares three commonly used SQL Server functions for handling **`NULL`** values, highlighting their arguments, behavior, data type rules, common use cases, and SQL standard compliance.

Feature	`ISNULL`	`COALESCE`	`NULLIF`
Arguments	2 only	2 or more	Exactly 2
Behavior	Replaces NULL with value	Returns the first non-NULL	Returns NULL if two values are equal
Data type Rules	First argument's type	Data type precedence	Data type of the first argument
Common Use Cases	Simple defaults	Multiple fallback values	Avoid division errors, normalize values
SQL Standard	Proprietary (SQL Server only)	ANSI standard	ANSI standard

***Table 2.10**: Comparison of ISNULL, COALESCE, and NULLIF Functions in SQL Server*

Performance Considerations

The following points compare **`ISNULL`** and **`COALESCE`**, besides providing guidance for using them effectively in SQL Server queries:

- **`ISNULL` versus `COALESCE`**:
  - **`ISNULL`** is slightly faster since it is simpler, and is limited to two arguments.
  - **`COALESCE`** may introduce additional overhead due to type precedence checks.
- **Indexes and Predicates**:
  - Be careful while using **`ISNULL`** or **`COALESCE`** in **`WHERE`** clauses, as it may prevent index usage.
  - **Example**:

    ```
    SELECT * FROM Orders
    WHERE ISNULL(Discount, 0) = 0;
    ```

    This may result in a table scan instead of an index seek.
- **Best Practice**: Perform **`NULL`** handling in the **`SELECT`** clause, instead of in **`WHERE`** clauses whenever possible.

Real-World Scenarios

The following examples demonstrate best practices for handling **NULL** values in financial, customer, analytical, and data science scenarios:

- **Financial Applications:**
  - Always use **DECIMAL** with **ISNULL** or **COALESCE** for monetary amounts.
  - **Example**:

```
SELECT AccountID,
ISNULL(Balance, 0.00) + ISNULL(Interest, 0.00) AS NetBalance
FROM Accounts;
```

- **Customer Data Normalization:**
  - Replace missing customer details with defaults.
  - **Example**:

```
SELECT CustomerName,
COALESCE(Email, Phone, 'No Contact Info') AS PrimaryContact
FROM Customers;
```

- **Analytics and Reporting:**
  - Avoid skewed reports by treating missing values consistently.
  - **Example**:

```
SELECT Region,
SUM(ISNULL(SalesAmount, 0)) AS TotalSales
FROM Sales
GROUP BY Region;
```

- **Machine Learning (ML) and Data Science (DS) Pipelines:**
  - Many ML pipelines do not require missing values. Use **COALESCE** to replace **NULL** with defaults during ETL.

Best Practices

The following best practices provide guidance on how to choose and use **ISNULL**, **COALESCE**, and **NULLIF** effectively in SQL Server:

- Prefer **COALESCE** whenever multiple fallback values are possible.
- Use **ISNULL** for simplicity when only a single replacement is needed.
- Use **NULLIF** instead of verbose CASE expressions while normalizing data.
- Always consider data type precedence while using **COALESCE**.
- Avoid using **ISNULL/COALESCE** in WHERE clauses whenever indexing is critical.
- Document the reason behind choosing a specific default value (for example, replacing **NULL** with 0 may not always be logically correct).

Type Conversions

SQL Server performs implicit conversions automatically, and explicit conversions using functions.

Implicit Conversions

In SQL Server, implicit conversions occur automatically when the database engine needs to convert data from one type to another to perform an operation. These conversions happen behind the scenes, and hence do not require explicit instructions from the user. While convenient, implicit conversions can sometimes affect query performance, especially when they are applied to large tables or indexed columns. Therefore, understanding how and when SQL Server performs implicit conversions is important for writing efficient queries, and avoiding unexpected results.

```
DECLARE @x INT = 100;
DECLARE @y DECIMAL(10,2) = 50.55;
SELECT @x + @y; -- Implicitly converts INT to DECIMAL
```

Explicit Conversions (CAST and CONVERT)

Explicit conversions in SQL Server allow you to intentionally change a value from one data type to another via functions such as **CAST** and **CONVERT**. Unlike implicit conversions, these require you to specify the target data type, and thus give you greater control over how data is transformed. Explicit conversions are commonly used when formatting data for presentation, performing calculations between different data types, or ensuring compatibility between columns during queries and joins. Hence, proper use of CAST and **CONVERT** can help you prevent data loss, besides improving the clarity of a given query.

```
//
SELECT CAST('2025-01-01' AS DATETIME);
SELECT CONVERT(VARCHAR(20), GETDATE(), 120); -- Formatting
```

Tip: *Always use explicit conversions in production code to avoid hidden errors.*

Choosing Optimal Data Types

Choosing the right data type is crucial for database performance, storage efficiency, and accuracy. Using oversized or inappropriate types can lead to wasted space, slower queries, and even precision issues in calculations. Thus, by selecting the most appropriate data type for each column, you can optimize both storage and query performance, besides maintaining data integrity.

The following guidelines outline the best practices for selecting SQL Server data types:

1. Always use the smallest type that fits.
2. Avoid **NVARCHAR(MAX)** and **VARBINARY(MAX)**, unless they are required.
3. Use **DECIMAL** for money instead of **FLOAT**.
4. Use **DATE** instead of **DATETIME** whenever possible.

Case Study: E-Commerce

Selecting appropriate data types is a fundamental part of database design. The right choices ensure efficient storage, maintain data integrity, and optimize query performance. Moreover, using data types that are too large or imprecise can lead to wasted space, slower queries, and potential errors in calculations or comparisons. Therefore, understanding the nature of the data and its usage patterns is the key to making informed decisions.

The following examples illustrate typical data type choices for common database columns in an e-commerce system:

- Product IDs: **INT**
- Order IDs: **BIGINT**

- Prices: **DECIMAL(18,2)**
- Customer Emails: **NVARCHAR(255)**
- Order Notes: **NVARCHAR(MAX)**

Identity and Sequence Objects

Identity Columns

Identity columns and sequence objects in SQL Server are used to automatically generate incremental values for primary keys and other unique identifiers.

```
CREATE TABLE Orders (
    OrderID INT IDENTITY(1,1) PRIMARY KEY,
    OrderDate DATETIME2
);
```

Sequences

Sequence objects in SQL Server act as independent number generators, and produce unique numeric values that can be used across multiple tables or columns.

```
CREATE SEQUENCE InvoiceSeq START WITH 1000 INCREMENT BY 1;

CREATE TABLE Invoices (
    InvoiceID INT PRIMARY KEY DEFAULT NEXT VALUE FOR InvoiceSeq,
    Amount DECIMAL(18,2)
);
```

Conclusion

In this chapter, we explored the foundational concepts of SQL Server data types such as numeric, character, binary, and date/time types. We examined how NULL works, and discussed strategies for managing it effectively, as well as the use of functions such as **ISNULL**, **COALESCE**, and **NULLIF**. The chapter also covered type conversions, both implicit and explicit, using core functions like **CAST** and **CONVERT**, along with guidelines for selecting the most appropriate data types to ensure efficiency and accuracy. Additionally, we reviewed identity columns and sequence objects for automatic key generation. Hence, mastering these concepts will equip you to design databases that are efficient, reliable, and scalable.

In the next chapter, we will dive into **SELECT** statements and filtering logic, while learning how to retrieve, sort, and filter data effectively, along with practical tips for writing optimized queries.

Practice Exercises

1. Create a Countries table with **CountryCode CHAR(3)** and **CountryName NVARCHAR(100)**. Insert 10 countries, and include multilingual names.
2. Insert "**José**" into a **VARCHAR** column without specifying collation, and compare its behavior when inserted into **NVARCHAR**.
3. Create a table with **VARCHAR(50)** and insert names of varying lengths. Then, compare the actual storage with **CHAR(50)**.
4. Demonstrate a collation conflict error by joining two tables with different collations. Resolve it using explicit **COLLATE**.
5. Create a Products table with **ProductDescription NVARCHAR(MAX)**, and practice inserting and retrieving very large text values.

CHAPTER 3

SELECT Statements and Filtering Logic

Introduction

This chapter focuses on one of the most fundamental and widely used features of SQL Server: the `SELECT` statement. While previous chapters introduced data types and their role in structuring information, this chapter turns to the practical task of retrieving and shaping data. The `SELECT` statement is at the heart of T-SQL, and enables developers to extract meaningful results from raw data, filter records with conditions, rename columns, and construct queries that reflect real-world business requirements. In addition to covering the basic syntax of `SELECT`, we will explore the logical flow of query execution, filtering techniques with `WHERE`, the use of comparison and logical operators, and methods to handle duplicates and sorting. Hence, by mastering these concepts, you will gain the ability to write precise, efficient, and maintainable queries that form the foundation for more advanced SQL techniques in the chapters that follow.

Structure

In this chapter, we will cover the following topics:

- Column Aliases and Computed Columns
- `WHERE` Clause Predicates and Logical Operators

  Therefore, this section explores:
  - Role of the `WHERE` Clause
  - Different Types of Predicates (Conditions)
  - Combining Conditions Using Logical Operators (AND, OR, NOT)
  - Importance of Operator Precedence and Parentheses
  - Performance Considerations and Indexing Best Practices
  - Advanced Usage Scenarios with Examples
- `TOP`, `OFFSET-FETCH`, and `ROW_NUMBER` Pagination
- `CASE` Expressions and Conditional Logic
- `EXISTS`, `IN`, and `JOIN` Filters
- Window Functions
- Eliminating Duplicates with `DISTINCT`

Column Aliases and Computed Columns

When writing SQL queries, one of the main goals is not only to retrieve the correct data but also to present it in a way that is readable, understandable, and meaningful to both developers and end-users. Thus, the two most important techniques that support this are the use of column aliases, and computed columns.

These features may look small compared to joins or filtering logic, but they play a critical role in query readability, maintainability, and performance optimization. Hence, in real-world applications, a well-named alias or a carefully defined computed column can drastically reduce confusion, simplify code, and avoid repeated calculations across queries.

Column Aliases

A column alias is a temporary name assigned to a column or expression in a SQL query. Instead of displaying the database's actual column name (which might be cryptic, technical, or too long), you can rename it using an alias, so that the result set is easier to read.

Aliases exist only for the duration of the query result; they do not rename columns in the actual table.

Hence, they are especially useful when:

- Columns have non-intuitive names.
- Expressions or calculations are used in the **SELECT** clause.
- Queries are exposed to end-users, reports, or exported datasets.

Before diving into the actual syntax, it is important to understand that column aliases act as a bridge between technical database structures and human readability. They allow developers to present query results in a way that aligns with business terminology or reporting requirements, which makes queries not only functional, but also easier to interpret by non-technical users.

Syntax:

```
SELECT column_name AS alias_name
FROM table_name;
```

The **FROM** clause plays a foundational role in any **SELECT** statement because it tells SQL Server which dataset or table to retrieve information from. Without this clause, SQL would have no context on where the requested columns or expressions should come from. As queries grow in complexity spanning multiple tables, views, or even derived sets the **FROM** clause remains the anchor that establishes the scope of the query.

Moreover, the AS keyword is optional, but including it improves readability.

Example 1: Simple Alias

Suppose you have a table Employees with a column named **Emp_FName**. Instead of returning **Emp_FName**, you can rename it for better readability, as shown here:

```
SELECT Emp_FName AS FirstName
FROM Employees;
```

Aliases become even more powerful in real-world scenarios, particularly when you are dealing with large-scale enterprise databases. They not only simplify reporting, but also help avoid conflicts when you are working with joined tables that might contain columns with identical names. Therefore, by clearly defining aliases, you can enhance both the clarity and maintainability of your SQL queries, while ensuring that your code can be easily understood and reused by others.

Output:

```
FirstName
John
Sarah
Michael
```

At this point, you can see how the alias makes the query results more intuitive. Rather than exposing technical column names that may not align with business terminology, aliases provide a user-friendly output that can be directly consumed in reports or dashboards. Here, the alias makes the result set clearer, especially for users who are not familiar with the table schema. Before moving on, it is worth noting that while aliases improve readability, their absence in simple queries might not always create confusion. However, as queries grow in size and complexity, explicitly defining aliases helps establish consistent naming conventions, besides avoiding ambiguity.

Here, the alias makes the result set clearer, especially for users who are not familiar with the table schema.

Example 2: Aliases Without AS

You can also write:

```
SELECT Emp_FName FirstName
FROM Employees;
```

Although this shorthand is supported by SQL Server, it leaves room for misinterpretation. Developers and analysts reviewing the query might mistake it for something else, which can cause unnecessary confusion. Hence, using **AS** eliminates that ambiguity and sets a clear standard.

While valid, this style can be confusing in complex queries. Hence, the best practice is to always use **AS** for clarity, particularly when you are working in teams.

Example 3: Aliasing Expressions

Aliases become particularly powerful when working with expressions in the SELECT clause, as shown here:

```
SELECT Salary * 0.1 AS Bonus
FROM Employees;
```

It can be seen that while applying expressions, aliases transform raw calculations into meaningful labels. This ensures that the output is not only accurate, but is also easy to interpret for business users who may not understand the underlying formulas.

Here, **Salary * 0.1** is an expression, and Bonus is the alias. Without the alias, SQL Server would return a column header like (No column name), which will be unhelpful.

Example 4: Aliases with Spaces

Aliases can include spaces, but then you must enclose them in square brackets or double quotes like the example here:

```
SELECT Emp_FName AS [First Name],
       Emp_LName AS [Last Name]
FROM Employees;
```

This flexibility is particularly useful in scenarios where query results are intended for direct presentation, such as exporting to Excel or feeding into BI tools. It ensures that the column headers are looking professional, and that they are matching the formatting expectations of end-users.

Output:

First Name	Last Name
John	Smith
Sarah	Lee

Therefore, by making use of aliases with spaces, SQL developers can balance technical database schemas against the expectations of business stakeholders. This small adjustment improves usability, and also ensures that exported or displayed data aligns with the language that is used in reports, dashboards, and documentation.

This technique is often used in reporting systems where column headers must be human-readable.

Best Practices for Column Aliases:

- **Always use meaningful names.**
  - **Bad**: `SELECT Salary * 0.1 AS col1`
  - **Good**: `SELECT Salary * 0.1 AS Bonus`
- **Follow consistent naming conventions.** Use **`CamelCase`**, **`PascalCase`**, or **`snake_case`** consistently, depending on project standards.
- **Avoid spaces unless required.** Instead of **`[First Name]`**, use **`FirstName`** unless the output is directly for reporting.
- **Document Alias Usage.** In large queries, include comments explaining why certain aliases are chosen, especially for computed expressions. Taking the time to document alias usage is not just good practice, but it helps future developers quickly understand the purpose behind each alias. This becomes especially critical in enterprise environments where queries may be reused, extended, or audited. Hence, a well-documented alias strategy reduces confusion, prevents errors, and also improves collaboration across teams.

Computed Columns

A computed column is a column in a query or table whose value is derived from other columns using an expression, formula, or function. Unlike a normal column, you do not store values directly, but compute them dynamically.

There are two major scenarios where you use computed columns, which are:

- **In Queries**: Temporary computed values are returned by the **`SELECT`** statement.
- **In Tables**: Permanently defined computed columns are a part of the table schema.

Example 1: Computed Column in Query

```
SELECT FirstName,
       LastName,
       Salary,
       Salary * 0.10 AS Bonus
FROM Employees;
```

Here, `Bonus` is a computed column. It does not exist in the Employees table, but is created dynamically during query execution. Computed columns like this are especially useful when you want to avoid storing redundant data in your tables. Instead of persisting values such as bonuses, taxes, or discounts, you can calculate them on the fly, while ensuring that the results always reflect the latest source data. Therefore, this approach not only saves storage space, but also reduces the risk of data inconsistencies between base and derived values.

Example 2: Computed Column in Table Schema

You can also define computed columns inside a table. For example, suppose you want to store a full name without explicitly entering it every time. Therefore, you will execute this code:

```
CREATE TABLE Employees (
    EmpID INT PRIMARY KEY,
    FirstName NVARCHAR(50),
    LastName NVARCHAR(50),
    FullName AS (FirstName + ' ' + LastName)
);
```

Now, **FullName** will be automatically computed whenever you query the table:

SELECT FullName FROM Employees; Defining computed columns at the schema level helps enforce consistency across all queries and applications that use the table. Now, instead of repeating the same concatenation logic in multiple queries, the database guarantees that the calculation is applied uniformly. This approach improves maintainability, reduces the chance of errors, and simplifies client-side code by centralizing logic directly in the table design.

Persisted vs. Non-Persisted Computed Columns

Hence, computed columns are non-persisted by default, which means that SQL Server calculates them on the fly each time they are queried. However, you can mark them as persisted, so that the result is stored on disk.

```
ALTER TABLE Employees
ADD AnnualSalary AS (Salary * 12) PERSISTED;
```

- Persisted columns consume storage, but improve performance for repeated calculations.
- Non-persisted columns save storage, but may slow down queries with frequent calculations.

Therefore, when you are deciding to choose between persisted and non-persisted, the choice usually comes down to a trade-off between storage space and performance. If the calculation is complex or frequently referenced in queries, persisting the column can significantly reduce execution time. On the other hand, if the column is rarely used or involves lightweight calculations, leaving it non-persisted helps conserve storage, and also keeps the schema lean.

Example 3: Complex Computed Column

```
CREATE TABLE Orders (
    OrderID INT PRIMARY KEY,
    UnitPrice DECIMAL(10,2),
    Quantity INT,
    Discount DECIMAL(4,2),
    TotalAmount AS ((UnitPrice * Quantity) - Discount) PERSISTED
);
```

Here, **TotalAmount** is always derived from **UnitPrice**, **Quantity**, and **Discount**. You do not need to update it manually. This approach is particularly useful in transactional systems where derived values, such as totals or margins, are repeatedly queried. Therefore, by storing **TotalAmount** as a persisted computed column, SQL Server ensures consistency across all queries without requiring developers to manually recalculate it each time. This not only simplifies application logic, but also reduces the risk of data anomalies caused by human error or forgotten updates.

Advantages of Computed Columns:

- **Reduce Repetition**: There is no need to repeatedly write formulas in every query.
- **Consistency**: Computed columns eliminate calculation errors by centralizing logic.
- **Performance**: Persisted computed columns can be indexed for faster lookups.
- **Readability**: Computed columns make queries cleaner and more intuitive.

In addition to these benefits, computed columns also encourage better schema design by separating raw data storage from derived business logic. This separation allows queries and reports to focus on using ready-to-go values, rather than recalculating them on the fly. Over time, this can significantly improve maintainability, especially in environments with complex reporting or analytics requirements.

Limitations of Computed Columns:

- They cannot always include non-deterministic functions (for example, `GETDATE()`).
- Some computed columns cannot be persisted if they rely on other non-deterministic functions.
- Overuse of computed columns may increase storage requirements (when persisted).

While these restrictions may seem limiting, they exist to ensure database consistency and predictable behavior. Developers should weigh the trade-offs between convenience and performance when deciding whether to use computed columns. In many cases, a combination of well-chosen computed columns and carefully designed queries provides the best balance between flexibility and efficiency.

Real-World Example: Computed Columns in Business Scenarios:

- **E-Commerce Systems**
  - `TotalPrice = UnitPrice * Quantity`
  - `DiscountedPrice = TotalPrice - (TotalPrice * DiscountRate)`
- **Payroll Systems**
  - `NetPay = GrossPay - (Tax + Insurance + OtherDeductions)`
  - `AnnualSalary = MonthlySalary * 12`
- **Healthcare Systems**
  - `BMI = Weight/(Height * Height)`
  - `Age = DATEDIFF (YEAR, DateOfBirth, GETDATE())`

Combining Aliases and Computed Columns

Aliases and computed columns are often used together to make query results more user-friendly, as shown here:

```
SELECT FirstName + ' ' + LastName AS FullName,
       Salary * 0.15 AS BonusAmount,
       (Salary * 12) AS AnnualSalary
FROM Employees;
```

Here,

- **`FullName`** is a computed expression with an alias.
- **`BonusAmount`** and **`AnnualSalary`** are both computed expressions with descriptive aliases.

Hence, this combination produces self-explanatory output, which is useful for reports, dashboards, or APIs.

Common Mistakes and Avoiding Them

When working with aliases and computed columns, developers often commit common mistakes that can affect readability, maintainability, and performance. The following points highlight some of the most frequent mistakes, as well as how to avoid them:

- **Using Vague Aliases**
  - **Bad**: `SELECT Salary * 0.10 AS x`
  - **Good**: `SELECT Salary * 0.10 AS Bonus`
- **Overusing Spaces in Aliases**
  - While `[Total Sales Amount]` is fine for reports, in development environments, we prefer `TotalSalesAmount`.
- **Forgetting to Persist Frequently Used Computed Columns**
  - If you calculate (`Salary * 12`) in every query, define it as a persisted computed column in the schema.
- **Performance Issues with Complex Expressions**
  - **Example**: `FullName` = `FirstName + ' ' + LastName` is cheap.
  - However, `TaxBracket = CASE ... END` with many conditions may be expensive. Therefore, you must persist it, if it is queried frequently.

Key Takeaways:

- Aliases improve readability and produce user-friendly output.
- Computed columns allow derived data to be generated dynamically or stored persistently.
- Use descriptive aliases to avoid ambiguity.
- For performance, persist computed columns if they are used frequently.
- Together, aliases and computed columns simplify reporting, reduce repetition, and improve consistency.

WHERE Clause Predicates and Logical Operators

The `WHERE` clause is one of the most fundamental and powerful components of a `SELECT` statement in SQL Server. It allows developers to filter rows based on specific conditions so that only the relevant subset of data is retrieved. Without the `WHERE` clause, a query retrieves all rows from the specified tables, which can be inefficient, and also overwhelming when you are dealing with large datasets. Hence, by applying carefully designed filtering logic, you can dramatically improve both performance and usability of your queries.

Role of the WHERE Clause

The `WHERE` clause appears immediately after the `FROM` clause in a `SELECT` statement, as well as before grouping or ordering clauses. Its purpose is to filter the dataset, and return only the rows that satisfy the specified condition(s).

Basic Syntax:

```
SELECT column1, column2
FROM TableName
WHERE condition;
```

For example:

```
SELECT FirstName, LastName, Age
FROM Employees
WHERE Age > 40;
```

This query returns only the employees who are older than 40 years.

Key Point: *The `WHERE` clause does not affect the columns retrieved; it only filters rows.*

Predicates in the WHERE Clause

A predicate is simply a condition that evaluates to **TRUE**, **FALSE**, or **UNKNOWN** (when you are dealing with **NULL**). Only rows for which the predicate evaluates to **TRUE** are included in the results.

Types of Predicates:

- **Comparison Predicates**: Use standard operators: =, <, >, <=, >=, <>.

  ```
  SELECT *
  FROM Products
  WHERE Price >= 100;
  ```

- **Range Predicates (BETWEEN)**: They filter rows within a specific range (inclusive).

  ```
  SELECT *
  FROM Orders
  WHERE OrderDate BETWEEN '2025-01-01' AND '2025-06-30';
  ```

- **Set Predicates (IN/NOT IN)**: They check whether a value exists in a specified set.

  ```
  SELECT *
  FROM Employees
  WHERE DepartmentID IN (1, 2, 3);
  ```

- **Pattern Matching (LIKE)**: Used for string searches with wildcards (%, _).

  ```
  SELECT *
  FROM Customers
  WHERE LastName LIKE 'Sm%';
  ```

- **Null Check Predicates (IS NULL/IS NOT NULL)**: They handle missing values explicitly.

  ```
  SELECT *
  FROM Employees
  WHERE ManagerID IS NULL;
  ```

- **Boolean Predicates**: Some columns may naturally store BIT values (0, 1).

  ```
  SELECT *
  FROM Flags
  WHERE IsActive = 1;
  ```

Logical Operators: AND, OR, NOT

When multiple conditions are required, logical operators allow developers to combine or negate them.

AND Operator

It requires all the conditions to be **TRUE**.

```
SELECT *
FROM Employees
WHERE Age > 30 AND DepartmentID = 2;
```

Here, only the employees who are older than 30, and work in Department 2 are returned.

OR Operator

It requires at least one condition to be **TRUE**.

```
SELECT *
FROM Employees
WHERE DepartmentID = 2 OR DepartmentID = 5;
```

Here, the employees from Department 2 or Department 5 are included.

The OR operator allows you to combine multiple conditions in a **WHERE** clause, and returns the rows that meet any of the specified criteria. While it is straightforward to use, queries with many OR conditions can become harder to read. This may impact performance if the indexes are not properly utilized. Therefore, for large datasets, consider rewriting complex OR conditions using IN, or separate queries with UNION to improve clarity and efficiency.

NOT Operator

It negates a condition.

```
SELECT *
FROM Employees
WHERE NOT (Age < 25);
```

Here, it excludes all the employees who are under 25.

***Warning**: Use **NOT** carefully with **NULL** values. For example, **NOT** (Salary > 50000) will not include rows where Salary is **NULL**, as **NULL** yields **UNKNOWN** in comparisons. The **NOT** operator reverses the result of a condition, which will allow you to exclude rows that meet certain criteria. However, you must take care while using **NOT** with columns that can contain **NULL** values. This is because the comparisons involving **NULL** produce **UNKNOWN**, which can lead to unexpected results. Therefore, you should always test queries with possible **NULL**s to ensure accurate filtering.*

Operator Precedence and Parentheses

When multiple logical operators are used, SQL Server follows precedence rules, which are:

- **NOT** is evaluated first.
- **AND** is evaluated after that.
- **OR** is evaluated at the very last.

For example:

```
SELECT *
FROM Employees
WHERE Age > 30 OR DepartmentID = 2 AND IsActive = 1;
```

This is equivalent to:

```
WHERE Age > 30 OR (DepartmentID = 2 AND IsActive = 1);
```

If the intention was different, parentheses must be used. This is shown here:

```
WHERE (Age > 30 OR DepartmentID = 2) AND IsActive = 1;
```

Tip: *Always use parentheses when mixing* **AND** *and* **OR** *to ensure clarity. Understanding operator precedence is essential to ensure that SQL queries return the expected results. While SQL Server applies a standard order of evaluation* **NOT** *first,* **AND** *second, and* **OR** *last, using parentheses explicitly improves readability and prevents logical errors. Therefore, in complex queries, always group conditions with parentheses to clearly indicate the intended logic, and to make the query easier for others to understand and maintain.*

Practical Examples of WHERE Logic

Example 1: Filtering by Multiple Criteria

```
SELECT OrderID, CustomerID, OrderDate
FROM Orders
WHERE OrderDate >= '2025-01-01'
      AND OrderDate <= '2025-06-30'
      AND TotalAmount > 500;
```

- This retrieves high-value orders from the first half of 2025.

This example demonstrates how combining multiple conditions in the **WHERE** clause allows precise filtering of data. By using logical operators like **AND**, as well as comparison operators, you can target specific subsets of rows based on multiple criteria. Thus, applying these techniques consistently ensures that queries return accurate and meaningful results for analysis or reporting.

Example 2: Complex Business Rules

```
SELECT *
FROM Employees
WHERE (DepartmentID = 3 OR DepartmentID = 5)
      AND HireDate < '2020-01-01'
      AND IsActive = 1;
```

- Here, the employees from departments 3 or 5, who are hired before 2020 and are still active, will be filtered.

This example illustrates how combining **OR** and **AND** conditions with parentheses enables the implementation of complex business rules. Proper use of grouping ensures that SQL Server evaluates conditions in the intended order, which allows for precise filtering of employees who meet multiple criteria. Hence, such techniques are essential for real-world queries where multiple conditions must be satisfied simultaneously.

Example 3: Handling Missing Data

```
SELECT *
FROM Products
WHERE Discontinued = 1 OR Discontinued IS NULL;
```

- This captures discontinued products even if the column is not populated.

Performance Considerations

When designing queries for performance, understanding how SQL Server uses indexes is crucial. Poorly written filters or misuse of functions can prevent the optimizer from taking advantage of indexes, which can lead to full table scans and degraded performance. Therefore, the following best practices highlight how to write index-friendly queries:

- **Index Usage**: Conditions in the `WHERE` clause often rely on indexes. Therefore, you must ensure that filtering columns are properly indexed. **Example**: Filtering on `LastName` is efficient if there is an index on `LastName`.
- **`SARGability` (Search ARGument able)**: Queries should be written to allow indexes to be used. For example:

  ❌ Bad (Non-SARGable):

  ```
  WHERE YEAR(OrderDate) = 2025;
  ```

  ✅ Good (SARGable):

  ```
  WHERE OrderDate >= '2025-01-01' AND OrderDate < '2026-01-01';
  ```
- **Avoid Functions on Columns**: Wrapping columns in functions prevents index usage.
- **Statistics and Histograms**: Ensure that all the statistics are up to date, as SQL Server uses them to generate efficient query plans.

Best Practices

Writing effective filtering logic in SQL Server is not just about correctness, but also about clarity, maintainability, and performance. Ambiguous or inefficient conditions can make queries harder to understand, and can significantly reduce execution speed. Therefore, the following best practices will help you design filters that are both accurate and efficient:

- Use clear and explicit conditions with parentheses.
- Prefer `IN` for multiple equality checks, and not multiple ORs.
- Handle `NULL` explicitly with `IS NULL` or `IS NOT NULL`.
- Optimize range searches with proper indexing.
- Keep queries SARGable to leverage indexes.
- Test filtering logic against realistic datasets to confirm performance.

Pagination: `TOP, OFFSET-FETCH, ROW_NUMBER`

When you are working with large datasets in SQL Server, returning all rows at once is neither efficient, nor it is user-friendly. Instead, applications often need to retrieve subsets of rows, or "**pages**" of data, at a time. This concept is known as pagination.

Pagination is crucial in:

- Web Applications (For example, displaying search results, product listings, or customer records)
- Reporting Systems (For example, showing rows in chunks for readability)
- Performance Optimization (For example, retrieving only what is needed, instead of full tables)

SQL Server provides multiple tools to achieve pagination, which are:

- `TOP` Clause
- `OFFSET-FETCH` Clause (Introduced in SQL Server 2012)
- `ROW_NUMBER()` Function with Windowing

Pagination with the TOP Clause

The TOP clause limits the number of rows returned by a query. It is the simplest way to implement pagination when you only need the "first N rows".

Syntax:

```
SELECT TOP (N) column1, column2
FROM TableName
ORDER BY column_name;
```

Example 1: Retrieving the Top 10 Employees by Salary

```
SELECT TOP (10) EmployeeID, FirstName, LastName, Salary
FROM Employees
ORDER BY Salary DESC;
```

- Here, it returns only the 10 highest-paid employees.

Example 2: Using `PERCENT` with `TOP`

```
SELECT TOP (5) PERCENT *
FROM Customers
ORDER BY CustomerID;
```

- Here, it retrieves the top 5% of all customers.

Note: *Using* **`PERCENT`** *is less common in production because the exact number of rows depends on the dataset size, which can be unpredictable.*

Limitations of `TOP`:

- It only retrieves the first N rows, as it cannot directly implement "page 2, 3, and so on".
- It requires careful use of **`ORDER BY`**. Without it, results may be inconsistent because SQL Server does not guarantee row order, unless it is explicitly specified.

Pagination with `OFFSET-FETCH`

To address the limitations of TOP, SQL Server 2012 introduced the **`OFFSET-FETCH`** clause as part of the **`ORDER BY`** clause. This allows developers to skip a certain number of rows (**`OFFSET`**), and then retrieve the next set of rows (**`FETCH`**).

Syntax:

```
SELECT column1, column2
FROM TableName
ORDER BY column_name
OFFSET X ROWS
FETCH NEXT Y ROWS ONLY;
```

Here

- **`OFFSET X ROWS`**: Skips the first X rows
- **`FETCH NEXT Y ROWS ONLY`**: Returns the next Y rows after the skipped ones

Example 1: Retrieving Rows 11–20

```
SELECT EmployeeID, FirstName, LastName
FROM Employees
```

```
ORDER BY EmployeeID
OFFSET 10 ROWS FETCH NEXT 10 ROWS ONLY;
```

- Skips the first 10 rows, and returns the next 10 (from 11 to 20).

Example 2: Implementing Page Numbers

Suppose each page should display 25 records. This will look like:

```
DECLARE @PageNumber INT = 3;
DECLARE @PageSize INT = 25;

SELECT OrderID, CustomerID, OrderDate
FROM Orders
ORDER BY OrderDate DESC
OFFSET (@PageNumber - 1) * @PageSize ROWS
FETCH NEXT @PageSize ROWS ONLY;
```

Here:

- Page 1 returns rows 1-25.
- Page 2 returns rows 26–50.
- Page 3 returns rows 51–75.

Advantages of `OFFSET-FETCH`:

- Cleaner, built-in pagination support
- Easy integration with applications (pass in page number and size)
- Works seamlessly with **`ORDER BY`**

Limitations:

- Requires **`ORDER BY`**
- Performance can degrade for large **`OFFSET`** values (for example, skipping 1 million rows still requires SQL Server to scan and count them)

Pagination with `ROW_NUMBER()`

Before **`OFFSET-FETCH`** was introduced, the most common pagination method in SQL Server used the **`ROW_NUMBER()`** window function.

Syntax:

```
SELECT column1, column2,
       ROW_NUMBER() OVER (ORDER BY column_name) AS RowNum
FROM TableName;
```

The **`ROW_NUMBER()`** function assigns a unique sequential number to each row based on the **`ORDER BY`** clause.

Example 1: Numbering Rows

```
SELECT EmployeeID, FirstName, LastName,
       ROW_NUMBER() OVER (ORDER BY LastName) AS RowNum
FROM Employees;
```

- Each employee is assigned a row number based on the alphabetical order of **`LastName`**.

Example 2: Extracting Pages with ROW_NUMBER()

```
WITH EmployeeCTE AS
(
    SELECT EmployeeID, FirstName, LastName,
           ROW_NUMBER() OVER (ORDER BY EmployeeID) AS RowNum
    FROM Employees
)
SELECT *
FROM EmployeeCTE
WHERE RowNum BETWEEN 11 AND 20;
```

- This retrieves page 2, while assuming a page size of 10.

Advantages of ROW_NUMBER():

- Very flexible, as you can filter based on ranges (**BETWEEN**, >, <)
- Can be combined with other window functions for advanced reporting
- Works on older versions of SQL Server (before 2012)

Limitations:

- More verbose than **OFFSET-FETCH**
- Requires a CTE or subquery
- May have extra overhead compared to the simpler **OFFSET-FETCH** for small datasets

Choosing between TOP, OFFSET-FETCH, and ROW_NUMBER()

The following table summarizes the main pagination techniques in SQL Server, and also highlights their best use cases, advantages, and limitations:

Method	Best Use Case	Pros	Cons
TOP	Quick retrieval of the first N rows	Simple syntax, efficient	Cannot retrieve arbitrary "pages"
OFFSET-FETCH	Standard pagination (page 2, 3, and so on)	Built-in, clean syntax	Poor performance with a large OFFSET
ROW_NUMBER()	Flexible, advanced paging with filters	Works in older versions; is immensely powerful	Verbose, requires subqueries

***Table 3.1**: Comparison of Pagination Methods in SQL Server*

Performance Considerations

Efficient pagination in SQL Server requires careful consideration of indexes, query structure, and dataset size. Poorly designed pagination queries can result in wasted resources, slow response times, and poor user experience. Therefore, the following best practices will help you implement scalable and efficient pagination logic:

- Indexes: Always use ORDER BY on indexed columns for better performance.

  ```
  CREATE INDEX IX_Employees_LastName ON Employees(LastName);
  ```

  It helps speed up pagination queries significantly.

- Avoid Large OFFSETs: Skipping millions of rows wastes resources. Instead: Consider providing a concrete example or alternative approach to illustrate this point for readers.
- Use keyset pagination (filter on the last retrieved key).

```
SELECT TOP (25) *
FROM Employees
WHERE EmployeeID > @LastEmployeeID
ORDER BY EmployeeID;
```

Balance Query Complexity:

```
TOP: Is the fastest, but limited
OFFSET-FETCH: Is the standard for modern apps
ROW_NUMBER(): Is powerful for advanced filters
```

Best Practices

Pagination in SQL Server must be implemented carefully to ensure both performance and consistency of results. Without proper design, queries can return inconsistent data or degrade in speed as datasets grow. Therefore, you should follow the mentioned best practices outline reliable approaches for handling pagination efficiently:

- Always use **ORDER BY** to ensure consistent results.
- Prefer **OFFSET-FETCH** for simple, modern pagination.
- Use **ROW_NUMBER()** when pagination needs to combine with complex filters.
- Use keyset pagination instead of large OFFSETs for scalable solutions.
- Index the column(s) used in **ORDER BY** for the best performance.

CASE Expressions and Conditional Logic

In real-world database applications, queries often require conditional logic, that is, the ability to return different values depending on certain conditions. In T-SQL, this is achieved using the CASE expression, which allows you to implement if-then-else logic directly within queries.

The **CASE** expression is extremely versatile and is often used to:

- Categorize data into groups.
- Replace complex joins or subqueries.
- Implement derived or computed columns.
- Handle NULLs or substitute default values.
- Perform pivoting-like operations.

Syntax of CASE

There are two main forms of **CASE** in T-SQL, which are:

- **Simple CASE Expression**

  It compares an expression to a series of possible values.

  ```
  CASE input_expression
      WHEN value1 THEN result1
      WHEN value2 THEN result2
  ```

```
    ...
    ELSE default_result
END
```

- This example checks the equality between the **input_expression** and each **WHEN** value.
- It returns the corresponding **THEN** result for the first match.
- If no match is found, then the **ELSE** value is returned (optional).

- **Searched CASE Expression**

  It evaluates a series of Boolean conditions (logical expressions).

```
CASE
    WHEN condition1 THEN result1
    WHEN condition2 THEN result2
    ...
    ELSE default_result
END
```

  - Each **WHEN** is a condition in this example.
  - It is evaluated in order until one is true.
  - If none are true, it returns the **ELSE** value (if provided).

Examples of Simple CASE

Example 1: Assign Labels Based on Department

```
SELECT EmployeeID, DepartmentID,
       CASE DepartmentID
           WHEN 1 THEN 'Finance'
           WHEN 2 THEN 'Human Resources'
           WHEN 3 THEN 'IT'
           ELSE 'Other'
       END AS DepartmentName
FROM Employees;
```

- This example maps department IDs to readable names.
- It prevents repeated joins when a small lookup table is not necessary.

Example 2: Grade Classification

```
SELECT StudentID, Score,
       CASE Score
           WHEN 100 THEN 'Perfect'
           WHEN 90 THEN 'Excellent'
           WHEN 80 THEN 'Good'
           ELSE 'Average/Other'
       END AS GradeCategory
FROM StudentScores;
```

- This example translates numeric values into descriptive labels.

Examples of Searched CASE

Example 1: Categorize Employees by Salary Range

```
SELECT EmployeeID, FirstName, LastName, Salary,
       CASE
           WHEN Salary >= 100000 THEN 'High Earner'
           WHEN Salary BETWEEN 60000 AND 99999 THEN 'Mid-level'
           WHEN Salary < 60000 THEN 'Entry-level'
           ELSE 'Unknown'
       END AS SalaryCategory
FROM Employees;
```

- This example uses logical conditions to classify employees.
- It is more flexible than simple `CASE`, as it supports ranges.

Example 2: Handling NULL Values

```
SELECT OrderID, ShipDate,
       CASE
           WHEN ShipDate IS NULL THEN 'Not Yet Shipped'
           ELSE 'Shipped'
       END AS ShippingStatus
FROM Orders;
```

- The example replaces **`NULL`** with a meaningful label.
- It is more readable than using **`ISNULL`** or **`COALESCE`** in some cases.

Example 3: Conditional Discounts

```
SELECT OrderID, TotalAmount,
       CASE
           WHEN TotalAmount > 500 THEN TotalAmount * 0.90  -- 10% discount
           WHEN TotalAmount > 200 THEN TotalAmount * 0.95  -- 5% discount
           ELSE TotalAmount
       END AS FinalAmount
FROM Orders;
```

- This example demonstrates calculations inside CASE.
- It applies discounts conditionally.

Using CASE in ORDER BY

You can use **`CASE`** expressions to customize sorting logic.

Example: Sort Students by Pass/Fail before Score

```
SELECT StudentID, Score,
       CASE WHEN Score >= 50 THEN 'Pass' ELSE 'Fail' END AS Result
FROM Students
ORDER BY
       CASE
           WHEN Score >= 50 THEN 1
           ELSE 2
       END,
       Score DESC;
```

- This example ensures that all "**Pass**" students appear first, and are sorted by score, followed by "**Fail**" students.

Using CASE in GROUP BY/Aggregates

You can use CASE inside aggregate functions to compute conditional totals.

Example 1: Count Orders by Shipping Status

```
SELECT
    SUM(CASE WHEN ShipDate IS NULL THEN 1 ELSE 0 END) AS PendingOrders,
    SUM(CASE WHEN ShipDate IS NOT NULL THEN 1 ELSE 0 END) AS ShippedOrders
FROM Orders;
```

- This example counts orders based on shipping status in a single query.

Example 2: Sales by Category

```
SELECT
    SUM(CASE WHEN Category = 'Electronics' THEN Amount ELSE 0 END) AS
ElectronicsSales,
    SUM(CASE WHEN Category = 'Clothing' THEN Amount ELSE 0 END) AS ClothingSales,
    SUM(CASE WHEN Category = 'Other' THEN Amount ELSE 0 END) AS OtherSales
FROM Sales;
```

- This example demonstrates pivot-style aggregation using **CASE**.
- It avoids the need for the **PIVOT** operator in simpler scenarios.

Nested CASE Expressions

You can nest **CASE** expressions inside each other, even though readability should be considered.

```
SELECT EmployeeID, Salary,
       CASE
           WHEN Salary >= 100000 THEN
                CASE
                    WHEN Salary > 200000 THEN 'Executive'
                    ELSE 'Senior'
                END
           WHEN Salary >= 60000 THEN 'Mid-level'
           ELSE 'Entry-level'
       END AS PositionLevel
FROM Employees;
```

- This example demonstrates multi-level decision making.
- Sometimes, it is better handled with separate conditions for clarity.

Best Practices for CASE

When you are working with conditional logic in SQL Server, you will find that the **CASE** expression is a versatile tool that can be applied in filtering, calculations, and reporting. Therefore, to use it effectively, keep the following practices in mind:

- Use Searched **CASE** for Complex Conditions.
    - It is more flexible than simple equality checks.

- Keep Readability in Mind.
  - Long, deeply nested **CASE** statements can reduce clarity.
  - Hence, you must consider breaking logic into computed columns or views.
- Use with Aggregates Carefully.
  - It is very powerful for conditional counts and sums.
- Factor in Performance Conditions.
  - **CASE** is evaluated for SQL Server to stop at the first match.
  - Ensure that conditions are written efficiently.
- Consider Alternative Functions.
  - To handle **NULLs**, **ISNULL**, **COALESCE**, or **IIF** may be a better approach sometimes.
  - SQL Server 2012 introduced IIF (**condition**, **true_value**, **false_value**) as shorthand for a simple two-way **CASE**.

Key Takeaways

The CASE expression is one of the most important tools for embedding conditional logic directly into SQL queries. It allows developers to transform raw data into meaningful categories, apply dynamic formulas, and control sorting and grouping behavior. Therefore, you must remember the following points:

- **CASE** expressions introduce conditional logic into SQL queries.
- They are of two types: Simple **CASE** (equality checks) and Searched **CASE** (boolean conditions).
- They can be used in **SELECT**, **ORDER BY**, **GROUP BY**, and aggregate functions.
- They are essential for categorization, handling **NULLs**, applying conditional formulas, and custom sorting.
- **Best Practice**: Keep expressions simple and readable; use with aggregates for powerful conditional summaries.

EXISTS, IN, and JOIN Filters

When working with relational data, queries often require filtering rows based on values that exist in other tables or subqueries. T-SQL provides several mechanisms for achieving this:

- **EXISTS**: Tests whether a subquery returns at least one row
- **IN**: Checks if a value exists within a set of values
- **JOIN Filters**: Combine rows from multiple tables and filters based on matching conditions

Although these constructs often serve similar purposes, each has unique performance implications, use cases, and readability trade-offs.

The EXISTS Operator

The **EXISTS** operator is used to test the existence of rows returned by a subquery. If the subquery returns at least one row, the condition evaluates to **TRUE**.

Syntax

```
WHERE EXISTS (subquery)
```

- The subquery is typically a correlated subquery, while referencing columns from the outer query.
- SQL Server stops processing once the first row is found, which makes it efficient in many scenarios.

Example 1: Employees with Orders

```
SELECT e.EmployeeID, e.FirstName, e.LastName
FROM Employees e
WHERE EXISTS (
    SELECT 1
    FROM Orders o
    WHERE o.EmployeeID = e.EmployeeID
);
```

- This returns only those employees who have placed at least one order.
- **SELECT 1** is used in this example, as the actual column list inside the subquery is irrelevant; only the existence of rows matters.

Example 2: Customers with No Orders

```
SELECT c.CustomerID, c.CompanyName
FROM Customers c
WHERE NOT EXISTS (
    SELECT 1
    FROM Orders o
    WHERE o.CustomerID = c.CustomerID
);
```

- This example uses NOT EXISTS to find customers with no orders.
- Here, you may observe a common pattern for anti-joins.

The IN Operator

The IN operator is used to check whether a value matches any value in a list or subquery result set.

Syntax

```
WHERE column IN (value1, value2, ..., valueN)
```

or

```
WHERE column IN (SELECT column FROM Table)
```

Using the **IN** operator simplifies queries when checking for membership in a predefined set of values or the result of a subquery. It is especially useful for filtering data against small static lists, or when the subquery returns a limited number of rows. However, for large datasets, **EXISTS** or properly indexed joins may provide better performance. Always be mindful of **NULL** values, as **NOT IN** can produce unexpected results if the set contains any **NULLs**.

Example 1: Static List

```
SELECT FirstName, LastName, DepartmentID
FROM Employees
WHERE DepartmentID IN (1, 2, 3);
```

- This filters employees in departments 1, 2, or 3.
- This is very readable for small static sets.

Example 2: Subquery

```
SELECT FirstName, LastName
FROM Employees
WHERE EmployeeID IN (SELECT EmployeeID FROM Orders);
```

- This example finds employees who appear in the Orders table.
- It is functionally similar to the `EXISTS` example earlier.

Notes on `IN`:

- `IN` works well for small sets.
- For large subqueries, performance with `IN` may degrade when it is compared to `EXISTS` or `JOIN`.
- `NOT IN` requires caution with `NULLs`, as they can cause unexpected results (rows may be excluded if the subquery contains `NULL` values).

JOIN Filters

`JOIN` filters combine rows from two or more tables based on a related column. Unlike `EXISTS` or `IN`, which test membership or existence, JOIN actually brings in data from multiple tables.

Types of Joins Used in Filtering:

- `INNER JOIN`: Returns rows with matching values in both tables
- `LEFT JOIN` + `WHERE` ... `IS NULL`: This is often used to filter rows that do not have a match (anti-join).

Example 1: `INNER JOIN` Filter

```
SELECT e.EmployeeID, e.FirstName, e.LastName
FROM Employees e
INNER JOIN Orders o
    ON e.EmployeeID = o.EmployeeID;
```

- It returns employees who have at least one order.
- It is similar to `EXISTS` and `IN`, but joins bring actual order data into scope.

Example 2: `LEFT JOIN` with Anti-Filter

```
SELECT c.CustomerID, c.CompanyName
FROM Customers c
LEFT JOIN Orders o
    ON c.CustomerID = o.CustomerID
WHERE o.CustomerID IS NULL;
```

- It returns customers with no matching orders.
- It is equivalent to the `NOT EXISTS` example seen earlier.

EXISTS versus IN versus JOIN – Comparison

Although `EXISTS`, `IN`, and `JOIN` can often be used interchangeably, choosing the right one improves both readability and performance.

Therefore, the following table summarizes the key differences, use cases, and performance considerations for **EXISTS**, **IN**, and **JOIN** while filtering or combining data in SQL Server queries:

Feature / Use Case	EXISTS	IN	JOIN
Purpose	Tests the existence of rows	Checks membership in a set	Combines rows from multiple tables
Best For	Large datasets, correlated subqueries	Small static sets, membership tests	When additional data from the related table is required
Performance	Stops at first match (Efficient)	May degrade with large subqueries	Can produce duplicates unless handled
NULL Handling	Safe with NULLs	**NOT** IN fails if **NULL** exists	**NULLs** handled naturally
Anti-Join (No Match)	NOT EXISTS (Preferred)	NOT IN (Caution with NULLs)	LEFT JOIN ... WHERE NULL
Readability	Good for existence logic	Simple for small lists	Clear when pulling extra columns

***Table 3.2**: Comparison of EXISTS, IN, and JOIN in SQL Server*

Performance Considerations

When deciding between **EXISTS**, **IN**, and **JOIN** for subquery logic or filtering, it is important to understand their performance characteristics and ideal use cases:

- **EXISTS**
  - Generally, it is more efficient for large tables, since it short-circuits at the first match.
  - It works best with correlated subqueries and proper indexes.
- **IN**
  - It is fast for small lists (static values).
  - When it is combined with subqueries, its performance depends on SQL Server's execution plan.
  - However, it can be slower than **EXISTS** when it comes to large sets.
- **JOIN**
  - It is useful when retrieving additional columns from the related table.
  - It might produce duplicates unless **DISTINCT** or aggregation is applied.
  - It can be more expensive if unnecessary and extra data is brought in.

Practical Use Cases

Use Case 1: Security Filtering with EXISTS

```
SELECT UserID, UserName
FROM Users u
WHERE EXISTS (
    SELECT 1 FROM Permissions p
    WHERE p.UserID = u.UserID
      AND p.PermissionType = 'Admin'
);
```

- **EXISTS** checks if a user has admin permissions.

Use Case 2: Static Lookup with IN

```
SELECT ProductID, ProductName
FROM Products
WHERE CategoryID IN (1, 4, 7);
```

- `IN` filters products belonging to specific categories.

Use Case 3: Data Enrichment with JOIN

```
SELECT o.OrderID, c.CompanyName, o.TotalAmount
FROM Orders o
INNER JOIN Customers c
    ON o.CustomerID = c.CustomerID;
```

- `JOIN` pulls in customer names along with order details.

Best Practices

When choosing between `EXISTS`, `IN`, and `JOIN`, you must follow these best practices to ensure efficiency and correctness:

- **Use `EXISTS` for Large Data.** Use it especially when you are checking for the presence of related rows.
- **Use `IN` for `Small`, Readable Lists.** It is great for filtering against static sets of values.
- **Use `JOIN` When You Need Extra Columns.** Do not use `JOIN` just for filtering; if you do not need additional data, it may add unnecessary overhead.
- **Beware of `NULLs` with `NOT IN`.** A single `NULL` in the subquery result can invalidate the whole condition. You must prefer `NOT EXISTS` instead.
- **Always Check the Execution Plans.** SQL Server may internally optimize `EXISTS`, `IN`, or `JOIN` into similar plans. Hence, testing it with actual data is essential.

Window Functions

Window functions are one of the most powerful features in T-SQL. Unlike aggregate functions that collapse multiple rows into a single result, window functions allow you to perform calculations across a set of rows related to the current row, while it returns a row for each input. This means that you can compute running totals, rankings, moving averages, and percentiles, all without losing the details fed in individual rows.

Moreover, window functions are widely used in analytical queries, reporting systems, and dashboards because they allow complex calculations in a declarative and efficient way.

Window Function

A window function performs a calculation across a set of rows called a window that is defined by the `OVER()` clause. Each row can "see" other rows in the defined window, but the row itself remains in the result.

For example, if you want to calculate the total sales for each region, but still see each individual order, then a window function is ideal.

General Syntax:

```
function_name (expression)
OVER (
    [PARTITION BY partition_column]
    [ORDER BY order_column]
    [ROWS BETWEEN ...]
)
```

Here:

- **`function_name(expression)`**: Indicates the aggregate or ranking function to apply
- **`OVER()`**: Defines the window scope
- **`PARTITION BY`**: Divides the dataset into groups (like a grouped aggregate, but without collapsing rows)
- **`ORDER BY`**: Determines the order of rows within the partition for calculations such as ranking or running totals
- **`ROWS BETWEEN …`** : Specifies the frame of rows (for example, the current row and the next two rows)

Categories of Window Functions

There are three broad categories of window functions in SQL Server, which are:

- **Aggregate Window Functions**: They extend aggregate functions (**`SUM`**, **`AVG`**, **`MIN`**, **`MAX`**, **`COUNT`**) over a window.
- **Ranking Window Functions**: They assign ranking values to rows (**`ROW_NUMBER`**, **`RANK`**, **`DENSE_RANK`**, **`NTILE`**).
- **Analytic/Value Window Functions**: They provide value-based insights (**`LEAD`**, **`LAG`**, **`FIRST_VALUE`**, **`LAST_VALUE`**).

Aggregate Window Functions

`Aggregate` functions inside a window context let you calculate totals, averages, and other aggregates, while maintaining detail rows.

Example: Total Sales per Region:

```
SELECT
    Region,
    OrderID,
    Amount,
    SUM(Amount) OVER (PARTITION BY Region) AS TotalRegionSales,
    AVG(Amount) OVER (PARTITION BY Region) AS AvgOrderAmount
FROM Orders;
```

Here:

- **`SUM(Amount)`** computes the total sales per region.
- **`AVG(Amount)`** calculates the average order size in the region.
- Each row still shows the individual order.

Ranking Functions

```
ROW_NUMBER()
SELECT
      CustomerID,
      OrderDate,
      ROW_NUMBER() OVER (PARTITION BY CustomerID ORDER BY OrderDate) AS
OrderSequence
FROM Orders;
```

- It assigns unique sequential numbers.

```
RANK()
SELECT
      EmployeeID,
      Sales,
      RANK() OVER (ORDER BY Sales DESC) AS SalesRank
FROM SalesSummary;
```

- The ties receive the same rank, while the sequence may skip numbers.

```
DENSE_RANK()
SELECT
      EmployeeID,
      Sales,
      DENSE_RANK() OVER (ORDER BY Sales DESC) AS SalesRank
FROM SalesSummary;
```

- There are no gaps in rank numbers.

```
NTILE(n)
SELECT
      CustomerID,
      OrderAmount,
      NTILE(4) OVER (ORDER BY OrderAmount DESC) AS Quartile
FROM Orders;
```

- It divides rows into n groups.

Analytic Functions

LEAD() and **LAG()**

```
SELECT
      EmployeeID,
      OrderDate,
      LAG(OrderDate) OVER (PARTITION BY EmployeeID ORDER BY OrderDate) AS PrevOrder,
      LEAD(OrderDate) OVER (PARTITION BY EmployeeID ORDER BY OrderDate) AS NextOrder
FROM Orders;
```

- **LAG** looks behind, while **LEAD** looks ahead.

```
FIRST_VALUE() and LAST_VALUE()
SELECT
      Department,
      EmployeeName,
```

```
        Salary,
        FIRST_VALUE(Salary) OVER (PARTITION BY Department ORDER BY Salary DESC)
    AS HighestSalary,
        LAST_VALUE(Salary) OVER (PARTITION BY Department ORDER BY Salary DESC
        ROWS BETWEEN UNBOUNDED PRECEDING AND UNBOUNDED FOLLOWING) AS
    LowestSalary
    FROM Employees;
```

- It retrieves the first or the last value in the window.

Window Frames

Window frames define the rows that are included relative to the current row. These can be:

- **Running Total**: The rows between the unbounded preceding and the current row
- **Sliding Window**: The rows between the one that is preceding and the one that is following
- **Full Partition**: The range between unbounded preceding and unbounded following

Example: Running Total

```
SELECT
    OrderID,
    OrderDate,
    Amount,
    SUM(Amount) OVER (ORDER BY OrderDate
    ROWS BETWEEN UNBOUNDED PRECEDING AND CURRENT ROW) AS RunningTotal
FROM Orders;
```

Real-World Use Cases

- **Sales Reporting**: This includes running totals and ranking sales representatives.
- **Customer Analytics**: These are used to segment customers and measure the days since they made their last purchase.
- **Financial Analysis**: This consists of moving averages and comparing quarter performance.
- **Operational Dashboards**: They calculate time gaps and detect trends.

Performance Considerations

- **Indexes Matter**: `ORDER BY` can be expensive without proper indexes.
- **Large Partitions**: Computing rankings on millions of rows is resource-intensive.
- **Frame Clauses**: Specify explicitly for clarity.
- **Batch Mode**: SQL Server 2019+ optimizes some window functions.

Best Practices

- Always specify `PARTITION BY` and `ORDER BY`.
- Use `ROW_NUMBER` for deduplication.
- Avoid using window functions in subqueries without filtering.
- Prefer `DENSE_RANK` for consistent grouping.
- Validate `LAST_VALUE` when using frames.

Eliminating Duplicates with DISTINCT

When you are querying data, duplicates may appear due to join operations or poorly normalized structures. **DISTINCT** removes them by collapsing identical rows.

Example:

```
SELECT DISTINCT DepartmentID
FROM Employees;
```

This yields a unique list of departments.

Multi-Column Distinct

DISTINCT applies across all selected columns, as shown here:

```
SELECT DISTINCT FirstName, LastName
FROM Employees;
```

This removes duplicate name combinations.

You can count unique values through:

```
SELECT COUNT(DISTINCT DepartmentID) AS UniqueDepartments
FROM Employees;
```

Best Practices

When removing duplicates in SQL Server queries, it is important to use the right approach to maintain performance and correctness. Therefore, you must consider the following guidelines:

- Use **DISTINCT** only when necessary.
- For large queries, investigate duplicates at the source (bad join, redundant data).
- Sometimes **GROUP BY** with aggregates is more appropriate.

Conclusion

This chapter covered the essentials of the **SELECT** statement, including column aliases, computed columns, filtering with WHERE, conditional logic with **CASE**, pagination, window functions, and techniques for handling duplicates. Hence, mastering these concepts enables you to write clear, efficient, and maintainable queries. In the next chapter, we will explore joins, set operations, and subqueries. Additionally, we will learn how to combine data from multiple tables, manipulate result sets, and solve more complex business problems.

CHAPTER 4
Joins, Set Operations, and Subqueries

Introduction

In relational database systems, data is rarely stored in a single table; instead, information is distributed across multiple normalized tables. For example, a sales system might have one table for Customers, another for Orders, and yet another for Products. Hence, to retrieve meaningful insights such as "all customers who purchased a particular product in the last quarter", we must combine data from multiple sources. SQL provides three primary mechanisms for data combination and retrieval: joins, which combine rows from two or more tables based on related columns; set operators, which merge entire result sets into one by stacking rows (such as `UNION`, `INTERSECT`, and `EXCEPT`); and subqueries, which embed queries inside others to perform lookups, filtering, or calculations. These tools are the backbone of relational querying, and allow us to integrate information across multiple entities such as customers, orders, and payments, filter intelligently using conditions that depend on multiple tables, as well as model complex business logic like hierarchies, exclusions, or conditional inclusion. Without mastery of joins, sets, and subqueries, SQL querying remains incomplete. Therefore, this chapter aims to provide deep coverage of these features, their use cases, and best practices.

Structure

In this chapter, we will cover the following topics:

- `CROSS JOIN` and `SELF JOIN`
- Set Operators: `UNION`, `INTERSECT`, `EXCEPT`
- Correlated and Non-Correlated Subqueries
- Derived Tables and Common Table Expressions (CTEs)
- Handling `NULL`s in Joins and Set Operations

CROSS JOIN and SELF JOIN

In SQL, joins are among the most powerful tools available to query writers. While **`INNER`**, **`LEFT`**, **`RIGHT`**, and **`FULL JOIN`**s are used extensively in everyday applications, there are two special join types that often confuse beginners, but are extremely powerful when used correctly. These are **`CROSS JOIN`** and **`SELF JOIN`**. Both of them allow you to approach data in unique ways, while offering solutions to business requirements that traditional joins may not handle efficiently.

Hence, this section will explore the mechanics, syntax, and real-world applications of **`CROSS JOIN`** and **`SELF JOIN`** in great detail, along with performance considerations, best practices, and common pitfalls that you might encounter.

CROSS JOIN

A **CROSS JOIN** returns the Cartesian product of two tables. In simple terms, it pairs every row from the first table with every row from the second table. Hence, if Table A has *m* rows and Table B has *n* rows, the result set will contain $m \times n$ rows.

Unlike **INNER** or **OUTER** joins, a **CROSS JOIN** does not require a join condition (**ON** clause). It is purely combinatorial.

Syntax:

```
SELECT
    a.Column1,
    b.Column2
FROM
    TableA a
CROSS JOIN
    TableB b;
```

Example: Generating Combinations

Imagine you are a retailer that sells T-shirts in multiple colors and sizes. You want to generate all possible color-size combinations to ensure that your product catalog is complete. Therefore, you will create this:

```
CREATE TABLE Colors (
    ColorID INT PRIMARY KEY,
    ColorName VARCHAR(50)
);

CREATE TABLE Sizes (
    SizeID INT PRIMARY KEY,
    SizeName VARCHAR(50)
);

INSERT INTO Colors VALUES (1, 'Red'), (2, 'Blue'), (3, 'Green');
INSERT INTO Sizes VALUES (1, 'Small'), (2, 'Medium'), (3, 'Large');
```

Now, you want every possible combination, such as what is shown here:

```
SELECT
    c.ColorName,
    s.SizeName
FROM
    Colors c
CROSS JOIN
    Sizes s;
```

Result:

```
Red   Small
Red   Medium
Red   Large
Blue  Small
Blue  Medium
Blue  Large
```

```
Green Small
Green Medium
Green Large
```

With 3 colors and 3 sizes, you will get 9 combinations. If the number of colors or sizes grows, the combinations will also grow multiplicatively.

Use Cases of CROSS JOIN

- **Generating Test Data:** Developers often use **CROSS JOIN** to quickly generate large volumes of test data. For example, pairing thousands of customers with hundreds of products creates millions of test transactions.
- **Scenario Analysis:** Businesses may use **CROSS JOIN** to simulate all possible scenarios. For instance, they may pair possible interest rates with loan terms to analyze financial outcomes.
- **Matrix Reports: CROSS JOIN** is helpful when building pivot-style or matrix reports, where you need all possible row-column intersections, even if some intersections may have no actual data.
- **Scheduling Systems:** In schools or organizations, **CROSS JOIN** can be used to generate all possible time-slot and room combinations, before filtering with business rules.

Performance Considerations

- **Result Size Explosion: CROSS JOIN** can generate enormous result sets. Joining a table of 1,000 rows with a table of 1,000 rows will produce 1,000,000 rows. Hence, it may overwhelm memory and disk I/O.
- **Filtering after CROSS JOIN:** Usually, **CROSS JOIN** is combined with a **WHERE** clause to restrict results. For example, after generating all combinations, you may only keep valid or allowed ones.
- **Best Practice:** You must always estimate row counts before running **CROSS JOIN** in production systems.

Example with Filtering:

```
-- Generate all potential staff-to-project assignments.

SELECT
    e.EmployeeName,
    p.ProjectName
FROM
    Employees e
CROSS JOIN
    Projects p
WHERE
    e.Department = p.Department; -- Only allow matching departments.
```

Here, **CROSS JOIN** generates all combinations first, but the **WHERE** clause filters down to generate only logically valid results.

SELF JOIN

A **SELF JOIN** occurs when a table is joined to itself. This is often used when rows in the same table need to be compared, or when hierarchical/recursive relationships exist within a single dataset.

Although there is no keyword **SELF JOIN** in SQL, you can implement it by giving aliases to the same table, and then join it as if it was composed of two different tables.

Syntax

```
SELECT
    a.Column1,
    b.Column1
FROM
    TableName a
JOIN
    TableName b
ON
    a.SomeColumn = b.OtherColumn;
```

Example: Employee Hierarchies

Suppose that you have an Employees table that records each employee's manager. The table is structured as follows:

```
CREATE TABLE Employees (
    EmployeeID INT PRIMARY KEY,
    EmployeeName VARCHAR(100),
    ManagerID INT NULL
);
```

Sample Data:

```
EmployeeID | EmployeeName | ManagerID
-----------|--------------|----------
1          | Alice        | NULL
2          | Bob          | 1
3          | Carol        | 1
4          | Dave         | 2
```

- Alice is the CEO (no manager).
- Bob and Carol report to Alice.
- Dave reports to Bob.

To find employees and their managers, you will use:

```
SELECT
    e.EmployeeName AS Employee,
    m.EmployeeName AS Manager
FROM
    Employees e
LEFT JOIN
    Employees m
ON
    e.ManagerID = m.EmployeeID;
```

Result:

```
Employee | Manager
---------|--------
Alice    | NULL
Bob      | Alice
Carol    | Alice
Dave     | Bob
```

This is a `SELF JOIN` because the Employees table is joined to itself.

Use Cases of `SELF JOIN`

1. **Hierarchical Data**: It is commonly used to represent organizational charts, product categories, or family trees.
2. **Comparing Rows within a Table**: Find pairs of students in the same class, or employees in the same department.
3. **Detecting Relationships: `SELF JOIN`s** help identify related records within the same dataset (for example, customers referring other customers).

Example: Finding Colleagues

Suppose we want to find employees who share the same manager. In that case, we will use:

```
SELECT
    e1.EmployeeName AS Employee1,
    e2.EmployeeName AS Employee2,
    m.EmployeeName AS Manager
FROM
    Employees e1
JOIN
    Employees e2
    ON e1.ManagerID = e2.ManagerID
JOIN
    Employees m
    ON e1.ManagerID = m.EmployeeID
WHERE
    e1.EmployeeID < e2.EmployeeID;
```

This query lists unique employee pairs under the same manager.

Advanced SELF JOIN: Detecting Hierarchies beyond One Level

Sometimes, you will need to go beyond one manager level. While recursive Common Table Expressions (CTEs) are often better suited, `SELF JOIN`s can still help if the depth is limited.

Example: The table for employees and their "grand-managers" (manager's manager) will look like:

```
SELECT
    e.EmployeeName AS Employee,
    m.EmployeeName AS Manager,
    gm.EmployeeName AS GrandManager
FROM
    Employees e
LEFT JOIN Employees m
    ON e.ManagerID = m.EmployeeID
LEFT JOIN Employees gm
    ON m.ManagerID = gm.EmployeeID;
```

Performance Considerations

- `SELF JOIN`s on large tables can be expensive because they effectively double the dataset being processed.

- Adding indexes on join keys (for example, **`ManagerID`**) is crucial for good performance.
- For deeply hierarchical data (like hundreds of levels), use recursive CTEs instead of multiple **`SELF JOIN`**s.

Key Differences: CROSS JOIN vs. SELF JOIN

Feature	`CROSS JOIN`	`SELF JOIN`
Purpose	It gives the Cartesian product of two tables.	It compares or relates rows within the same table.
Syntax Requirement	No join condition is required.	It requires a join condition (usually on a key).
Common Use Cases	It is used for generating combinations and test data.	It is used in hierarchies, self-comparisons, and relationships.
Result Size	It is multiplicative (m × n rows).	It is dependent on internal relationships.

***Table 4.1**: Comparison of Cross Join and Self Join*

Advanced Considerations for CROSS JOIN and SELF JOIN

While **`CROSS JOIN`**s and **`SELF JOIN`**s are conceptually straightforward, their advanced usage requires careful attention to performance, scalability, and practical application in real-world scenarios. Hence, this section provides deeper insight into optimizing, structuring, and applying these joins effectively.

`CROSS JOIN`: Advanced Use Cases

- **Simulating All Possible Combinations**
  - **`CROSS JOIN`** is ideal for generating all possible pairings of two sets.
  - **Example**: A product pricing matrix for multiple sizes and colors will look like:

    ```
    SELECT p.ProductName, s.Size, c.Color
    FROM Products p
    CROSS JOIN Sizes s
    CROSS JOIN Colors c;
    ```

  - It produces every possible combination of product, size, and color.
  - It can be filtered later using a **`WHERE`** clause to focus on feasible combinations.
- **Generating Test Data**
  - It is useful for creating dummy or synthetic datasets to validate reports or ETL pipelines.

    ```
    SELECT s.StudentID, c.CourseID
    FROM Students s
    CROSS JOIN Courses c;
    ```

  - Every student is paired with every course, which is useful for stress testing.
- **Performance Considerations**
  - The number of rows equals to **`rows_in_first_table`** multiplied by **`rows_in_second_table`**.
  - Always estimate the result set size to avoid performance bottlenecks or memory issues.
  - Use filtering early with **`WHERE`** conditions to reduce generating unnecessary rows.

SELF JOIN: Advanced Use Cases

1. **Hierarchical Relationships:** They represent parent-child relationships, such as employee-manager or category-subcategory.

```
SELECT e1.Name AS Employee, e2.Name AS Manager
FROM Employees e1
LEFT JOIN Employees e2
ON e1.ManagerID = e2.EmployeeID;
```

   Hence, they include **NULL** for employees without a manager to preserve all rows.

2. **Finding Sequential Patterns:** They compare adjacent rows or trends in time-series data.

```
SELECT s1.Date AS CurrentDate, s1.Sales AS CurrentSales, s2.Sales AS
PreviousSales
FROM Sales s1
LEFT JOIN Sales s2
ON s1.EmployeeID = s2.EmployeeID
AND s1.Date = DATEADD(day, 1, s2.Date);
```

3. **Detecting Duplicates or Conflicts:** You may do this to identify potential duplicate records in a table.

```
SELECT e1.EmployeeID, e1.Name
FROM Employees e1
JOIN Employees e2
  ON e1.Name = e2.Name
 AND e1.EmployeeID <> e2.EmployeeID;
```

NULL Handling in SELF JOINs

- Columns used in join conditions may contain **NULL**.
- For **LEFT JOIN** self-joins, unmatched rows result in **NULL** on the joined side.
- Therefore, you must always handle **NULL**s explicitly using **ISNULL** or **COALESCE**, whenever necessary. This is shown as follows:

```
SELECT e1.Name AS Employee, COALESCE(e2.Name, 'No Manager') AS Manager
FROM Employees e1
LEFT JOIN Employees e2
ON e1.ManagerID = e2.EmployeeID;
```

Combining with Other SQL Features

- **CROSS JOIN with Aggregates:** It can be combined with **GROUP BY** or **HAVING** for advanced reporting

```
SELECT p.ProductName, c.Color, COUNT(o.OrderID) AS TotalOrders
FROM Products p
CROSS JOIN Colors c
LEFT JOIN Orders o
  ON p.ProductID = o.ProductID
 AND c.ColorID = o.ColorID
GROUP BY p.ProductName, c.Color;
```

- **`SELF JOIN` with Window Functions**: It can replace some self-joins for sequential comparisons using **`LAG()`** or **`LEAD()`** for performance optimization.

```
SELECT EmployeeID, SaleDate, SaleAmount,
       LAG(SaleAmount) OVER (PARTITION BY EmployeeID ORDER BY SaleDate) AS
PreviousSale
FROM Sales;
```

- **Best Practices**
   a. Always alias tables to avoid confusion, especially in **`SELF JOIN`**s.
   b. Filter early in **`CROSS JOIN`**s to avoid massive intermediate result sets.
   c. Consider window functions as an alternative to **`SELF JOIN`**s while comparing sequential data.
   d. Validate **`NULL`** behavior in join conditions to ensure accurate results.
   e. Use **`CROSS JOIN`**s only when necessary; otherwise, **`INNER`** or **`LEFT JOIN`**s with conditions are a safer choice.

- **Real-World Examples**
   - **Inventory Management:** Generate all potential product configurations with **`CROSS JOIN`**.
   - **Organizational Charts:** Build employee-manager hierarchy with **`SELF JOIN`**.
   - **Historical Comparisons:** Compare current and previous records to identify trends using **`SELF JOIN`**.

Best Practices

When working with different types of joins in SQL, it is important to follow certain best practices to ensure clarity, accuracy, and performance. Therefore, you must implement these practices:

1. Always use **`WHERE`** clauses with **`CROSS JOIN`** to limit results.
2. In **`SELF JOIN`**s, make column aliases clear (Employee versus Manager) to avoid confusion.
3. Index join columns (**`ManagerID`**, **`EmployeeID`**) to improve performance.
4. Prefer recursive CTEs over multiple **`SELF JOIN`**s for complex hierarchies.

Set Operators: UNION, INTERSECT, EXCEPT

SQL Server (and relational databases in general) often requires working with multiple result sets from different queries. While JOINs combine rows horizontally (by relating columns across tables), set operators combine results vertically, which stacks or filters rows across multiple queries.

Set operators are rooted in the principles of set theory from mathematics, where collections of elements can be merged, intersected, or subtracted. SQL brings these ideas into the relational world, and gives us **`UNION`**, **`INTERSECT`**, and **`EXCEPT`** as the primary tools.

Rules for Set Operators

Before we explore each operator, it is important to understand the rules that govern their use. These rules are:

1. **Column Count Must Match.**
   - Both queries must return the same number of columns.

   - **Example**:You cannot use UNION to combine a query that returns both ID and Name with a query that returns only ID.

2. **Data Types Must Be Compatible.**
   - Corresponding columns must have compatible data types (for example, **INT** with **BIGINT**, **VARCHAR** with **NVARCHAR**).
   - Implicit conversions may occur, but mismatched data types (like **DATE** with **VARCHAR**) will fail.

3. **Column Names Will be Derived from the First Query.**
   - The output column names come from the first query, regardless of the second query.
   - Always use alias for clarity.
   - **Order Results.**
   - **ORDER BY** can only appear once at the end of the entire set operation (and not within each query).

UNION Operator

The **UNION** operator combines the results of two queries into a single result set, which eliminates duplicates by default.

Syntax:

```
SELECT column_list
FROM Table1
UNION
SELECT column_list
FROM Table2;
```

Key Properties:

- Removes duplicate rows (acts like **DISTINCT**)
- Useful for merging datasets with possible overlap
- Performs implicit sorting during duplicate elimination, which may impact performance

Example 1: Combining Customer Lists

Suppose we have two customer tables from merged businesses, which look like:

```
SELECT CustomerName, Email
FROM Customers_2024
UNION
SELECT CustomerName, Email
FROM Customers_2025;
```

This query produces a deduplicated list of all customers across both years.

UNION ALL Variant

If duplicates are acceptable (or desired for performance reasons), use **UNION ALL**. This will look like:

```
SELECT CustomerName, Email
FROM Customers_2024
UNION ALL
```

```
SELECT CustomerName, Email
FROM Customers_2025;
```

- It keeps duplicates.
- It is faster, as no deduplication step is applied.
- Use this when you know datasets do not overlap, or when you explicitly need duplicates.

INTERSECT Operator

The **INTERSECT** operator returns only rows that exist in both queries.

Syntax:

```
SELECT column_list
FROM Table1
INTERSECT
SELECT column_list
FROM Table2;
```

Key Properties

- It is equivalent to a logical **AND** between sets.
- It always removes duplicates, even without **DISTINCT**.
- It is useful for finding common records across datasets.

Example 2: Customers in Both Years

```
SELECT CustomerName, Email
FROM Customers_2024
INTERSECT
SELECT CustomerName, Email
FROM Customers_2025;
```

This query identifies customers present in datasets from 2024 and 2025.

Behind the Scenes

- SQL Server internally deduplicates and compares rows.
- For large datasets, consider indexes on the intersected columns to optimize performance.

EXCEPT Operator

The **EXCEPT** operator returns rows from the first query that do not exist in the second query.

Syntax:

```
SELECT column_list
FROM Table1
EXCEPT
SELECT column_list
FROM Table2;
```

Key Properties

- Equivalent to a logical MINUS operation in mathematics
- Removes duplicates automatically

- Order matters; it may look like this:

  `A EXCEPT B ≠ B EXCEPT A.`

Example 3: Customers Lost between Years

```
SELECT CustomerName, Email
FROM Customers_2024
EXCEPT
SELECT CustomerName, Email
FROM Customers_2025;
```

This query identifies customers who were in the 2024 dataset, but not in 2025 (that is, lost customers).

Reverse Example: New Customers

```
SELECT CustomerName, Email
FROM Customers_2025
EXCEPT
SELECT CustomerName, Email
FROM Customers_2024;
```

This query finds customers who have been newly acquired in 2025.

Comparison of Operators

The following table summarizes the main set operators in SQL, including their purpose, how they handle duplicates, and their typical use cases:

Operator	Purpose	Duplicate Handling	Typical Use Case
`UNION`	Combine results, remove duplicates	Removes Duplicates	Merging lists from multiple tables/sources
`UNION ALL`	Combine results, keep duplicates	Keeps Duplicates	Appending datasets with no need for deduplication
`INTERSECT`	Common rows across both queries	Removes Duplicates	Finding overlapping customer bases
`EXCEPT`	Rows in first query, but not in second	Removes Duplicates	Identifying lost or missing records

Table 4.2: *Overview of SQL Set Operators*

Performance Considerations

Set operators involve sorting and deduplication, which can be expensive. Hence, the performance considerations to keep in mind while using them are:

1. **Use `UNION ALL` When Possible.**
   - Avoids sorting, as it is significantly faster for large datasets.
   - Use if duplicates do not matter, or if the datasets do not overlap.
2. **Index the Compared Columns.**
   - **`INTERSECT`** and **`EXCEPT`** benefit from indexes on involved columns.
3. **Consider `JOIN` Alternatives.**
   - Sometimes, **`JOIN`** with **`DISTINCT`** performs better than **`INTERSECT`**.

- **Example**:

```
SELECT DISTINCT a.CustomerName, a.Email
FROM Customers_2024 a
JOIN Customers_2025 b
ON a.CustomerName = b.CustomerName AND a.Email = b.Email;
```

4. **Consider Large Data Scenarios.**
   - Partition the data before applying set operators.
   - Avoid combining massive result sets unnecessarily—filter them early on.

Practical Business Use Cases

While applying SQL set operators in real-world scenarios, several common use cases stand out from others. Hence, we have mentioned a few of them to strengthen your understanding of the concept:

- **Marketing Campaign Analysis**
  - **INTERSECT**: Customers who responded to both campaigns
  - **EXCEPT**: Customers lost after a campaign
  - **UNION**: Total reach of all campaigns
- **Data Migration/Integration**
  - Use **EXCEPT** to identify missing rows between old and new systems.
  - Use **INTERSECT** to confirm consistency across systems.
- **Auditing and Reconciliation**
  - Compare transactions across two sources.
  - Example: Banking systems often use **EXCEPT** to detect mismatched records.

Example: Employee Union, Intersect, Except

Consider two tables, which are:

```
Employees_2024 (EmployeeID, Name, Department)
Employees_2025 (EmployeeID, Name, Department)
```

Find all unique employees across both years.

```
SELECT EmployeeID, Name, Department
FROM Employees_2024
UNION
SELECT EmployeeID, Name, Department
FROM Employees_2025;
```

Find employees who stayed both years.

```
SELECT EmployeeID, Name, Department
FROM Employees_2024
INTERSECT
SELECT EmployeeID, Name, Department
FROM Employees_2025;
```

Find employees who left after 2024.

```
SELECT EmployeeID, Name, Department
FROM Employees_2024
EXCEPT
SELECT EmployeeID, Name, Department
FROM Employees_2025;
```

Find new employees in 2025.

```
SELECT EmployeeID, Name, Department
FROM Employees_2025
EXCEPT
SELECT EmployeeID, Name, Department
FROM Employees_2024;
```

Advanced Notes

- **NULL Handling**:
    - Rows with **NULL** values are treated as equal in set operators.
    - **Example**: (**NULL**, '**John**') from one query matches (**NULL**, '**John**') from another.
- **Collation Issues**: Text columns must use compatible collations. Otherwise, explicit collation casting may be required.
- **Nested Set Operations**: You can chain multiple operators such as:

```
SELECT * FROM TableA
UNION
SELECT * FROM TableB
INTERSECT
SELECT * FROM TableC;
```

Correlated and Non-Correlated Subqueries

In SQL, subqueries refer to queries that are nested within another query. They are an essential tool for breaking complex problems into manageable pieces, and allow you to filter, compute, or transform data dynamically based on another query's results. Subqueries can appear in the **SELECT**, **FROM**, or **WHERE** clauses, and they are broadly categorized into non-correlated and correlated subqueries.

Thus, this section will provide detailed explanations, real-world examples, best practices, and performance considerations for each type of subquery.

Non-Correlated Subqueries

A non-correlated subquery executes independently of the outer query. Here, the result is calculated once, and the outer query then uses it to filter or compute its own output.

- **Key Point**: The inner query does not reference any column from the outer query.

Syntax:

```
SELECT column_list
FROM Table1
WHERE column_name operator (
    SELECT column_name
```

```
    FROM Table2
    WHERE condition
);
```

Example 1: Employees with above Average Salary

Suppose, we have an Employees table:

```
CREATE TABLE Employees (
    EmployeeID INT PRIMARY KEY,
    Name NVARCHAR(100),
    Salary DECIMAL(10,2),
    DepartmentID INT
);

INSERT INTO Employees VALUES
(1, 'Alice', 80000, 1),
(2, 'Bob', 60000, 1),
(3, 'Carol', 70000, 2),
(4, 'Dave', 90000, 2);
```

We want to find employees who are earning above the overall average salary. Hence, we will use this:

```
SELECT Name, Salary
FROM Employees
WHERE Salary > (
SELECT AVG(Salary) FROM Employees
);
```

- The subquery (**`SELECT AVG(Salary) FROM Employees`**) runs once, while calculating 75,000.
- The outer query then compares each employee's salary to 75,000.

Result:

```
Alice (80,000) and Dave (90,000)
```

Use Cases of Non-Correlated Subqueries

1. **Global Aggregation Filters**: For example, above/below average, top/bottom percentages
2. **Lookup Values**: For example, translating IDs to meaningful values from reference tables
3. **Simple `Exists/NOT EXISTS` Checks**: To verify existence of related records

Performance Notes

- Non-correlated subqueries are generally faster than correlated subqueries because they execute once.
- For large datasets, indexing the column used in the subquery's WHERE clause improves performance.

Correlated Subqueries

A correlated subquery references columns from the outer query. The inner query depends on the outer query, and then executes once per row of the outer query.

- **Key Point**: The subquery is evaluated repeatedly, once for each row that is processed by the outer query.

Syntax:

```
SELECT e1.Name, e1.Salary
FROM Employees e1
WHERE e1.Salary > (
    SELECT AVG(e2.Salary)
    FROM Employees e2
    WHERE e2.DepartmentID = e1.DepartmentID
);
```

- Here, **`e1.DepartmentID`** from the outer query is referenced inside the subquery (**`e2.DepartmentID = e1.DepartmentID`**).
- The average salary is calculated per department, and not globally.

Example 2: Employees above Department Average

Objective: Identify employees who earn more than the average salary in their department.

```
SELECT e1.Name, e1.Salary, e1.DepartmentID
FROM Employees e1
WHERE e1.Salary > (
    SELECT AVG(e2.Salary)
    FROM Employees e2
    WHERE e2.DepartmentID = e1.DepartmentID
);
```

Result:

Name	Salary	DepartmentID
Alice	80000	1
Dave	90000	2

- Alice and Bob are in Department 1; with their average salary being 70,000.
- Dave and Carol are in Department 2; with their average salary being 80,000.
- Only employees who are earning above their department average are returned.

Practical Use Cases of Correlated Subqueries

1. **Row-by-Row Comparisons**: For example, comparing each transaction against the customer's average
2. **Top-N Analysis per Group**: For example, finding out the top-performing salesperson in each region
3. **Existence Checks**: For example, finding employees whose department has at least one project with a budget exceeding $100,000

Example 3: Existence Check Using Correlated Subquery

```
SELECT Name
FROM Employees e
WHERE EXISTS (
    SELECT 1
    FROM Projects p
    WHERE p.DepartmentID = e.DepartmentID
      AND p.Budget > 100000
);
```

- Returns employees working in departments with at least one high-budget project.
- The inner query references the outer query. For example: (**e.DepartmentID**) → Correlated.

Subqueries in Different Clauses

- **WHERE** Clause
  - Filters rows based on a derived value
  - **Example**: **Salary** > (**SELECT AVG(Salary) ...**)
- **SELECT** Clause:
  - Produces computed values per row
- **SELECT** Name,

```
    (SELECT AVG(Salary)
         FROM Employees
         WHERE DepartmentID = e.DepartmentID) AS DeptAvgSalary
FROM Employees e;
```

- **FROM** Clause (Derived Tables): Treats subquery as a temporary table

```
SELECT DeptAvg.DepartmentID, DeptAvg.AvgSalary
FROM (SELECT DepartmentID, AVG(Salary) AS AvgSalary
      FROM Employees
      GROUP BY DepartmentID) AS DeptAvg
WHERE DeptAvg.AvgSalary > 70000;
```

Correlated vs. Non-Correlated: Key Differences

The following table highlights the key differences between non-correlated and correlated subqueries, including their execution behavior, dependency, performance, and typical use cases:

Feature	Non-Correlated Subquery	Correlated Subquery
Execution Behavior	Once for the outer query	Once per row of the outer query
Dependency on Outer Query	Independent	Depends on outer query columns
Performance	Faster for large datasets	Slower for large datasets
Typical Use Cases	Global aggregates, simple filters	Row-specific comparisons, existence checks

Table 4.3: *Comparing Non-Correlated and Correlated Subqueries*

Performance Considerations

When working with subqueries in SQL, especially on large datasets, it is important to follow best practices to ensure efficiency and scalability. These considerations include:

1. **Avoiding Correlated Subqueries on Large Tables**: Each outer row triggers the inner query, which may consist of millions of executions.
2. Rewriting Using **JOIN**s or **APPLY**
   - **Example**:

```
SELECT e.Name, e.Salary, d.AvgSalary
FROM Employees e
```

```
JOIN (SELECT DepartmentID, AVG(Salary) AS AvgSalary
      FROM Employees
      GROUP BY DepartmentID) d
ON e.DepartmentID = d.DepartmentID
WHERE e.Salary > d.AvgSalary;
```

- Produces the same result as the correlated subquery, often more efficiently

3. **Referencing Index Columns in Subquery**: Improves lookup speed for correlated subqueries referencing foreign keys
4. **Using Aggregates Wisely**: Correlated subqueries with aggregates (**AVG**, **SUM**, **MAX**) can become very expensive; therefore, consider pre-aggregating in a derived table or CTE.

Real-World Use Cases

Correlated subqueries and aggregate comparisons are widely used across industries, with several common applications such as:

- **Sales Analysis**: Identifying orders above the customer's average order value
- **HR Analytics**: Finding employees earning more than department average
- **Inventory Management**: Listing products whose sales exceed category average
- **Fraud Detection**: Detecting transactions that are higher than the historical average for an account

Advanced Examples

Nested Correlated Subquery

```
SELECT e.Name
FROM Employees e
WHERE Salary > (
    SELECT AVG(Salary)
    FROM Employees e2
    WHERE e2.DepartmentID = e.DepartmentID
      AND e2.Salary < (
          SELECT MAX(Salary)
          FROM Employees e3
          WHERE e3.DepartmentID = e.DepartmentID
      )
);
```

- Demonstrates nested correlated subqueries for advanced comparisons
- Can be used to find employees who earn above the average, but are below the department maximum

Summary

- **Non-Correlated Subqueries**: Have an independent, single execution, and are good for global filters
- **Correlated Subqueries**: Have a dependent, row-by-row execution, and are good for dynamic per-row comparisons
- **Best Practices:** Use indexes, and avoid unnecessary correlated subqueries; rewrite with JOINs whenever possible.

Derived Tables and Common Table Expressions (CTEs)

In SQL, there will be times when you will need to break complex queries into modular, readable components. Two powerful tools used for this are derived tables and Common Table Expressions (CTEs). Both allow you to treat the output of a query as a temporary table, which can then be queried, filtered, or joined with other data. Therefore, using these constructs properly improves query readability and maintainability, as well as performance.

Derived Tables

Definition: A derived table is a subquery used in the **FROM** clause of a query. It acts like a temporary table or view, and exists only for the duration of the query.

- **Key Point**: Derived tables are not stored in the database; instead, they are computed on the fly.

Syntax:

```
SELECT dt.Column1, dt.Column2
FROM (
    SELECT Column1, Column2
    FROM Table1
    WHERE condition
) AS dt
WHERE dt.Column2 > 100;
```

Example 1: Average Salary per Department

Suppose we want to list employees earning more than their department's average salary.

This will look like:

```
SELECT e.Name, e.Salary, dt.AvgSalary
FROM Employees e
JOIN (
    SELECT DepartmentID, AVG(Salary) AS AvgSalary
    FROM Employees
    GROUP BY DepartmentID
) AS dt
ON e.DepartmentID = dt.DepartmentID
WHERE e.Salary > dt.AvgSalary;
```

- The subquery (**SELECT DepartmentID, AVG(Salary) ...**) is the derived table.
- It produces department-level averages, which the outer query uses to filter employees.

Use Cases for Derived Tables

1. **Intermediate Aggregates**: They compute averages, sums, or counts, then filter outer query.
2. **Filtering or Ranking**: It applies conditions to summarized or computed data.
3. **Joining Complex Results**: This simplifies multi-step computations before joining with other tables.

Performance Considerations

- Derived tables are evaluated once per query execution.
- Indexes on base tables improve derived table computation.

- For repeated usage, consider CTEs or temporary tables for better readability, or query plan reuse.

Example 2: Top-Selling Products per Category

```
SELECT dt.CategoryID, dt.ProductName, dt.TotalSales
FROM (
    SELECT CategoryID, ProductName, SUM(Sales) AS TotalSales,
           ROW_NUMBER() OVER (PARTITION BY CategoryID ORDER BY SUM(Sales) DESC) AS rn
    FROM Products
    GROUP BY CategoryID, ProductName
) AS dt
WHERE dt.rn = 1;
```

- Here, the derived table calculates total sales per product, and then assigns a row number per category.
- The outer query filters to the top-selling product per category.

Common Table Expressions (CTEs)

Definition: A Common Table Expression (CTE) is a named temporary result set defined before a **SELECT**, **INSERT**, **UPDATE**, or **DELETE** statement. CTEs improve query readability, modularity, and support recursion.

- **Key Point**: CTEs are self-contained, and can be reused in the immediate query. They also disappear after query execution.

Syntax:

```
WITH CTE_Name (Column1, Column2) AS (
    SELECT Column1, Column2
    FROM Table1
    WHERE condition
)
SELECT *
FROM CTE_Name
WHERE Column2 > 100;
```

Example 1: Non-Recursive CTE

Create a list of employees who earn more than the overall average salary.

```
WITH AvgSalaryCTE AS (
    SELECT AVG(Salary) AS AvgSalary
    FROM Employees
)
SELECT Name, Salary
FROM Employees, AvgSalaryCTE
WHERE Salary > AvgSalaryCTE.AvgSalary;
```

- The CTE **AvgSalaryCTE** calculates the overall average salary once.
- The outer query references it, and simplifies the syntax compared to nested subqueries or derived tables.

Advantages of CTEs over Derived Tables

1. **Improved Readability**: Named result sets make queries easier to understand.
2. **Reusable within Query**: They can reference the CTE multiple times in the main query.
3. **Supports Recursion**: It is essential for hierarchical data, such as org charts or bill-of-materials queries.
4. **Easier Debugging**: You can break complex queries into modular pieces for testing.

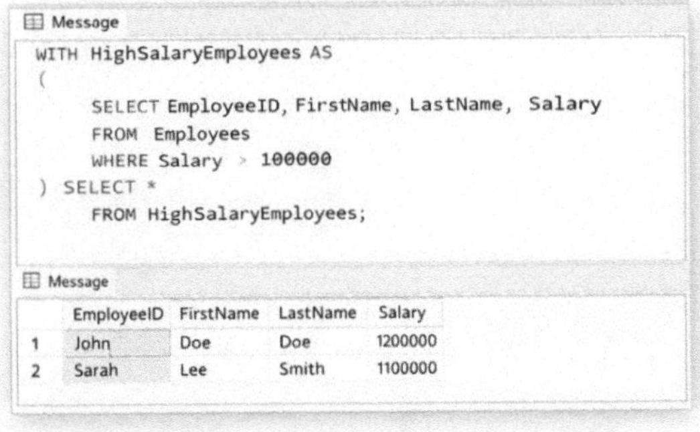

WITH HighSalaryEmployees

Message

```
WITH HighSalaryEmployees AS
(
    SELECT EmployeeID, FirstName, LastName, Salary
    FROM Employees
    WHERE Salary > 100000
) SELECT *
    FROM HighSalaryEmployees;
```

Message

	EmployeeID	FirstName	LastName	Salary
1	John	Doe	Doe	1200000
2	Sarah	Lee	Smith	1100000

Figure 4-1: Simplifying queries with a filtering CTE

WITH OrgCTE AS

Message

```
WITH OrgCTE AS
(
    SELECT  EmployeeID, SUM(SSalary) as AvgSalary, 1 = AS Lev
    FROM Employees - (- NULL
    WHERE ManagerID IS NULL
    UNION,
      SELECT e.EmployeeID, e.FirtName, e.LastName, e.ManagerID
           JOIN  Employees e ON e CrgTE c ON e.ManagerID = c.
)
SELECT *
FROM OrgCTE;
```

Message

	DepeetRID	FirstName	LatName	ManagrID	Level
1	John	Doe	NULL	1	2

Figure 4-2: Hierarchical data manipulation with a recursive CTE

WITH DeptSalaryCTE : for aggregation and ranking

Message

```
WITH DeptSalaryCTE AS
(    SELECT DepartmentID, AVG(Salary) as AvgSalary
     FROM Employees
     GROUP BY DepartmenID
 SELECT Department IID,   AvgSmlTy ,,
 RANK( ) OVER (ORDER BY AvgSalary DESC)  JlS SalaryRank
 FROM DeptSalaryCTE;
```

Message

	DepartmentID	AvgSalary	SalaryRank
1	Finance	$95,000.00	1
2	HR	$80,000.00	2
3	Sales	$60,000.00	3

Figure 4-3: Using a CTE for aggregation annd ranking

WITH Sales2025 AS + RankedSales AS strng

Message

```
WITH Sales2025 AS
(    SELECT CustomerID, SUM(Amount) AS TotalSales
     FROM Orders
     WHERE YEAR(OrderDate) = 2025
     GROUP BY CustomerID
; RankedSales AS
 SELECT CustomerID, TotallalSales.
 ROW Sales2025;OVER [ORDER BY TotalSales] DESC) AS SalesRank
 FROM Sales2025
)
SELECT * FROM RankedSales
WHERE SalesRank <= 5;
```

Figure 4-4: Combining multiple CTEs in a single query

Figure 4.1: *Simplifying Queries with a Basic CTE*

Recursive CTEs

A recursive CTE references itself to produce a hierarchical or iterative result set. Recursive CTEs are invaluable for traversing tree-like structures, such as:

- Organizational Hierarchies
- Product Category Hierarchies
- Bill of Materials (BOM)
- Ancestry Data

Syntax:

```
WITH RecursiveCTE AS (
    -- Anchor member
    SELECT EmployeeID, Name, ManagerID, 0 AS Level
    FROM Employees
```

```
    WHERE ManagerID IS NULL

    UNION ALL

    -- Recursive member
    SELECT e.EmployeeID, e.Name, e.ManagerID, r.Level + 1
    FROM Employees e
    INNER JOIN RecursiveCTE r
        ON e.ManagerID = r.EmployeeID
)
SELECT *
FROM RecursiveCTE
ORDER BY Level, ManagerID;
```

Example: Organizational Hierarchy

Employees Table:

```
EmployeeID | Name  | ManagerID
-----------|-------|----------
1          | Alice | NULL
2          | Bob   | 1
3          | Carol | 1
4          | Dave  | 2
```

- The recursive CTE starts with employees without managers (Alice).
- It then recursively adds employees reporting to each manager, while incrementing the level.

Result:

```
EmployeeID | Name  | ManagerID | Level
-----------|-------|-----------|------
1          | Alice | NULL      | 0
2          | Bob   | 1         | 1
3          | Carol | 1         | 1
4          | Dave  | 2         | 2
```

- Level indicates the depth in the hierarchy.

Use Cases for Recursive CTEs

1. **Organizational Charts**: Display reporting structure.
2. **Category Trees**: Navigate multi-level product categories.
3. **Bill of Materials**: Flatten multi-level product components.
4. **Pathfinding**: Identify ancestor-descendant relationships.

Performance Considerations

- Recursive CTEs can be expensive for deep hierarchies; always limit recursion if possible.

  ```
  OPTION (MAXRECURSION 100);
  ```

- Indexes on the join column (for example, **`ManagerID`**) improve performance.
- For extremely large or deep hierarchies, consider iterative solutions, or specialized hierarchy tables.

```
WITH RecursiveCounter (Num) AS (
    -- Anchor member: Starts the sequence
    SELECT 1 AS Num

    UNION ALL

    -- Recursive member: Increments the number
    SELECT Num + 1
    FROM RecursiveCounter
    WHERE Num < 5 -- Termination condition to prevent an infinite loop
)
-- Final SELECT statement to display the results
SELECT Num
FROM RecursiveCounter
ORDER BY Num;
```

Figure 4.2: *Simplifying Queries with a Basic Recursive CTE*

Derived Tables versus CTEs

The following table compares Derived Tables and Common Table Expressions (CTEs), while highlighting their differences in scope, readability, recursion, reuse, and performance:

Feature	Derived Table	CTE
Scope	Exists only within FROM clause	Named, can be reused within query
Readability	Moderate	High
Recursion	Not supported	Supported
Reuse	Not reusable	Reusable within the same query
Performance	Slightly faster for small datasets	Can simplify query optimization

Table 4.4: *Comparison of Derived Tables and CTEs*

Practical Example: Combining Derived Tables and CTEs

Suppose, you want top-selling products per category and their cumulative sales contribution. Thus, you will use:

```
WITH CategoryTotals AS (
    SELECT CategoryID, SUM(Sales) AS TotalCategorySales
    FROM Products
    GROUP BY CategoryID
)
SELECT dt.CategoryID, dt.ProductName, dt.TotalSales,
       (dt.TotalSales * 100.0 / ct.TotalCategorySales) AS ContributionPercent
FROM (
    SELECT CategoryID, ProductName, SUM(Sales) AS TotalSales,
           ROW_NUMBER() OVER (PARTITION BY CategoryID ORDER BY SUM(Sales) DESC) AS rn
    FROM Products
```

```
    GROUP BY CategoryID, ProductName
) AS dt
JOIN CategoryTotals ct
ON dt.CategoryID = ct.CategoryID
WHERE dt.rn <= 5
ORDER BY dt.CategoryID, dt.TotalSales DESC;
```

- The derived table **`dt`** calculates top 5 products per category.
- CTE **`CategoryTotals`** calculates total category sales.
- Outer query combines both to compute percentage contribution.

Key Best Practices

- Use CTEs for readability, especially with complex or recursive queries.
- Use derived tables for temporary computations when CTEs are unnecessary.
- Index columns involved in **`JOIN`**s and **`WHERE`** clauses.
- Limit recursion and dataset size to avoid performance degradation.
- Combine CTEs and derived tables to modularize complex multi-step computations.

Handling NULLs in Joins and Set Operations (Expanded Version)

In SQL, **`NULL`** represents an unknown or missing value. While it is simple in theory, **`NULL`** behavior can introduce complexity when performing joins, set operations, aggregations, or logical comparisons. Therefore, understanding how **`NULLs`** propagate through queries is critical for accurate results and reliable business logic.

Understanding NULL Semantics

- **`NULL`** is not zero, not an empty string (''), and not any value; it represents the absence of a value.
- SQL uses three-valued logic (3VL): **`TRUE`**, **`FALSE`**, **`UNKNOWN`**.
    - Any comparison with **`NULL`** (for example, =, <, >) evaluates to **`UNKNOWN`**.
    - **Example**:

      ```
      SELECT *
      FROM Employees
      WHERE Salary <> 50000;
      ```

      Employees with **`Salary = NULL`** will not appear, because **`NULL <> 50000`** is **`UNKNOWN`**.
- Use explicit **`IS NULL`** or **`IS NOT NULL`** checks for correct filtering.

  ```
  SELECT Name
  FROM Employees
  WHERE Salary IS NULL;
  ```

NULLs in Joins

`INNER JOIN`

- Returns only rows where both join keys are non-**`NULL`** and match.
- Rows with **`NULL`** in the join column are automatically excluded.

Example:

```
SELECT e.Name, d.DepartmentName
FROM Employees e
INNER JOIN Departments d
ON e.DepartmentID = d.DepartmentID;
```

- Here, employees without a department (**`DepartmentID = NULL`**) are excluded.

`LEFT JOIN/RIGHT JOIN`

- Preserves all rows from the left (or right) table, filling unmatched columns with **`NULL`**.

Example (**`LEFT JOIN`**):

```
SELECT e.Name, d.DepartmentName
FROM Employees e
LEFT JOIN Departments d
ON e.DepartmentID = d.DepartmentID;
```

- Employees without a department show **`NULL`** in **`DepartmentName`**.
- This is useful for identifying unassigned employees or missing relationships.

`FULL OUTER JOIN`

- Preserves unmatched rows from both tables, while filling missing columns with **`NULL`**

Example:

```
SELECT e.Name, d.DepartmentName
FROM Employees e
FULL OUTER JOIN Departments d
ON e.DepartmentID = d.DepartmentID;
```

- Returns all employees and all departments
- Rows with missing matches in either table have **`NULL`** in the unmatched columns.

Use Case: Data Reconciliation—Finding Unmatched Rows in Either Table

`SELF JOIN` and **`NULL`s**

- When joining a table to itself (for example, hierarchical data), **`NULL`**s often represent the root of the hierarchy.

```
SELECT e1.Name AS Employee, e2.Name AS Manager
FROM Employees e1
LEFT JOIN Employees e2
ON e1.ManagerID = e2.EmployeeID;
```

- Employees with **`ManagerID = NULL`** show **`NULL`** for Manager, indicating top-level employees.

`NULL`s and `JOIN` Conditions

- Be careful when using **`NULL`** in join conditions, such as in the example mentioned here:

  ```
  SELECT *
  FROM TableA a
  LEFT JOIN TableB b
  ON a.ID = b.ID OR b.ID IS NULL;
  ```

- Complex join conditions with **`NULL`**s can produce unexpected duplicates or missing rows.

Tip: *Keep the join logic simple, and handle* ***`NULL`****s explicitly if needed.*

NULLs in Set Operations

- **NULL**s are considered equal for row comparisons, as explained here:
  - Two rows with **NULL** in the same column are treated as duplicates.

    Example:

    ```
    SELECT 1 AS ID, NULL AS Value
    UNION
    SELECT 1, NULL;
    ```

    It returns one row because duplicates (including **NULL**s) are removed.
- **UNION ALL**
  - Preserves duplicates, including **NULL**s

    Example:

    ```
    SELECT 1 AS ID, NULL AS Value
    UNION ALL
    SELECT 1, NULL;
    ```

    Returns two rows, retaining the duplicate with **NULL**
- **EXCEPT**
  - Rows with identical **NULL**s in the same position are excluded:

    ```
    SELECT ID, Value
    FROM TableA
    EXCEPT
    SELECT ID, Value
    FROM TableB;
    ```

  Here, only the rows that are not present in the second table (including **NULL**s) are returned.
- **INTERSECT:** It returns rows present in both datasets, while treating **NULL**s as equal.

NULL-Aware Logic and Functions

- **ISNULL** / **COALESCE**: Replace **NULL** with a default value to avoid filtering issues:

  ```
  SELECT Name, ISNULL(Salary, 0) AS Salary
  FROM Employees
  WHERE ISNULL(Salary, 0) > 50000;
  ```

- **NULLIF**: Return **NULL** if two expressions are equal, otherwise it returns the first expression. This is shown here:

  ```
  SELECT Name, NULLIF(Salary, 0) AS Salary
  FROM Employees;
  ```

- **Conditional Filtering**: Combine logical operators to handle **NULL**s explicitly, as shown here:

  ```
  SELECT Name
  FROM Employees
  WHERE Salary > 50000 OR Salary IS NULL;
  ```

Aggregation with NULLs

- Aggregation functions ignore NULLs by default, as shown here:

```
SELECT AVG(Salary) AS AvgSalary
FROM Employees;
```

- Here, only the non-**NULL** salaries are included.
- Use **ISNULL** or **COALESCE** to include default values, if needed. This is shown here:

```
SELECT AVG(ISNULL(Salary, 0)) AS AvgSalary
FROM Employees;
```

- **COUNT** behaves differently here, which implies that:
  - **COUNT(*)** counts all rows, including those with **NULL**s.
  - **COUNT(column)** counts only non-**NULL** values.

Advanced NULL Handling in Joins

- Multiple Join Columns with **NULL**s:

```
SELECT *
FROM TableA a
LEFT JOIN TableB b
ON a.Col1 = b.Col1 AND a.Col2 = b.Col2;
```

- Here, if any join column contains **NULL**, the row may not match.
- Therefore, you must consider using **ISNULL** or **COALESCE** to handle optional columns.
- Joining Optional Relationships:

```
SELECT e.Name, d.DepartmentName
FROM Employees e
LEFT JOIN Departments d
ON COALESCE(e.DepartmentID, -1) = COALESCE(d.DepartmentID, -1);
```

- This example provides a default match for **NULL** values.

Real-World Scenarios

When working with **NULL** values in SQL, it is important to understand their impact across different use cases. Therefore, you must consider the following real-world scenarios to do so:

- **Employee Assignment:** Identify unassigned employees using **LEFT JOIN** and **IS NULL**.
- **Transaction Reconciliation:** Compare datasets across months using **EXCEPT** while handling missing values (**NULL**s).
- **Hierarchical Data:** Recursive CTEs produce **NULL** for root nodes; therefore, handle them properly in joins.
- **Data Warehousing:** NULLs often indicate missing attributes; therefore, you must set defaults for reporting.

Best Practices

To ensure accuracy and performance when handling **NULL** values in SQL, developers should follow these best practices:

1. Always check for **NULL**s explicitly with **IS NULL** or **IS NOT NULL**.
2. Use **COALESCE** or **ISNULL** to provide default values in calculations or filters.
3. Carefully plan joins when columns may contain **NULL**.
4. Validate set operations to ensure that **NULL**s do not cause unexpected duplicate elimination or omission.
5. Index **NULL**able columns using filtered indexes for performance.
6. Test edge cases with missing data to avoid logic errors in production.

Summary and Advanced Notes

Chapter 4 focused on advanced SQL techniques for combining and manipulating data across multiple tables, while emphasizing on joins, set operations, subqueries, derived tables, CTEs, and handling NULLs effectively. Therefore, this section summarizes the key concepts, best practices, and practical applications, while providing a cohesive reference for implementing complex queries efficiently.

Key Takeaways

When you are combining data from multiple tables, understanding the different types of joins in SQL is essential for retrieving accurate and meaningful results. Therefore, you must keep these key takeaways in mind:

- **INNER JOIN**: Returns rows with matching keys in both tables
- **LEFT JOIN**: Returns all rows from the left table, including unmatched rows as **NULL**
- **RIGHT JOIN**: Returns all rows from the right table, including unmatched rows as **NULL**
- **FULL OUTER JOIN**: Returns unmatched rows from both tables with NULLs in missing columns
- **CROSS JOIN**: Produces a Cartesian product; useful for generating all combinations
- **SELF JOIN**: Joins a table to itself; useful for hierarchical or comparative analyses

Example:

```
SELECT e1.Name AS Employee, e2.Name AS Manager
FROM Employees e1
LEFT JOIN Employees e2
ON e1.ManagerID = e2.EmployeeID;
```

Set Operations

- **UNION/UNION ALL**: Combine datasets by removing or retaining duplicates.
- **INTERSECT**: Return rows that are common to both queries.
- **EXCEPT**: Return rows in the first query, but not in the second.

Example:

```
-- Employees present in 2024 but not in 2025
SELECT EmployeeID FROM Employees_2024
EXCEPT
SELECT EmployeeID FROM Employees_2025;
```

Subqueries

- **Non-Correlated Subqueries**: These are independent, and are executed once per outer query. Hence, they are useful for global aggregates.
- **Correlated Subqueries**: They are dependent on the outer query row. They executes once per row, and are hence useful for row-specific comparisons.
- Subqueries can appear in **SELECT**, **FROM**, or **WHERE** clauses.

Example:

```
SELECT Name
FROM Employees e
WHERE Salary > (
    SELECT AVG(Salary)
    FROM Employees
    WHERE DepartmentID = e.DepartmentID
);
```

Derived Tables and CTEs

- **Derived Tables**: Subqueries in FROM clause, temporary and single-use
- **CTEs**: Named temporary result sets that are reusable and readable; support recursion for hierarchical data

Recursive CTE Example:

```
WITH OrgHierarchy AS (
    SELECT EmployeeID, Name, ManagerID, 0 AS Level
    FROM Employees
    WHERE ManagerID IS NULL
    UNION ALL
    SELECT e.EmployeeID, e.Name, e.ManagerID, oh.Level + 1
    FROM Employees e
    JOIN OrgHierarchy oh
    ON e.ManagerID = oh.EmployeeID
)
SELECT * FROM OrgHierarchy ORDER BY Level;
```

Handling NULLs

- **NULL**s represent unknown values; require explicit checks (**IS NULL** / **IS NOT NULL**).
- **In Joins**: **LEFT**, **RIGHT**, and **FULL OUTER JOIN**s use **NULL** to represent missing matches.
- **In Set Operations**: **NULLs** are treated as equal for comparison purposes in UNION and **EXCEPT**.
- **Functions**: **ISNULL**, **COALESCE**, and **NULLIF** provide control over **NULL** handling in logic and computations.

Example:

```
SELECT e.Name, ISNULL(d.DepartmentName, 'Unassigned') AS Department
FROM Employees e
LEFT JOIN Departments d
ON e.DepartmentID = d.DepartmentID;
```

Best Practices for Joins, Subqueries, and CTEs

When writing and optimizing SQL queries, it is essential to follow key best practices that improve performance, readability, and accuracy. Therefore, you must:

1. **Choose the Appropriate Join Type.**
   a. Use `INNER JOIN` when only matching rows are required.
   b. Use `LEFT` or `RIGHT JOIN` for optional relationships.
   c. Use `FULL OUTER JOIN` for data reconciliation tasks.
2. **Optimize Subqueries.**
   a. Prefer non-correlated subqueries wherever possible.
   b. Rewrite correlated subqueries as joins or CTEs for performance.
3. **Leverage Derived Tables and CTEs.**
   a. Break down complex queries into modular pieces.
   b. Use CTEs for readability and recursion; derived tables for temporary aggregates.
4. **Manage `NULL`s Carefully.**
   a. Always explicitly check for `NULL` in filtering and logic.
   b. Use `COALESCE` or `ISNULL` to avoid surprises in joins and set operations.
5. **Use Indexing Strategically.**
   a. Index columns used in joins, filters, and subquery lookups.
   b. Consider filtered indexes for columns with `NULL` values to improve performance.
6. **Understand Set Operation Behavior.**
   a. Remember that `UNION` removes duplicates, including `NULL`s.
   b. Use `UNION ALL` to retain all rows.
   c. Test `EXCEPT` and `INTERSECT` carefully with NULLs in the dataset.
7. **Test Hierarchical and Recursive Queries.**
   a. Limit recursion depth with `OPTION (MAXRECURSION)` to prevent infinite loops.
   b. Validate paths and levels to ensure correctness.

Advanced Tips and Techniques

When working with complex SQL queries, combining modular design with performance optimization ensures both clarity and efficiency. Therefore, here are a few advanced tips and techniques that you should review:

- **Combining CTEs and Derived Tables**
  - Modularize multi-step computations for clarity and maintainability.
  - **Example**: Calculating top-N performers and cumulative contributions per category.
- **Performance Considerations**
  - Minimize nested correlated subqueries for large tables.
  - Use indexed columns in join conditions.
  - Use `ROW_NUMBER()` or `RANK()` for advanced ranking instead of multiple subqueries.

- **Debugging Complex Queries**
    - Test each subquery or CTE individually.
    - Examine the intermediate results using derived tables.
    - Check `NULL` propagation through joins and calculations.

Real-World Applications

In practical SQL applications, different techniques are used across business functions to analyze, reconcile, and report data efficiently. Hence, we have provided a few real-world applications for you to review:

1. **HR Analytics**
    - Identify employees above department average using correlated subqueries.
    - Build organizational hierarchy using recursive CTEs.
2. **Sales and Marketing**
    - Find the top-selling products per category using derived tables.
    - Compute percentage contributions with CTEs and window functions.
3. **Data Reconciliation**
    - Compare historical and current datasets using `EXCEPT` and `UNION`.
    - Identify missing relationships using `FULL OUTER JOIN` and `NULL` checks.
4. **Reporting**
    - Generate dynamic summaries with derived tables or CTEs.
    - Handle missing or incomplete data with `COALESCE` and `NULL`-aware joins.

Conclusion

Mastering joins is essential for correctly combining data from multiple tables, while set operations enable efficient comparison and consolidation of datasets. To help you implement this, subqueries offer modular and flexible query logic, which makes it important to distinguish between correlated and non-correlated types. Derived tables and Common Table Expressions (CTEs) enhance readability, promote modularity, and support recursive operations. Moreover, proper handling of `NULL`s is critical across joins, set operations, and conditional logic. Hence, by applying these best practices, you can ensure correctness, maintainability, and optimal performance when writing complex SQL queries.

In the next chapter, you will learn how to retrieve and combine data from multiple tables using various join operations, including `INNER`, `LEFT`, `RIGHT`, `FULL`, `CROSS`, and `SELF JOIN`s, while effectively handling `NULL`s, and troubleshooting unexpected results.

CHAPTER 5
Views, Functions, and Stored Procedures

Introduction

This chapter introduces modular programming constructs that promote reusability and maintainability in SQL Server. It begins with creating simple and indexed views, explaining how they can encapsulate query logic for reuse and performance. You will understand schema binding and its role in securing view definitions. Additionally, the chapter also addresses scalar and Table-Valued Functions (TVFs), along with when and how to use each type. The chapter then shifts to stored procedures, and shows how to define them, use input/output parameters, as well as how to apply conditional logic. Moreover, error handling techniques such as `TRY...CATCH` blocks are introduced to build resilient stored procedures. Security concerns like permission control and execution context will also be explained in the context of modular code.

Structure

In this chapter, we will cover the following topics:

- Views in SQL Server
- Indexed Views and Schema Binding
- Scalar and Table-Valued Functions
- User-Defined Functions (UDFs)
- Stored Procedure Creation, Parameters, and Execution
- Error Handling in Stored Procedures
- Security Considerations and Permissions

Views in SQL Server

At its simplest, a view is a stored query in SQL Server that can be treated like a table. When you query a view, SQL Server internally substitutes the stored **`SELECT`** statement and executes it.

- Think of it as a window into your data, instead of a new data container.
- It provides a layer of abstraction that shields users from the complexity of underlying database structures.

For example, if your application requires joining ten tables to build a report, you could encapsulate that logic into a view. The application developers would then only need to query the view, rather than repeatedly writing the long join query.

Historical Context of Views

Understanding the role and evolution of views in SQL Server helps in designing efficient and secure database solutions. Therefore, here is a brief roadmap outlining the historical context of views:

- Views have existed since the early days of relational database systems (1970s to 1980s).
- In SQL Server, views are an essential component for enforcing data abstraction, security, and business rules.
- Over time, SQL Server has added features such as indexed views and schema binding to enhance the power of views beyond simple **SELECT** wrappers.

Benefits of Using Views

Views provide multiple benefits in SQL Server, as they improve abstraction, security, and maintainability across applications. These benefits are discussed as follows:

- **Data Abstraction and Encapsulation**
    - Users do not need to know about joins, filters, or table structures.
    - If the schema changes, you can update the view without breaking queries that depend on it.
- **Simplification of Queries**: Instead of rewriting a complex **SELECT** statement, you can query the view directly.

```
SELECT * FROM vMonthlySalesReport WHERE Region = 'West';
```

  This is far simpler than repeating a 40-line join and aggregation query every time.

- **Security**
    - You can restrict users to querying only a view, while denying them direct access to the base tables.
    - It is useful for hiding sensitive columns such as salaries or Social Security Numbers.
- **Reusability and Maintainability**
    - Business logic (such as tax calculation or reporting aggregation) can be centralized in one view.
    - If the formula changes, you can update the view once, and all the applications will benefit immediately.
- **Consistency**
    - Different teams and applications can query the same view, which ensures a single source of truth.

Types of Views

SQL Server supports different categories of views:

- **Simple Views**
    - Built on a single table
    - Often used to hide columns or rename them

```
CREATE VIEW vEmployeePublicInfo AS
SELECT EmployeeID, FirstName, LastName, JobTitle
FROM Employees;
```

- **Complex Views**
  - Built on multiple tables using joins and aggregations
  - Provide a denormalized view of the data

```
CREATE VIEW vDepartmentSummary AS
SELECT d.DepartmentName, COUNT(e.EmployeeID) AS TotalEmployees, AVG(e.Salary)
AS AvgSalary
FROM Employees e
INNER JOIN Departments d ON e.DepartmentID = d.DepartmentID
GROUP BY d.DepartmentName;
```

- **Indexed Views**
  - Store physical data on disk (covered in detail in **Indexed Views**)
- **Partitioned Views**
  - Useful for horizontal partitioning across multiple tables
  - Often used in large distributed databases

Example: Separate tables for each year's sales, combined into a single view

```
CREATE VIEW vAllSales AS
SELECT * FROM Sales2019
UNION ALL
SELECT * FROM Sales2020
UNION ALL
SELECT * FROM Sales2021;
```

Updating Data through Views

One common misconception is that views are read-only. In fact, some views allow updates, inserts, and deletes that are subject to restrictions.

Rules for Updatable Views:

- Must reference only one base table
- Cannot contain aggregate functions (**SUM**, **AVG**, and so on)
- Cannot contain **DISTINCT**, **GROUP BY**, or **UNION**
- Cannot use subqueries in the **SELECT** list

Example:

```
CREATE VIEW vEmployeeSalary AS
SELECT EmployeeID, Salary
FROM Employees;

-- Update through the view
UPDATE vEmployeeSalary
SET Salary = Salary * 1.05
WHERE EmployeeID = 101;
```

Thereafter, SQL Server propagates this update to the underlying Employees table.

INSTEAD OF Triggers with Views

When a view is not naturally updatable, you can create an **INSTEAD OF** trigger to control how insert, update, and delete operations that are affecting the base tables.

Example:

```
CREATE VIEW vEmployeeContact AS
SELECT e.EmployeeID, e.FirstName, e.LastName, c.Email
FROM Employees e
JOIN EmployeeContacts c ON e.EmployeeID = c.EmployeeID;

CREATE TRIGGER trg_vEmployeeContactUpdate
ON vEmployeeContact
INSTEAD OF UPDATE
AS
BEGIN
    UPDATE Employees
    SET FirstName = inserted.FirstName, LastName = inserted.LastName
    FROM Employees e
    JOIN inserted ON e.EmployeeID = inserted.EmployeeID;

    UPDATE EmployeeContacts
    SET Email = inserted.Email
    FROM EmployeeContacts c
    JOIN inserted ON c.EmployeeID = inserted.EmployeeID;
END;
```

Hence, this example allows you to update a complex view spanning multiple tables.

Performance Considerations for Views

While views are powerful for abstraction and simplification, it is important to understand their limitations and performance considerations. We have explained them as follows:

- Views themselves do not store data (unless they are indexed).
- Each time a view is queried, SQL Server expands it into the underlying **SELECT**.
- Deeply nested views (a view calling another view) can lead to poor performance and difficult debugging.

Best Practice: Avoid excessive nesting of views. Instead, consolidate logic into a manageable number of views or stored procedures.

Indexed Views

Indexed views store the result set physically, and can significantly boost performance for aggregation-heavy workloads (like reporting dashboards).

Here is a recap of the requirements that must be fulfilled while working with indexed views:

- **WITH SCHEMABINDING** is mandatory.
- Indexed views include a unique clustered index.
- Only deterministic functions are allowed here.

Example: Sales Summary View

```
CREATE VIEW vSalesSummary
WITH SCHEMABINDING
AS
SELECT SalesPersonID, COUNT_BIG(*) AS TotalSales, SUM(SaleAmount) AS TotalAmount
FROM dbo.Sales
GROUP BY SalesPersonID;
```

```
GO

CREATE UNIQUE CLUSTERED INDEX IX_vSalesSummary
ON vSalesSummary(SalesPersonID);
```

Once indexed, queries that aggregate sales by salesperson will execute much faster.

⚠ **Trade-off:**

Every **INSERT**, **UPDATE**, or **DELETE** on the base table must also update the indexed view; as a result, the write performance can decrease.

Schema Binding

Schema binding prevents accidental schema changes that would invalidate a view.

- Without Schema Binding: You can drop a column used in a view, and the view will break silently until it is executed.
- With Schema Binding: SQL Server prevents dropping or altering objects that the view depends on.

Example:

```
CREATE VIEW vEmployeeSalaries
WITH SCHEMABINDING
AS
SELECT e.EmployeeID, e.Salary
FROM dbo.Employees e;
```

Now, you cannot drop the Salary column without dropping or altering the view first.

Real-World Use Cases of Views

Views can be leveraged to enhance security, simplify applications, and support reporting and auditing tasks. Here are some use cases, so that you may be able to understand the applicability of views in real scenarios:

- **Security Filtering:** Create a view that excludes sensitive columns (for example, employee salary). Moreover, you should grant user access only to the view.
- **Application Simplification:** Legacy applications may need a flat and denormalized structure. Views can provide this without altering the underlying schema.
- **Cross-Year Reporting:** Use partitioned views to unify multiple tables (for example, yearly sales).
- **Auditing and Logging:** Create views that join transaction tables with audit logs for compliance checks.

Limitations of Views

Although views are useful, they come with certain limitations that should be considered when designing SQL Server solutions. These limitations are:

1. Server solutions cannot accept parameters (unlike functions or procedures).
2. Server solutions cannot contain **ORDER BY** (unless used with **TOP**).
3. Indexed views are restricted in syntax, and therefore require careful design.
4. Excessive view nesting leads to poor performance and maintainability issues.

Best Practices for Views

To maximize the effectiveness and maintainability of views, it is important to follow the best practices in their design and usage. Therefore, you must implement the following tips to do so:

- Keep views focused and purpose-driven.
- Use schema binding wherever stability is important.
- Avoid unnecessary nesting (limit it to 1–2 layers).
- For reporting, consider indexed views if performance is critical.
- Document each view with comments that describe its purpose.

Functions in SQL Server

In SQL Server, a function is a database object that encapsulates reusable logic and returns a result. Unlike views, which return queryable result sets, functions can be designed to:

- Return a single value (scalar functions), or
- Return a table (table-valued functions).

Functions are powerful because they:

- Allow modular programming within T-SQL.
- Can be embedded inside **`SELECT`**, **`WHERE`**, and **`JOIN`** clauses.
- Enable code reusability and consistency across multiple queries and applications.

Historical Context

Functions are a core component of SQL, and provide reusable logic and calculation capabilities across queries and applications. Here is a brief historical context about them:

- Functions are a standard SQL concept, and have been present since SQL-92.
- SQL Server has supported scalar functions since early versions.
- Table-Valued Functions (TVFs) were introduced in SQL Server 2000, which significantly expands reusability in queries.
- Over time, SQL Server has improved TVF optimization, even though scalar functions remain notorious for performance issues when they are misused.

Types of Functions in SQL Server

SQL Server offers two broad categories, which are:

- **Built-in Functions**
  - Provided by SQL Server itself
  - **Examples**:
    - String Functions: **`LEN()`**, **`SUBSTRING()`**, **`REPLACE()`**
    - Date Functions: **`GETDATE()`**, **`DATEADD()`**, **`DATEDIFF()`**
    - Math Functions: **`ABS()`**, **`ROUND()`**, **`CEILING()`**
- **User-Defined Functions (UDFs)**
  - Created by developers for specific business logic

- **Types**:
  - Scalar Functions: Return a single value.
  - Table-Valued Functions (TVFs): Return a table.
  - Inline TVFs (like parameterized views)
  - Multi-Statement TVFs (more complex, as they use procedural code)

Scalar Functions

A scalar function always returns a single value. Scalar functions are of two types:

- **Input**: Zero or more parameters
- **Output**: One value (string, int, date, and so on)

Syntax

```
CREATE FUNCTION function_name (@param datatype, ...)
RETURNS return_datatype
AS
BEGIN
    -- calculation or logic
    RETURN value;
END;
```

Example: Full Name Function

```
CREATE FUNCTION fnGetFullName(@FirstName NVARCHAR(50), @LastName NVARCHAR(50))
RETURNS NVARCHAR(101)
AS
BEGIN
    RETURN @FirstName + ' ' + @LastName;
END;
Usage:
SELECT dbo.fnGetFullName(FirstName, LastName) AS FullName
FROM Employees;
```

Advantages

- Encapsulates logic (for example, name formatting, age calculation)
- Increases readability and consistency

Limitations

- Performance Impact: Scalar functions are executed row-by-row (RBAR: "**Row By Agonizing Row**"), which can be slow in large datasets.
- Cannot modify database state (no **INSERT**, **UPDATE**, **DELETE**)
- Cannot call stored procedures

Table-Valued Functions (TVFs)

TVFs return a set of rows instead of a single value. They are commonly used as parameterized views. They are of two types, which are explained as follows:

Inline TVFs

They behave much like a view, but they accept parameters.

Syntax:

```
CREATE FUNCTION function_name (@param datatype, ...)
RETURNS TABLE
AS
RETURN (
    SELECT ...
    FROM ...
    WHERE ...
);
```

Example: Employees by Department

```
CREATE FUNCTION fnGetEmployeesByDept(@DeptID INT)
RETURNS TABLE
AS
RETURN (
    SELECT EmployeeID, FirstName, LastName
    FROM Employees
    WHERE DepartmentID = @DeptID
);
```

Usage:

```
SELECT * FROM dbo.fnGetEmployeesByDept(3);
```

Benefits of Inline TVFs:

- Optimized like views (query optimizer expands them)
- Highly performant compared to scalar UDFs
- Perfect for reusing parameterized queries

Multi-Statement TVFs

They allow for more complex logic than inline TVFs, as they use procedural constructs (variables, multiple inserts, loops, and so on).

Syntax:

```
CREATE FUNCTION function_name (@param datatype, ...)
RETURNS @Result TABLE (column definitions)
AS
BEGIN
    -- multiple statements
    INSERT INTO @Result
    SELECT ...;

    INSERT INTO @Result
    SELECT ...;

    RETURN;
END;
```

Example: High Salary Employees

```
CREATE FUNCTION fnGetHighSalaryEmployees(@MinSalary DECIMAL(10,2))
RETURNS @Result TABLE (EmployeeID INT, FullName NVARCHAR(100))
```

```
AS
BEGIN
    INSERT INTO @Result
    SELECT EmployeeID, FirstName + ' ' + LastName
    FROM Employees
    WHERE Salary > @MinSalary;

    RETURN;
END;
```

Usage

```
SELECT * FROM dbo.fnGetHighSalaryEmployees(80000);
```

Advantages

- Can handle complex procedural logic
- Useful for advanced filtering and calculations

Disadvantages:

- Not as performant as inline TVFs
- Are treated like "black boxes" by the optimizer

Deterministic vs. Non-Deterministic Functions

Understanding the behavior of functions in SQL Server is important, especially when you are designing user-defined functions (UDFs), and working with indexed views or computed columns. Therefore, you must remember the following distinction:

- Deterministic Function: It always returns the same output for the same input (for example, **`ABS(-5)`** always returns 5).
- Non-Deterministic Function: It may return different results for the same input (for example, **`GETDATE()`**, **`NEWID()`**).

Impact on UDFs:

- Indexed views and persisted computed columns require deterministic functions.
- Using non-deterministic functions in these contexts will raise errors.

Functions vs. Views vs. Stored Procedures

The following table compares views, functions (UDFs), and stored procedures, while highlighting their key features, usage, and capabilities in SQL Server:

Feature	View	Function (UDF)	Stored Procedure
Returns Data	Table (Virtual)	Scalar (Single Value) or Table	Any Shape (Multiple Sets, or Values)
Accepts Parameters	❌ No	✅ Yes	✅ Yes
Used in **`SELECT`**	✅ Yes	✅ Yes	❌ No
Updates Data	Sometimes (If Simple)	❌ No	✅ Yes
Error Handling	❌ No	❌ No	✅ Yes (**`TRY...CATCH`**)

Table 5.1: *Comparison of Views, Functions, and Stored Procedures*

Performance Considerations

Different types of user-defined functions (UDFs) in SQL Server have varying performance characteristics. Therefore, understanding these differences is crucial for writing efficient queries.

- **Scalar UDFs**
  - Biggest performance risk
  - Executed row-by-row, which may cause slowdowns in large queries
  - SQL Server 2019 introduced scalar UDF inlining, which dramatically improves performance by converting UDF logic into inline expressions.
- **Inline TVFs**
  - Highly optimized
  - Best performance choice among UDFs
- **Multi-Statement TVFs**
  - Slower than inline TVFs, as they materialize intermediate results
  - Avoid them unless it is absolutely necessary.

Real-World Use Cases for Functions

User-defined functions (UDFs) in SQL Server can be tailored for specific tasks, ranging from simple calculations to complex data retrieval, depending on the function type. Therefore, it is also important to understand the real-world cases for UDFs.

- **Scalar Functions**
  - **`fnCalculateAge(@BirthDate)`**: Returns employee's age
  - **`fnFormatPhoneNumber(@Phone)`**: Ensures that phone numbers follow company standards
- **Inline TVFs**
  - **`fnGetOrdersByCustomer(@CustomerID)`**: Returns all orders for a given customer
  - They are good for reporting and parameterized queries.
- **Multi-Statement TVFs**
  - **`fnGetInventoryStatus(@WarehouseID)`**: Combines stock, pending shipments, and backorders into a single result set

Security Considerations

Functions in SQL Server not only encapsulate logic, but they also play a role in security and permission management. Therefore, you must know about the following security considerations associated with them:

- Functions run with the caller's permissions, unless they are defined with **`EXECUTE AS`**.
- **Permissions**:
  - `GRANT EXECUTE ON FUNCTION fnGetEmployeesByDept TO SalesRole;`
  - Functions can help secure sensitive business logic by exposing results without revealing the underlying table structure.

Best Practices for Functions

To maximize performance and maintainability when using user-defined functions, it is important to follow these best practices:

- Use inline TVFs instead of scalar functions whenever possible.
- Avoid multi-statement TVFs, unless procedural logic is unavoidable.
- Do not perform row-by-row operations inside scalar functions for large datasets.
- Document deterministic and non-deterministic functions.
- Keep functions small and focused.

Exercises

1. Write a scalar function `fnCalculateTax` that takes an amount and returns the value with 7% tax applied.
2. Create an inline TVF `fnGetOrdersByYear(@Year INT)` that returns all orders for a specific year.
3. Implement a multi-statement TVF `fnGetTopCustomers(@TopN INT)` that returns the top N customers by sales.
4. Test performance differences by running a scalar function and an inline TVF on a large dataset.
5. Identify whether the function `GETDATE()` can be used in an indexed view, and explain why or why not.

Stored Procedures in SQL Server

A stored procedure (often shortened to *proc*) is a precompiled collection of SQL statements stored in the database. It can contain:

- `SELECT` Queries
- DML Statements (`INSERT`, `UPDATE`, `DELETE`)
- Control-of-Flow Logic (`IF`, `WHILE`, `CASE`)
- Error Handling (`TRY...CATCH`)
- Calls to Other Procedures/Functions

Hence, stored procedures are one of the most powerful modular programming features in SQL Server.

Stored Procedures

Stored procedures in SQL Server offer several advantages that improve efficiency, security, and maintainability in database applications. These advantages are:

1. **Reusability**: Encapsulate frequently used logic once, and then call it multiple times.
2. **Maintainability**: If business rules change, update the procedure once.
3. **Performance**: Procedures are compiled and cached, which reduces repeated parsing overhead.
4. **Security**: Grant `EXECUTE` permissions without exposing underlying tables.
5. **Abstraction**: Applications call stored procedures without needing to know database schema.
6. **Transaction Control**: Combine multiple statements into one atomic unit.

Creating Stored Procedures

Basic Syntax

```
CREATE PROCEDURE procedure_name
AS
BEGIN
    -- T-SQL statements
END;
```

Example: Simple Procedure

```
CREATE PROCEDURE spGetAllEmployees
AS
BEGIN
    SELECT EmployeeID, FirstName, LastName, DepartmentID
    FROM Employees;
END;
Execution:
EXEC spGetAllEmployees;
```

Parameters in Stored Procedures

Stored procedures can accept parameters, which makes them dynamic and reusable.

Input Parameters

```
CREATE PROCEDURE spGetEmployeesByDept
    @DeptID INT
AS
BEGIN
    SELECT EmployeeID, FirstName, LastName
    FROM Employees
    WHERE DepartmentID = @DeptID;
END;
```

Execution:

```
EXEC spGetEmployeesByDept @DeptID = 3;
```

Output Parameters

Procedures can also return values via output parameters.

```
CREATE PROCEDURE spGetEmployeeSalary
    @EmployeeID INT,
    @Salary DECIMAL(10,2) OUTPUT
AS
BEGIN
    SELECT @Salary = Salary
    FROM Employees
    WHERE EmployeeID = @EmployeeID;
END;

DECLARE @EmpSalary DECIMAL(10,2);
EXEC spGetEmployeeSalary 101, @EmpSalary OUTPUT;
PRINT @EmpSalary;
```

Default Parameters

```
CREATE PROCEDURE spGetEmployeesByStatus
    @IsActive BIT = 1
AS
BEGIN
    SELECT EmployeeID, FirstName, LastName
    FROM Employees
    WHERE IsActive = @IsActive;
END;

-- Uses default
EXEC spGetEmployeesByStatus;
-- Override default
EXEC spGetEmployeesByStatus @IsActive = 0;
```

Returning Values from Procedures

A stored procedure can return an integer value with **RETURN**. This is often used for status codes, such as:

```
CREATE PROCEDURE spCheckEmployeeExists
    @EmployeeID INT
AS
BEGIN
    IF EXISTS(SELECT 1 FROM Employees WHERE EmployeeID = @EmployeeID)
        RETURN 1;  -- Employee exists
    ELSE
        RETURN 0;  -- Not found
END;

DECLARE @Result INT;
EXEC @Result = spCheckEmployeeExists 101;
PRINT @Result;
```

Conditional Logic in Procedures

Procedures can include control-of-flow logic such as **IF...ELSE** and **CASE**. They look like:

```
CREATE PROCEDURE spGetEmployeeBonus
    @EmployeeID INT
AS
BEGIN
    DECLARE @Salary DECIMAL(10,2);
    SELECT @Salary = Salary FROM Employees WHERE EmployeeID = @EmployeeID;

    IF @Salary > 100000
        PRINT 'Eligible for high bonus';
    ELSE IF @Salary > 50000
        PRINT 'Eligible for standard bonus';
    ELSE
        PRINT 'No bonus';
END;
```

Transactions in Stored Procedures

Procedures often manage transactions to ensure data integrity. You can see the following example to understand how this happens:

```
CREATE PROCEDURE spTransferFunds
    @FromAccount INT,
    @ToAccount INT,
    @Amount DECIMAL(10,2)
AS
BEGIN
    BEGIN TRANSACTION;

    UPDATE Accounts
    SET Balance = Balance - @Amount
    WHERE AccountID = @FromAccount;

    UPDATE Accounts
    SET Balance = Balance + @Amount
    WHERE AccountID = @ToAccount;

    IF @@ERROR <> 0
    BEGIN
        ROLLBACK TRANSACTION;
        PRINT 'Transaction failed';
        RETURN;
    END

    COMMIT TRANSACTION;
END;
```

Error Handling with TRY...CATCH

SQL Server provides structured error handling with **TRY...CATCH** blocks.

```
CREATE PROCEDURE spSafeInsertEmployee
    @FirstName NVARCHAR(50),
    @LastName NVARCHAR(50),
    @Salary DECIMAL(10,2)
AS
BEGIN
    BEGIN TRY
        INSERT INTO Employees (FirstName, LastName, Salary)
        VALUES (@FirstName, @LastName, @Salary);
    END TRY
    BEGIN CATCH
        PRINT 'Error: ' + ERROR_MESSAGE();
    END CATCH;
END;
```

Some useful error functions in **CATCH** block are:

- `ERROR_NUMBER()`
- `ERROR_MESSAGE()`
- `ERROR_LINE()`
- `ERROR_PROCEDURE()`

Dynamic SQL in Stored Procedures

Sometimes, SQL needs to be built dynamically. This can be seen in the following example:

```
CREATE PROCEDURE spSearchEmployees
    @ColumnName NVARCHAR(50),
    @SearchValue NVARCHAR(100)
AS
BEGIN
    DECLARE @SQL NVARCHAR(MAX);
    SET @SQL = 'SELECT EmployeeID, FirstName, LastName FROM Employees WHERE '
               + QUOTENAME(@ColumnName) + ' = @Value';

    EXEC sp_executesql @SQL, N'@Value NVARCHAR(100)', @SearchValue;
END;

EXEC spSearchEmployees 'FirstName', 'John';
```

Best Practice: Always use **sp_executesql** with parameters to avoid SQL injection.

Performance Considerations

To ensure stored procedures perform efficiently and predictably, it is important to consider execution behavior and best practices. Therefore, you must remember the following considerations:

- **Execution Plan Caching**: Stored procedures reuse cached plans, while improving performance.
- **SET Options**: Certain session settings can affect execution plan reuse.
- **Avoid Over-Complex Logic**: Use procedures for business rules, but avoid turning them into "mini-applications."
- **Parameter Sniffing**: SQL Server may optimize a plan based on the first parameter value. Use **OPTION (RECOMPILE)** if needed.

Security Considerations

Stored procedures can enhance security in SQL Server by controlling permissions, execution context, and guarding against SQL injection. Therefore, you must remember the following security considerations to use them effectively:

1. **Granular Permissions:** Users can be given **EXECUTE** permission on a procedure without any access to underlying tables.

   ```
   GRANT EXECUTE ON spGetEmployeesByDept TO SalesRole;
   ```

2. **Execution Context:** Procedures can run under a specific security context:

   ```
   CREATE PROCEDURE spSecureInsert
   WITH EXECUTE AS OWNER

       AS
   BEGIN
       -- It runs with the owner's permissions.
   END;
   ```

3. **SQL Injection Protection**: Use parameterized queries (**sp_executesql**) instead of concatenating strings.

Real-World Use Cases

Stored procedures serve a variety of practical purposes in SQL Server, as they support business processes, reporting, and secure application interactions. Therefore, here are a few real-world use cases for you to consider:

1. **Business Transactions:** Transfer funds, approve leave requests, and manage inventory.
2. **Batch Processing:** Generate end-of-day reports, payroll calculations, and ETL pipelines.
3. **Security Wrappers:** Provide data access without exposing tables directly.
4. **Application Interfaces:** Middleware calls stored procedures, instead of embedding SQL inside the application code.

Best Practices for Stored Procedures

To ensure stored procedures are reliable, maintainable, and easy to use, follow these best practices:

- Use meaningful names (**`prefix sp_`** is discouraged, except for system procs).
- Always include error handling (**`TRY...CATCH`**).
- Use transactions for multi-step operations.
- Avoid hardcoding values; use parameters instead.
- Document purpose and expected parameters.
- Keep procedures focused; avoid monolithic "**`God procedures`**".

Exercises

1. Write a stored procedure that returns employees earning above a specified salary.
2. Add error handling to the above procedure using **`TRY...CATCH`**.
3. Create a procedure that accepts **`DepartmentID`** and returns employees in that department, ordered by last name.
4. Create a procedure that transfers funds between accounts with transaction handling.
5. Modify a procedure to include an output parameter that returns the number of rows affected.
6. Test SQL injection protection by comparing string concatenation and parameterized dynamic SQL.

Security Considerations

When working with modular programming constructs in SQL Server such as views, functions, and stored procedures security is a critical aspect that developers and DBAs must consider. Poorly designed security models can lead to unauthorized access, privilege escalation, and data leaks. SQL Server provides several mechanisms to secure modular code, while ensuring that access to underlying objects and data is controlled, and that it is audited properly.

Therefore, in this section, we will explore key security practices related to modular programming in SQL Server, including permissions, execution context, schema binding, ownership chaining, and encryption.

Principle of Least Privilege

The foundation of database security is the Principle of Least Privilege (PoLP). This principle states that users should only be given the minimum rights that are necessary to perform their tasks.

- Instead of granting direct access to tables, you can create views and stored procedures as controlled access points.
- Users interact with these higher-level abstractions, while direct access to sensitive tables can be restricted.

Example:

```
-- Create a sensitive table
CREATE TABLE HR.Employees
(
    EmployeeID INT PRIMARY KEY,
    FullName NVARCHAR(100),
    Salary DECIMAL(10,2)
);

-- Instead of granting SELECT on HR.Employees,
-- Create a view that hides salary information
CREATE VIEW HR.EmployeePublicInfo
AS
SELECT EmployeeID, FullName
FROM HR.Employees;

-- Grant SELECT only on the view
GRANT SELECT ON HR.EmployeePublicInfo TO PublicUsers;
```

Here, users with access to the view cannot see the Salary column, even though it exists in the underlying table.

Ownership Chaining

Ownership chaining is a security feature in SQL Server that allows users to access objects (such as tables) indirectly through other objects (such as views or stored procedures), without requiring direct permissions on the underlying objects.

- If all objects in a chain are owned by the same schema owner, SQL Server does not check permissions on the underlying objects.
- This allows developers to centralize access control at the top layer (views, procedures, functions), instead of every base object.

Example:

```
-- Stored procedure accessing the Employees table
CREATE PROCEDURE HR.GetAllEmployees
AS
BEGIN
    SELECT * FROM HR.Employees;
END;

-- Grant EXECUTE to a user
GRANT EXECUTE ON HR.GetAllEmployees TO HRUser;
```

Here, the `HRUser` does not need `SELECT` rights on `HR.Employees`. Ownership chaining thus ensures that permissions on the procedure are sufficient.

Caution: While ownership chaining simplifies security, it must be carefully managed. If ownership changes or objects cross schemas with different owners, the chain breaks, and requires explicit permissions.

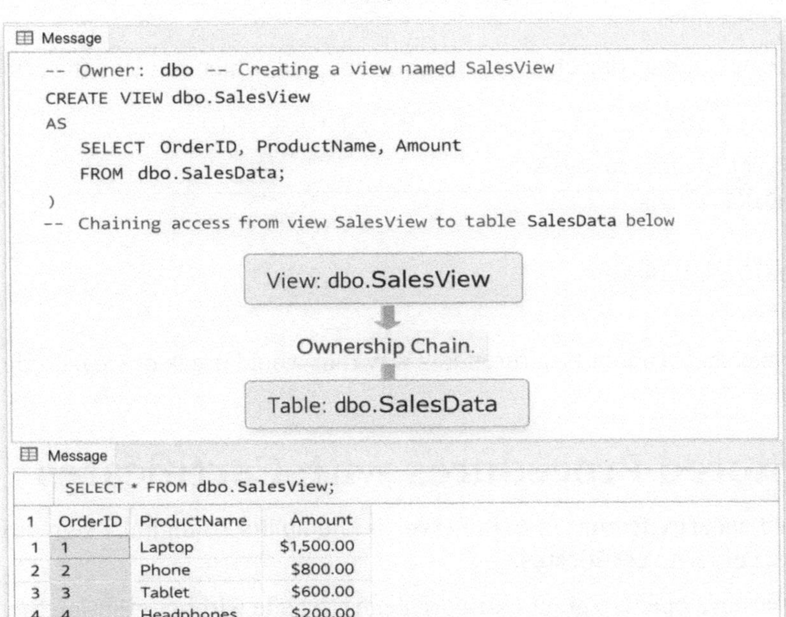

Figure 5.1: *Simplifying Ownership Chaining*

Execution Context (EXECUTE AS)

Stored procedures and functions can be executed under different execution contexts, and allow for flexibility in permission management. Therefore, you must know about them. We have explained them as follows:

- **`EXECUTE AS CALLER`** (Default): Runs under the caller's permissions
- **`EXECUTE AS OWNER`**: Runs under the module owner's permissions
- **`EXECUTE AS SELF`**: Runs under the creator's permissions
- **`EXECUTE AS 'UserName'`**: Runs under a specified user's permissions

Example:

```
CREATE PROCEDURE HR.GetConfidentialSalaries
WITH EXECUTE AS OWNER
AS
BEGIN
    SELECT FullName, Salary
    FROM HR.Employees;
END;
```

Here, even if the caller does not have direct access to the Salary column, the procedure executes with the owner's permissions, which allows for controlled access.

This approach is particularly useful when sensitive data must be accessed, but it should not be broadly exposed.

Schema Binding for Security

We previously discussed schema binding in the context of views and indexed views. From a security perspective, schema binding prevents unauthorized schema changes that could compromise security.

- Without schema binding, someone could drop or alter an underlying table, and can potentially bypass access rules.
- With schema binding, objects remain tightly coupled, which reduces the attack surface.

Example:

```
CREATE VIEW HR.EmployeeSecureView
WITH SCHEMABINDING
AS
SELECT EmployeeID, FullName
FROM HR.Employees;
```

Now, the Employees table cannot be altered in a way that would break or weaken the security of this view.

Signing Stored Procedures with Certificates

Another advanced security feature in SQL Server is the ability to digitally sign stored procedures, functions, and triggers with certificates.

- This allows developers to grant extra privileges to code without granting them to the user.
- Users can execute a procedure that has elevated rights (via certificate signing) without having those rights themselves.

Hence, this technique is especially useful for operations like writing audit logs, or accessing highly privileged objects.

Encryption of Stored Procedures, Functions, and Views

SQL Server allows you to encrypt the definition of views, functions, and stored procedures using the **`WITH ENCRYPTION`** option.

Example:

```
CREATE PROCEDURE HR.SecureProcedure
WITH ENCRYPTION
AS
BEGIN
    SELECT TOP 1 * FROM HR.Employees;
END;
```

Advantages:

- Prevents casual users from viewing the source code via tools like SSMS
- Adds a layer of intellectual property protection

Limitations:

- It is not true cryptographic protection, as advanced users can still reverse-engineer definitions.
- Encrypted definitions cannot be easily debugged or modified.

⚠ **Best Practice**: Use encryption only when necessary, and always keep source code backed up outside the SQL Server.

Row-Level Security (RLS)

SQL Server also supports Row-Level Security, which restricts access to specific rows in a table based on user context.

- Instead of granting blanket access to a table, you can define security policies that filter rows per user or role.
- This can be combined with views and functions for powerful, fine-grained control.

Example:

```
-- Create predicate function
CREATE FUNCTION HR.EmployeePredicate(@EmployeeID INT)
RETURNS TABLE
WITH SCHEMABINDING
AS
RETURN SELECT 1 AS AccessResult
WHERE @EmployeeID = USER_ID();

-- Apply Row-Level Security Policy
CREATE SECURITY POLICY HR.EmployeeFilter
ADD FILTER PREDICATE HR.EmployeePredicate(EmployeeID)
ON HR.Employees
WITH (STATE = ON);
```

Now, users will only see the rows that match their identity, even if they query directly.

Auditing and Monitoring

Security is not complete without auditing and monitoring. SQL Server provides features like SQL Server Audit and Extended Events to track access and execution of modular code.

Best Practices:

- Audit execution of sensitive stored procedures.
- Monitor failed permission attempts.
- Log changes to objects such as views, functions, and procedures.

Best Practices for Security in Modular Code

To enhance security and control when working with SQL Server, consider the following best practices for stored procedures:

- Use stored procedures instead of ad-hoc queries to reduce SQL injection risk.
- Grant **EXECUTE** instead of broad **SELECT/UPDATE** permissions.
- Leverage ownership chaining for simplified access management.
- Apply schema binding for stronger control.
- Use **EXECUTE AS** and certificate signing carefully to manage elevated rights.
- Encrypt definitions only when necessary, and also maintain backups.
- Implement Row-Level Security (RLS) for fine-grained data control.
- Audit and monitor execution activity continuously.

✅ **Key Takeaway**: Security in SQL Server modular programming is not just about granting or denying permissions; it is about creating controlled entry points (views, functions, and stored procedures), using features like execution context, ownership chaining, schema binding, and encryption to protect both data and logic, while maintaining usability and performance.

Error Handling in Stored Procedures

Error handling is a critical aspect of writing robust and production-ready stored procedures in SQL Server. Therefore, while writing procedural code, you must anticipate invalid inputs, violations of constraints, deadlocks, permission issues, or unexpected system failures. Without proper handling, these errors can cause partial transactions, data inconsistencies, or confusing messages for users and applications.

SQL Server provides powerful constructs like **TRY...CATCH** blocks, system error functions, transaction handling, and logging mechanisms to capture and manage errors gracefully. Hence, a well-designed error handling strategy not only ensures data integrity, but also improves maintainability and debugging.

The title has been slightly adjusted to better align with the style guide.

Implementing proper error handling in SQL Server provides multiple benefits for data integrity, user experience, and system security. These benefits are:

- **Data Integrity:** Prevents half-completed operations from corrupting data
- **User Experience:** Returns meaningful error messages instead of cryptic system errors
- **System Reliability:** Enables developers to log issues and diagnose problems easily
- **Security:** Avoids leaking sensitive details through unhandled errors

To understand these benefits, you can consider the example of a banking system, where a stored procedure transferring money between accounts must either succeed fully, or fail completely. If only the debit succeeds and the credit fails, the system will be out of balance. Error handling prevents such scenarios.

TRY...CATCH Structure

The **TRY...CATCH** block is the fundamental mechanism for error handling in T-SQL.

Syntax:

```
BEGIN TRY
    -- Statements that may cause an error
END TRY
BEGIN CATCH
    -- Error handling logic
END CATCH
```

When an error occurs inside the **TRY** block, SQL Server immediately transfers control to the **CATCH** block.

Example: Handling Division by Zero

```
CREATE PROCEDURE usp_SafeDivision
    @Dividend INT,
    @Divisor INT
AS
BEGIN
    BEGIN TRY
```

```
        DECLARE @Result DECIMAL(10,2);
        SET @Result = @Dividend / @Divisor;
        PRINT 'Result: ' + CAST(@Result AS VARCHAR(20));
    END TRY
    BEGIN CATCH
        PRINT 'Error occurred: Division by zero is not allowed.';
    END CATCH
END;
```

If **@Divisor = 0**, execution jumps to the **CATCH** block.

Functions Available in CATCH Block

Inside the **CATCH** block, SQL Server exposes several functions to capture details about the error:

T-SQL Error Handling System Functions:

Function	Description
ERROR_NUMBER()	Returns the error number
ERROR_SEVERITY()	Returns the severity level
ERROR_STATE()	Returns the state number associated with the error
ERROR_PROCEDURE()	Returns the name of the procedure or trigger where it occurred
ERROR_LINE()	Returns the line number where the error occurred
ERROR_MESSAGE()	Returns the full error message text

***Table 5.2**: SQL Server System Functions Used within TRY...CATCH Blocks to Capture and Analyze Runtime Errors*

Example: Logging Error Details

```
CREATE PROCEDURE usp_InsertCustomer
    @CustomerName NVARCHAR(100),
    @Email NVARCHAR(200)
AS
BEGIN
    BEGIN TRY
        INSERT INTO Customers (CustomerName, Email)
        VALUES (@CustomerName, @Email);
    END TRY
    BEGIN CATCH
        INSERT INTO ErrorLog (ErrorNumber, ErrorMessage, ErrorProcedure, ErrorLine,
ErrorDate)
        VALUES (
            ERROR_NUMBER(),
            ERROR_MESSAGE(),
            ERROR_PROCEDURE(),
            ERROR_LINE(),
            GETDATE()
        );
        PRINT 'An error occurred. Please check ErrorLog table.';
    END CATCH
END;
```

Hence, this approach allows you to build a central error logging framework.

Transactions and Error Handling

Most critical operations require transactions to ensure atomicity (all-or-nothing execution). Therefore, if an error occurs, you can **ROLLBACK** the transaction.

Pattern: TRY...CATCH with Transactions

```
CREATE PROCEDURE usp_TransferFunds
    @FromAccount INT,
    @ToAccount INT,
    @Amount DECIMAL(10,2)
AS
BEGIN
    BEGIN TRY
        BEGIN TRANSACTION;

        UPDATE Accounts
        SET Balance = Balance - @Amount
        WHERE AccountID = @FromAccount;

        UPDATE Accounts
        SET Balance = Balance + @Amount
        WHERE AccountID = @ToAccount;

        COMMIT TRANSACTION;
    END TRY
    BEGIN CATCH
        ROLLBACK TRANSACTION;

        PRINT 'Transaction failed: ' + ERROR_MESSAGE();
    END CATCH
END;
```

Here, if either update fails, the entire transaction rolls back, which ensures that no account is left in an inconsistent state.

Nested TRY...CATCH Blocks

Stored procedures may contain nested **TRY...CATCH** blocks to handle different types of errors at different levels.

Example:

```
BEGIN TRY
    -- Outer transaction
    BEGIN TRANSACTION;

    BEGIN TRY
        -- Inner logic
        EXEC usp_InsertCustomer 'John Doe', NULL;
    END TRY
    BEGIN CATCH
        PRINT 'Inner Error: ' + ERROR_MESSAGE();
        ROLLBACK TRANSACTION;
        RETURN;
    END CATCH;
```

```
    COMMIT TRANSACTION;
END TRY
BEGIN CATCH
    PRINT 'Outer Error: ' + ERROR_MESSAGE();
    ROLLBACK TRANSACTION;
END CATCH;
```

Hence, this layered approach is useful for complex procedures that combine multiple operations.

Rethrowing Errors

Sometimes, you want to re-raise an error after logging it. This process is called rethrowing, and is illustrated in the following examples.

Using `THROW`:

```
BEGIN CATCH
    INSERT INTO ErrorLog (ErrorNumber, ErrorMessage, ErrorDate)
    VALUES (ERROR_NUMBER(), ERROR_MESSAGE(), GETDATE());

    -- Rethrow the error
    THROW;
END CATCH;
```

As you can see, **`THROW`** re-raises the original error, while preserving its severity and state.

Best Practices in Error Handling

To ensure robust and secure error handling in SQL Server stored procedures, follow these best practices:

1. Always use **`TRY...CATCH`** in production stored procedures.
2. Combine error handling with transactions for data integrity.
3. Log errors in a central table (**`ErrorLog`**) with timestamps.
4. Use custom error messages for clarity, but log system messages for diagnostics.
5. Rollback before rethrowing errors to avoid leaving open transactions.
6. Do not expose sensitive details (for example, server paths, system errors) directly to end-users.
7. Gracefully handle expected errors (for example, division by zero, duplicate keys).
8. Use **`THROW`** over **`RAISERROR`** for rethrowing, since **`THROW`** is the modern approach.

Summary: Error handling in stored procedures is not just a defensive coding practice; it is essential for maintaining data consistency, application stability, and system reliability. Therefore, by leveraging **`TRY...CATCH`**, error functions, transactions, logging, and best practices, you can design stored procedures that fail gracefully, assist in troubleshooting, and safeguard your SQL Server environment.

Real-World Case Studies

Case Study 1: E-Commerce Order Processing

Scenario: An online retail platform uses a stored procedure to handle order placement. When a customer places an order:

1. The order must be inserted into the Orders table.

2. The inventory must be updated.
3. A payment record must be logged.

Risk:

- If payment succeeds but inventory update fails, the system would record a sale without deducting the stock.
- If order creation fails after payment, the money is debited, but no order is shipped.

Solution (With `TRY...CATCH` and Transactions):

```
CREATE PROCEDURE usp_ProcessOrder
    @CustomerID INT,
    @ProductID INT,
    @Quantity INT,
    @PaymentAmount DECIMAL(10,2)
AS
BEGIN
    BEGIN TRY
        BEGIN TRANSACTION;

        INSERT INTO Orders (CustomerID, ProductID, Quantity, OrderDate)
        VALUES (@CustomerID, @ProductID, @Quantity, GETDATE());

        UPDATE Products
        SET Stock = Stock - @Quantity
        WHERE ProductID = @ProductID;

        INSERT INTO Payments (CustomerID, Amount, PaymentDate)
        VALUES (@CustomerID, @PaymentAmount, GETDATE());

        COMMIT TRANSACTION;
    END TRY
    BEGIN CATCH
        ROLLBACK TRANSACTION;

        INSERT INTO ErrorLog (ErrorMessage, ErrorDate, Module)
        VALUES (ERROR_MESSAGE(), GETDATE(), 'Order Processing');

        THROW; -- Let the application know that the transaction failed
    END CATCH;
END;
```

Impact: *This ensures that orders, inventory, and payments always stay in sync—either all succeed, or none are applied.*

Case Study 2: Healthcare Patient Records

Here is a complete **T-SQL code example** you can include in the case study to illustrate the sequence and its impact:

Case Study 2: Healthcare Patient Records (Code Example)

```
BEGIN TRY
    BEGIN TRANSACTION;

    -- Step 1: Insert visit details
    INSERT INTO Visits (PatientID, VisitDate, DoctorID, Notes)
```

```
    VALUES (101, GETDATE(), 12, 'Routine check-up');

    -- Step 2: Update patient's last visit date
    UPDATE Patients
    SET LastVisitDate = GETDATE()
    WHERE PatientID = 101;

    -- Step 3: Record billing information
    INSERT INTO Billing (PatientID, Amount, BillingDate)
    VALUES (101, 150.00, GETDATE());

    COMMIT TRANSACTION;
END TRY
BEGIN CATCH
    ROLLBACK TRANSACTION;

    PRINT 'An error occurred. Transaction has been rolled back.';
END CATCH;
```

Explanation

This example demonstrates how multiple dependent operations are executed in a specific sequence within a transaction. The BEGIN TRANSACTION ensures that all steps—recording the visit, updating the patient record, and inserting billing information—are treated as a single unit of work. If any step fails, the ROLLBACK statement prevents partial updates, thereby maintaining data consistency and integrity.

Risk:

- If the visit is recorded but billing fails, the hospital loses revenue.
- If billing succeeds but the visit fails, the patient history stays incomplete.

Solution: Error handling ensures that patient care records and billing remain consistent. Therefore, if an error occurs, a rollback is triggered, and the issue is logged for manual resolution.

Case Study 3: Airline Reservation System

Scenario: When a passenger books a flight:

1. A record is inserted into the Bookings table.
2. A seat is reserved in the Seats table.
3. A payment is processed.

Risk:

- If a seat is reserved but payment fails, the airline loses revenue, and blocks a seat unnecessarily.
- If payment succeeds but no seat is reserved, the customer has paid, but they will have no ticket.

Solution (With Nested `TRY...CATCH`): The airline system uses nested error handling the inner block ensures seat reservation is valid, while the outer block ensures payment and booking are consistent. If anything fails, the seat is released, and the customer is notified to retry.

Case Study 4: Banking Funds Transfer

Scenario: Transferring money between accounts requires:

1. Debiting the sender's account
2. Crediting the recipient's account

3. Recording the transaction in the Ledger

Risk:

- If only the debit succeeds, the money disappears from the sender's account.
- If only the credit succeeds, the money is created from nowhere.

Solution: A stored procedure with a transaction rollback guarantees that both debit and credit either succeed or fail together. If a deadlock or constraint violation occurs, the procedure logs the error, and then rethrows it for retry.

Case Study 5: Financial Reporting (End-of-Month Closing)

Scenario: A financial services company runs a stored procedure to generate monthly reports that:

1. Aggregates all transactions
2. Updates summary tables
3. Archives detailed data

Risk: If archiving fails after summaries are updated, the report shows double-counted or missing transactions.

Solution: Error handling ensures that if archiving fails, the entire reporting cycle rolls back, and the previous month's data remains untouched until the issue is fixed.

Lessons from Case Studies

Across industries, error handling in stored procedures protects:

- **E-Commerce**: Prevents double-charging or stock mismanagement.
- **Healthcare**: Ensures patient data and billing are in sync.
- **Airlines**: Guarantees seat reservations match payments.
- **Banking**: Enforces atomic transfers to maintain trust.
- **Finance**: Preserves reporting accuracy and compliance.

Security Considerations and Permissions

SQL Server security is a multi-layered defense system, which ensures that only the right users, processes, and applications can access or modify data. Therefore, while working with views, functions, and stored procedures, you are not just writing modular code, but also building security boundaries.

Without proper security, even the best-written procedures can become attack vectors for SQL injection, data leaks, or privilege escalation. Hence, this section will expand on best practices and showcases real-world applications where permissions and execution context play a critical role.

Security Concepts in SQL Server

Implementing proper security in SQL Server involves managing permissions, ownership, and execution context to protect data and ensure appropriate access. Therefore, it is important to know about the following security concepts with regards to SQL Server:

- **Principle of Least Privilege (PoLP)**
  - Users should have the minimum level of access that is required to perform their tasks.
  - **Example**: A cashier in a retail system should update sales data, but they should not delete products.

- **Permissions Granularity**
  - Permissions can be applied at the server, database, schema, table, or column level.
  - Developers often use stored procedures and views to encapsulate logic, while granting users access only to these modules, and not to underlying tables.
- **Ownership Chaining**
  - If a stored procedure or view references a table owned by the same schema owner, SQL Server does not check additional permissions on that table.
  - This improves performance, but it must be monitored carefully to avoid accidental privilege leaks.
- **Execution Context (`EXECUTE AS`)**
  - Procedures and functions can run under different security contexts:
    - **Caller**: Uses the caller's permissions
    - **Self/Owner**: Uses the module owner's permissions
    - **Specific User**: Executes under a defined user

Common Security Practices for Views, Functions, and Stored Procedures

To enforce secure and controlled access to data in SQL Server, follow these best practices while designing views and stored procedures:

- Use schema binding in views to prevent accidental changes to underlying tables.
- Avoid granting direct table access to end users; instead, expose data through stored procedures or views.
- Parameterize stored procedures to reduce SQL injection risk.
- Audit access logs to monitor who runs sensitive procedures.
- Use role-based security to group permissions logically.

Real-World Case Studies

Case Study 1: Healthcare Patient Privacy (HIPAA Compliance)

Scenario: A hospital database stores sensitive patient records in the Patients table. The nurses need to view only non-sensitive data (name, age, and visit history), while the doctors need full access.

Solution:

- A view called **`vw_PatientSummary`** exposes only the non-sensitive columns.
- Nurses are granted SELECT permission on the view only, and not the underlying table.
- Doctors have access to the full Patients table through secured stored procedures.

Impact:

- This practice ensures HIPAA compliance.
- It prevents unauthorized staff from viewing sensitive patient information like SSNs or diagnoses.

Case Study 2: Banking Transactions (SOX Compliance)

Scenario: In a bank's system, tellers must execute withdrawals and deposits, but they should never be able to see customers' account balances beyond the transactions they process.

Solution:

- Stored procedures **usp_Deposit**, and **usp_Withdraw** are created.
- Tellers have **EXECUTE** permissions only on these procedures.
- Any direct access to the Accounts table is denied.

Impact:

- Tellers can perform their job without exposing customer balances.
- This helps maintain Sarbanes-Oxley (SOX) compliance by restricting access to financial records.

Case Study 3: E-Commerce Inventory Control

Scenario: An e-commerce platform has multiple vendors updating product stock. However, vendors should only be able to update their own inventory.

Solution:

- Stored procedure **usp_UpdateStock** enforces row-level filtering, which looks like this:

```
CREATE PROCEDURE usp_UpdateStock
    @VendorID INT,
    @ProductID INT,
    @Quantity INT
AS
BEGIN
    UPDATE Products
    SET Stock = Stock + @Quantity
    WHERE ProductID = @ProductID
      AND VendorID = @VendorID;  -- Prevents cross-vendor updates
END;
```

- Vendors only have **EXECUTE** permission on this procedure, and not **UPDATE** access on the table.

Impact:

- This prevents malicious or accidental modification of another vendor's stock.
- This protects business integrity.

Case Study 4: Airline Reservation System

Scenario: Airline booking agents process reservations, but they should not directly manipulate seat assignments.

Solution:

- Agents only have **EXECUTE** permission on a stored procedure **usp_BookSeat**.
- The procedure validates payment and seat availability before showing a confirmation.

Impact:

- This prevents fraudulent seat bookings.
- It ensures that only valid and verified transactions can reserve seats.

Case Study 5: Finance and Data Warehousing

Scenario: A financial services firm runs monthly risk reports. Analysts should only be able to run stored procedures that generate reports, and should not query raw transactional data.

Solution:

- Analysts are granted EXECUTE permission on reporting procedures.
- The underlying transactional tables remain restricted.
- Procedures use WITH EXECUTE AS OWNER, so that analysts can run reports without needing table access.

Impact:

- It protects raw financial data.
- It ensures that analysts have the tools they need without the risk of overexposure.

Lessons from Case Studies

Different industries leverage SQL Server security features to protect sensitive data and enforce compliance in the following ways:

- Healthcare: Views restrict sensitive columns to ensure privacy.
- Banking: Stored procedures enforce compliance and prevent data misuse.
- E-Commerce: Row-level filtering protects vendor data.
- Airlines: Stored procedures safeguard transactional integrity.
- Finance: Execution context enables reporting without over-permissioning.

Key Takeaways

To maintain strong security practices in SQL Server, it is important to follow consistent guidelines for permissions and access control. Therefore, you must factor in the following while using permissions and access control:

- Always apply the principle of least privilege.
- Use views and stored procedures as security boundaries.
- Favor role-based permissions over individual user assignments.
- Carefully choose EXECUTE AS context to balance usability and safety.
- Regularly audit permissions and logs to detect misuse.

Conclusion

In this chapter, you have learned how to retrieve and combine data from multiple tables using various join operations, including `INNER`, `LEFT`, `RIGHT`, `FULL`, `CROSS`, and `SELF JOIN`s, while effectively handling `NULL`s and troubleshooting unexpected results. You also explored set-based operations such as `UNION`, `INTERSECT`, and `EXCEPT` to combine and compare datasets efficiently, and gained hands-on experience with correlated and non-correlated subqueries, derived tables, and Common Table Expressions (CTEs) for modular and reusable query design, including recursive operations. Hence, by mastering these techniques, you are now able to write complex queries that integrate data across multiple tables, filter and aggregate information accurately, as well as optimize query performance, forming a solid foundation for advanced SQL programming and analytics.

Therefore, after building on this knowledge, the next chapter will introduce modular programming constructs in SQL Server, including views, functions, and stored procedures. It will teach you how to encapsulate query logic for reuse, implement error handling, manage permissions securely, and develop resilient, maintainable database routines that enhance both performance and security.

CHAPTER 6

CTEs, MERGE, Pivoting, JSON, and XML

Introduction

This chapter focuses on advanced SQL Server features that extend beyond traditional relational operations into more sophisticated querying, transformation, and integration of structured and semi-structured data. We will begin with Common Table Expressions (CTEs), which can be recursive and non-recursive, and will see how they simplify complex nested queries, while allowing hierarchical operations. We will then cover the MERGE statement, a powerful tool for performing insert, update, and delete logic in a single operation. The chapter then explores PIVOT and UNPIVOT transformations for reshaping data. Finally, we will dive into semi-structured data JSON and XML showing how to parse, generate, and integrate them seamlessly into SQL Server.

Structure

In this chapter, we will cover the following topics:

- Introduction to Advanced SQL Features
- Writing Recursive and Non-Recursive CTEs
- MERGE Statement for `UPSERT` Operations
- `PIVOT` and `UNPIVOT` Transformations
- Working with JSON: `OPENJSON`, `JSON_VALUE`, `FOR JSON`
- XML Parsing and Generation

Introduction to Advanced SQL Features

As relational databases evolve, SQL Server continues to provide advanced features to handle modern business needs. In earlier chapters, we covered modularity (views, functions, procedures). Now, we will explore tools that help with the following:

- **Simplifying Queries**: CTEs make deeply nested or hierarchical queries readable and maintainable.
- **Efficient Data Modification**: `MERGE` performs multiple operations in a single statement.
- **Data Reshaping**: `PIVOT/UNPIVOT` convert data between row-based and column-based forms.
- **Integrating Semi-Structured Data**: JSON and XML allow SQL Server to interact with APIs, documents, and applications.

Therefore, by the end of this chapter, you will be able to combine these features to build powerful data pipelines inside SQL Server.

Writing Recursive and Non-Recursive CTEs

A **Common Table Expression (CTE)** is a temporary, named result set that exists only during the execution of a single query. CTEs improve readability, reduce complexity, and provide a powerful way to express queries that would otherwise require deeply nested subqueries or multiple derived tables.

CTEs can be categorized into non-recursive and recursive CTEs, which are explained as follows:

- **Non-Recursive CTEs**: They are useful for simplifying complex queries, improving readability, and reusing query logic.
- **Recursive CTEs**: They are useful for handling hierarchical or graph-like data structures, such as organizational charts, folder trees, or bill of materials.

Hence, this section explores both in detail. It will also show how to build, apply, and optimize them in SQL Server.

Syntax of a CTE

The basic structure of a CTE is as follows:

```
WITH CTE_Name (Column1, Column2, ...)
AS
(
    -- Anchor Query (for recursive CTEs) OR regular query (for non-recursive CTEs)
    SELECT ...
)
-- Reference the CTE in the main query
SELECT *
FROM CTE_Name;
```

Key Points:

- A CTE must be immediately followed by a query that references it.
- The name given to the CTE acts like a virtual table or view, and is valid only for that query execution.
- Multiple CTEs can be chained together with commas.

Non-Recursive CTEs

Non-recursive CTEs are equivalent to inline views or derived tables, but they usually improve readability. They are commonly used to:

- Break down complex queries into steps.
- Remove repeated subquery logic.
- Improve query maintainability.

Example 1: Simplifying a Subquery

Without a CTE:

```
SELECT DepartmentID, AVG(Salary) AS AvgSalary
FROM Employees
```

```
WHERE DepartmentID IN (
    SELECT DepartmentID
    FROM Departments
    WHERE Location = 'New York'
)
GROUP BY DepartmentID;
```

Using a **CTE**:

```
WITH DeptNY AS
(
    SELECT DepartmentID
    FROM Departments
    WHERE Location = 'New York'
)
SELECT e.DepartmentID, AVG(e.Salary) AS AvgSalary
FROM Employees e
JOIN DeptNY d ON e.DepartmentID = d.DepartmentID
GROUP BY e.DepartmentID;
```

Benefit: This query is more modular and reusable. In case if you wanted to add Chicago sometime in the future, you would only update the CTE.

Example 2: Multi-Step Query

You can stack multiple CTEs for stepwise calculations, as shown here:

```
WITH Sales_CTE AS
(
    SELECT SalesPersonID, SUM(SalesAmount) AS TotalSales
    FROM Sales
    GROUP BY SalesPersonID
),
RankedSales AS
(
    SELECT SalesPersonID, TotalSales,
           RANK() OVER (ORDER BY TotalSales DESC) AS SalesRank
    FROM Sales_CTE
)
SELECT *
FROM RankedSales
WHERE SalesRank <= 5;
```

This two-step CTE first aggregates, and then ranks, while producing a clear logical flow.

Recursive CTEs

Recursive CTEs are the most useful when you are dealing with hierarchical data. They allow you to reference the CTE inside its own definition, and enable iterative processing until a termination condition is met.

Syntax Pattern:

```
WITH RecursiveCTE (columns)
AS
(
```

```
    -- Anchor Member (starting point)
    SELECT ...
    FROM ...
    WHERE ... -- Base condition

    UNION ALL

    -- Recursive Member (iterates)
    SELECT ...
    FROM RecursiveCTE
    JOIN ...
    ON ...
)
SELECT *
FROM RecursiveCTE;
```

- **`Anchor Member`:** The initial dataset
- **`Recursive Member`:** The query that refers back to the CTE, while progressively building results
- **`UNION ALL`:** Combines anchor and recursive steps (**`ALL`** is common, whereas **`DISTINCT`** may be used, but is slower)
- The recursion continues until no more rows are returned.

Example 1: Employee Hierarchy

Imagine that you want to get the full reporting hierarchy starting from a manager.

```
WITH EmployeeHierarchy AS
(
    -- Anchor: top-level manager
    SELECT EmployeeID, ManagerID, Name, 0 AS Level
    FROM Employees
    WHERE ManagerID IS NULL

    UNION ALL

    -- Recursive: employees reporting to the manager
    SELECT e.EmployeeID, e.ManagerID, e.Name, h.Level + 1
    FROM Employees e
    INNER JOIN EmployeeHierarchy h
    ON e.ManagerID = h.EmployeeID
)
SELECT *
FROM EmployeeHierarchy
ORDER BY Level, ManagerID;
```

Explanation:

- Start with the CEO (no manager).
- Iteratively find direct reports, while increasing the Level each time.
- Using the example produces a tree traversal of the organization.

Example 2: Bill of Materials (BOM)

Recursive CTEs are also used in manufacturing scenarios, which can be seen in the following example:

```
WITH BOM_CTE AS
```

```
(
    -- Base product
    SELECT ComponentID, ParentComponentID, ComponentName, 1 AS Level
    FROM Components
    WHERE ParentComponentID IS NULL

    UNION ALL

    -- Recursive expansion
    SELECT c.ComponentID, c.ParentComponentID, c.ComponentName, b.Level + 1
    FROM Components c
    INNER JOIN BOM_CTE b
    ON c.ParentComponentID = b.ComponentID
)
SELECT *
FROM BOM_CTE;
```

This query expands all child components from the root assembly down to the smallest part.

Limiting Recursion

To prevent infinite loops (for example, circular references in data), SQL Server provides:

- **`MAXRECURSION`** option in queries, which can be seen here:

```
WITH Numbers AS
(
    SELECT 1 AS n
    UNION ALL
    SELECT n + 1
    FROM Numbers
    WHERE n < 1000
)
SELECT *
FROM Numbers
OPTION (MAXRECURSION 100);
```

Here, the recursion stops at 100 iterations by default. You can override with **`MAXRECURSION 0`** (infinite), but make sure that you use it cautiously.

Practical Use Cases

Recursive queries and CTEs are powerful tools in SQL Server, as they allow you to handle hierarchical data, generate sequences, traverse graphs, and also perform iterative calculations efficiently. Here are some practical use cases of recursive queries and CTEs:

1. **Hierarchical Data Navigation**
   - Employees, Managers, and Organizational Charts
   - Folder Structures (Like File Systems)
   - Parent-Child Relationships
2. **Generating Sequences**
   - Numbers, dates, or ranges without permanent tally tables
3. **Graph Traversals**
   - Finding the shortest path or connectivity in a network of nodes

4. **Recursive Calculations**
   - Factorials, Fibonacci, and Cumulative Totals

Best Practices for CTEs

To ensure efficient and safe use of recursive CTEs in SQL Server, you may follow these best practices:

- Use non-recursive CTEs to simplify multi-step queries.
- Check recursion carefully to avoid infinite loops.
- Always set **MAXRECURSION** for production safety.
- Recursive CTEs can be slow on very deep hierarchies; therefore, you can consider alternatives like hierarchyid data type or adjacency list models for efficiency.
- Keep CTEs modular, with meaningful names, to enhance readability.

Best Practices for Using CTEs

While CTEs make SQL queries more modular and readable, following these best practices ensures efficiency and maintainability:

- **Limit Recursion Depth**: Use the **MAXRECURSION** option to avoid infinite loops.
- **Optimize Joins inside CTEs**: Keep CTEs focused; avoid unnecessary joins that make the execution sluggish.
- **Avoid Multiple Re-references**: Each reference to a CTE causes it to be re-executed unless materialized; therefore, you should consider using temp tables for repeated use.
- **Use Meaningful Names**: Naming CTEs descriptively improves readability for complex queries.

Example:

```
WITH SalesSummary AS (
    SELECT SalesPersonID, SUM(SalesAmount) AS TotalSales
    FROM Sales
    GROUP BY SalesPersonID
)
SELECT s.SalesPersonID, s.TotalSales
FROM SalesSummary s
ORDER BY s.TotalSales DESC
OPTION (MAXRECURSION 50);
```

Performance Considerations with CTEs

CTEs are not materialized objects; SQL Server treats them like inline views. This has implications for performance, which can show up as:

- **Recalculation per Reference**: If you reference the same CTE multiple times, SQL Server may recompute it each time.
- **Indexes Do Not Apply Directly**: Since CTEs are virtual, indexes cannot be created directly on them. Use indexed temp tables if any performance issues arise.
- **Execution Plans**: Always check the execution plan to see how the CTE is expanded. Sometimes choosing query rewriting or temporary storage might be better.

💡 **Tip**: *For very large recursive hierarchies, consider alternatives like indexed adjacency lists or nested sets for performance gains.*

Real-Life Use Cases for Recursive CTEs

Recursive CTEs are particularly useful in business scenarios such as:

1. **Organizational Hierarchies**: You can find managers, subordinates, and reporting chains.
2. **Bill of Materials (BOM)**: You can represent parent-child relationships in manufacturing.
3. **Folder Structures**: You can navigate directory trees for document storage systems.
4. **Network Graphs**: You can explore connected nodes in logistics or social networks.

📌 **Example: An employee hierarchy with levels will look like**:

```
WITH OrgChart AS (
    SELECT EmployeeID, ManagerID, 0 AS Level
    FROM Employees
    WHERE ManagerID IS NULL
    UNION ALL
    SELECT e.EmployeeID, e.ManagerID, oc.Level + 1
    FROM Employees e
    INNER JOIN OrgChart oc ON e.ManagerID = oc.EmployeeID
)
SELECT EmployeeID, ManagerID, Level
FROM OrgChart
ORDER BY Level, EmployeeID;
```

Using CTEs vs. Temp Tables vs. Views

When you are deciding between Common Table Expressions (CTEs), temporary tables, and views, it is useful to understand their scope, performance implications, maintainability, and support for recursion. The following table highlights the key differences between them:

Feature	CTEs	Temp Tables	Views
Scope	Single query only	Session-wide	Permanent object in schema
Performance	Recomputed each time	Can be indexed	Precompiled query logic
Maintainability	Great for modular readability	Good for large intermediates	Best for code reuse
Recursion Support	Yes	No	No

Table 6.1: *Comparison of CTEs, Temp Tables, and Views*

Here are a few rules you should remember while using either of the elaborated options:

- Use CTEs for readability and recursion.
- Use temp tables for large datasets or repeated use.
- Use views for reusable query encapsulation.

Summary: CTEs are an essential tool in T-SQL for writing clean, modular, and powerful queries. Non-recursive CTEs simplify query complexity, while recursive CTEs unlock solutions for hierarchical and graph-like data problems. When they are combined with safeguards like MAXRECURSION, they can infuse both elegance and safety in SQL design.

MERGE Statement for UPSERT Operations

The **MERGE** statement in SQL Server is a powerful T-SQL construct that allows developers to perform **INSERT**, **UPDATE**, and **DELETE** operations in a single statement. This makes it especially useful when synchronizing two tables, handling incremental loads in data warehouses, or performing **UPSERT** (update if the record exists, and insert if it does not).

Before **MERGE**, developers often had to write multiple queries using combinations of **IF EXISTS**, **INSERT**, and **UPDATE**. While this works, it leads to verbose code, and also introduces race conditions sometimes. **MERGE** simplifies this process, reduces code duplication, and ensures that operations are performed atomically.

MERGE Statement Syntax

The general syntax for **MERGE** is as follows:

```
MERGE target_table AS target
USING source_table AS source
ON target.KeyColumn = source.KeyColumn
WHEN MATCHED THEN
    UPDATE SET target.Column1 = source.Column1,
               target.Column2 = source.Column2
WHEN NOT MATCHED BY TARGET THEN
    INSERT (Column1, Column2, Column3)
    VALUES (source.Column1, source.Column2, source.Column3)
WHEN NOT MATCHED BY SOURCE THEN
    DELETE;
```

Key Components

1. **Target Table**: The table that will be modified (inserted into, updated, or deleted from)
2. **Source Table**: The dataset that will be compared against the target (can be a table, view, or subquery)
3. **ON Clause**: Defines the join condition between source and target
4. **WHEN MATCHED**: Defines what happens when rows exist in both source and target
5. **WHEN NOT MATCHED BY TARGET**: Defines what happens when a row exists in source, but it does not in target (usually an **INSERT**)
6. **WHEN NOT MATCHED BY SOURCE**: Defines what happens when a row exists in target, but it does not in source (usually a **DELETE**)

Simple UPSERT Example

Consider the following tables:

- **Customers** (Target)
- **Customers_Staging** (Source)

We want to update the existing customers if they already exist in the main table, or insert new customers if they do not.

```
MERGE Customers AS target
USING Customers_Staging AS source
ON target.CustomerID = source.CustomerID
```

```
WHEN MATCHED THEN
    UPDATE SET target.Name = source.Name,
               target.Email = source.Email,
               target.Phone = source.Phone
WHEN NOT MATCHED BY TARGET THEN
    INSERT (CustomerID, Name, Email, Phone)
    VALUES (source.CustomerID, source.Name, source.Email, source.Phone);
```

Explanation

- If a **CustomerID** exists in both tables, an **UPDATE** occurs.
- If a **CustomerID** exists only in **Customers_Staging**, then **INSERT** happens.

This is a textbook **UPSERT** operation.

Adding DELETE Logic

Sometimes, the requirement is to also **remove rows** from the target that no longer exist in the source. In that case, we will extend the **MERGE**, as shown here:

```
MERGE Customers AS target
USING Customers_Staging AS source
ON target.CustomerID = source.CustomerID
WHEN MATCHED THEN
    UPDATE SET target.Name = source.Name,
               target.Email = source.Email,
               target.Phone = source.Phone
WHEN NOT MATCHED BY TARGET THEN
    INSERT (CustomerID, Name, Email, Phone)
    VALUES (source.CustomerID, source.Name, source.Email, source.Phone)
WHEN NOT MATCHED BY SOURCE THEN
    DELETE;
```

Here:

- Rows that are not found in **Customers_Staging**, but are present in **Customers**, as they are deleted.

Hence, this is useful in data synchronization scenarios where the source is considered the "**single source of truth**".

MERGE with OUTPUT Clause

The **OUTPUT** clause can be combined with **MERGE** to log changes or audit modifications, as shown here:

```
MERGE Customers AS target
USING Customers_Staging AS source
ON target.CustomerID = source.CustomerID
WHEN MATCHED THEN
    UPDATE SET target.Name = source.Name
WHEN NOT MATCHED BY TARGET THEN
    INSERT (CustomerID, Name) VALUES (source.CustomerID, source.Name)
OUTPUT $action AS MergeAction, inserted.*, deleted.*;
```

- **$action** returns **INSERT**, **UPDATE**, or **DELETE**.

- `inserted.*` shows the new row values.
- deleted.* shows the old row values.

Thus, this illustration is particularly useful for change tracking and ETL pipelines.

Real-World Use Cases

In data warehousing, SQL Server techniques such as ETL processes, slowly changing dimensions, and incremental loads are essential for maintaining accurate and up-to-date data. These use cases are explained as follows:

1. **Data Warehousing ETL:** You can synchronize staging tables with fact/dimension tables.

   Example: Nightly jobs updating a `DimCustomer` table.
2. **Slowly Changing Dimensions (SCD) Type 1:** You can update existing dimension rows with the latest attribute values.
3. **Master Data Management**: You can consolidate data from multiple systems into a single master table.
4. **Incremental Loads**: Instead of truncating and reloading, `MERGE` can handle only changed data.

Common Pitfalls and Best Practices

While MERGE is powerful, it comes with caveats. These pitfalls are elaborated here, followed by the best practices that can address them:

Pitfalls

1. **Concurrency Issues:** `MERGE` can cause race conditions in high-concurrency environments if it is not used with proper isolation levels.
2. **Unintended Deletes:** Careless use of `WHEN NOT MATCHED BY SOURCE THEN DELETE` can wipe out critical rows.
3. **Performance Issues**
   - `MERGE` may perform worse than separate `UPDATE + INSERT` statements for very large datasets.
   - Therefore, you must always index join columns that are used in the ON clause.
4. **Incorrect Matching Logic:** A wrong `ON` condition can result in mass updates or deletes.

Best Practices

- Always test `MERGE` on a small dataset before applying it to production.
- Use the `OUTPUT` clause to verify the number of affected rows.
- Use transaction control (`BEGIN TRAN/COMMIT/ROLLBACK`) to ensure data safety.
- Apply appropriate indexes on the ON clause columns.
- Consider separate statements (`INSERT/UPDATE/DELETE`) for highly concurrent OLTP systems.

MERGE vs. Traditional Approach

When they are performing `INSERT`, `UPDATE`, or `DELETE` operations based on conditions, developers often use separate statements in the traditional approach. However, SQL Server's `MERGE` statement allows you to combine these operations into a single and more efficient command. Hence, this not only simplifies code, but can also improve performance and maintainability while handling complex data synchronization tasks.

Traditional Method (before MERGE)

```
IF EXISTS (SELECT 1 FROM Customers WHERE CustomerID = @CustomerID)
    UPDATE Customers SET Name = @Name WHERE CustomerID = @CustomerID;
ELSE
    INSERT INTO Customers (CustomerID, Name) VALUES (@CustomerID, @Name);
```

MERGE Method

```
MERGE Customers AS target
USING (SELECT @CustomerID AS CustomerID, @Name AS Name) AS source
ON target.CustomerID = source.CustomerID
WHEN MATCHED THEN
    UPDATE SET target.Name = source.Name
WHEN NOT MATCHED THEN
    INSERT (CustomerID, Name) VALUES (source.CustomerID, source.Name);
```

Hence, we can conclude that MERGE is more concise, scalable, and easier to maintain.

Summary: The **`MERGE`** statement in SQL Server is a powerful tool for simplifying data synchronization, and performing conditional operations efficiently. It can thus be summarized that:

- **`MERGE`** simplifies complex synchronization logic by combining **`INSERT`**, **`UPDATE`**, and **`DELETE`** in a single statement.
- It is ideal for **`UPSERT`** operations, ETL processes, and data synchronization.
- You must be careful about avoiding performance bottlenecks and unintended data loss.
- With proper indexing, transaction handling, and testing, **`MERGE`** can become an indispensable tool for database developers.

Best Practices for Using MERGE

The MERGE statement is powerful, but it requires careful use. Therefore, you must implement the following best practices for using it. These are explained as follows:

- **Always Include a `WHEN NOT MATCHED BY SOURCE THEN DELETE` Clause Only If Intended**: If you do not heed this, you may risk deleting rows accidentally.
- **Use Filters in the `ON` Condition**: Ensure that you only match the correct rows, as vague conditions may lead to duplicate updates.
- **Test with Small Datasets First:** Confirm the logic before applying it to millions of rows.
- **Use Transaction Control**: Wrap the **`MERGE`** in a transaction to rollback in case of logic errors.

Example (With Transaction Safety):

```
BEGIN TRANSACTION;

MERGE TargetTable AS T
USING SourceTable AS S
ON (T.ID = S.ID)
WHEN MATCHED THEN
    UPDATE SET T.Value = S.Value
WHEN NOT MATCHED THEN
    INSERT (ID, Value) VALUES (S.ID, S.Value);

COMMIT TRANSACTION;
```

Common Pitfalls with MERGE

While MERGE simplifies UPSERTs, its misuse can cause unexpected results such as:

1. **Duplicate Rows in Source**: If the source has duplicates, MERGE may fail or update multiple times.
2. **Missing Semicolon**: `MERGE` must be the last statement in a batch, or it should be terminated with.
3. **Incorrect ON Clause**: Overly broad conditions may update unintended rows.
4. **Triggers Firing Unexpectedly**: `MERGE` executes triggers as a combination of `INSERT`, `UPDATE`, and `DELETE`.

Tip: *De-duplicate your source table with a* `ROW_NUMBER()` *filter before running* `MERGE`.

Performance Considerations with MERGE

To optimize the performance and reliability of MERGE operations in SQL Server, consider the following best practices:

- **Indexes are Critical**: Ensure that the join keys in the `ON` clause are indexed on both the source and the target tables.
- **Batch Operations**: For very large datasets, split `MERGE` into smaller batches to reduce locking and transaction log pressure.
- **Statistics Updates**: Outdated statistics can cause poor plans; therefore, you should update them before big `MERGE` operations.
- **Parallelism**: SQL Server may parallelize `MERGE`, but you must watch out for unexpected deadlocks with concurrent processes.

Example of Batching:

```
WHILE 1=1
BEGIN
    MERGE TOP (10000) TargetTable AS T
    USING (SELECT TOP (10000) * FROM SourceTable ORDER BY ID) AS S
    ON (T.ID = S.ID)
    WHEN MATCHED THEN
        UPDATE SET T.Value = S.Value
    WHEN NOT MATCHED THEN
        INSERT (ID, Value) VALUES (S.ID, S.Value);

    IF @@ROWCOUNT = 0 BREAK;
END
```

Real-Life Use Cases for MERGE

The `MERGE` statement can be applied across various business scenarios to simplify data synchronization and maintain consistency. These scenarios can be:

1. **Data Warehouse Loads**: Sync dimension tables from staging to production.
2. **Customer Master Data**: Insert new customers, update the existing ones, and remove inactive ones in one statement.
3. **Inventory Management**: Adjust stock counts when items are shipped or returned.
4. **Reference Data Sync**: Keep lookup tables (for example, country lists) updated automatically.

Example: Updating a product dimension table in a warehouse can look like:

```
MERGE DimProduct AS T
USING StagingProduct AS S
ON (T.ProductKey = S.ProductKey)
WHEN MATCHED THEN
    UPDATE SET T.ProductName = S.ProductName,
               T.Category = S.Category
WHEN NOT MATCHED THEN
    INSERT (ProductKey, ProductName, Category)
    VALUES (S.ProductKey, S.ProductName, S.Category)
WHEN NOT MATCHED BY SOURCE THEN
    DELETE;
```

PIVOT and UNPIVOT Transformations

In relational databases, data is usually stored in a normalized, row-oriented format. However, for reporting, analytics, and visualization, data often needs to be transformed into a columnar or "crosstab" format. Therefore, SQL Server provides two powerful operators for this: PIVOT and **UNPIVOT**. These transformations are explained as follows:

- **PIVOT** allows you to rotate the data from rows into columns, and enables summarization of data in a matrix-style layout.
- **UNPIVOT** does the opposite; it takes columns, and then converts them back into rows.

Hence, these transformations are especially useful when preparing datasets for reporting tools (such as Power BI, SSRS, or Excel), or when you are restructuring raw transactional data into human-readable forms.

PIVOT Transformation

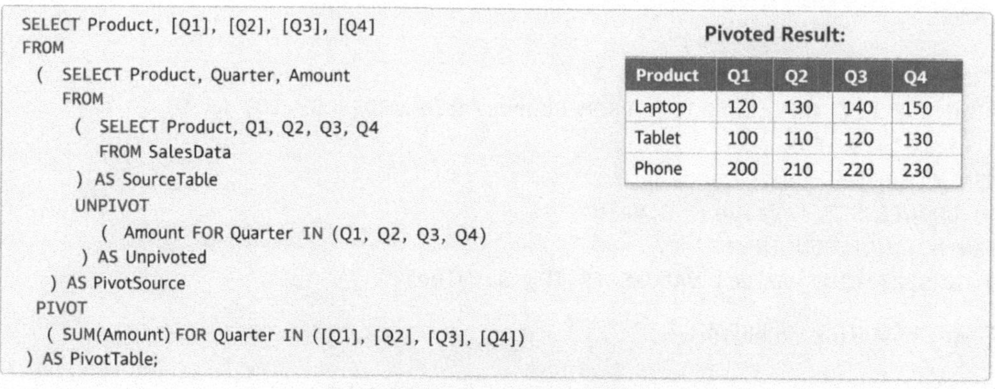

Product	Q1	Q2	Q3	Q4
Laptop	120	130	140	150
Tablet	100	110	120	130
Phone	200	210	220	230

UNPIVOT Transformation

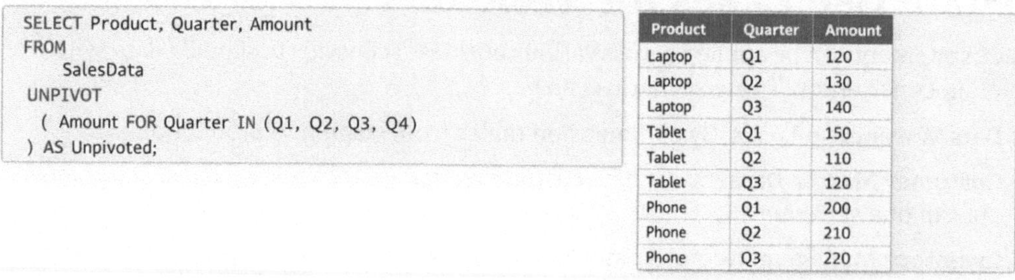

Product	Quarter	Amount
Laptop	Q1	120
Laptop	Q2	130
Laptop	Q3	140
Tablet	Q1	150
Tablet	Q2	110
Tablet	Q3	120
Phone	Q1	200
Phone	Q2	210
Phone	Q3	220

***Figure 6.1**: PIVOT and UNPIVOT Transformations in SQL Server*

Understanding PIVOT

The PIVOT operator allows you to aggregate and display data where unique values from one column become new column headers, and the corresponding aggregated values are displayed as their contents.

Therefore, you may think of **`PIVOT`** as a way of creating a pivot table in Excel, but you do so directly in the SQL Server.

Syntax of PIVOT:

```
SELECT <non-pivoted columns>,
       [FirstColumn], [SecondColumn], ... [NthColumn]
FROM
(
    SELECT <columns>
    FROM <table>
) AS SourceTable
PIVOT
(
    <aggregation_function>(<value_column>)
    FOR <column_to_pivot>
    IN ([FirstColumn], [SecondColumn], ... [NthColumn])
) AS PivotTable;
```

- **`<non-pivoted columns>`**: Columns that remain unchanged in the result
- **`<aggregation_function>`**: An aggregate function such as **`SUM()`**, **`COUNT()`**, or **`AVG()`**
- **`<value_column>`**: The column containing values you want to aggregate
- **`<column_to_pivot>`**: The column whose distinct values become new columns

Example 1: Sales Data Transformation

Suppose you have a table '**`Sales`**' with the following data:

Region	Quarter	SalesAmount
North	Q1	5000
North	Q2	7000
South	Q1	4000
South	Q2	6000

***Table 6.2:** Sample Dataset Representing Quarterly Sales Amounts by Region, Commonly Used in GROUP BY*

You want to transform this so that quarters (**`Q1`**, **`Q2`**) become columns, and the sales amounts are displayed accordingly.

Query:

```
SELECT Region, [Q1], [Q2]
FROM
(
    SELECT Region, Quarter, SalesAmount
    FROM Sales
) AS SourceTable
PIVOT
```

```
(
    SUM(SalesAmount)
    FOR Quarter IN ([Q1], [Q2])
) AS PivotTable;
```

Result:

Region	Q1	Q2
North	5000	7000
South	4000	6000

Table 6.3: *Pivoted Result Set Showing Quarterly Sales Amounts by Region, Produced Using the PIVOT Operator in T-SQL*

Here, the rows for quarters have been **pivoted** into separate columns for better readability.

Example 2: Pivot with `COUNT()`

If you have an Orders table with order statuses, you can pivot on the Status column to count how many orders fall into each category. This will look like:

```
SELECT CustomerID, [Pending], [Shipped], [Cancelled]
FROM
(
    SELECT CustomerID, Status
    FROM Orders
) AS SourceTable
PIVOT
(
    COUNT(Status)
    FOR Status IN ([Pending], [Shipped], [Cancelled])
) AS PivotTable;
```

This query shows the number of orders per status for each customer.

Understanding UNPIVOT

While **`PIVOT`** rotates rows into columns, **`UNPIVOT`** transforms columns back into rows. This is useful when dealing with denormalized or cross-tab data that needs to be flattened for further processing.

Syntax of `UNPIVOT`:

```
SELECT <non-unpivoted columns>, <unpivoted_column>, <value_column>
FROM
(
    SELECT <columns>
    FROM <table>
) AS SourceTable
UNPIVOT
(
    <value_column> FOR <unpivoted_column> IN ([col1], [col2], [col3], ...)
) AS UnpivotTable;
```

- **`<non-unpivoted columns>`**: Columns that remain unchanged
- **`<unpivoted_column>`**: The new column representing the names of the original pivoted columns
- **`<value_column>`**: The values from the pivoted columns

Example 1: Flattening Sales Data

Using the pivoted **SalesSummary** table:

Region	Q1	Q2
North	5000	7000
South	4000	6000

Table 6.4: *Quarterly Sales Figures by Region Displayed in a Cross-Tabular Format, Commonly Used in Reporting and Analytical Queries*

You can **unpivot** it back into row-based format.

Query:

```
SELECT Region, Quarter, SalesAmount
FROM
(
    SELECT Region, [Q1], [Q2]
    FROM SalesSummary
) AS SourceTable
UNPIVOT
(
    SalesAmount FOR Quarter IN ([Q1], [Q2])
) AS UnpivotTable;
```

Result:

Region	Quarter	SalesAmount
North	Q1	5000
North	Q2	7000
South	Q1	4000
South	Q2	6000

Table 6.5: *Sample Dataset Showing Sales Amounts by Region and Quarter, Commonly Used for GROUP BY, Aggregation, and Reporting Examples in T-SQL*

Now, the data is back in a normalized structure suitable for joins, filters, and aggregations.

Example 2: Unpivoting Exam Scores

Consider the provided Scores table:

Student	Math	Science	History
Alice	90	85	88
Bob	78	92	80

Table 6.6: *Sample Dataset Showing Student Scores across Multiple Subjects, Useful for Illustrating Aggregation, Ranking, or Pivot/Unpivot Operations in T-SQL*

To transform subjects into rows, you can implement the following:

```
SELECT Student, Subject, Score
FROM
(
```

```
    SELECT Student, Math, Science, History
    FROM Scores
) AS SourceTable
UNPIVOT
(
    Score FOR Subject IN ([Math], [Science], [History])
) AS UnpivotTable;
```

Result:

Student	Subject	Score
Alice	Math	90
Alice	Science	85
Alice	History	88
Bob	Math	78
Bob	Science	92
Bob	History	80

***Table 6.7**: Sample Dataset Showing Student Scores in Long Format, Suitable for Aggregation, Ranking, or Pivot/Unpivot Operations in T-SQL*

Best Practices for PIVOT and UNPIVOT

When working with **PIVOT** and **UNPIVOT** in SQL Server, it is important to understand their requirements, performance considerations, and typical use cases. These use cases are explained as follows:

1. **Use with Aggregate Functions: PIVOT** requires an aggregate function. Therefore, you must ensure that the aggregation matches business needs (**SUM**, **AVG**, **COUNT**, and so on).
2. **Static Column Names:** Columns created by PIVOT must be explicitly listed (**[Q1]**, **[Q2]**). Therefore, dynamic SQL is needed for dynamic columns.
3. **Performance Considerations:**
    - **PIVOT** and **UNPIVOT** may create large intermediate result sets.
    - Therefore, you must ensure that the indexing on the base columns is appropriate to improve query performance.
4. **Use Cases:**
    - **PIVOT** is ideal for reporting, dashboards, and crosstab summaries.
    - **UNPIVOT** is useful for normalizing denormalized data, especially when you are importing it from Excel or CSV files.

Best Practices for Using PIVOT

To ensure efficient and maintainable use of PIVOT in SQL Server, consider the following best practices:

- **Limit the Number of Pivoted Columns**: Pivoting thousands of columns can lead to unwieldy result sets.
- **Pre-Aggregate before Pivoting**: If you have multiple rows per category, consider using **SUM** or **MAX** to avoid duplicates.
- **Use Dynamic Pivoting Cautiously: D**ynamic SQL is powerful, but introduces complexity and potential security risks.

- **Index Your Pivoted Column Source**: This reduces sorting and grouping costs.

Here is an example of pre-aggregation before **PIVOT**:

```
;WITH SalesSummary AS (
    SELECT ProductID, YEAR(OrderDate) AS SalesYear, SUM(Amount) AS TotalSales
    FROM Sales
    GROUP BY ProductID, YEAR(OrderDate)
)
SELECT ProductID, [2023], [2024]
FROM SalesSummary
PIVOT (
    SUM(TotalSales) FOR SalesYear IN ([2023], [2024])
) AS PivotTable;
```

Common Pitfalls with PIVOT and UNPIVOT

When working with **PIVOT** and **UNPIVOT**, it is important to handle special cases and potential pitfalls to avoid unexpected results. These pitfalls are mentioned here, followed by tips to tackle them:

1. **NULL Values**: Pivoted columns without matching data return **NULL**, and not 0. Therefore, make it a point to always wrap with **ISNULL()** if needed.
2. **Fixed Column List**: The **IN** clause of **PIVOT** requires fixed values; you cannot pivot unknown future categories without dynamic SQL.
3. **Data Explosion**: **UNPIVOT** may create far more rows than expected, if it is applied to wide tables.
4. **Duplicate Values**: Pivoting without aggregation may result in errors. Therefore, an aggregate function must be specified.

Tip*: Use a staging table to sanitize and deduplicate data before pivoting.*

Performance Considerations with PIVOT/UNPIVOT

To optimize performance when using PIVOT with large datasets, consider these practical strategies:

- **Memory Pressure**: Pivoting large datasets consumes significant **tempdb** resources.
- **Batch Pivoting**: For massive data, consider pivoting in chunks, or filtering with a **WHERE** clause.
- **Index Strategy**: Create indexes on pivot columns to speed up grouping and sorting.
- **Precompute Common Pivots**: For reporting dashboards, materialize pivoted results into summary tables that are refreshed every night.

Here is an example of handling **NULL**s and optimizing:

```
SELECT ProductID,
       ISNULL([2023],0) AS Sales2023,
       ISNULL([2024],0) AS Sales2024
FROM (
    SELECT ProductID, YEAR(OrderDate) AS SalesYear, Amount
    FROM Sales
) src
PIVOT (
    SUM(Amount) FOR SalesYear IN ([2023], [2024])
) AS PivotTable;
```

Real-Life Use Cases of PIVOT and UNPIVOT

PIVOT and **UNPIVOT** are widely used in business scenarios to restructure data for reporting, analysis, and analytics. These cases can be:

1. **Financial Reporting**: Convert monthly expense rows into side-by-side columns for dashboards.
2. **Survey Data Analysis**: Pivot survey responses where each question is stored as a row.
3. **Inventory Levels**: Show stock by product across multiple warehouses as columns.
4. **Data Normalization**: Use **UNPIVOT** to transform denormalized wide tables into tall, narrow structures for analytics.

📌 **Example: UNPIVOT Survey Data**

```
SELECT RespondentID, Question, Answer
FROM SurveyResults
UNPIVOT (
    Answer FOR Question IN (Q1, Q2, Q3, Q4)
) AS Unpivoted;
```

Summary: PIVOT and **UNPIVOT** are essential SQL Server operators for reshaping and summarizing data in versatile ways. Therefore, we can summarize the section into the following points:

- **PIVOT** transforms rows into columns, while creating cross-tab style results.
- **UNPIVOT** flattens multiple columns back into row-based format.
- Together, these operators provide powerful tools for reshaping data for reporting, analysis, and integration.
- While these operators are extremely useful, they require explicit column handling, and may also need dynamic SQL for flexibility.

In the next section, we will move from relational reshaping to handling semi-structured data, and will focus on JSON in SQL Server.

Working with JSON: OPENJSON, JSON_VALUE, FOR JSON

Modern applications frequently exchange and store data in JSON (JavaScript Object Notation) format because of its lightweight structure, human readability, and compatibility with web technologies. SQL Server provides first-class support for JSON, which makes it possible to store, query, and manipulate JSON data inside relational databases. Unlike XML, which has long been integrated into SQL Server, JSON support is more recent (introduced in SQL Server 2016, and beyond), and it aligns SQL Server with modern development needs.

This section covers the following:

- Understanding JSON in SQL Server
- Storing and Querying JSON Data
- Using **OPENJSON** to Parse JSON Arrays and Objects
- Extracting Specific Values with **JSON_VALUE** and **JSON_QUERY**
- Generating **JSON** Output with **FOR JSON**
- Indexing and Performance Considerations with JSON Data

Understanding JSON in SQL Server

JSON is commonly used to represent hierarchical and semi-structured data, such as:

```
{
  "CustomerID": 101,
  "Name": "Sarah Connor",
  "Orders": [
    { "OrderID": 5001, "Amount": 120.50 },
    { "OrderID": 5002, "Amount": 75.00 }
  ]
}
```

Here, SQL Server does not have a dedicated JSON data type (unlike PostgreSQL or MongoDB). Instead, the JSON data is stored as an **NVARCHAR** column. This provides flexibility, but it also requires developers to validate and query JSON through built-in functions.

JSON support in SQL Server includes:

- **Parsing** JSON text into rows and columns (**OPENJSON**)
- **Extracting** values from JSON documents (**JSON_VALUE** and **JSON_QUERY**)
- **Modifying** JSON using **JSON_MODIFY**
- **Generating** JSON directly from query results (**FOR JSON**)

Storing JSON Data

A **JSON** string can be stored in any **NVARCHAR** column, as shown here:

```
CREATE TABLE Customers
(
    CustomerID INT PRIMARY KEY,
    CustomerData NVARCHAR(MAX) -- stores JSON
);
```

```
INSERT INTO Customers (CustomerID, CustomerData)
VALUES
(101, '{
    "Name": "Sarah Connor",
    "City": "Los Angeles",
    "Orders": [
        {"OrderID": 5001, "Amount": 120.50},
        {"OrderID": 5002, "Amount": 75.00}
    ]
}');
```

To ensure that the string is valid JSON, SQL Server provides the **ISJSON()** function, which shows up as:

```
SELECT CustomerID, ISJSON(CustomerData) AS IsValidJSON
FROM Customers;
```

If the result is 1, the value is a valid JSON document.

Extracting Values from JSON: JSON_VALUE and JSON_QUERY

JSON_VALUE extracts scalar values (like strings, numbers, or Booleans) from a JSON document. It will look something like this:

```
SELECT
    CustomerID,
    JSON_VALUE(CustomerData, '$.Name') AS CustomerName,
    JSON_VALUE(CustomerData, '$.City') AS City
```

FROM Customers;

- **$** represents the root of the JSON document.
- **$.Name** extracts the "**Name**" field.
- **$.City** extracts the "**City**" field.

Output:

CustomerID	CustomerName	City
101	Sarah Connor	Los Angeles

***Table 6.8**: Sample Dataset Showing Basic Customer Information, Useful for Illustrating SELECT Queries, Filtering, or Joins in T-SQL*

JSON_QUERY

While **JSON_VALUE** extracts scalars, **JSON_QUERY** retrieves JSON objects or arrays. **This looks like:**

```
SELECT
    CustomerID,
    JSON_QUERY(CustomerData, '$.Orders') AS OrdersArray
FROM Customers;
```

Output:

CustomerID	OrdersArray
101	[{"OrderID":5001,"Amount":120.50},{"OrderID":5002,"Amount":75.00}]

***Table 6.9**: Sample Dataset Showing a Customer's Orders Stored as a JSON Array, Commonly Used to Demonstrate JSON Parsing, OPENJSON, or JSON_VALUE Functions in T-SQL*

This is useful when you want to keep the nested structure intact.

Parsing JSON into Rows and Columns: OPENJSON

OPENJSON transforms JSON arrays and objects into a relational rowset, which makes it easier to query the nested data.

Example: Expanding Orders

```
SELECT *
FROM OPENJSON('[
    {"OrderID": 5001, "Amount": 120.50},
```

```
    {"OrderID": 5002, "Amount": 75.00}
]');
```

Output:

key	value	type
0	{"OrderID":5001,"Amount":120.50}	5
1	{"OrderID":5002,"Amount":75.00}	5

Table 6.10: *Sample Dataset Showing Key-Value Pairs for JSON Objects, Useful for Illustrating JSON Parsing and Manipulation in T-SQL Using OPENJSON, or Related Functions*

Therefore, **OPENJSON** returns key-value pairs by default. Therefore, to shape this into columns, use a **WITH clause, as shown here**:

```
SELECT ORDERID, AMOUNT
FROM OPENJSON('[
    {"ORDERID": 5001, "AMOUNT": 120.50},
    {"ORDERID": 5002, "AMOUNT": 75.00}
]')
WITH (
    ORDERID INT '$.ORDERID',
    AMOUNT  DECIMAL(10,2) '$.AMOUNT'
);
```

Output:

OrderID	Amount
5001	120.50
5002	75.00

Table 6.11: *Sample Dataset Showing Individual Orders with Their Amounts, Commonly Used for Aggregation, Joins, and Basic SQL Operations in T-SQL*

This makes it possible to integrate JSON arrays into relational queries seamlessly.

Generating JSON from Queries: FOR JSON

SQL Server can generate JSON output directly using the `FOR JSON` clause. This is useful when building APIs, or exporting structured data to applications.

Example: Auto Mode

```
SELECT CustomerID, Name, City
FROM CustomersBasic
FOR JSON AUTO;
Output (JSON format):
[
  { "CustomerID": 101, "Name": "Sarah Connor", "City": "Los Angeles" },
  { "CustomerID": 102, "Name": "John Reese", "City": "New York" }
]
```

Example: Path Mode

PATH mode provides finer control over JSON keys and nesting.

```
SELECT
    CustomerID AS "Customer.CustomerID",
    Name AS "Customer.Name",
    City AS "Customer.City"
FROM CustomersBasic
FOR JSON PATH, ROOT('Customers');
```

Output:

```
{
  "Customers": [
    {
      "Customer": {
        "CustomerID": 101,
        "Name": "Sarah Connor",
        "City": "Los Angeles"
      }
    }
  ]
}
```

Modifying JSON Data: JSON_MODIFY

SQL Server allows you to update parts of a JSON document without replacing the entire string.

```
UPDATE Customers
SET CustomerData = JSON_MODIFY(CustomerData, '$.City', 'San Francisco')
WHERE CustomerID = 101;
```

Now, Sarah Connor's City field is updated inside the JSON column.

Performance and Indexing with JSON

Since JSON is stored in **NVARCHAR**, SQL Server does not automatically optimize JSON queries. To improve performance, implement the following practices:

1. **Use Computed Columns**: Extract values from JSON into computed columns that can be indexed.

   ```
   ALTER TABLE Customers
   ADD City AS JSON_VALUE(CustomerData, '$.City');

   CREATE INDEX IX_Customers_City ON Customers(City);
   ```

2. **Avoid Storing Unbounded JSON**: Use **NVARCHAR(4000)** instead of **NVARCHAR(MAX)** whenever possible.
3. **Validate with ISJSON**: Ensure data integrity at insertion.

Best Practices for JSON in SQL Server

When working with semi-structured data in SQL Server, JSON provides a flexible way to store, exchange, and query complex data. Therefore, you must remember some best practices while working with JSON, which are:

- Use JSON whenever data exchange with APIs or modern applications is required.

- Avoid overusing JSON for relational data, as it can hurt performance if it is used as a substitute for proper normalization.
- Extract frequently queried fields into indexed computed columns.
- Use **FOR JSON PATH** for API-friendly formatting.
- Combine JSON with OPENJSON to seamlessly bridge semi-structured and structured data worlds.

SQL Server provides comprehensive support for working with JSON, while enabling seamless integration of semi-structured data with relational tables. Thus, a few important points to remember are:

- SQL Server supports reading, parsing, and generating JSON using built-in functions.
- **JSON_VALUE** extracts scalars, **JSON_QUERY** retrieves objects/arrays.
- **OPENJSON** turns JSON into tabular data.
- **FOR JSON** generates JSON output directly from queries.
- Indexing JSON with computed columns improves performance.

XML Parsing and Generation

XML (Extensible Markup Language) is a widely used standard for representing semi-structured data. Before JSON became the dominant choice for modern web APIs, XML was the backbone of many enterprise integrations, SOAP-based web services, and configuration systems. SQL Server has robust support for XML data, which allows developers to store, query, generate, and shred XML documents directly within the database engine.

This section explores how to store XML data, query XML nodes and attributes, use XML data type methods, and generate XML from relational data. Therefore, by the end of this section, you will be able to seamlessly integrate XML into your T-SQL workflows.

Storing XML Data in SQL Server

SQL Server provides a native xml data type that can store XML documents or fragments. Unlike varchar(max) or nvarchar(max), the xml data type enforces proper XML structure by ensuring that the data is well-formed. It can also support schema validation when required, allowing you to maintain consistency and integrity in your XML data.

Creating Tables with XML Columns:

```
CREATE TABLE OrdersXML
(
    OrderID INT PRIMARY KEY,
    OrderDetails XML
);
```

Here, **OrderDetails** stores XML content.

Inserting XML Data:

```
INSERT INTO OrdersXML (OrderID, OrderDetails)
VALUES (1,
N'<Order>
     <CustomerID>CUST001</CustomerID>
     <OrderDate>2025-08-23</OrderDate>
```

```
    <Items>
        <Item>
            <ProductID>101</ProductID>
            <Quantity>2</Quantity>
        </Item>
        <Item>
            <ProductID>202</ProductID>
            <Quantity>5</Quantity>
        </Item>
    </Items>
</Order>');
```

Hence, this example shows how to insert an XML document into the **OrderDetails** column.

Querying XML Data

SQL Server provides the **XQuery language** and **XML methods** for retrieving values from XML columns. The key methods are:

- **.value()**: It extracts a single scalar value.
- **.query()**: It returns an XML fragment.
- **.nodes()**: It shreds XML into relational rows.
- **.exist()**: It checks if an element/attribute exists.

Extracting a Single Value:

```
SELECT OrderDetails.value('(/Order/CustomerID/text())[1]', 'NVARCHAR(50)') AS
CustomerID
FROM OrdersXML
WHERE OrderID = 1;
```

This returns **CUST001**.

Extracting Multiple Items with .nodes():

```
SELECT
    Item.value('(ProductID/text())[1]', 'INT') AS ProductID,
    Item.value('(Quantity/text())[1]', 'INT') AS Quantity
FROM OrdersXML
CROSS APPLY OrderDetails.nodes('/Order/Items/Item') AS T(Item);
```

Output:

ProductID	Quantity
101	2
202	5

***Table 6.12**: Sample Dataset Showing Product IDs with Their Corresponding Quantities, Useful for Aggregation, Joins, and Inventory Calculations in T-SQL*

Here, **.nodes()** breaks down XML into rows, which make it easy to join them with relational tables.

Modifying XML Data

XML data can be updated using the **.modify()** method, which supports inserting, deleting, or replacing XML nodes.

Updating an XML Node:

```
UPDATE OrdersXML
SET OrderDetails.modify('replace value of (/Order/CustomerID/text())[1] with
"CUST999"')
WHERE OrderID = 1;
```

This updates the **<CustomerID>** from **CUST001** to **CUST999**.

Inserting New XML Elements:

```
UPDATE OrdersXML
SET OrderDetails.modify('insert <Status>Shipped</Status> as last into (/Order)[1]')
WHERE OrderID = 1;
```

Now, the XML includes a <Status> element.

Generating XML from Relational Data

SQL Server makes it easy to create XML from query results if you use the FOR XML clause.

FOR XML AUTO:

Generates XML where each table row becomes an element with attributes.

```
SELECT OrderID, CustomerID
FROM Orders
FOR XML AUTO;
```

Output:

```
<Orders OrderID="1" CustomerID="CUST001" />
<Orders OrderID="2" CustomerID="CUST002" />
```

FOR XML RAW:

Generates generic **<row>** elements.

```
SELECT OrderID, CustomerID
FROM Orders
FOR XML RAW;
```

Output:

```
<row OrderID="1" CustomerID="CUST001" />
<row OrderID="2" CustomerID="CUST002" />
```

FOR XML PATH:

This is the most flexible option, as it allows custom element names.

```
SELECT
    OrderID AS "Order/@ID",
    CustomerID AS "Order/Customer",
    OrderDate AS "Order/Date"
```

```
FROM Orders
FOR XML PATH(''), ROOT('Orders');
```

Output:

```
<Orders>
  <Order ID="1">
    <Customer>CUST001</Customer>
    <Date>2025-08-23</Date>
  </Order>
  <Order ID="2">
    <Customer>CUST002</Customer>
    <Date>2025-08-23</Date>
  </Order>
</Orders>
```

Validating XML with Schema Collections

SQL Server allows you to define XML Schema Collections for validation.

Defining an XML Schema Collection:

```
CREATE XML SCHEMA COLLECTION OrderSchema AS N'
<xs:schema xmlns:xs="http://www.w3.org/2001/XMLSchema">
  <xs:element name="Order">
    <xs:complexType>
      <xs:sequence>
        <xs:element name="CustomerID" type="xs:string"/>
        <xs:element name="OrderDate" type="xs:date"/>
      </xs:sequence>
    </xs:complexType>
  </xs:element>
</xs:schema>';
```

Applying Schema Validation:

```
CREATE TABLE OrdersWithSchema
(
    OrderID INT PRIMARY KEY,
    OrderDetails XML(OrderSchema)
);
```

Now, only XML documents that conform to `OrderSchema` will be stored.

Performance Considerations with XML

While SQL Server's XML features are powerful, they should be used carefully. Therefore, you must factor in the following performance considerations while using them:

- **Indexing XML:** Use primary XML indexes (for path navigation) and secondary XML indexes (for queries filtering by values).
- **Storage Size:** XML can consume significant space use compression or JSON, if and when they are appropriate.

- **Avoid Overuse:** For structured data, you must prefer relational design. Additionally, do not forget to use XML for semi-structured or hierarchical data.

Key Takeaways

- The xml data type allows you to store and query XML documents natively in SQL Server.
- Use `.value()`, `.nodes()`, `.query()`, and `.exist()` to extract and manipulate XML.
- `FOR XML (AUTO, RAW, PATH)` allows you to generate XML directly from relational queries.
- XML Schema Collections enforce validation rules on stored XML.
- Indexing XML improves query performance, but it should be applied strategically.

Conclusion

In this chapter, you explored several advanced SQL Server features that are essential for handling complex data manipulation and semi-structured formats. You learned how to use Common Table Expressions (CTEs) to simplify deeply nested queries, and also how to implement recursive logic for hierarchical data. The `MERGE` statement was introduced as a powerful alternative to multiple `INSERT`, `UPDATE`, and `DELETE` statements, which will allow you to streamline `upsert` operations in a singular efficient command.

Beyond traditional relational data, the chapter also covered techniques for reshaping and transforming datasets with `PIVOT` and `UNPIVOT`, which will allow you to switch between row- and column-oriented perspectives. Finally, you gained hands-on knowledge about working with JSON and XML, and learned how to parse, query, and integrate semi-structured data into relational models using SQL Server's built-in functions and operators.

Therefore, by completing this chapter, you have strengthened your ability to perform advanced transformations, integrate modern data formats, and simplify complex business logic. These skills will prepare you to move beyond static queries and create more dynamic, automated, and reusable database solutions.

In the next chapter, we will explore Dynamic SQL, Triggers, and Table-Valued Functions (TVFs). You will learn how to safely build and execute dynamic queries, design triggers for enforcing rules and auditing. Additionally, you shall also create TVFs for reusable data logic, to extend SQL Server's flexibility and power.

CHAPTER 7

Dynamic SQL, Triggers, and Table-Valued Functions (TVFs)

Introduction

In this chapter, we will explore three powerful areas of T-SQL: dynamic SQL, triggers, and Table-Valued Functions (TVFs). You will learn how to construct dynamic queries securely, how to leverage triggers for enforcing business rules and auditing, and how to build reusable TVFs to encapsulate logic for complex queries. Along the way, we will emphasize performance optimization, security best practices, and real-world use cases that demonstrate the right way to apply these features in production environments.

Structure

In this chapter, we will cover the following topics:

- Introduction to Dynamic SQL, Triggers, and TVFs
- Executing Dynamic SQL Safely with `sp_executesql`
- Preventing SQL Injection Attacks
- Using `AFTER` and `INSTEAD OF` Triggers
- Implementing Auditing with Triggers
- Designing and Optimizing Inline and Multi-Statement TVFs

Introduction to Dynamic SQL, Triggers, and TVFs

SQL Server developers often face scenarios where static SQL is insufficient. Examples include:

- Building queries with conditional filters at runtime
- Automatically enforcing rules when data changes
- Reusing logic across multiple queries while maintaining performance

Therefore, dynamic SQL allows queries to be generated and executed at runtime. Triggers provide automated responses to DML operations (**`INSERT`**, **`UPDATE`**, **`DELETE`**). Table-Valued Functions (TVFs) allow developers to write reusable query logic that returns sets of data like tables.

Executing Dynamic SQL Safely with `sp_executesql`

Dynamic SQL is the process of constructing SQL statements as strings, and executing them at runtime. While it is powerful, it comes with risks such as SQL injection and performance degradation, if not used carefully. SQL Server provides the **`sp_executesql`** system stored procedure to execute dynamic SQL safely and efficiently. Unlike the **`EXEC()`** command, **`sp_executesql`** supports parameterization, which improves both security and query plan reuse.

sp_executesql

There are two common approaches to dynamic SQL in SQL Server:

1. **`EXEC()`**: Executes a string as SQL
   - Easy to use, but does not support parameterized queries
   - Carries a higher risk of SQL injection
   - Poor query plan caching
2. **`sp_executesql`**: Executes a SQL string with support for parameters
   - Supports input and output parameters
   - Allows SQL Server to reuse cached execution plans
   - Safer against SQL injection when parameters are properly defined

Key Point: Use **`sp_executesql`** instead of **`EXEC()`** whenever you need dynamic SQL with parameters.

Syntax of `sp_executesql`

The **`sp_executesql`** system stored procedure allows execution of dynamic SQL with parameterization. This improves security by reducing SQL injection risks, and enhances performance by allowing SQL Server to reuse execution plans instead of recompiling queries every time.

```
sp_executesql
    @stmt = N'SQL_statement',
    @params = N'@parameter_declarations',
    @param1 = value1,
    @param2 = value2, ...
```

- **`@stmt`**: The SQL statement to execute
- **`@params`**: A string that defines parameter names, data types, and directions (input/output)
- **`@param1 = value1, …`**: The actual values passed into the query

Simple Example

Suppose you want to filter data from the **`Sales.Orders`** table based on **`CustomerID`**.

Therefore, while using **`EXEC()`** (Not Safe):

```
DECLARE @sql NVARCHAR(MAX);
DECLARE @CustomerID INT = 42;

SET @sql = 'SELECT * FROM Sales.Orders WHERE CustomerID = ' + CAST(@CustomerID AS
NVARCHAR(10));
EXEC(@sql);  -- Not recommended
```

On the other hand, if you use **sp_executesql (Safe)**:

```
DECLARE @sql NVARCHAR(MAX);
DECLARE @CustomerID INT = 42;

SET @sql = N'SELECT * FROM Sales.Orders WHERE CustomerID = @CustID';
EXEC sp_executesql @sql, N'@CustID INT', @CustID = @CustomerID;
```

Here:

- **@CustID** is declared inside the parameter definition string.
- The actual value (**42**) is passed separately, which further prevents injection.

Using Multiple Parameters

When building dynamic SQL, parameterization is key to improving both security and performance. Therefore, by declaring parameters separately and passing them into the query, SQL Server can safely reuse execution plans across different inputs and reduce compilation overhead, while protecting against SQL injection.

```
DECLARE @sql NVARCHAR(MAX);
DECLARE @StartDate DATE = '2025-01-01';
DECLARE @EndDate DATE = '2025-03-31';

SET @sql = N'SELECT OrderID, OrderDate, TotalAmount
             FROM Sales.Orders
             WHERE OrderDate BETWEEN @FromDate AND @ToDate';

EXEC sp_executesql
    @sql,
    N'@FromDate DATE, @ToDate DATE',
    @FromDate = @StartDate,
    @ToDate = @EndDate;
```

- **@FromDate** and **@ToDate** are declared once and reused in the SQL.
- SQL Server can reuse the execution plan even for different date ranges.

Output Parameters in sp_executesql

You can also retrieve values using output parameters, as shown in the following example:

```
DECLARE @sql NVARCHAR(MAX);
DECLARE @TotalOrders INT;
DECLARE @CustomerID INT = 42;

SET @sql = N'SELECT @OrderCount = COUNT(*)
             FROM Sales.Orders
             WHERE CustomerID = @CustID';

EXEC sp_executesql
    @sql,
    N'@CustID INT, @OrderCount INT OUTPUT',
    @CustID = @CustomerID,
    @OrderCount = @TotalOrders OUTPUT;

PRINT 'Total Orders = ' + CAST(@TotalOrders AS NVARCHAR(10));
```

Hence, this query counts the orders for a given customer, and stores the result in **@TotalOrders**.

Benefits of sp_executesql

Parameterized queries in SQL Server offer several advantages that improve security, performance, and code maintainability. Let us explore these aspects in detail:

1. **Security**: It means that parameterized queries prevent SQL injection by separating SQL code from parameters.
2. **Performance**: Through parameterized queries, execution plans are cached and reused.
3. **Maintainability**: Parameterized queries generate leaner code compared to concatenating strings.
4. **Flexibility**: They support input and output parameters.

Common Mistakes to Avoid

When using parameterized queries in SQL Server, it is important to avoid common mistakes that can lead to errors or security issues. We have provided a brief overview of these issues, along with the fixes you can employ to avoid them:

- Forgetting N prefix for Unicode strings

  Always write **`N'String'`** instead of '**`String`**'.

- Encountering mismatched parameter types

  Ensure that declared parameter types match the actual table column types.

- Concatenating user input into the query string

  This defeats the purpose of parameterization.

Bad Example (Still Vulnerable):

```
SET @sql = N'SELECT * FROM Sales.Orders WHERE CustomerID = ' + @UserInput;
```

Real-World Use Cases

Therefore, Dynamic SQL in SQL Server is useful for constructing flexible queries that adapt to runtime requirements. Here are some real-world use cases:

- **Dynamic Filtering**: Where clause conditions depend on user input
- **Dynamic Table/Column Selection**: Generating queries for reporting systems
- **Parameterized Search**: Building search functionality across multiple columns
- **Auditing Queries**: Logging SQL statements that are executed dynamically

Comparing sp_executesql with EXEC()

While both **`EXEC()`** and **`sp_executesql`** can run dynamic SQL, they behave differently in the following ways:

- **`EXEC()`** simply executes a string and cannot parameterize queries, which makes it more vulnerable to SQL injection, and also harder to optimize.
- **`sp_executesql`** supports parameters, and allows queries to reuse execution plans, which improves performance.

Example: Using `EXEC()` (Not Recommended):

```
DECLARE @sql NVARCHAR(MAX) =
    N'SELECT * FROM Employees WHERE EmployeeID = ' + CAST(5 AS NVARCHAR(10));

EXEC(@sql);
```

Example: Using `sp_executesql` (Recommended):

```
DECLARE @sql NVARCHAR(MAX) =
    N'SELECT * FROM Employees WHERE EmployeeID = @EmpID';

EXEC sp_executesql @sql, N'@EmpID INT', @EmpID = 5;
```

☑ As you may observe, the second approach is both safer and faster because SQL Server can cache and reuse execution plans.

Using Dynamic SQL with OUTPUT Parameters

Dynamic SQL can return scalar values using OUTPUT parameters.

Example:

```
DECLARE @sql NVARCHAR(MAX);
DECLARE @EmployeeName NVARCHAR(100);

SET @sql = N'SELECT @EmpName = FirstName + '' '' + LastName
             FROM Employees WHERE EmployeeID = @EmpID';

EXEC sp_executesql
     @sql,
     N'@EmpID INT, @EmpName NVARCHAR(100) OUTPUT',
     @EmpID = 5,
     @EmpName = @EmployeeName OUTPUT;

PRINT @EmployeeName;
```

Here, the employee's full name is retrieved, and is then stored in **`@EmployeeName`**.

Handling Dynamic Column Names

Sometimes, column names must be dynamic. Since they cannot be parameterized, you must build them carefully.

Example:

```
DECLARE @sql NVARCHAR(MAX);
DECLARE @ColumnName NVARCHAR(50) = N'LastName';

SET @sql = N'SELECT ' + QUOTENAME(@ColumnName) + ' FROM Employees';

EXEC sp_executesql @sql;
```

☑ Therefore, **`QUOTENAME()`** protects against injection by wrapping column names in brackets.

Dynamic SQL for Search Queries (Optional Parameters)

Dynamic SQL is often used to implement flexible search queries with optional filters.

Example:

```
DECLARE @sql NVARCHAR(MAX) = N'SELECT * FROM Employees WHERE 1=1';
DECLARE @params NVARCHAR(MAX) = N'@DeptID INT, @City NVARCHAR(50)';
DECLARE @DeptID INT = 3, @City NVARCHAR(50) = NULL;

IF @DeptID IS NOT NULL
    SET @sql += N' AND DepartmentID = @DeptID';
IF @City IS NOT NULL
    SET @sql += N' AND City = @City';

EXEC sp_executesql @sql, @params, @DeptID = @DeptID, @City = @City;
```

This creates a reusable search procedure without having you write separate queries for each case.

Performance Monitoring of Dynamic SQL

To analyze dynamic SQL performance:

- Use **SET STATISTICS IO ON** and **SET STATISTICS TIME ON** to measure execution.
- Check execution plans in SSMS.
- Monitor **sys.dm_exec_cached_plans** to see how well queries reuse the cached plans. The following example demonstrates how to retrieve cached execution plans and analyze their reuse:

```
SELECT cp.objtype, cp.usecounts, st.text
FROM sys.dm_exec_cached_plans AS cp
CROSS APPLY sys.dm_exec_sql_text(cp.plan_handle) AS st
WHERE st.text LIKE '%Employees%';
```

Therefore, this helps confirm if queries built with **sp_executesql** are being cached or not.

Best Practices Recap

To ensure safe and efficient use of dynamic SQL in SQL Server, follow these best practices:

1. Always use **sp_executesql** instead of **EXEC()** for safety and performance.
2. Parameterize whenever possible.
3. Use **QUOTENAME()** for dynamic identifiers.
4. Avoid concatenating user input directly.
5. Monitor execution plans to confirm caching.

Summary: Using **sp_executesql** in SQL Server provides a secure and efficient way to execute dynamic queries with parameters. Therefore, you must consider the following:

- Use **sp_executesql** instead of **EXEC()** for parameterized queries.
- Always declare parameters explicitly to prevent injection.
- **sp_executesql** supports input and output parameters, which makes it flexible for reporting and auditing.
- Execution plans are cached, which improves performance for repeated queries.

Preventing SQL Injection Attacks

SQL injection is one of the most dangerous vulnerabilities in database-driven applications. It occurs when untrusted input is concatenated directly into a SQL statement, and allows attackers to manipulate queries, as well as access the data they should not be seeing. Therefore, as a database developer, you must understand how injection attacks work, and apply proven techniques to prevent them.

SQL Injection

SQL injection (SQLi) is a code injection technique where malicious SQL statements are inserted into an input field or parameter, and are executed by the database.

For example, if user input is directly concatenated into a query:

```
DECLARE @sql NVARCHAR(MAX);
SET @sql = 'SELECT * FROM Users WHERE Username = ''' + @UserInput + '''';
EXEC(@sql);
```

If **`@UserInput = 'admin'`**, the query is safe.

However, if an attacker enters:

```
' OR 1=1 --
```

The query becomes:

```
SELECT * FROM Users WHERE Username = '' OR 1=1 --'
```

This returns all users, while bypassing authentication.

⚠ **Key Danger**: SQL injection exploits trust in user input. Therefore, you must never trust strings provided by a user, an application, or an external system.

Real-World Impact of SQL Injection

SQL injection attacks can have severe technical, financial, and legal consequences for organizations. These can give rise to the following:

- **Data Theft**: Attackers can extract sensitive customer or financial information.
- **Authentication Bypass**: Weak login systems can be bypassed by injecting conditions like **`OR 1=1`**.
- **Data Manipulation**: Attackers may insert, update, or delete critical records.
- **Escalation of Privileges**: With advanced techniques, attackers may gain admin-level access.
- **Reputation and Legal Consequences**: Many organizations face legal penalties and loss of customer trust after they encounter injection-related breaches.

Unsafe Dynamic SQL Example

The example given here demonstrates a vulnerable dynamic-SQL pattern that allows SQL injection by concatenating untrusted input into the query. It looks like this:

```
DECLARE @sql NVARCHAR(MAX);
DECLARE @CustID NVARCHAR(50);

-- Input from user
SET @CustID = '105 OR 1=1';
```

```
SET @sql = 'SELECT * FROM Sales.Orders WHERE CustomerID = ' + @CustID;
EXEC(@sql);  -- Vulnerable!
```

This returns all orders instead of just customer 105 because the injected text (**OR 1=1**) becomes a part of the executed SQL.

Preventing SQL Injection with sp_executesql

The safest way to execute dynamic SQL is by using parameters with **sp_executesql**. This looks like:

```
DECLARE @sql NVARCHAR(MAX);
DECLARE @CustID INT = 105;

SET @sql = N'SELECT * FROM Sales.Orders WHERE CustomerID = @Customer';
EXEC sp_executesql @sql, N'@Customer INT', @Customer = @CustID;
```

Here, the malicious string 105 OR 1=1 would be treated as a literal value, which is not executable SQL.

Parameterization in Stored Procedures

Another defense is to encapsulate queries inside stored procedures with parameters. It looks like this:

```
CREATE PROCEDURE GetCustomerOrders
    @CustomerID INT
AS
BEGIN
    SELECT * FROM Sales.Orders WHERE CustomerID = @CustomerID;
END;
```

Now, attackers cannot inject SQL into the query string.

Input Validation

While parameterization is the strongest defense, input validation is an important additional safeguard. Therefore, you must consider the following:

- **Whitelist Validation**: Only allow expected values (for example, numeric IDs, specific status codes).
- **Length Checks**: Reject overly long inputs that might indicate malicious intent.
- **Data type enforcement**: Ensure that input variables match the expected types (**INT**, **DATE**, and so on).

Here is an example of numeric validation:

```
IF ISNUMERIC(@CustID) = 0
BEGIN
   RAISERROR('Invalid input', 16, 1);
   RETURN;
END;
```

Least Privilege Principle

Restrict the permissions of application accounts by following these tips:

- Do not let them connect with **sa or db_owner** rights.
- Use separate accounts for read-only queries, updates, and admin operations.

- If an attacker injects SQL, enabling limited permissions minimizes the damage.

Escaping User Input (Last Resort)

Escaping user input is not a substitute for parameterization, but in rare cases (for example, dynamic table names), you may need to sanitize input. This can look like:

```
DECLARE @TableName SYSNAME = QUOTENAME(@UserTable);
SET @sql = N'SELECT COUNT(*) FROM ' + @TableName;
EXEC sp_executesql @sql;
```

In this example:

- **QUOTENAME()** ensures that only valid SQL identifiers are used, while wrapping names in brackets (**[TableName]**).
- You must also remember to never concatenate raw user input without sanitization.

Defense-in-Depth Checklist

To reduce the risk of SQL injection and harden your database environment, follow these defensive measures:

- Always use parameterized queries with **sp_executesql** or stored procedures.
- Validate and sanitize all inputs.
- Apply the least privilege access to application accounts.
- Monitor logs for suspicious SQL activity.
- Use database firewalls or application-level security filters.
- Regularly test with penetration tools (for example, simulate injection attempts).

Using QUOTENAME() for Dynamic Identifiers

When column names, table names, or schema names should be dynamic, they cannot be passed as parameters. In these cases, use **QUOTENAME()** to sanitize identifiers.

Example:

```
DECLARE @TableName NVARCHAR(50) = 'Employees';
DECLARE @sql NVARCHAR(MAX);

SET @sql = N'SELECT * FROM ' + QUOTENAME(@TableName);

EXEC sp_executesql @sql;
```

☑ As you can see, this prevents injection by wrapping names in brackets: **[Employees]**. Without **QUOTENAME()**, an attacker could pass malicious input like **Employees; DROP TABLE Employees**.

Escaping Strings with REPLACE()

If you must build a query with string concatenation (not recommended), you must remember to always escape single quotes.

Example (Escaping the Input Safely):

```
DECLARE @City NVARCHAR(50) = 'O''Reilly';  -- User input with single quote
DECLARE @sql NVARCHAR(MAX);

SET @sql = N'SELECT * FROM Customers WHERE City = '''
```

```
        + REPLACE(@City, '''', '''''') + '''';

EXEC sp_executesql @sql;
```

This ensures that the query remains valid without breaking into injected SQL.

Least Privilege Principle

One of the most overlooked defenses against SQL injection is reducing permissions. You can ensure this via the following tips:

- Do not let the application account use **sa** or **db_owner**.
- Grant only the needed rights (**SELECT**, **INSERT**, or **UPDATE** on specific tables).
- Therefore, even if SQL injection occurs, the damage is limited.

Example:

```
-- Instead of granting db_owner:
GRANT SELECT, INSERT, UPDATE ON dbo.Orders TO AppUser;
```

This prevents attackers from dropping tables, or accessing the unrelated data.

Using Parameterized Stored Procedures

Stored procedures with parameters eliminate injection risks and provide better maintainability.

Example:

```
CREATE PROCEDURE GetCustomerOrders
    @CustomerID INT
AS
BEGIN
    SELECT OrderID, OrderDate, TotalAmount
    FROM Orders
    WHERE CustomerID = @CustomerID;
END;
```

Call:

```
EXEC GetCustomerOrders @CustomerID = 102;
```

☑ Therefore, using parameters ensures that the input is treated as data, and not as executable SQL.

White-Listing User Input

For user-driven queries (for example, sorting, filtering), only allow expected safe values.

Example:

```
DECLARE @SortColumn NVARCHAR(50) = 'LastName';
IF @SortColumn NOT IN ('FirstName', 'LastName', 'HireDate')
    SET @SortColumn = 'LastName'; -- fallback safe default

DECLARE @sql NVARCHAR(MAX) =
    N'SELECT * FROM Employees ORDER BY ' + QUOTENAME(@SortColumn);

EXEC sp_executesql @sql;
```

Therefore, it ensures that only pre-approved columns can be sorted.

Detecting SQL Injection Attempts

SQL Server can log unusual activity for review. For example, checking **sys.dm_exec_requests** for suspicious queries can look like:

```
SELECT session_id, text, start_time
FROM sys.dm_exec_requests
CROSS APPLY sys.dm_exec_sql_text(sql_handle)
WHERE text LIKE '%; DROP%' OR text LIKE '%--%';
```

Hence, this helps detect attempts where attackers try **DROP**, comments (--), or stacked queries (;).

Using TRY...CATCH for Safer Error Handling

Attackers often exploit error messages to learn about schema details. Therefore, you must hide internal errors with **TRY...CATCH** blocks, and return user-friendly messages.

Example:

```
BEGIN TRY
    EXEC sp_executesql N'SELECT * FROM Employees WHERE EmployeeID = @EmpID',
        N'@EmpID INT', @EmpID = 5;
END TRY
BEGIN CATCH
    PRINT 'An error occurred. Please contact support.';
END CATCH;
```

This prevents leaking sensitive details like table names or constraints.

Continuous Monitoring and Auditing

Preventing SQL injection is not just about writing secure code. You also need ongoing monitoring, which you can ensure by:

- Enabling SQL Server Audit to capture suspicious commands
- Monitoring login failures and unusual activity
- Setting alerts on dangerous keywords (**DROP**, **ALTER**, **xp_cmdshell**).

Best Practices Recap

Good security hygiene for dynamic SQL and inputs protects your database and users; therefore, you must follow these practical measures to reduce risk and improve robustness:

1. Always use parameterized queries (**sp_executesql**, stored procedures).
2. Sanitize identifiers with **QUOTENAME()**.
3. Escape strings if concatenation is unavoidable.
4. Apply least privilege permissions.
5. Implement white-listing for dynamic options.
6. Monitor logs for suspicious activity.
7. Hide error details with proper error handling.

Summary:

- SQL injection is one of the most serious database vulnerabilities.
- Avoid string concatenation—use parameterized queries with **sp_executesql**.
- Stored procedures with strict parameter definitions provide an additional defense.
- Input validation, least privilege, and logging further strengthen security.
- Always assume that the user input is untrusted, and protect queries accordingly.

Using AFTER and INSTEAD OF Triggers

Triggers are special types of stored procedures that automatically run in response to data modification events (**INSERT**, **UPDATE**, **DELETE**) on a table or view. They are essential when you want to enforce business rules, maintain audit trails, or prevent invalid changes without requiring client applications to implement the logic.

In SQL Server, the two most common trigger types are **AFTER** triggers and **INSTEAD OF** triggers. While both respond to DML operations, they behave differently, besides serving distinct purposes.

AFTER Triggers

An **AFTER** trigger fires *after* the triggering statement (**INSERT**, **UPDATE**, or **DELETE**) has executed successfully. This also implies that:

- They execute only if the original DML operation completes without errors.
- They are commonly used for auditing, cascading logic, or enforcing complex business rules.
- Multiple AFTER triggers can be defined on the same table for the same event, and the execution order can be controlled with **sp_settriggerorder**.

Syntax for **AFTER** Trigger:

```
CREATE TRIGGER trg_AfterInsertOrder
ON Sales.Orders
AFTER INSERT
AS
BEGIN
    SET NOCOUNT ON;

    INSERT INTO Audit.OrderLog (OrderID, Action, ActionDate)
    SELECT OrderID, 'INSERT', GETDATE()
    FROM inserted;
END;
```

In this example:

- **inserted** and **deleted** are pseudo-tables that store the before/after images of rows affected by the DML operation.
- In this example, every new order automatically creates an audit log entry.

Real-World Use Case: Enforcing Business Rules

Suppose, a company requires that all orders must have a positive total amount. Therefore, a table will look like:

```
CREATE TRIGGER trg_AfterInsertOrderValidation
```

```
ON Sales.Orders
AFTER INSERT
AS
BEGIN
    IF EXISTS (SELECT 1 FROM inserted WHERE TotalAmount <= 0)
    BEGIN
        RAISERROR ('Order amount must be greater than zero.', 16, 1);
        ROLLBACK TRANSACTION;
    END
END;
```

In this example:

- The trigger rolls back the entire insert if invalid data is detected.
- This ensures that business integrity is maintained, even if the front-end fails to enforce the rule.

INSTEAD OF Triggers

An **INSTEAD OF** trigger is fired *in place of* the triggering statement. You should also note the following features about such triggers:

- They are commonly used on views, since views generally do not support direct modifications.
- They allow you to define custom logic for **INSERT**, **UPDATE**, or **DELETE** operations on views or tables.
- Unlike **AFTER** triggers, they prevent the original DML from executing unless you explicitly include it in the trigger.

Syntax for **INSTEAD OF** Trigger

```
CREATE TRIGGER trg_InsteadOfInsertOrder
ON Sales.Orders
INSTEAD OF INSERT
AS
BEGIN
    SET NOCOUNT ON;

    INSERT INTO Sales.Orders (CustomerID, OrderDate, TotalAmount)
    SELECT CustomerID,
           ISNULL(OrderDate, GETDATE()), -- Default to today if NULL
           CASE WHEN TotalAmount < 0 THEN 0 ELSE TotalAmount END
    FROM inserted;
END;
```

Here:

- Any attempt to insert into **Sales.Orders** goes through the trigger first.
- The trigger replaces **NULL** dates with today's date.
- Negative order amounts are corrected to zero.

Real-World Use Case: Updating an Updatable View

Suppose, we have a view that combines customer and order information. This will look like:

```
CREATE VIEW vCustomerOrders
AS
```

```
SELECT c.CustomerID, c.Name, o.OrderID, o.TotalAmount
FROM Sales.Customers c
JOIN Sales.Orders o ON c.CustomerID = o.CustomerID;
```

By default, you cannot insert directly into this view. However, with an **INSTEAD OF** trigger, you can redirect inserts to the underlying tables, which will look like this:

```
CREATE TRIGGER trg_InsteadOfInsert_vCustomerOrders
ON vCustomerOrders
INSTEAD OF INSERT
AS
BEGIN
    INSERT INTO Sales.Customers (CustomerID, Name)
    SELECT DISTINCT CustomerID, Name FROM inserted;

    INSERT INTO Sales.Orders (OrderID, CustomerID, TotalAmount)
    SELECT OrderID, CustomerID, TotalAmount FROM inserted;
END;
```

Thus, this makes the view updatable, even though it pulls from multiple tables.

Differences between AFTER and INSTEAD OF Triggers

SQL Server supports different types of triggers, with each being designed for specific use cases. The comparison provided here highlights the key differences between **AFTER** triggers and **INSTEAD OF** triggers. This table will help you determine when to use each for auditing, validation, or custom logic.

Feature	AFTER Trigger	INSTEAD OF Trigger
Execution	Runs **after** the triggering DML succeeds	Runs **instead of** the DML
Typical Use	Auditing, validation, logging, and cascading updates	Making views updatable, custom insert/update logic
Can Rollback?	Yes	Yes
Works on Views?	No	Yes
Are Multiple Triggers Allowed?	Yes	Yes (Usually one per event)

Table 7.1: AFTER *vs.* INSTEAD OF *Triggers*

Best Practices for Using Triggers

When using triggers in SQL Server, you must follow the provided best practices to ensure maintainability, predictability, and performance:

- **Use Triggers Sparingly**: Triggers add hidden logic that may be difficult to maintain or debug.
- **Avoid Complex Logic Inside Triggers**: Keep them lightweight.
- **Do Not Use Triggers as a Replacement for Constraints**: Use foreign keys, check constraints, and defaults first.
- **Always Handle Multi-Row Operations**: inserted and deleted can contain multiple rows; therefore, you must avoid assuming single-row behavior.
- **Document triggers clearly**, since their effects are not obvious in the schema.

Common Pitfalls of Triggers

While triggers are powerful, developers often misuse them by:

- **Hidden Logic**: Business rules in triggers are not always obvious, making debugging harder.
- **Performance Issues**: Row-by-row operations or recursion can slow down transactions.
- **Unintended Consequences**: Multiple triggers on the same table may cause conflicts.

☞ Hence, to combat these pitfalls, you can document all the triggers, and keep logic as simple as possible.

Recursive Trigger Control

By default, a trigger can fire another trigger, which can cause recursion (direct or indirect).

Therefore, to prevent infinite loops:

```
ALTER DATABASE MyDB
SET RECURSIVE_TRIGGERS OFF;
```

Or, you may use this inside the trigger:

```
IF TRIGGER_NESTLEVEL() > 1
    RETURN; -- exit to prevent recursion
```

☑ This ensures that the triggers do not call themselves repeatedly.

Trigger Execution Order

SQL Server lets you define the execution order if multiple triggers exist on the same table.

Example:

```
EXEC sp_settriggerorder
    @triggername = 'trg_LogChanges',
    @order = 'First',
    @stmttype = 'UPDATE';
```

This guarantees that your auditing trigger runs before other business logic triggers.

Using Triggers for Complex Validation

Triggers can enforce validation rules that are too complex for **CHECK** constraints.

Example: Preventing Negative Balances

```
CREATE TRIGGER trg_PreventNegativeBalance
ON Accounts
AFTER UPDATE
AS
BEGIN
    IF EXISTS (
        SELECT 1
        FROM inserted i
        WHERE i.Balance < 0
    )
    BEGIN
        RAISERROR('Balance cannot be negative.', 16, 1);
```

```
        ROLLBACK TRANSACTION;
    END
END;
```

☑ This ensures that no transaction commits if it violates the rule.

Auditing User Actions with CONTEXT_INFO()

Sometimes, you want to know who triggered the change. Applications can set context information, which triggers can log.

Application Side:

```
DECLARE @bin VARBINARY(128) = CAST('User123' AS VARBINARY(128));
SET CONTEXT_INFO @bin;
```

Trigger Side:

```
CREATE TRIGGER trg_LogUserAction
ON Orders
AFTER INSERT
AS
BEGIN
    DECLARE @User VARBINARY(128) = CONTEXT_INFO();
    INSERT INTO AuditLog(OrderID, ActionUser, ActionDate)
    SELECT i.OrderID, CAST(@User AS NVARCHAR(50)), GETDATE()
    FROM inserted i;
END;
```

This way, your audit table records application-level user IDs.

Preventing DML on Sensitive Tables with INSTEAD OF

Sometimes, you want a table to appear editable, but it blocks changes.

Example:

```
CREATE TRIGGER trg_BlockDelete
ON Employees
INSTEAD OF DELETE
AS
BEGIN
    RAISERROR('Deleting employees is not allowed.', 16, 1);
END;
```

☑ The **DELETE** statement runs, but the trigger intercepts, and then cancels it.

Performance Considerations

To optimize trigger performance and ensure reliable execution in SQL Server, follow these guidelines:

- Keep trigger logic short and set-based.
- Avoid calling long-running stored procedures.
- Use inserted/deleted virtual tables wisely (never loop row by row).
- Index the columns being checked inside triggers for speed.

☞ Therefore, a poorly written trigger can turn a millisecond operation into a multi-second delay.

Real-World Example: Audit and Enforcement Together

The following trigger demonstrates the best practices for enforcing business rules and auditing changes in SQL Server:

```
CREATE TRIGGER trg_OrderValidation
ON Orders
AFTER INSERT, UPDATE
AS
BEGIN
    -- Enforce: TotalAmount must be positive
    IF EXISTS (SELECT 1 FROM inserted WHERE TotalAmount <= 0)
    BEGIN
        RAISERROR('Order amount must be positive.', 16, 1);
        ROLLBACK TRANSACTION;
        RETURN;
    END;

    -- Audit: Record the change
    INSERT INTO OrdersAudit(OrderID, Action, ChangeDate)
    SELECT i.OrderID,
           CASE WHEN d.OrderID IS NULL THEN 'INSERT' ELSE 'UPDATE' END,
           GETDATE()
    FROM inserted i
    LEFT JOIN deleted d ON i.OrderID = d.OrderID;
END;
```

☑ This trigger both enforces business rules and audits changes in a single operation.

Best Practices Recap

To ensure maintainable and efficient use of triggers in SQL Server, follow these key guidelines:

1. Use triggers only when constraints or application logic cannot achieve the goal.
2. Keep them short, set-based, and documented.
3. Avoid recursion, and explicitly control execution order.
4. Use auditing triggers for history instead of heavy logic.
5. Consider alternatives (stored procedures, constraints, computed columns) whenever possible.

Summary: SQL Server provides different types of triggers that serve distinct purposes, and understanding their behavior is key to using them effectively:

- `AFTER` triggers execute after a DML statement, which is useful for auditing, validation, and enforcing rules.
- `INSTEAD OF` triggers replace the triggering statement, and are commonly used to make complex views updatable.
- Both can roll back transactions if necessary.
- Use Triggers with Caution: They are powerful, but can obscure business logic if overused.

Auditing with Triggers

Auditing is a critical aspect of database management, especially in systems where compliance, security, and accountability are mandatory. Triggers are a natural fit for auditing because they automatically respond to data modifications, without requiring you to make changes to application code. Therefore, by capturing details about who changed what, when, and how, triggers help maintain a reliable audit trail.

Triggers for Auditing

While SQL Server provides built-in tools like Change Data Capture (CDC) and Temporal Tables, triggers remain valuable when:

- You need fine-grained control over what gets audited.
- You want to enforce business-specific audit rules (for example, only audit changes to critical columns).
- You need to log user actions in real time with full flexibility.
- You are working in environments where CDC or temporal tables are unavailable.

Designing an Audit Table

Before writing audit triggers, you need an audit table to store historical records. Thus, a common schema includes the following:

```
CREATE TABLE Audit.EmployeeChanges
(
    AuditID       INT IDENTITY PRIMARY KEY,
    EmployeeID    INT,
    ActionType    VARCHAR(10),       -- INSERT, UPDATE, DELETE
    ChangedBy     SYSNAME,           -- Login name
    ChangedDate   DATETIME DEFAULT GETDATE(),
    OldValue      NVARCHAR(MAX),
    NewValue      NVARCHAR(MAX)
);
```

This table records:

- The primary key of the affected row (**EmployeeID**)
- The type of action performed
- Who performed the action
- When the change occurred
- The before/after values

Example: Auditing `INSERT` Operations

The following trigger illustrates how to capture audit information for newly inserted employee records in SQL Server:

```
CREATE TRIGGER trg_AuditEmployeeInsert
ON HR.Employees
AFTER INSERT
AS
BEGIN
    SET NOCOUNT ON;
    INSERT INTO Audit.EmployeeChanges (EmployeeID, ActionType, ChangedBy, OldValue,
NewValue)
```

```
    SELECT i.EmployeeID,
           'INSERT',
           SUSER_SNAME(),
           NULL,                                   -- No old value
           CONCAT('Name: ', i.FirstName, ' ', i.LastName,
                  ', Title: ', i.JobTitle,
                  ', Salary: ', i.Salary)
    FROM inserted i;
END;
```

- Every new employee insertion is logged.
- **SUSER_SNAME()** records the current SQL Server login.
- Only new values are captured because old values do not exist for inserts.

Example: Auditing UPDATE Operations

The following trigger demonstrates how to audit updates to employee records by capturing both old and new values in SQL Server:

```
CREATE TRIGGER trg_AuditEmployeeUpdate
ON HR.Employees
AFTER UPDATE
AS
BEGIN
    SET NOCOUNT ON;

    INSERT INTO Audit.EmployeeChanges (EmployeeID, ActionType, ChangedBy, OldValue,
NewValue)
    SELECT d.EmployeeID,
           'UPDATE',
           SUSER_SNAME(),
           CONCAT('Name: ', d.FirstName, ' ', d.LastName,
                  ', Title: ', d.JobTitle,
                  ', Salary: ', d.Salary),
           CONCAT('Name: ', i.FirstName, ' ', i.LastName,
                  ', Title: ', i.JobTitle,
                  ', Salary: ', i.Salary)
    FROM deleted d
    JOIN inserted i ON d.EmployeeID = i.EmployeeID;
END;
```

- Both deleted and inserted pseudo-tables are used.
- The deleted table stores the old values, while inserted stores the new values.
- Only the changed rows are captured.

Example: Auditing DELETE Operations

The following trigger captures deletions from the Employees table, and logs old values into the audit table for traceability. This is demonstrated as follows:

```
CREATE TRIGGER trg_AuditEmployeeDelete
ON HR.Employees
AFTER DELETE
```

```
AS
BEGIN
    SET NOCOUNT ON;

    INSERT INTO Audit.EmployeeChanges (EmployeeID, ActionType, ChangedBy, OldValue,
NewValue)
    SELECT d.EmployeeID,
           'DELETE',
           SUSER_SNAME(),
           CONCAT('Name: ', d.FirstName, ' ', d.LastName,
                  ', Title: ', d.JobTitle,
                  ', Salary: ', d.Salary),
           NULL   -- No new value
    FROM deleted d;
END;
```

- Deleted rows are captured from the deleted pseudo-table.
- New values are null, as the row no longer exists.

Consolidating into a Single Trigger

Instead of creating separate triggers for **INSERT**, **UPDATE**, and **DELETE**, you can combine them into one, as shown here:

```
CREATE TRIGGER trg_AuditEmployees
ON HR.Employees
AFTER INSERT, UPDATE, DELETE
AS
BEGIN
    SET NOCOUNT ON;

    -- INSERT actions
    INSERT INTO Audit.EmployeeChanges (EmployeeID, ActionType, ChangedBy, OldValue,
NewValue)
    SELECT i.EmployeeID, 'INSERT', SUSER_SNAME(), NULL,
           CONCAT('Name: ', i.FirstName, ' ', i.LastName, ', Title: ', i.JobTitle, ',
Salary: ', i.Salary)
    FROM inserted i
    LEFT JOIN deleted d ON i.EmployeeID = d.EmployeeID
    WHERE d.EmployeeID IS NULL;

    -- UPDATE actions
    INSERT INTO Audit.EmployeeChanges (EmployeeID, ActionType, ChangedBy, OldValue,
NewValue)
    SELECT i.EmployeeID, 'UPDATE', SUSER_SNAME(),
           CONCAT('Name: ', d.FirstName, ' ', d.LastName, ', Title: ', d.JobTitle, ',
Salary: ', d.Salary),
           CONCAT('Name: ', i.FirstName, ' ', i.LastName, ', Title: ', i.JobTitle, ',
Salary: ', i.Salary)
    FROM inserted i
    JOIN deleted d ON i.EmployeeID = d.EmployeeID;

    -- DELETE actions
    INSERT INTO Audit.EmployeeChanges (EmployeeID, ActionType, ChangedBy, OldValue,
NewValue)
```

```
    SELECT d.EmployeeID, 'DELETE', SUSER_SNAME(),
           CONCAT('Name: ', d.FirstName, ' ', d.LastName, ', Title: ', d.JobTitle, ',
Salary: ', d.Salary),
           NULL
    FROM deleted d
    LEFT JOIN inserted i ON d.EmployeeID = i.EmployeeID
    WHERE i.EmployeeID IS NULL;
END;
```

Hence, this approach reduces redundancy and centralizes auditing logic.

Best Practices for Audit Triggers

Moreover, when you are working with triggers, it is important to follow best practices to maintain performance and avoid unnecessary overhead. Here are the key guidelines you should keep in mind:

- Keep triggers lightweight, as heavy logic can slow down transactions.
- Avoid auditing every column unnecessarily; instead, focus on sensitive or critical ones.
- Store only necessary details, since excessive logging can bloat audit tables.
- Archive old audit records to maintain performance.
- Combine with indexing on Audit tables for faster queries.
- Consider built-in alternatives like Change Data Capture (CDC) or temporal tables, if the requirements are complex.

Capturing the Host and Application Name

SQL Server allows you to capture the host machine, the program, and the login that are responsible for the change. This looks like:

```
CREATE TRIGGER trg_AuditOrderUpdates
ON Orders
AFTER UPDATE
AS
BEGIN
    INSERT INTO AuditLog(OrderID, OldValue, NewValue, ChangedBy, HostName,
ProgramName, ChangeDate)
    SELECT
        d.OrderID,
        d.Status,
        i.Status,
        SUSER_SNAME(),
        HOST_NAME(),
        PROGRAM_NAME(),
        GETDATE()
    FROM deleted d
    JOIN inserted i ON d.OrderID = i.OrderID;
END;
```

☑ Hence, this provides contextual audit information beyond just the data.

Auditing with Extended Events Integration

Instead of relying only on audit tables, triggers can write events into Extended Events or the SQL Server Error Log. This is demonstrated in the following example:

```
CREATE TRIGGER trg_AuditToErrorLog
ON Customers
AFTER DELETE
AS
BEGIN
    DECLARE @msg NVARCHAR(4000);
    SELECT @msg = 'Customer deleted: ' + CAST(d.CustomerID AS NVARCHAR(10))
    FROM deleted d;

    RAISERROR(@msg, 10, 1) WITH LOG;
END;
```

☑ Therefore, this ensures that administrators can monitor changes outside of the database tables.

Partial Auditing (Only Key Columns)

Auditing *every* column can lead to huge audit tables. Instead, you should log only important attributes, just as in the example here:

```
CREATE TRIGGER trg_AuditKeyColumns
ON Employees
AFTER UPDATE
AS
BEGIN
    IF UPDATE(Salary) OR UPDATE(Position)
    BEGIN
        INSERT INTO EmployeeAudit(EmployeeID, OldSalary, NewSalary, OldPos, NewPos,
ChangeDate)
        SELECT
            d.EmployeeID, d.Salary, i.Salary, d.Position, i.Position, GETDATE()
        FROM inserted i
        JOIN deleted d ON i.EmployeeID = d.EmployeeID;
    END
END;
```

☑ Hence, this keeps the audit log lightweight and focused.

Soft Deletes with Audit Triggers

Instead of deleting records, you can mark them as inactive while still auditing the action. This can be seen in the example here:

```
CREATE TRIGGER trg_SoftDeleteOrders
ON Orders
INSTEAD OF DELETE
AS
BEGIN
    UPDATE Orders
    SET IsActive = 0, DeletedDate = GETDATE()
```

```
    WHERE OrderID IN (SELECT OrderID FROM deleted);

    INSERT INTO OrdersAudit(OrderID, Action, ChangeDate)
    SELECT OrderID, 'SOFT DELETE', GETDATE()
    FROM deleted;
END;
```

☑ Hence, this preserves the data for compliance and investigation.

Compliance-Driven Auditing (GDPR, SOX, HIPAA)

For industries like finance, healthcare, and government, auditing must meet strict legal standards. Some of them are mentioned here:

- **SOX**: Audit trails for financial transactions.
- **HIPAA**: Medical record changes must log user, timestamp, and reason.
- **GDPR**: Right-to-erasure logs require retention policies.

☞ Therefore, triggers can be paired with encryption and partitioned audit tables for compliance.

Auditing DDL Changes (Schema Changes)

Most triggers audit DML, but you can also audit DDL with DDL TRIGGERS, as shown in this example:

```
CREATE TRIGGER trg_AuditDDL
ON DATABASE
FOR CREATE_TABLE, ALTER_TABLE, DROP_TABLE
AS
BEGIN
    INSERT INTO DDL_Audit(EventType, ObjectName, ExecutedBy, ChangeDate)
    SELECT EVENTDATA().value('(/EVENT_INSTANCE/EventType)[1]', 'NVARCHAR(100)'),
           EVENTDATA().value('(/EVENT_INSTANCE/ObjectName)[1]', 'NVARCHAR(200)'),
           SUSER_SNAME(),
           GETDATE();
END;
```

☑ Hence, this ensures that the schema modifications are tracked, along with the data changes.

Archiving Old Audit Data

Since audit logs can grow quite large, you must implement partitioning and archiving.

Example Strategy:

- Keep 90 days of audit logs in the main table.
- Move older logs to an archive database or cold storage.

```
INSERT INTO AuditLogArchive
SELECT * FROM AuditLog WHERE ChangeDate < DATEADD(DAY, -90, GETDATE());

DELETE FROM AuditLog WHERE ChangeDate < DATEADD(DAY, -90, GETDATE());
```

☑ Keeps performance high, while maintaining compliance.

Real-World Case Study: Banking Transactions

A banking system uses auditing triggers to prevent fraud, where:

- Every `WITHDRAWAL` is logged with old balance, new balance, and teller ID.
- Large withdrawals (> $10,000) trigger an alert log entry.
- Soft deletes ensure that the transactions are never physically removed.

☞ Hence, this creates a tamper-proof audit trail critical for regulators.

Best Practices Recap for Auditing with Triggers

When implementing auditing in SQL Server, it is important to balance thoroughness with efficiency to ensure compliance without harming performance. Therefore, you must remember following these practices:

1. Audit only what is necessary (avoid bloated logs).
2. Store who, when, what changed (user, timestamp, old and new values).
3. Use DDL triggers for schema-level auditing.
4. Plan archiving for large audit tables.
5. Test audit triggers under high transaction loads.
6. Always document audit logic for compliance reviews.

Summary: Moreover, in SQL Server, triggers can be leveraged to capture data changes in real time, which makes them a flexible but sensitive tool for auditing:

- Triggers provide a powerful way to implement custom auditing logic.
- Inserted and deleted pseudo-tables enable capturing old and new values.
- Audit triggers can log inserts, updates, and deletes either separately, or in a consolidated trigger.
- They are flexible, but they must be carefully designed to avoid performance issues.

Inline and Multi-Statement Table-Valued Functions

Table-Valued Functions (TVFs) are a powerful extension of SQL Server's user-defined functions that return a dataset (a table), instead of a scalar value. They play a vital role in promoting code reusability, modularization, and composability within queries. Unlike views, which are limited to static SQL definitions, TVFs can encapsulate more dynamic logic and accept parameters, which makes them excellent candidates for reusable query patterns.

There are two main types of TVFs in SQL Server:

- Inline TVFs
- Multi-Statement TVFs (MSTVFs)

Therefore, this section explores both in detail, along with their benefits, trade-offs, and performance implications.

Inline Table-Valued Functions

An Inline TVF is essentially a parameterized view. It consists of a single RETURN statement that defines the query. It also behaves much like a view with added flexibility because it can take parameters.

Syntax Example:

```
CREATE FUNCTION dbo.GetOrdersByCustomer(@CustomerID INT)
RETURNS TABLE
AS
RETURN
(
    SELECT OrderID, OrderDate, TotalAmount
    FROM Sales.Orders
    WHERE CustomerID = @CustomerID
);
```

Key Points about Inline TVFs:

- They return the result of a single **SELECT** query.
- They are read-only (cannot perform **INSERT**, **UPDATE**, or **DELETE**).
- The query optimizer can inline the function into the outer query, which results in excellent performance.
- They behave similarly to parameterized views, and offer modularity with minimal performance cost.

Usage Example:

```
SELECT *
FROM dbo.GetOrdersByCustomer(102);
```

Here, SQL Server replaces the function with the underlying query during execution, which means that no intermediate storage is required.

Multi-Statement Table-Valued Functions

A Multi-Statement Table-Valued Function (MSTVF) allows you to define complex procedural logic that cannot be expressed in a single SELECT statement. Unlike Inline TVFs, MSTVFs can contain multiple T-SQL statements, intermediate transformations, conditional logic, and data manipulation before they return a final result set.

While MSTVFs offer flexibility, they come with important performance trade-offs that every SQL Server developer must understand. Hence, you must pay attention to the following sections:

Syntax Example:

```
CREATE FUNCTION dbo.GetHighValueOrders(@MinAmount DECIMAL(10,2))
RETURNS @HighValueOrders TABLE
(
    OrderID INT,
    CustomerID INT,
    TotalAmount DECIMAL(10,2),
    OrderDate DATE
)
AS
```

```
BEGIN
    INSERT INTO @HighValueOrders
    SELECT OrderID, CustomerID, TotalAmount, OrderDate
    FROM Sales.Orders
    WHERE TotalAmount >= @MinAmount;

    -- Additional procedural logic
    UPDATE @HighValueOrders
    SET TotalAmount = TotalAmount * 1.05
    WHERE OrderDate < '2023-01-01';

    RETURN;
END;
```

Usage Example:

```
SELECT *
FROM dbo.GetHighValueOrders(1000);
```

Key Characteristics of Multi-Statement TVFs

Explicit Table Variable Return: MSTVFs return a table variable that is explicitly defined in the function body as:

```
RETURNS @TableVar TABLE (...)
```

This table variable exists only within the function, and is populated step by step using procedural logic.

Support for Complex Procedural Logic: MSTVFs allow for the following elements:

- Multiple **INSERT**, **UPDATE**, and **DELETE** Operations
- Conditional Logic (IF/ELSE)
- Loops and Control-of-Flow Statements
- Step-by-Step Data Shaping

Hence, this makes them suitable for complex transformations that cannot be expressed in a single query.

Major Performance Consideration (Critical): MSTVFs can introduce significant performance problems, if used incorrectly.

SQL Server treats MSTVFs as opaque "**black boxes**" during query optimization. Therefore, the following holds true:

- The query optimizer cannot see inside the function logic.
- SQL Server assumes the function returns one row (prior to SQL Server 2019).
- Cardinality estimates are often wildly inaccurate.
- Poor estimates can lead to:
    - Bad join strategies
    - Inefficient execution plans
    - Unexpected performance degradation on large datasets

Therefore, even in newer versions of SQL Server, MSTVFs still do not optimize as well as inline TVFs.

Comparison with Inline TVFs

Feature	Inline TVF	Multi-Statement TVF
Optimizer Visibility	Full	Very Limited
Cardinality Estimation	Accurate	Often Inaccurate
Execution Plan	Inlined into query	Separate Operator
Performance	Excellent	Often Slower
Procedural Logic	No	Yes

Table 7.2: *Comparison of Inline TVFs and Multi-Statement TVFs in T-SQL*

Rule of Thumb: If the logic can be written as a single `SELECT`, do not use an MSTVF.

When to Use Multi-Statement TVFs (Safely)

MSTVFs are appropriate when:

- The logic is inherently procedural.
- Multiple transformation steps are required.
- Result sets are small and well-bounded.
- Performance impact has been tested and accepted.

They should **not** be used:

- In high-volume OLTP queries
- Inside joins on large tables
- As a replacement for Inline TVFs or views

Performance Best Practices

To minimize performance risks when using MSTVFs, follow these best practices:

1. Prefer Inline TVFs whenever possible.
2. Keep returned row counts small and predictable.
3. Avoid using MSTVFs inside large joins.
4. Test execution plans with realistic data volumes.
5. Consider alternatives such as:
    - Inline TVFs
    - Views
    - Stored Procedures
    - Temporary Tables in Calling Code

Comparing Inline vs. Multi-Statement TVFs

Before using Table-Valued Functions (TVFs), it is important to understand their differences in definition, optimization, and performance. The table given here compares inline TVFs and multi-statement TVFs to help you choose the right approach based on your workload and requirements.

Feature	Inline TVF	Multi-Statement TVF
Definition	Single query (like parameterized view)	Multiple queries with procedural logic
Return Type	Direct query result	Table variable
Optimization	Can be inlined and optimized by SQL Server	Acts as a black box, limited optimization
Performance	Fast, highly optimized	Slower for large datasets
Complexity	Simple logic only	Complex logic, transformations allowed
Use Case	Simple filters, projections, reusable queries	Complex transformations, aggregations, business rules

Table 7.3: *Inline vs. Multi-Statement TVFs*

Performance Considerations

While TVFs provide great flexibility, performance should always be carefully considered. Therefore, you must factor in the following:

1. Inline TVFs are generally preferred because the SQL optimizer can fully expand them into the execution plan, while enabling index usage, joins, and filtering optimizations.
2. Multi-Statement TVFs can be slower due to the use of table variables:
    - Table variables do not maintain distribution statistics.
    - SQL Server often assumes a row count of 1, leading to poor query plans.
    - For larger datasets, this can severely impact performance.

Best Practices:

- Use inline TVFs whenever possible.
- Reserve MSTVFs only for scenarios requiring procedural logic that cannot be expressed in a single query.

Practical Use Cases

Inline TVF Example: Filtering Data by Date Range

```
CREATE FUNCTION dbo.GetOrdersInDateRange(@StartDate DATE, @EndDate DATE)
RETURNS TABLE
AS
RETURN
(
    SELECT OrderID, CustomerID, TotalAmount, OrderDate
    FROM Sales.Orders
    WHERE OrderDate BETWEEN @StartDate AND @EndDate
);
```

Multi-Statement TVF Example: Custom Business Rules

```
CREATE FUNCTION dbo.GetPreferredCustomers(@MinTotal DECIMAL(10,2))
RETURNS @Preferred TABLE
(
    CustomerID INT,
    TotalSpent DECIMAL(10,2),
    Tier VARCHAR(10)
```

```
)
AS
BEGIN
    INSERT INTO @Preferred
    SELECT CustomerID, SUM(TotalAmount) AS TotalSpent, 'Silver'
    FROM Sales.Orders
    GROUP BY CustomerID
    HAVING SUM(TotalAmount) >= @MinTotal;

    -- Upgrade top customers
    UPDATE @Preferred
    SET Tier = 'Gold'
    WHERE TotalSpent >= @MinTotal * 5;

    RETURN;
END;
```

Best Practices

Table-Valued Functions (TVFs) can encapsulate reusable query logic, but their design directly impacts performance and maintainability. Therefore, you must follow these best practices:

- ☑ Prefer Inline TVFs for performance.
- ☑ Use parameters to make TVFs reusable.
- ☑ Apply proper naming conventions (for example, **`Get*`**, **`fn*`**).
- ☑ Keep MSTVFs as lean as possible—avoid large temporary logic, if possible.
- ✕ Avoid using MSTVFs for large datasets that require frequent joins.

Conclusion

In this chapter, you gained an in-depth understanding of how to extend SQL Server's flexibility using Dynamic SQL, Triggers, and Table-Valued Functions (TVFs). You also learned how to securely build and execute parameterized dynamic SQL statements using **`sp_executesql`**, while ensuring both reusability and protection against SQL injection. Additionally, the chapter introduced DML triggers, including **`AFTER`** and **`INSTEAD OF`** triggers, which can automate enforcement of business rules, support auditing, and also maintain data integrity in real-world applications.

Furthermore, you explored TVFs as a way to encapsulate reusable query logic. Both inline and multi-statement TVFs were covered, along with their advantages and trade-offs compared to views. Hence, by combining dynamic SQL, triggers, and TVFs, you are now equipped to create more modular, automated, and adaptable database solutions that can evolve alongside changing business requirements.

The next chapter focuses on query optimization and performance tuning. There, you will learn how to design efficient queries, analyze execution plans, optimize indexes, and avoid common performance pitfalls.

Chapter 8

Query Optimization and Performance Tuning

Introduction

In the previous chapter, we explored dynamic SQL, triggers, and Table-Valued Functions (TVFs), focusing on how to build reusable logic, enforce business rules, and apply the best practices in real-world scenarios. Building on that foundation, this chapter shifts focus toward optimizing the performance of those solutions. This chapter is essential for developers aiming to write efficient and scalable T-SQL code. Here, you will learn how to read and interpret execution plans to uncover performance bottlenecks. Various indexing strategies, including clustered, non-clustered, filtered, and covering indexes, are explained with practical examples. We will then dive deeper into the concept of SARGability (Search Argument Ability), which involves writing predicates that make queries index-friendly. Additionally, you will explore statistics management, query rewrites, optimization hints, and performance monitoring through Dynamic Management Views (DMVs). Finally, we will review common pitfalls that cause slow queries, along with strategies to avoid them.

The goal of this chapter is to make you confident in analyzing, diagnosing, and improving SQL query performance in real-world workloads.

Structure

In this chapter, we will cover the following topics:

- Introduction: The Importance of Performance Tuning
- Reading and Interpreting Execution Plans
- Index Design and Usage (Clustered, Nonclustered, Filtered, and Covering)
- SARGability and Predicate Optimization
- Statistics Management and Query Selectivity
- Query Rewrites and Optimization Hints
- Performance Monitoring Using DMVs
- Avoiding Common Pitfalls

Introduction: The Importance of Performance Tuning

Most SQL developers know how to write queries that "work", but in large-scale systems, being able to write working queries is not enough on its own. They must also be efficient, scalable, and predictable.

As an example, consider this:

- A query that runs in 100 milliseconds may be fine for small tables, but when the table grows from 1 million to 100 million rows, it could suddenly take 10 minutes or more to process them.
- A poor join strategy might perform acceptably in development, but it will fail under production load.

Therefore, performance tuning ensures that queries:

- Scale with data growth.
- Minimize CPU, memory, and I/O usage.
- Are meeting the SLAs (Service Level Agreements) for response time.

SQL Server includes powerful tools for optimization, including execution plans, indexing, statistics, DMVs, and query rewrites. Hence, this chapter will teach you how to use them effectively.

Reading Execution Plans

Execution plans are one of the most powerful tools in SQL Server for understanding query performance. An execution plan shows how the SQL Server query optimizer has decided to execute your query, which indexes it uses, the join algorithms it applies, and the relative cost of each step. Hence, by carefully reading execution plans, developers and database administrators (DBAs) can pinpoint emerging and existent performance bottlenecks, and will be able to optimize queries effectively.

SQL Server offers two types of execution plans:

- **Estimated Execution Plan**: Displays how SQL Server *thinks* that it will execute the query, based on statistics and metadata, without actually running the query.
- **Actual Execution Plan**: Displays the real steps SQL Server took when executing the query, including runtime metrics such as the number of rows processed.

Therefore, understanding how to interpret both is the key to mastering query performance tuning.

Execution Plan

An execution plan is essentially a map of operations SQL Server follows to retrieve or manipulate data.

For example, when you write:

```
SELECT FirstName, LastName
FROM Employees
WHERE DepartmentID = 5;
Here, SQL Server must decide:
```

- If should it scan the whole Employees table.
- If it can use an index on **`DepartmentID`**.
- If it should apply a filter first, and then the project (select) columns.

The execution plan answers these questions by showing which operators are chosen (for example, Index Seek, Nested Loops, or Hash Match).

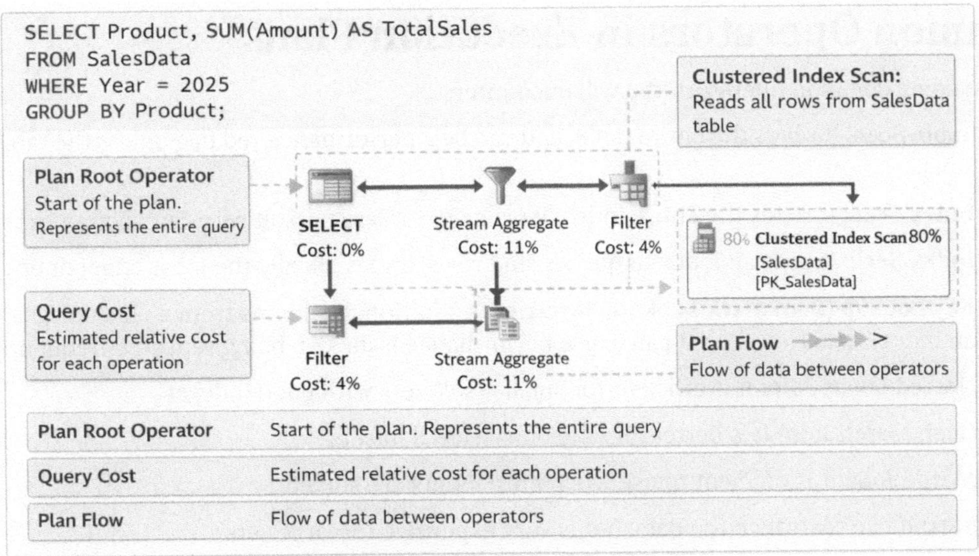

Figure 8.1: *Reading an Execution Plan*

Generating Execution Plans

There are several ways to view execution plans, such as:

1. In SQL Server Management Studio (SSMS):
    - **Estimated Plan**: Press Ctrl+L, or click on *Display Estimated Execution Plan.*
    - **Actual Plan**: Press Ctrl+M before running the query, or click on *Include Actual Execution Plan.*
2. When you use T-SQL Commands:

```
SET SHOWPLAN_XML ON;
GO
SELECT * FROM Employees WHERE DepartmentID = 5;
GO
SET SHOWPLAN_XML OFF;
```

    - **`SHOWPLAN_XML`** and **`STATISTICS XML`** can produce plans in XML format.
3. When you use Dynamic Management Views (DMVs): **`sys.dm_exec_query_plan`** and **`sys.dm_exec_requests`** can retrieve cached or running plans.

Logical vs. Physical Operators

Execution plans consist of operators. These operators are building blocks representing SQL Server's actions.

- **Logical Operators**: They represent the conceptual operation (for example, *join, filter, and so on*).
- **Physical Operators**: They show the actual method used (for example, *Nested Loops Join*, or the *Hash Match Join*).

For example,

- A logical join may be required, but SQL Server might choose a Nested Loop (which is efficient for small sets), or a Hash Match (which is better for larger, unsorted sets).

Common Operators in Execution Plans

Here are some common operators you will encounter:

- **Table Scan**: It reads the entire table, and can be a performance red flag unless the table is very small.
- **Index Scan**: It reads the entire index; it is useful for large result sets, but is quite expensive.
- **Index Seek**: It uses an index to quickly find rows, and is usually the most efficient operation.
- **Key Lookup (Bookmark Lookup)**: It retrieves additional columns from a clustered index after an Index Seek. However, it can cause performance issues on being repeated frequently.
- **Nested Loops Join**: It is efficient for small result sets with good indexes.
- **Hash Match Join**: It is better for large, unsorted datasets.
- **Merge Join**: It is efficient to use when both inputs are sorted.
- **Sort**: It can rearrange the data, but is very expensive for large sets.
- **Compute Scalar**: It performs calculations.
- **Filter**: It applies conditions to rows.

Reading an Execution Plan Flow

Execution plans should be read from right to left, top to bottom.

- **Right-Most Operator**: Reflects the first operation performed
- **Left-Most Operator**: Reflects the final output returned to the client

Example:

```
[Clustered Index Scan] → [Filter] → [SELECT]
```

This means that SQL Server scanned the clustered index, applied a filter, and then returned the results.

Estimated vs. Actual Execution Plans

- **Estimated Plan**: It is based only on statistics, and is useful when you do not want to run the query (for example, in production).
- **Actual Plan**: It shows the real execution path and the runtime row counts. This helps in identifying issues such as:
    - **Row Estimation Errors**: SQL Server thought that it would process 100 rows, but actually processed 1,000,000 instead.
    - **Wrong Choice of Operator**: An unnecessary Hash Join might be chosen when a Nested Loop would have been better.

Here is an example of how we can estimate rows incorrectly:

```
SELECT *
FROM Orders
WHERE YEAR(OrderDate) = 2022;
```

Here, due to the function `YEAR(OrderDate)`, SQL Server may estimate the row counts and scan more than expected, which would be incorrect. Additionally, this is a non-SARGable query.

Costs and Percentages in Execution Plans

Each operator in a plan has a cost percentage. These percentages are estimates of relative cost, and not of the exact execution time.

Example:

- An Index Seek may carry 10% of the cost.
- A Hash Match Join may carry 90% of the cost.

Therefore, you must focus on the highest-cost operators first as you optimize queries.

Identifying Bottlenecks

When you are analyzing execution plans, look out for the following bottlenecks:

1. **Table Scans on Large Tables**: Consider adding indexes.
2. **Key Lookups**: Consider a covering index.
3. **Expensive Sorts**: This can be avoided with proper indexing.
4. **Row Estimation Errors**: This may require you to update the statistics.
5. **Parallelism**: Multiple threads can speed up queries, but excessive parallelism may indicate inefficiency.

Execution Plan Formats

Execution plans can be viewed in three formats:

1. **Graphical Plan (SSMS Default)**: It is easy to read visually.
2. **Text Plan**: It shows the operations in text format.

   ```
   SET SHOWPLAN_TEXT ON;
   ```
3. **XML Plan**: It provides detailed information, such as runtime statistics.

Practical Example: Comparing Plans

Now, let us compare two queries:

Query 1 (Non-SARGable):

```
SELECT *
FROM Orders
WHERE YEAR(OrderDate) = 2022;
```

Execution Plan: Clustered Index Scan (Inefficient).

Query 2 (SARGable):

```
SELECT *
FROM Orders
WHERE OrderDate >= '2022-01-01'
  AND OrderDate < '2023-01-01';
```

Execution Plan: Index Seek (Efficient; Uses Date Index).

Hence, these queries demonstrate how reading execution plans can reveal inefficiencies that are caused by non-SARGable predicates.

Best Practices for Reading Execution Plans

Execution plans are essential for diagnosing and tuning query performance. Therefore, reviewing them systematically helps identify inefficiencies, and also prevents long-term performance issues. Here are the best practices you should follow while reading them:

- Always compare estimated and actual row counts.
- Focus on operators with high costs.
- Eliminate Key Lookups whenever possible.
- Watch out for warnings (for example, "`Missing Index`", or "`Spill to TempDB`").
- Save execution plans over time to monitor performance regressions.

Interpreting Parallelism in Execution Plans

When SQL Server detects that a query can benefit from parallel execution, the execution plan may include operators such as Parallelism (which may include Distribute Streams, Repartition Streams, and Gather Streams).

- **Distribute Streams**: Splits input rows across multiple threads
- **Repartition Streams**: Redistributes rows across threads based on a hash or key
- **Gather Streams**: Combines parallel streams back into a single output

Parallelism can speed up large queries, but it comes at the cost of synchronization overhead. Therefore, monitoring the **`CXPACKET`** and **`CXCONSUMER`** waits can help identify if parallelism is overused.

Tip: *If you see excessive parallelism on small queries, consider adjusting the* ***`MAXDOP`*** (Maximum Degree of Parallelism), *or query the rewrites.*

Identifying Missing Indexes from Execution Plans

Execution plans often include Missing Index Recommendations, which are visible as a green hint in Management Studio. For example:

"*Missing Index (Impact 89.63): `Create NonClustered Index on [dbo].Sales INCLUDE([Amount])`*"

- These suggestions are based on query workload, but are not always optimal.
- Therefore, you must always test them before implementing them, as SQL Server may suggest redundant or overlapping indexes.
- Use DMVs like **`sys.dm_db_missing_index_details`** to collect missing index recommendations across the workload.

Detecting Implicit Conversions

Execution plans can expose implicit conversions when SQL Server converts a value to match data types during comparison. This can cause index scans instead of seeks, which slows down performance.

Example:

```
WHERE CAST(CustomerID AS NVARCHAR) = '123'
```

- If **`CustomerID`** is stored as **`INT`**, this conversion will prevent index usage.
- The execution plan will show the **`CONVERT_IMPLICIT`** warning.

Fix: Align data types in schema and queries.

Understanding Estimated vs. Actual Execution Plans

- Estimated Execution Plan: It is generated without running the query, and uses SQL Server's statistics and cost model.
- Actual Execution Plan: It is produced after executing the query, and shows the true row counts and operators used.

Discrepancies between estimated and actual row counts can indicate the presence of:

- Outdated Statistics
- Skewed Data Distribution
- Non-SARGable Predicates

Best Practice: Always compare estimated and actual execution plans while troubleshooting.

Spotting Parameter Sniffing Issues

As execution plans are cached, the parameter values at first execution may heavily influence plan choice (which is also known as parameter sniffing). You will also see that:

- A plan that is optimized for one parameter value might be inefficient for another.
- Symptoms: Query runs fast sometimes but extremely slow with different parameters.

Execution Plan Clues:

- High row estimate variance as compared to the actual number of rows.
- Execution plans are being reused, but their performance varies drastically.

Fixes:

- Use `OPTION (RECOMPILE)` for queries that need fresh plans.
- Apply `OPTIMIZE FOR` hints.
- Use local variables to decouple from parameter sniffing (however, do exercise caution while using them).

Identifying Expensive Operators

Execution plans can highlight the operators that are consuming most of the cost.
Examples:

- **Key Lookup (Clustered)**: It indicates the missing index that covers the requisite columns.
- Sort: It may appear due to `ORDER BY` or `DISTINCT`. Large sorts suggest adding indexes with sorted columns.
- Hash Match: It is commonly used for joins. However, you must watch out for excessive memory usage.

Tip: Tune efforts on high-cost operators (as per the 80/20 rule).

Execution Plan Caching and Reuse

SQL Server caches execution plans for reuse, which improves performance. However:

- Too many single-use plans can bloat the plan cache (which is known as "plan cache pollution").

- You can monitor with DMV in the following manner:

```
SELECT usecounts, objtype, size_in_bytes, text
FROM sys.dm_exec_cached_plans
CROSS APPLY sys.dm_exec_sql_text(plan_handle);
```

- Use parameterization to encourage reuse.
- Consider **sp_executesql** for safe dynamic SQL.

Using Live Query Statistics

SQL Server Management Studio (SSMS) offers Live Query Statistics, and shows real-time query execution and row flow.

Benefits:

- They identify long-running operators.
- They detect blocking operators in real time.
- They compare estimated and actual row processing while the query is running.

This tool is especially valuable for debugging slow-running production queries.

Best Practices for Reading Execution Plans

When reviewing execution plans, it is important to follow a structured approach, so that you can quickly spot upcoming performance issues. Therefore, here are the best practices you should follow while reading execution plans:

1. Start with root operator (**SELECT**, **INSERT**, and so on) ,and follow the arrows backward.
2. Identify highest-cost operators, and then investigate them.
3. Compare estimated and actual rows to check cardinality accuracy.
4. Look for warnings like missing indexes, implicit conversions, and spills.
5. Always analyze in the context of workload, and not just one query.

Understanding Key Lookups

- A key lookup occurs when the optimizer uses a non-clustered index, but it needs additional columns that are not included in the index.
- This generates a lookup to the clustered index or heap, which can be expensive on large tables.

  Example:

```
SELECT OrderID, CustomerID, TotalAmount
FROM Orders
WHERE CustomerID = 123;
```

- If **CustomerID** has a non-clustered index, but **TotalAmount** is not included. Hence, SQL Server performs a key lookup.

Optimization:

- You must include the required columns in the index, as shown here:

```
CREATE NONCLUSTERED INDEX IX_Orders_CustomerID
ON Orders(CustomerID)
INCLUDE (TotalAmount);
```

- This eliminates key lookups, and also improves query performance.

Bookmark Lookups vs. RID Lookups

Key lookups occur when SQL Server retrieves the additional columns that are not included in a non-clustered index. Therefore, understanding the type of lookup can help us optimize queries. These lookup types are:

- Bookmark Lookup: Occurs in clustered tables or tables with primary key indexes
- RID Lookup: Occurs in heap tables (tables without a clustered index)

Insight: Converting heaps to clustered tables often removes RID lookups, and reduces the I/O.

Nested Loops vs. Hash vs. Merge Joins

Execution plans reveal the join operator chosen by SQL Server. Some of these plans are:

1. **Nested Loops**: They are efficient for small data sets; they can become slow with large joins.
2. **Hash Joins**: They are efficient for large, unsorted sets; additionally, they may require memory allocation.
3. **Merge Joins**: They are efficient for pre-sorted inputs (for example, indexed columns).

Tip: Ensure that join keys are indexed appropriately to match the join type.

Understanding Scan vs. Seek

SQL Server uses different access methods to retrieve data. Therefore, understanding these can help optimize query performance. Here are a few types of seeks and scans you should know about:

- **Index Seek**: They are efficient, as they retrieve rows via index lookup.
- **Index Scan**: They are less efficient, as they read all the index rows.
- **Table Scan**: They read all the rows, and are usually employed as a last resort.

Example:

```
-- Index seek
SELECT * FROM Orders WHERE OrderID = 1001;

-- Table scan
SELECT * FROM Orders WHERE YEAR(OrderDate) = 2024;  -- Non-SARGable
```

Insight: Scans are acceptable for small tables. However, you must consider rewriting queries, or creating supporting indexes on large tables.

Looking at Estimated vs. Actual Rows

Understanding the difference between estimated and actual rows is crucial for diagnosing query performance problems. SQL Server's optimizer relies on estimates to choose an execution plan. However, mismatches can reveal deeper issues.

- Estimated rows and actual rows highlight cardinality estimation issues.
- A large mismatch often indicates:
  - Stale Statistics
  - Non-SARGable Predicates
  - Skewed data Distributions

Example in Execution Plan:

- Estimated: 100 Rows
- Actual: 100,000 Rows

Fix: *Update the statistics, or rewrite the predicates for SARGability.*

Warnings in Execution Plans

In SQL Server execution plans, yellow triangles highlight potential performance issues that should be investigated to prevent query bottlenecks. Common warnings include:

- Missing Statistics
- Implicit Conversions
- Spills to `tempdb`
- Triggers or Hash Joins that exceed memory grants

Tip: *Hover over the warning icon to see the details of every issue.*

Understanding Operator Costs

Understanding the relative costs in an execution plan helps prioritize which parts of a query to optimize for maximum performance impact. Therefore, you must know that:

- Execution plans show the relative cost percentages for each operator.
- Focus optimization efforts on operators with the highest cost.

Example:

- **Nested Loop Join**: 10%
- **Key Lookup**: 50%
- **Clustered Index Scan**: 40%

Insight: Optimizing the Key Lookup can drastically improve the total query performance.

Parallelism and Degree of Parallelism (DOP)

For large or resource-intensive queries, SQL Server may execute parts of the query in parallel to improve performance. Execution plans can include parallelism operators such as:

    - Gather Streams
    - Distribute Streams

- SQL Server may split work across multiple threads for large queries.

Best Practice: You should monitor `CXPACKET` waits, and then optimize the memory-intensive queries to reduce parallelism overhead.

Spill to `TempDB`

Execution plans can reveal when operators spill to `TempDB`, which typically occurs during sorts or hash joins whenever available memory is insufficient.

- Execution plans show if operators spill to `tempdb`, which usually occurs during sorts or hash joins when memory is insufficient.
- Signs: High cost and `tempdb` usage warning.

Optimization:

- Increase the memory grant, if possible.
- Add supporting indexes to reduce sort/hash requirements.
- Rewrite queries to limit the result sets early on.

Execution Plan Reuse

SQL Server caches execution plans to improve performance for queries that are executed repeatedly. However, certain factors like recompile hints or dynamic SQL can force it to generate new plans.

- SQL Server caches plans to improve performance for repeated queries.
- Recompiling hints or using dynamic SQL may force new plan generation.

Insight:

- Frequent recompilations can degrade performance.
- Cached plans are more efficient for consistent query patterns.

Reading Flow and Row Counts

Understanding the flow of an execution plan is essential to interpret how SQL Server processes a query. Here, you must know that graphical plans typically flow from right to left, while text-based plans flow top to bottom.

- Execution plans flow right-to-left (Graphical Plans), or from top-to-bottom (Text Plans).
- Look at:
    - Rows In/Rows Out
    - Estimated vs. Actual
    - Operator Cost

Tip: *Follow the flow to identify bottlenecks in joins, scans, and filters.*

Analyzing Execution Plan Operators

Execution plans include a variety of operators, each representing a step in SQL Server's query processing. Therefore, recognizing these operators helps in understanding performance characteristics, as well as in identifying bottlenecks.

- Seek vs. Scan
- Nested Loop/Hash Join/Merge Join
- Sort/Compute Scalar/Filter/Key Lookup
- Aggregate/Compute Scalar/Parallelism/Index Spool

Tip: *Understand what each operator does, and if it can be optimized via indexes, query rewrites, or statistics.*

Using Actual Execution Plan vs. Estimated

SQL Server provides two types of execution plans to help analyze query performance. The estimated plan uses the query optimizer's predictions without executing the query, while the actual plan runs the query, and also shows the true row counts as well as runtime metrics.

- **Estimated Plan**: No query execution; uses optimizer estimates
- **Actual Plan**: Runs the query and shows true row counts

Recommendation: Use Actual Plan for diagnosing performance issues.

Saving and Comparing Plans

Saving execution plans allows you to track query performance over time and compare the effects of changes such as query modifications, updated statistics, or index adjustments.

- Save execution plans as **`.sqlplan`** files.
- Compare before/after changes to queries, statistics updates, or index modifications.

-- Save plan from SSMS:

Ctrl + M -> Include the **`Actual Execution Plan`** -> **`Execute`** -> **`Save`** the plan.

Plan Guides

Plan guides are helpful when you cannot directly change the query text such as with third-party applications because they allow you to influence query behavior through forced hints or options, all without modifying the original code.

- They are useful when you cannot modify the query text (for example, third-party apps).
- They can force hints or plan options without having you change application code.

```
EXEC sp_create_plan_guide
    @name = N'ForceIndex',
    @stmt = N'SELECT * FROM Orders WHERE CustomerID = 1',
    @type = N'SQL',
    @hints = N'OPTION (INDEX(IX_Orders_CustomerID))';
```

Index Design and Usage

Indexes are one of the most critical components of query performance in SQL Server. A well-designed index can reduce query execution times from minutes to milliseconds, while a poorly designed or missing index can cripple performance. Hence, this section covers the concepts, strategies, and best practices for index design and usage in T-SQL.

Introduction to Indexes

To fully leverage SQL Server performance, it is essential to understand how indexes work and why they accelerate data retrieval. Therefore, you must know that:

- An index is a database structure that improves data retrieval speed by providing a quick lookup path.
- Think of it like a book's index: instead of flipping through every page, you can jump directly to the topic you want to access.
- SQL Server indexes are built on B-Tree structures, which make searches, lookups, and ordered scans faster.

There are two main types of indexes:

- **Clustered Index**: Determines the physical order of rows in a table
- **Non-Clustered Index**: Provides a separate lookup structure which points to clustered index or heap rows

Clustered Indexes

Clustered indexes determine the physical order of rows in a table, and are critical for improving query performance on sorted or range-based data.

- Every table can have one clustered index (since rows can be physically ordered only once).
- It is often created on the primary key by default.
- Best suited for columns that are:
    - Unique
    - Ever-increasing (like **IDENTITY** or datetime)
    - Used in range queries

Example:

```
CREATE CLUSTERED INDEX IX_Orders_OrderDate
ON Orders(OrderDate);
```

Pitfall: Avoid clustered indexes on columns that frequently update, as this causes page splits and fragmentation.

Non-Clustered Indexes

To enhance query performance without changing the physical table order, SQL Server uses non-clustered indexes as secondary access paths.

- They store a copy of selected columns and a pointer back to the base table.
- They are useful for filtering, joins, and **WHERE** clauses.
- They can include additional columns via **INCLUDE** to avoid lookups.

Example:

```
CREATE NONCLUSTERED INDEX IX_Orders_Customer
ON Orders(CustomerID)
INCLUDE (OrderDate, TotalAmount);
```

This eliminates key lookups when retrieving **OrderDate** and **TotalAmount**, as well as the **CustomerID**.

Covering Indexes

For queries that access multiple columns frequently, covering indexes can provide complete results without referencing the base table, which can greatly improve performance. Therefore, you must know that:

- Covering indexes include all columns that are required by a query.
- SQL Server can satisfy the query entirely from the index without touching the base table.
- Covering indexes reduce I/O and improve performance significantly.

Example Query:

```
SELECT CustomerID, OrderDate, TotalAmount
FROM Orders
WHERE CustomerID = 101;
```

Covering Index:

```
CREATE NONCLUSTERED INDEX IX_Orders_Cover
ON Orders(CustomerID)
INCLUDE (OrderDate, TotalAmount);
```

Filtered Indexes

When queries frequently target a specific subset of rows, filtered indexes provide an efficient way to index only relevant data. You must also remember the following points about them:

- These indexes are special ones with a `WHERE` clause that only include a subset of rows.
- They save storage and maintenance cost.
- They are best used for sparse columns or filtering queries on specific values.

Example:

```
CREATE NONCLUSTERED INDEX IX_Orders_Active
ON Orders(Status)
WHERE Status = 'Active';
```

This speeds up queries that only search for active orders.

Unique Indexes

Unique indexes prevent duplicate values in a column, and also serve as an optimization tool for query performance.

- They ensure the uniqueness of column values (like constraints).
- SQL Server enforces uniqueness, besides improving performance.

Example:

```
CREATE UNIQUE NONCLUSTERED INDEX IX_Customers_Email
ON Customers(Email);
```

Index Keys and Included Columns

Understanding the distinction between key and included columns will help you design efficient indexes that balance performance and storage. Therefore, you must remember the following:

- Index key columns define the sort order and lookup path.
- Included columns are the additional columns that are stored in the leaf level of the index, but are not a part of the key.
- Keep key columns small and stable; use included columns for wide or variable data.

Index Seek vs. Index Scan

Choosing the right access method is the key to query performance, as it determines how SQL Server retrieves data from indexes. Therefore, you must understand the following differences:

- **Seek**: SQL Server navigates directly to the rows using index keys, and is highly efficient.
- **Scan**: SQL Server reads the entire index (which is similar to a full table scan), and is hence slower.

Goal: Write queries that encourage seeks, and not scans.

Index Maintenance (Rebuild and Reorganize)

Indexes become fragmented due to inserts, updates, and deletes. Therefore, you must:

- **Reorganize**: This includes lightweight defragmentation (recommended for 5-30% fragmentation).
- **Rebuild**: This involves dropping and recreating the index (use for >30% fragmentation).

Example:

```
ALTER INDEX IX_Orders_Customer
ON Orders REBUILD WITH (ONLINE = ON);
```

Indexed Views

For queries involving frequent aggregations or joins, indexed views can significantly improve performance by storing the precomputed results.

- Indexed views are materialized views with indexes that persist aggregated or joined data.
- SQL Server automatically maintains them when base tables change.
- They are useful for aggregation-heavy queries.

Example:

```
CREATE VIEW SalesSummary
WITH SCHEMABINDING
AS
SELECT CustomerID, SUM(TotalAmount) AS TotalSpent
FROM dbo.Orders
GROUP BY CustomerID;

CREATE UNIQUE CLUSTERED INDEX IX_SalesSummary
ON SalesSummary(CustomerID);
```

Partitioned Indexes

Partitioning helps manage very large tables by dividing them into smaller, more manageable pieces. This improves query performance and maintenance. These indexes are useful in the following ways:

- Large tables can be partitioned by range (for example, by year).
- Partitioned indexes allow queries to target only relevant partitions.
- They improve performance and manageability for big data scenarios.

`Columnstore` Indexes

`Columnstore` indexes optimize analytical queries by storing data in a column-oriented format, and thus enable faster aggregations and reporting.

- They store data in a columnar format instead of row format.
- They are best for analytics and reporting workloads.
- They provide massive compression and batch execution improvements.

Example:

```
CREATE CLUSTERED COLUMNSTORE INDEX IX_Sales_Columnstore
ON Sales;
```

Covering Joins with Composite Indexes

Composite (multi-column) indexes can optimize joins.

Rule of Thumb: Order columns by selectivity (put the most selective at the very first).

Example:

```
CREATE NONCLUSTERED INDEX IX_Orders_CustDate
ON Orders(CustomerID, OrderDate);
```

Negative Impacts of Indexes on Performance

While indexes improve query performance, having too many or poorly designed indexes can negatively impact overall database efficiency. Therefore, you must be aware of the following challenges you might confront while using them:

- Too many indexes slow down DML operations (**INSERT**, **UPDATE**, **DELETE**).
- Wide indexes consume disk space and memory.
- Overlapping indexes increase maintenance overhead.

Best Practices for Index Design

Proper index design ensures optimal performance while minimizing storage and maintenance overhead. Hence, you must remember the following practices:

1. Keep clustered indexes narrow, static, and unique.
2. Create non-clustered indexes on frequently searched columns.
3. Use **INCLUDE** for extra columns instead of bloating index keys.
4. Consider filtered indexes for skewed or sparse data.
5. Monitor usage with:

   ```
   SELECT *
   FROM sys.dm_db_index_usage_stats;
   ```

6. Drop unused indexes after validation.
7. Balance read and write performance.

Optimizing LIKE Queries

The **LIKE** operator can prevent index usage if it is not written carefully.

Problematic Example:

```
SELECT *
FROM Customers
WHERE LastName LIKE '%son';
```

- Here, the leading wildcard (%) prevents index seeks.

Optimized Version:

- Avoid leading % whenever possible. This is shown as follows:

  ```
  SELECT *
  FROM Customers
  WHERE LastName LIKE 'John%';
  ```

- Consider computed columns or full-text search for patterns with leading wildcards.

Using BETWEEN Efficiently

BETWEEN is generally SARGable if it is used with compatible data types.

Example:

```
SELECT *
FROM Orders
WHERE OrderDate BETWEEN '2024-01-01' AND '2024-01-31';
```

- Ensure that column and literal types match exactly (**DATE** vs **DATETIME**) to avoid implicit conversions.

IN vs. EXISTS vs. JOIN

Understanding how these predicates behave helps optimizer pick better plans. Therefore, here is a brief explanation of each of them, along with relevant tips and illustrations:

1. **IN**: It is good for small static lists.

   Example: `WHERE CustomerID IN (1,2,3)`

2. **EXISTS**: It is efficient for correlated subqueries.

   Example: `WHERE EXISTS (SELECT 1 FROM Orders o WHERE o.CustomerID = c.CustomerID)`

3. **JOIN**: Sometimes better for large sets; avoid duplicates.

Tip: *Test all three options with* **SET STATISTICS IO, TIME ON** *to see which performs best in your scenario.*

Avoiding Functions on Columns

Applying functions to columns breaks SARGability in the following manner:

```
WHERE YEAR(OrderDate) = 2024   -- Not SARGable
```

Therefore, you must rewrite:

```
WHERE OrderDate >= '2024-01-01' AND OrderDate < '2025-01-01';
```

Optimizing OR Predicates

OR predicates often prevent index seeks.

Problem:

```
WHERE Country = 'USA' OR Country = 'Canada';
```

Therefore, you can employ the following rewrite options:

- **UNION ALL**:

  ```
  SELECT * FROM Customers WHERE Country = 'USA'
  UNION ALL
  SELECT * FROM Customers WHERE Country = 'Canada';
  ```

- Use filtered indexes for highly selective conditions.

Optimizing NOT Predicates

`NOT IN` and **`NOT LIKE`** often cause scans.

Problem:

```
WHERE ProductID NOT IN (1,2,3)
```

An alternative to use instead of them is:

- Use **`LEFT JOIN/IS NULL or EXCEPT`**, as shown here:

```
SELECT ProductID
FROM Products
EXCEPT
SELECT ProductID
FROM Products
WHERE ProductID IN (1,2,3);
```

Parameter Sniffing Awareness

When queries use parameters, SQL Server may generate an execution plan based on the first parameter value, which can be suboptimal for other values. Therefore, you must be aware of the following awareness parameters:

- Parameters in predicates can lead to non-optimal plans if the values vary widely.
- Using option (**`RECOMPILE`**) or **`OPTIMIZE FOR UNKNOWN`** can mitigate performance issues.

Handling Nullable Columns in Predicates

Predicates on nullable columns may prevent index usage.

Problem:

```
WHERE PhoneNumber = '123456' OR PhoneNumber IS NULL;
```

Optimization: Split logic or use computed columns that normalize NULLs to a constant for indexing.

Using CAST and CONVERT Wisely

- Avoid casting columns inside predicates, as shown here:

  ```
  WHERE CAST(OrderID AS VARCHAR(20)) = '1001'  -- Not SARGable
  ```

- Instead, cast the literal in the following way:

  ```
  WHERE OrderID = 1001
  ```

Combining SARGable Predicates

- Multiple SARGable predicates can be combined efficiently, as shown here:

  ```
  WHERE OrderDate >= '2024-01-01'
    AND CustomerID IN (1,2,3)
  ```

- Here, each condition allows index seeks, and results in better execution plans.

Dynamic SQL for Flexible Predicate Optimization

- For queries where predicates vary, dynamic SQL can maintain SARGability.

```
DECLARE @SQL NVARCHAR(MAX) = N'SELECT * FROM Orders WHERE 1=1';

IF @StartDate IS NOT NULL
    SET @SQL += ' AND OrderDate >= @StartDate';

EXEC sp_executesql @SQL, N'@StartDate DATE', @StartDate;
```

- Using this ensures that the indexes are used even with optional filters.

Best Practices Recap

To ensure that SQL Server can efficiently use indexes and execute queries, follow these best practices:

1. Make predicates SARGable (avoid functions on columns).
2. Match data types to prevent implicit conversions.
3. Replace OR with UNION ALL for indexed columns.
4. Use filtered indexes for skewed data.
5. Test alternatives: IN vs. EXISTS vs. JOIN.
6. Avoid leading % in LIKE patterns.
7. Monitor execution plans to verify optimizer choices.

Statistics Management

In SQL Server, statistics play a central role in query optimization. The Query Optimizer uses statistics to estimate how many rows (cardinality) a query will likely process. These estimates guide the optimizer's choice of indexes, join algorithms, and overall execution strategies. If statistics are inaccurate or outdated, SQL Server may choose an inefficient execution plan, which will eventually lead to poor performance.

Hence, this section explores how statistics are created, maintained, and leveraged by SQL Server, as well as the best practices for managing them effectively.

Statistics

- **Definition**: Statistics are lightweight metadata objects that describe the distribution of values in a column (or a set of columns).
- **Components**:
  - A histogram representing value distribution
  - Density information showing data uniqueness
  - Cardinality estimates for predicting row counts

Example: If a Customers table has a column Country, statistics can tell SQL Server how many rows belong to "`USA`" compared to "`Ethiopia`" or "`Germany`".

Creating Statistics with SQL Server

Statistics can be:

1. Automatically created (when `AUTO_CREATE_STATISTICS is ON`)

   - If you query a column without existing stats, SQL Server creates one.
   - **Example**: Running **`SELECT * FROM Orders WHERE CustomerID = 101`** will create statistics on **`CustomerID`** if they do not exist.

2. Manually created (via **`CREATE STATISTICS`**)

```
CREATE STATISTICS Stat_CustomerID
ON Orders (CustomerID);
```

Auto Update Statistics

To help the SQL Server query optimizer make accurate decisions, it is important to understand how statistics work:

1. SQL Server automatically updates statistics when it detects significant data changes.
2. However, auto updates are sample-based. Therefore, they may not always reflect the true distribution of large datasets.

Example: If 1 million rows exist in Orders and you insert 500,000 new ones, auto-update may only sample 10% of rows, and can miss skewed data distribution.

Full Scan vs. Sampled Statistics

Choosing the right method for updating statistics affects query optimization and performance. Therefore, you can employ the following techniques:

- **Full Scan**: SQL Server reads all rows for statistics accurate but expensive.
- **Sampled**: SQL Server samples a subset of rows faster, but may lead to poor estimates.

```
UPDATE STATISTICS Orders(CustomerID) WITH FULLSCAN;
```

Updating Statistics Manually

You can explicitly update statistics to improve accuracy, as shown here:

```
-- Update a specific table
UPDATE STATISTICS Orders;

-- Update all tables in a database
EXEC sp_updatestats;
```

Filtered Statistics

Filtered statistics are useful for skewed data distributions.

Example: In an Orders table, 95% of rows may be "**`Shipped`**", while 5% are "**`Pending`**".

```
CREATE STATISTICS Stat_PendingOrders
ON Orders (Status)
WHERE Status = 'Pending';
```

This ensures that SQL Server has accurate estimates, specifically for rare values.

Incremental Statistics

For very large tables, updating only the necessary portions can improve efficiency and reduce overhead. Therefore, you will learn how incremental statistics can be useful in the following ways:

- They are available in partitioned tables.
- Instead of recalculating all partitions, SQL Server updates only modified partitions.
- They are great for large data warehouses with billions of rows.

```
ALTER DATABASE MyDB SET AUTO_CREATE_STATISTICS_INCREMENTAL = ON;
```

Async Statistics Updates

Understanding how SQL Server handles statistics updates helps manage query performance and predictability. Therefore, you must know about:

- **Synchronous Updates**: Here, the query waits, while the statistics are updated.
- **Asynchronous Updates**: Here, the query proceeds using old statistics, while SQL Server updates them in the background.

```
ALTER DATABASE MyDB SET AUTO_UPDATE_STATISTICS_ASYNC ON;
```

Therefore, it is best for high-throughput environments where blocking must be avoided.

Impact of Outdated Statistics

If the statistics are outdated:

- SQL Server may overestimate row counts, while choosing Nested Loops Joins for huge datasets.
- SQL Server may underestimate row counts, while choosing Hash Joins when indexes would have sufficed.

Example Scenario:

- Query plan expects 1,000 rows, but receives 1,000,000.
- Memory grants and join algorithms are inefficient.
- **Result**: Slow queries and possible **`tempdb`** spills.

Monitoring Statistics Health

It is important to track when statistics were last updated to ensure the query optimizer has accurate information for execution plans. Therefore, to monitor statistics health, you must:

- Use Dynamic Management Views (DMVs), as shown here:

```
SELECT
    OBJECT_NAME(s.object_id) AS TableName,
    c.name AS ColumnName,
    s.name AS StatsName,
    STATS_DATE(s.object_id, s.stats_id) AS LastUpdated
FROM sys.stats s
JOIN sys.stats_columns sc ON s.stats_id = sc.stats_id AND s.object_id = sc.object_id
JOIN sys.columns c ON sc.column_id = c.column_id AND sc.object_id = c.object_id
WHERE OBJECTPROPERTY(s.object_id, 'IsUserTable') = 1;
```

- Here, **`STATS_DATE`** tells when the statistics were last refreshed.
- Additionally, you must review large or frequently updated tables often.

Best Practices for Statistics Management

Properly maintained statistics help the optimizer generate accurate execution plans and improve query performance. Therefore, you must follow these best practices:

1. Keep **AUTO_CREATE_STATISTICS** and **AUTO_UPDATE_STATISTICS** enabled (default).
2. Use **FULLSCAN** updates for critical queries.
3. Add filtered statistics for skewed data.
4. Enable incremental statistics for partitioned tables.
5. Periodically run **sp_updatestats** as part of maintenance jobs.
6. Monitor execution plans, as unexpected row count estimates often indicate that statistics are outdated or stale.

Common Misconceptions

It is important to understand what SQL Server statistics do and do not do. Therefore, you must be aware of the following misconceptions:

- "*Indexes automatically keep statistics updated.*"

  This is not true, as statistics can become stale even if indexes exist.
- "*Auto-update statistics is always enough.*"

  In massive OLTP systems, manual full scans are often needed. Hence, this is not true.

Troubleshooting Poor Performance Caused by Stale Statistics

A common scenario while using stale statistics can be:

- A query runs fast in the morning, but it slows down in the evening after millions of rows are inserted.
- The execution plan still assumes the old row distribution.

Example:

```
SELECT *
FROM Sales
WHERE OrderDate >= '2025-01-01';
```

- Here, when statistics were last updated, only 10,000 rows matched this condition.
- Now, 1,000,000 rows match, but SQL Server still thinks that the cardinality is 10,000.
- The optimizer chooses a Nested Loops Join instead of a Hash Join.

Fix:

```
UPDATE STATISTICS Sales(OrderDate) WITH FULLSCAN;
```

Lesson: Always suspect that stale statistics are at play whenever query performance degrades suddenly.

Statistics and Parameter Sniffing

Statistics interact with parameter sniffing in tricky ways, which can be:

- SQL Server builds a query plan based on the first parameter value it sees.

- If the value is common, the plan might work for most queries.
- If the value is rare, it can lead to suboptimal plans.

Example:

```
CREATE PROCEDURE GetOrdersByCustomer @CustomerID INT AS
BEGIN
   SELECT * FROM Orders WHERE CustomerID = @CustomerID;
END;
```

- Here, if the first execution uses a rare customer ID (10 rows), SQL Server may optimize for a Nested Loop.
- If the next execution uses a very common customer ID (100,000 rows), the plan may be inefficient.

Solutions:

1. Use **`OPTION (RECOMPILE)`** for critical queries.
2. Create filtered statistics on **`CustomerID`**.
3. Consider query hints or plan guides only as a last resort.

Statistics in Data Warehousing

For very large tables, especially partitioned fact tables, accurate statistics require special attention because:

- Large fact tables (consisting of hundreds of rows) often rely on partitioning.
- The statistics at the table level may not accurately represent specific partitions.
- Tip: Use incremental statistics for better accuracy.

Example:

```
ALTER DATABASE DWDB SET AUTO_CREATE_STATISTICS_INCREMENTAL = ON;
```

This ensures that new partitions get updated stats without forcing a full-table scan.

Statistics and Index Maintenance

Many DBAs run index rebuilds nightly, under the assumption that it also fixes statistics. Therefore, you must be aware of the following loopholes and how to tackle them.

- Index rebuilds update statistics with a full scan, but it applies only to indexed columns.
- Non-indexed columns might still need manual updates.

Best Practice:

After index maintenance, also run:

```
EXEC sp_updatestats;
```

Using Extended Events for Statistics Monitoring

You can capture events related to statistics updates in the following manner:

```
CREATE EVENT SESSION StatsSession
ON SERVER
ADD EVENT sqlserver.auto_stats
```

```
ADD TARGET package0.ring_buffer;
ALTER EVENT SESSION StatsSession ON SERVER STATE = START;
```

This lets you monitor when and how often SQL Server triggers auto statistics updates.

Comparing Statistics Histograms

To troubleshoot query misestimates, compare histograms before and after an update, as shown here:

```
DBCC SHOW_STATISTICS ('Orders', 'Stat_CustomerID');
```

- Check if the value distribution matches the reality.
- If it does not, a full scan update is required.

Automating Statistics Maintenance

In large environments, manual updates are impractical. Therefore, you must use jobs as follows:

```
-- Example: Weekly Full Scan Stats Update
EXEC sp_MSforeachtable
   'UPDATE STATISTICS ? WITH FULLSCAN';
```

You may also use maintenance tools like Ola Hallengren's SQL Server scripts, which include both index and statistics management.

Advanced Best Practices Recap

To ensure that query plans remain accurate and performance stays optimal, follow these key practices for managing statistics:

- Always keep auto-create and auto-update ON.
- Schedule manual full scans for large/critical tables.
- Use filtered stats for skewed data.
- Use incremental stats for partitioned tables.
- Monitor histograms and `STATS_DATE()` regularly.
- Watch for parameter sniffing issues where statistics are a key factor.

Statistics Management

Statistics are one of the most critical components in SQL Server's query optimization process. The Query Optimizer relies heavily on statistics to estimate the number of rows (cardinality) that will be processed at different stages of a query. These estimates directly influence execution plan choices, such as which indexes to use, whether to perform a Nested Loop Join or a Hash Join, and whether to scan or seek into a table.

As a result, without accurate and up-to-date statistics, the optimizer may make poor decisions. This can lead to suboptimal plans, high CPU usage, excessive I/O, and slow queries.

Therefore, in this section, we will cover the fundamentals of statistics, how they are created and maintained, and the best practices for managing them to ensure stable and high-performing queries.

Statistics

- **Definition**: Statistics are lightweight objects that store data distribution information about the values in a column or index.

- **Purpose**: They help the optimizer estimate row counts for query predicates (**WHERE**, **JOIN**, **GROUP BY**, and so on).
- **Structure of Statistics**:
    1. **Header**: Features metadata about when the statistics were last updated, the number of rows sampled, and so on
    2. **Histogram**: Distribution of values in a column, divided into up to 200 steps
    3. **Density Vector**: Helps estimate the selectivity of equality predicates (for example, **WHERE ProductID = 42**)

Example:

```
DBCC SHOW_STATISTICS ('Sales.SalesOrderDetail', 'IX_ProductID')
```

This command displays the histogram and density vector for the **IX_ProductID** index, which shows how the optimizer views the distribution of data.

Types of Statistics

Statistics help the SQL Server query optimizer estimate row counts and choose efficient execution plans. Key statistics types include:

- **Index Statistics**
    - Automatically created with indexes
    - Cover all key columns in the index
- **Column Statistics**
    - Automatically created when a column is used in a predicate (if **AUTO_CREATE_STATISTICS** is **ON**)
    - Stored as hidden stats (with a system-generated name like **_WA_Sys_00000004**)
- **Multi-Column Statistics**
    - Manually created to help the optimizer understand the correlation between columns
    - **Example**: Correlation between City and State

    ```
    CREATE STATISTICS Stats_City_State
    ON Customers (City, State);
    ```

Automatic Statistics Creation

By default, SQL Server automatically creates statistics when:

- A column without existing statistics is referenced in a query predicate.
- An index is created (which also generates stats on index columns).

You can check the current database setting, as shown here:

```
SELECT name, is_auto_create_stats_on
FROM sys.databases
WHERE name = 'YourDB';
```

To tackle this, you may enable automatic stats creation, as shown here:

```
ALTER DATABASE YourDB
SET AUTO_CREATE_STATISTICS ON;
```

Updating Statistics

Over time, as data changes, statistics become stale and lose accuracy.

Therefore, here are some methods to update statistics:

1. Manually Updating:
   ```
   UPDATE STATISTICS Sales.SalesOrderDetail (IX_ProductID);
   ```
2. Updating All Statistics in a Table:
   ```
   UPDATE STATISTICS Sales.SalesOrderDetail;
   ```
3. Updating All Statistics in a Database:
   ```
   EXEC sp_updatestats;
   ```

Sampling and Full Scan

When updating statistics, SQL Server can either sample rows or scan the entire table.

- **Sampled Stats**: It is faster, but it may miss skewed data distributions.
- **Full Scan**: It is more accurate, but is more expensive.

Example with a Full Scan:

```
UPDATE STATISTICS Sales.SalesOrderDetail (IX_ProductID)
WITH FULLSCAN;
```

Automatic Statistics Updates

SQL Server automatically updates statistics when:

- About 20% of rows, or 500 rows have changed (pre-SQL Server 2016).
- For SQL Server 2016 onwards (with Trace Flag 2371, or enabled by default in newer versions), the threshold is dynamic for large tables.

Therefore, to check if auto-update is enabled:

```
SELECT name, is_auto_update_stats_on
FROM sys.databases
WHERE name = 'YourDB';
```

Hence, to enable it, you should use:

```
ALTER DATABASE YourDB
SET AUTO_UPDATE_STATISTICS ON;
```

Asynchronous Statistics Updates

SQL Server can refresh statistics either synchronously or asynchronously to balance accuracy and query performance in the following ways:

- **Synchronous**: A query waits for statistics to update before executing.
- **Asynchronous**: The query runs with old statistics while SQL Server updates stats in the background.

To enable the async stats update, you should implement the following:

```
ALTER DATABASE YourDB
SET AUTO_UPDATE_STATISTICS_ASYNC ON;
```

This setting is useful in high-traffic OLTP systems where query delays are unacceptable.

Using sys.dm_db_stats_properties

Dynamic Management Views (DMVs) help monitor statistics health in the following manner:

```
SELECT
    OBJECT_NAME(s.object_id) AS TableName,
    s.name AS StatsName,
    sp.last_updated,
    sp.rows,
    sp.rows_sampled,
    sp.modification_counter
FROM sys.stats AS s
CROSS APPLY sys.dm_db_stats_properties(s.object_id, s.stats_id) AS sp
WHERE OBJECTPROPERTY(s.object_id, 'IsUserTable') = 1;
```

Hence, this query shows when the statistics were last updated, and how many rows have changed since then.

Filtered Statistics

Filtered statistics improve estimates for skewed data distributions.

Example:

```
CREATE STATISTICS Stats_ActiveOrders
ON Sales.Orders (Status)
WHERE Status = 'Active';
```

Thus, this is highly effective when a column has skewed values (for example, 99% '**Inactive**' and 1% '**Active**').

Incremental Statistics

For partitioned tables, you can enable incremental stats so that only affected partitions are updated, instead of rescanning the entire table.

```
CREATE STATISTICS Stats_SalesDate
ON Sales.BigSalesTable (SaleDate)
WITH INCREMENTAL = ON;
```

Hence, this saves time and resources for very large tables.

Best Practices for Statistics Management

Proper statistics maintenance ensures that the SQL Server optimizer has accurate information for generating efficient execution plans. Therefore, you must be aware of the following best practices:

1. Keep **AUTO_CREATE** and **AUTO_UPDATE** statistics enabled.
2. Consider manual updates during ETL loads or heavy batch operations.

3. Use **FULLSCAN** for highly critical queries or skewed distributions.
4. Monitor the statistics age and staleness using **sys.dm_db_stats_properties**.
5. Use filtered or multi-column statistics for correlated columns.
6. Leverage incremental stats for partitioned tables.
7. Consider asynchronous updates in OLTP workloads.
8. Schedule regular statistics maintenance as part of a SQL Agent job.

Query Rewrites and Optimization Hints

Query rewriting and optimization hints are powerful tools that allow developers and DBAs to influence how SQL Server generates and executes query plans. While the query optimizer in SQL Server is highly sophisticated, there can be scenarios where rewriting queries or applying hints can drastically improve performance. Therefore, this section explores query rewrites for performance gains, the proper use of query hints, and the advanced techniques for influencing execution plans.

Importance of Query Rewrites

The SQL Server optimizer attempts to automatically find the most efficient query execution plan. However, due to data skew, outdated statistics, or query complexity, the chosen plan may not always be optimal. Therefore, rewriting queries can:

- Improve SARGability (making predicates usable by indexes).
- Reduce unnecessary computations.
- Replace suboptimal constructs (for example, **OR** vs. **UNION ALL**).
- Simplify nested subqueries.

Example: Poor Query vs. Rewritten Query

```
-- Non-SARGable Query (Function Applied to Column):
SELECT *
FROM Orders
WHERE YEAR(OrderDate) = 2024;

-- Rewritten to be SARGable:
SELECT *
FROM Orders
WHERE OrderDate >= '2024-01-01'
  AND OrderDate < '2025-01-01';
```

Here, the second query enables index usage on **OrderDate**, while the first query forces a full table scan.

Common Query Rewrite Patterns

Optimizing queries can significantly improve performance by reducing I/O, and also boost index usage, besides simplifying execution plans. Therefore, you must implement the following rewrite patterns to optimize queries:

1. **Replacing OR with UNION ALL**

   ```
   -- Slower version with OR
   SELECT * FROM Customers
   WHERE Country = 'USA' OR Country = 'Canada';
   ```

```
-- Rewritten with UNION ALL
SELECT * FROM Customers WHERE Country = 'USA'
UNION ALL
SELECT * FROM Customers WHERE Country = 'Canada';
```

Hence, this will allow SQL Server to evaluate each branch separately with index seeks.

2. **Avoiding `SELECT *`**

   Use only the required columns to reduce I/O.

   ```
   -- Inefficient:
   SELECT * FROM Sales;

   -- Efficient:
   SELECT OrderID, CustomerID, TotalAmount FROM Sales;
   ```

3. **Removing Nested Views or Subqueries**

   Flattening query layers reduces overhead.

Query Hints

Query hints are directives appended to queries that override the optimizer's default decisions. While they are powerful, hints should be used cautiously because they can "lock" a query into a suboptimal plan if the data distribution changes.

Syntax Example:

```
SELECT *
FROM Orders WITH (INDEX(OrderDate_Index))
WHERE OrderDate >= '2024-01-01';
```

Types of Query Hints

SQL Server provides several types of hints that allow you to guide the query optimizer for performance tuning or specific behavior. These can be:

1. **Join Hints:** Use them to force specific join types.

   ```
   SELECT *
   FROM Orders O
   INNER HASH JOIN Customers C
   ON O.CustomerID = C.CustomerID;
   ```

2. **Table Hints:** Use them to control how SQL Server accesses or locks a table.

   ```
   SELECT *
   FROM Orders WITH (NOLOCK);
   ```

   Note: NOLOCK *can read uncommitted/dirty data. Therefore, you must use it carefully.*

3. **Optimizer Hints:** Use them to influence plan selection.
   - **`OPTION (FORCE ORDER)`:** Preserve join order.
   - **`OPTION (LOOP JOIN)`:** Enforce loop joins.
   - **`OPTION (MAXDOP 1)`:** Restrict the degree of parallelism.

Example:

```
SELECT CustomerID, SUM(TotalAmount)
FROM Orders
GROUP BY CustomerID
OPTION (HASH GROUP, MAXDOP 2);
```

Occasions to Use Query Hints

Query hints should be applied sparingly and only in specific scenarios where the optimizer does not produce the desired plan. These occasions can be:

- When the optimizer consistently chooses a suboptimal plan
- For edge cases where statistics do not represent the actual data distribution
- To force execution consistency in critical OLTP workloads
- As a last resort after testing rewrites, statistics updates, and indexing

Risks of Query Hints

While query hints can influence execution plans, they come with potential downsides that must be carefully considered. These risks are:

- Overriding the optimizer may lead to performance degradation if the data distribution changes.
- Hardcoding hints can make queries less portable across SQL Server versions.
- Excessive hints may complicate query maintenance.

Best Practice: Always validate with SET STATISTICS IO, TIME ON and execution plans before and after applying hints.

Combining Query Rewrites with Hints

Sometimes, both rewriting and hints are necessary.

Example: Optimizing a Join

```
-- Suboptimal
SELECT *
FROM LargeOrders L
JOIN Customers C ON L.CustomerID = C.CustomerID;
```

```
-- Rewriting It with Hint:
SELECT *
FROM LargeOrders L WITH (INDEX(CustomerID_Index))
JOIN Customers C WITH (INDEX(CustomerID_PK))
ON L.CustomerID = C.CustomerID
OPTION (HASH JOIN);
```

Here, the rewrite and hints guide SQL Server toward efficient index usage, besides employing a Hash Join for large datasets.

Using Query Store for Hinting

SQL Server Query Store (introduced in SQL Server 2016) provides a mechanism for plan forcing without embedding hints in the query text. This is:

```
EXEC sp_query_store_force_plan @query_id = 123, @plan_id = 456;
```

This mechanism allows DBAs to control plan selection dynamically, and also keeps query text clean.

Practical Example: Optimizing Reporting Queries

Filtering on functions of columns can prevent SQL Server from using indexes efficiently. Consider the following example:

Original Query

```
SELECT *
FROM Sales
WHERE DATEPART(MONTH, OrderDate) = 6;
```

- This is non-SARGable, and forces a scan.

When it is optimized with rewrite:

```
SELECT *
FROM Sales
WHERE OrderDate >= '2024-06-01'
  AND OrderDate < '2024-07-01';
```

Now, we will optimize it further with hint:

```
SELECT *
FROM Sales WITH (INDEX(OrderDate_Index))
WHERE OrderDate >= '2024-06-01'
  AND OrderDate < '2024-07-01'
OPTION (RECOMPILE);
```

This ensures a fresh statistics evaluation for monthly reports.

Best Practices for Query Rewrites and Hints

To maintain high performance, always prefer query rewrites instead of forcing hints. You may also follow these best practices:

- Prefer rewrites over hints whenever possible.
- Keep queries SARGable to maximize index usage.
- Use hints sparingly, and do not forget to document the reason they were applied.
- Leverage Query Store for persistent plan control, rather than embedding hints.
- Regularly monitor queries with execution plans and DMVs.

Advanced Hint Techniques

Sometimes the optimizer may produce suboptimal plans due to parameter sniffing or row goal assumptions.

- `OPTIMIZE FOR UNKNOWN`: It is useful when parameter sniffing causes unstable performance.

```
SELECT * FROM Orders
WHERE CustomerID = @CustomerID
OPTION (OPTIMIZE FOR UNKNOWN);
```

- **`FAST N Hint`**: It prioritizes the quick retrieval of the first N rows.

```
SELECT TOP 100 *
FROM Sales
ORDER BY OrderDate DESC
OPTION (FAST 100);
```

- **`USE HINT ('DISABLE_OPTIMIZER_ROWGOAL')`**: It disables the row goal optimization when SQL Server overestimates small result sets.

Avoiding Common Performance Pitfalls

Performance pitfalls in SQL Server often arise not because of bad hardware, but due to inefficient coding practices, poor schema design, or lack of awareness about how the query optimizer works. Developers may unintentionally write queries that appear correct on surface, but execute slowly at scale. Therefore, understanding these pitfalls allows you to avoid common mistakes, besides building queries that are both correct and efficient.

Therefore, this section highlights the most frequent issues developers encounter, and also provides practical strategies to detect and resolve them.

Scalar User-Defined Functions (UDFs)

Scalar UDFs return a single value, but they are notorious performance killers because they execute row-by-row within the query.

Problem:

```
SELECT OrderID, dbo.fn_GetOrderTotal(OrderID)
FROM Sales.Orders;
```

Here, if **`fn_GetOrderTotal`** queries multiple tables, this scalar function will execute once for *each row*. This will turn a set-based query into RBAR (Row By Agonizing Row).

Solution:

- Replace scalar UDFs with inline Table-Valued Functions (iTVFs), or incorporate the logic directly into the query.
- **Example of an Inline Rewrite**:

```
CREATE FUNCTION dbo.fn_GetOrderTotal_iTVF(@OrderID INT)
RETURNS TABLE
AS
RETURN
(
   SELECT SUM(UnitPrice * Quantity) AS Total
   FROM Sales.OrderDetails
   WHERE OrderID = @OrderID
);
```

Then:

```
SELECT o.OrderID, t.Total
FROM Sales.Orders o
CROSS APPLY dbo.fn_GetOrderTotal_iTVF(o.OrderID) t;
```

Hence, this executes in a set-based fashion, and allows SQL Server to optimize in a better manner.

Implicit Conversions

Implicit conversions occur when SQL Server must convert data types to evaluate a predicate. This prevents index usage and slows down queries.

Example:

```
SELECT * FROM Customers WHERE Phone = 1234567890;
```

Therefore, if Phone is stored as **`VARCHAR(20)`** and you compare it to an **`INT`**, SQL Server will implicitly convert it. This will make the index on Phone useless.

Fix: Always match data types in predicates, as shown here:

```
SELECT * FROM Customers WHERE Phone = '1234567890';
```

Tip: *Use Extended Events or Execution Plans to detect "**`CONVERT_IMPLICIT`**" warnings.*

Non-SARGable Predicates

Non-SARGable predicates prevent index seeks and force scans.

Bad Examples:

```
WHERE YEAR(OrderDate) = 2024
WHERE LEFT(Phone, 3) = '212'
```

These require SQL Server to evaluate functions row by row.

Fix: Reformulate them to make them SARGable, as shown here:

```
WHERE OrderDate >= '2024-01-01' AND OrderDate < '2025-01-01'
WHERE Phone LIKE '212%'
```

Now indexes on **`OrderDate`** or Phone can be used.

`SELECT *` (The Silent Killer)

Selecting all columns can negatively impact performance and resource usage.

Therefore, using **`SELECT *`** retrieves unnecessary columns, bloating I/O, network bandwidth, and memory usage.

Bad Example:

```
SELECT * FROM Sales.Orders;
```

Better Example:

```
SELECT OrderID, OrderDate, CustomerID
FROM Sales.Orders;
```

Always select only the columns you need. This reduces reads, improves index coverage, and enhances maintainability.

Overusing Cursors

Cursors process rows one at a time, and should be avoided unless it is absolutely necessary to do so.

Bad Example:

```
DECLARE cur CURSOR FOR
SELECT CustomerID FROM Customers;

OPEN cur;
FETCH NEXT FROM cur INTO @CustomerID;

WHILE @@FETCH_STATUS = 0
BEGIN
   EXEC ProcessCustomer @CustomerID;
   FETCH NEXT FROM cur INTO @CustomerID;
END

CLOSE cur;
DEALLOCATE cur;
```

Fix: *Rewrite it as a set-based logic. This is shown here:*

```
INSERT INTO ProcessedCustomers (CustomerID)
SELECT CustomerID FROM Customers;
```

Additionally, if you must use cursors, prefer **FAST_FORWARD** or **READ_ONLY** options.

Nested Loops on Large Joins

Nested Loops can be efficient for small datasets, but they can be disastrous when you are joining millions of rows without proper indexes.

Detection: Execution plan shows Nested Loop Join with a high cost.

Fix:

- Add supporting indexes on join keys.
- Force a hash join or merge join (only if it is appropriate).
- Rewrite query to reduce row counts early on.

Parameter Sniffing

Parameter sniffing occurs when SQL Server caches an execution plan based on the first parameter value, which may not be optimal for subsequent values.

Example:

```
CREATE PROCEDURE GetOrdersByCustomer @CustomerID INT
AS
SELECT * FROM Sales.Orders WHERE CustomerID = @CustomerID;
```

Therefore, if the first execution runs for a customer with 100,000 orders, the plan is cached. It can be reused even for customers with just a single order.

Solutions:

- Use **OPTION (RECOMPILE)** for queries with highly variable parameters.

- Use **OPTIMIZE FOR** hints.
- Consider dynamic SQL to avoid bad cached plans.

OR Conditions and IN Clauses

Using OR in WHERE clauses can prevent SQL Server from using indexes efficiently.

Problem:

```
WHERE City = 'New York' OR City = 'Boston'
```

may prevent index usage.

Fix: Use **UNION ALL** with the following indexed predicates:

```
SELECT * FROM Customers WHERE City = 'New York'
UNION ALL
SELECT * FROM Customers WHERE City = 'Boston';
```

- Another way can be to use indexed filtered indexes.

Overly Complex Joins

Joining too many tables or overusing subqueries makes queries harder to optimize.

Therefore, here are some tips to tackle such joins:

- Break queries into CTEs or temporary tables.
- Eliminate unnecessary joins.
- Verify if each join is required for the result.

Excessive tempDB Usage

Queries that use too many temporary tables, table variables, or large sorts spill to **tempdb** can slow down performance.

Therefore, you must employ the given fixes:

- Index temporary tables.
- Use table variables cautiously (they do not have statistics by default).
- Monitor tempdb contention with DMVs.

Misuse of DISTINCT and ORDER BY

Adding **DISTINCT** or **ORDER BY** without business justification wastes CPU and memory.

Bad Example:

```
SELECT DISTINCT CustomerID FROM Sales.Orders;
```

when **CustomerID** is already unique.

To tackle this, you can:

- Remove unnecessary **DISTINCT**s.
- Only **ORDER BY** if the application truly needs sorted results.

Wide Index Keys

Defining indexes on wide keys (like `VARCHAR(200)` or multiple columns) increases storage, but it ends up reducing performance.

Therefore, you must:

- Use narrow keys.
- Consider surrogate keys like integers for joins.

Common Table Pitfalls Recap

In SQL Server, poorly written queries or overlooked design patterns can lead to slow performance, excessive I/O, and high memory usage. Hence, understanding the common pitfalls helps developers and DBAs optimize queries, ensure efficient execution plans, and maintain overall system performance. The following list highlights frequent issues and practical fixes to improve query efficiency and scalability:

- **Scalar UDFs**: Rewrite as inline logic.
- **Implicit Conversions**: Match the data types.
- **Non-SARGable Filters**: Use index-friendly predicates.
- `SELECT *`: Select only the columns that are required.
- **Avoid cursors**: Use a set-based logic.
- **Watch Joins**: Ensure that indexes support them.
- **Parameter Sniffing**: Optimize for variability.
- `TempDB`: Avoid excessive spills.
- `DISTINCT/ORDER BY`: Use only when required.

Conclusion

This chapter has provided a comprehensive guide to writing efficient and high-performing T-SQL code. You have learned how to read and interpret execution plans, identify bottlenecks, and understand the impact of operators on query performance. Indexing strategies such as clustered, non-clustered, filtered, and covering indexes were explored in detail, which provided you practical knowledge on how to design indexes that support both read and write workloads effectively.

The chapter also emphasized writing SARGable predicates, managing and updating statistics, and applying query hints judiciously. You now understand how to compare estimated and actual execution plans, use dynamic management views (DMVs) to monitor query performance, and avoid common pitfalls such as scalar functions, implicit conversions, and inefficient joins. These skills will empower you to proactively tune queries, maintain system performance, and make data-driven optimization decisions.

Furthermore, the next chapter will build on these optimization techniques by focusing on execution plans and the Query Store. You will learn how to analyze plan cache reuse, identify expensive operators, and leverage Query Store to track historical performance, as well as enforce stable plans for critical queries. Hence, this will further enhance your ability to manage SQL Server performance in production environments.

Chapter 9
Execution Plans and Query Store

Introduction

This chapter focuses on Efficient SQL Server performance, which requires a deep understanding of how queries are executed internally. Execution plans and the Query Store feature provide invaluable insights into query behavior, which enable developers and DBAs to diagnose issues, prevent regressions, and optimize queries systematically.

Therefore, in this chapter, we will explore execution plans, the plan cache, operator costs, parameter sniffing, and query recompilation. We will then dive into Query Store, a robust feature that tracks historical query performance, allows plan analysis, and even enables forcing specific plans for critical queries. Hence, by the end of it, readers will have the tools to proactively manage performance and make data-driven decisions.

Structure

In this chapter, we will cover the following topics:

- Introduction to Estimated vs. Actual Execution Plans
- Estimated vs. Actual Execution Plans
- Plan Cache and Reuse
- Operators and Cost Analysis
- Query Store Setup and Usage
- Forcing Plans and Analyzing

Introduction to Estimated vs. Actual Execution Plans

Understanding how SQL Server executes queries is essential for writing efficient and high-performing T-SQL code. Execution plans provide a visual and analytical representation of the steps the SQL Server query optimizer chooses to retrieve and process data.

Execution plans come in two primary forms: estimated and actual. The estimated execution plan predicts how SQL Server intends to execute a query based on available statistics, without actually running it. In contrast, the actual execution plan is generated after the query runs and includes real metrics such as the number of rows processed, CPU and I/O usage, as well as any operator warnings.

Hence, by comparing estimated and actual execution plans, developers and DBAs can identify discrepancies between expectations and reality, uncover hidden performance issues, and make data-driven decisions to optimize queries. Therefore, this section dives into both types of plans, and explains their generation, interpretation, advantages, and limitations, while providing the foundation for effective query tuning and performance troubleshooting.

Estimated vs. Actual Execution Plans

Execution plans are a cornerstone of SQL Server performance analysis. They provide insight into how SQL Server retrieves and processes data for a given query. Hence, understanding the difference between estimated and actual execution plans is critical for diagnosing bottlenecks, optimizing queries, and ensuring efficient use of system resources.

Execution Plans

Execution plans are the roadmap SQL Server uses to execute a query. Each plan is a tree of operators that perform specific tasks, such as scans, seeks, joins, sorts, and aggregations. Operators are connected in a flow that shows how data moves from source tables to the query output.

Execution plans allow you to:

- Identify expensive operations.
- Detect missing indexes or statistics.
- Understand how joins and filters are processed.
- Determine why a query may be slower than expected.

Execution plans come in two main types: estimated and actual. These are explained in detail in the following sections.

Estimated Execution Plans

Estimated execution plans are predictions made by the SQL Server query optimizer without executing the query. They rely on statistics about the data distribution in tables and indexes.

Key Features:

- They show predicted row counts, costs, and operator sequence.
- They are generated instantly, no impact on database performance.
- They are useful for preliminary analysis of complex queries.

How to Generate in SSMS:

1. Open a new query window.
2. Click on Display Estimated Execution Plan (Ctrl + L).
3. View the graphical plan with operators, row estimates, and cost percentages.

Example:

```
SELECT *
FROM Orders
WHERE CustomerID = 123;
```

- An estimated plan shows an Index Seek on **`CustomerID`**.
- Estimated Rows: 10 (Based on Statistics)

Advantages:

- Quick to generate
- Safe for production systems, as the query is not executed

Limitations:

- Row estimates may be inaccurate if statistics are outdated.
- It does not reveal actual execution issues like memory spills or parallelism effects.

Actual Execution Plans

Actual execution plans are generated after a query executes and include real runtime metrics. They show the actual number of rows processed by each operator, as well as any warnings encountered during execution.

Key Features:

- Actual Row Counts
- CPU, IO, and Memory Usage per Operator
- Operator Warnings (for example, Key Lookup, Sort Spill, Missing Stats)
- True Cost of Each Operation

How to Generate in SSMS:

1. Open a new query window.
2. Click Include Actual Execution Plan (Ctrl + M).
3. Execute the query.
4. Examine the Execution Plan tab for runtime metrics.

Example:

```
SELECT *
FROM Orders
WHERE OrderDate >= '2024-01-01';
```

- An actual plan may reveal the following:
  - Clustered Index Scan instead of Index Seek due to non-SARGable predicate
  - Key Lookup for columns is not included in the index.
  - Actual Rows: 5,000 (different from estimated 1,000)

Key Differences between Estimated and Actual Plans

Understanding the difference between estimated and actual execution plans is essential for diagnosing query performance, and identifying potential optimization opportunities. Therefore, you must have a look at the table here to get an idea about it:

Feature	Estimated Plan	Actual Plan
Execution	Not executed	Executed
Row Counts	Predicted	Actual
Operator Costs	Estimated	Actual
Operator Warnings	Not shown	Shown (tempdb spills, missing stats)
Use Cases	Query design, preliminary analysis	Performance tuning, diagnosis

Table 9.1: *Estimated vs. Actual Execution Plans*

Insight: Comparing estimated and actual plans highlights cardinality estimation issues, besides helping pinpoint the operators that might need optimization.

Comparing Execution Plans in SQL Server

Execution plans show how SQL Server executes a query. Comparing plans helps identify performance regressions, inefficient operators, or optimizer changes.

1. **Compare Estimated Execution Plans.**

   It is used before execution to understand how SQL Server *intends* to run a query.

   ```
   SET SHOWPLAN_XML ON;
   GO
   -- Your query here
   SET SHOWPLAN_XML OFF;
   GO
   ```

   Therefore, you must use it while:

   - Analyzing query logic
   - Testing changes without executing the query

2. **Compare Actual Execution Plans.**

   This includes runtime statistics such as actual rows, I/O, and CPU.

   ```
   SET STATISTICS PROFILE ON;
   -- or
   SET STATISTICS XML ON;
   ```

   Therefore, you must use it while:

   - Diagnosing slow queries
   - Comparing estimated and actual row counts

3. **Key Plan Differences**

   When comparing two execution plans, focus on:

   - Index Usage (Seek vs. Scan)
   - Join Operators (Nested Loops, Hash Match, and Merge Join)
   - Estimated vs. Actual Rows
   - Costly Operators (that claim high percentage of the total cost)
   - Warnings (Implicit Conversions, Spills, Missing Indexes)

Forcing a Specific Execution Plan

SQL Server allows you to force a known good plan when the optimizer chooses a suboptimal one.

Option 1: Query Store (Recommended)

Step 1: Enable Query Store.

```
ALTER DATABASE YourDatabase
SET QUERY_STORE = ON;
```

Step 2: Identify the Query and Plans.

```
SELECT q.query_id, p.plan_id, p.is_forced_plan
FROM sys.query_store_query q
JOIN sys.query_store_plan p
  ON q.query_id = p.query_id;
```

Step 3: Force the Desired Plan.

```
EXEC sys.sp_query_store_force_plan
     @query_id = 10,
     @plan_id  = 25;
```

Step 4: Verify Forced Plan.

```
SELECT plan_id, is_forced_plan
FROM sys.query_store_plan
WHERE query_id = 10;
```

Hence, this is best for:

- Production systems
- Preventing performance regressions after upgrades or parameter sniffing issues

Option 2: Use Query Hints (Use with Caution).

Example: Force a specific join or index.

```
SELECT *
FROM Sales.SalesOrderHeader
WITH (INDEX(IX_OrderDate))
OPTION (HASH JOIN);
```

Limitations:

- Is hard-coded
- Can break as data changes
- Not recommended for long-term fixes

Option 3: Plan Guides (Advanced/Legacy).

These are used when you cannot modify the query text.

```
EXEC sp_create_plan_guide
     @name = N'ForceIndexGuide',
     @stmt = N'SELECT ...',
     @type = N'SQL',
     @hints = N'OPTION (HASH JOIN)';
```

Therefore, you should use them only when the Query Store is not available.

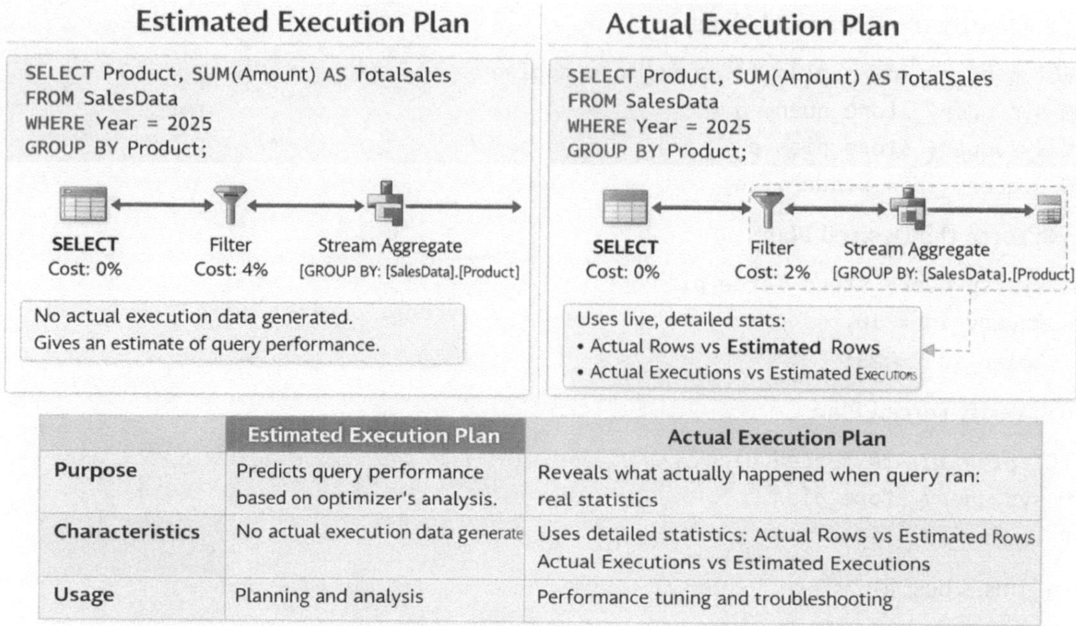

	Estimated Execution Plan	Actual Execution Plan
Purpose	Predicts query performance based on optimizer's analysis.	Reveals what actually happened when query ran: real statistics
Characteristics	No actual execution data generate	Uses detailed statistics: Actual Rows vs Estimated Rows Actual Executions vs Estimated Executions
Usage	Planning and analysis	Performance tuning and troubleshooting

Figure 9.1: *Estimated and Actual Execution Plan*

Interpreting Operator Costs

Execution plans in SQL Server provide a roadmap of how queries are executed and where resources are consumed. Each operator in a plan contributes a relative cost percentage, which helps developers and DBAs identify performance bottlenecks, as well as optimize queries effectively. Therefore, by analyzing these operators, you can focus your tuning efforts on the areas that will yield the most significant performance gains.

- Each operator in a plan shows a relative cost percentage
- Focus on operators with highest cost first
- **Example operators**:
    - **Index Seek/Scan**: Retrieval Efficiency
    - **Nested Loop/Hash/Merge Join**: Join Strategy Cost
    - **Sort/Aggregate**: Memory and CPU Usage

Tip: *High-cost operators that exist in the actual plan, but are low in the estimated plan indicate a wrong estimation by the optimizer.*

Common Pitfalls in Estimated Plans

SQL Server generates an estimated execution plan based on statistics and heuristics, as it predicts how many rows each operator will process. However, the actual execution plan reflects the true number of rows processed during query execution. Therefore, discrepancies between estimated and actual plans can indicate potential performance issues that need attention.

- **Stale Statistics**: SQL Server relies on outdated data distribution information.
- **Non-SARGable Predicates**: Functions on columns can force scans that are not predicted in estimated plan.
- **Skewed Data Distribution**: Highly uneven data can cause estimated rows to differ dramatically from actual rows.

- **Parameter Sniffing**: Estimated plan may be optimized for first parameter only.

Solution: Always verify estimated plans against actual plans to ensure accuracy.

Practical Tips

Understanding both estimated and actual execution plans is essential for effective SQL Server performance tuning. Estimated plans provide a quick prediction without executing the query, while actual plans show real runtime behavior. Therefore, comparing them helps identify discrepancies, and also optimize queries.

- **Use Estimated Plan**: For safe, fast query design checks.
- **Use Actual Plan**: When diagnosing slow queries or investigating unexpected operator costs.
- **Compare Plans**: Identify misestimations, missing indexes, or suboptimal joins.
- **Check Warnings**: Look for yellow triangles in SSMS execution plans to detect issues like `tempdb` spills.
- **Monitor Row Estimates**: Large differences between estimated and actual rows often indicate performance problems.

Advanced Considerations

To fully understand query performance, it's important to complement execution plans with actual resource metrics and advanced plan analysis.

- **`SET STATISTICS IO`, `TIME ON`**: Measure actual resource usage alongside execution plan.
- **Execution Plan XML**: Use XML plan for programmatic analysis and automation.
- **Plan Freezing**: Combine plan analysis with Query Store to prevent regressions.
- **Multiple Parameter Scenarios**: Verify plan performance across a range of parameter values.

Using Actual Execution Plans for Real Metrics

While the estimated execution plan predicts how SQL Server intends to execute a query, the actual execution plan provides real execution metrics such as:

- **Actual Rows vs. Estimated Rows**: Highlights cardinality estimation issues
- **I/O Statistics**: Logical and physical reads per operator
- **CPU Time**: Resource usage per operator

Example:

```
SET STATISTICS IO ON;
SET STATISTICS TIME ON;

SELECT *
FROM Orders
WHERE OrderDate >= '2025-01-01';

SET STATISTICS IO OFF;
SET STATISTICS TIME OFF;
```

- Compare actual row counts with estimated counts in the execution plan to identify performance discrepancies.

Identifying Cardinality Estimation Issues

A major reason queries perform poorly is misestimated rows. These can manifest in two variants, which are:

- **Underestimation**: Leads to insufficient memory grants, which can spill to tempdb.
- **Overestimation**: May cause overly cautious execution plans with unnecessary sorts or scans.

Tip: *Look for warning indicators in the actual plan like yellow triangles near the operators.*

Comparing Estimated and Actual Plans

Analyzing both estimated and actual execution plans helps identify discrepancies that can affect query performance. Hence, you can do the following:

- **Right-Click a Query in SSMS**: Display Estimated Execution Plan vs. Include Actual Execution Plan.
- Analyze the differences as follows:
    - Operators Used (Seek vs. Scan, and Join Type Changes)
    - Row Counts (Estimated vs. Actual)
    - Resource Usage per Operator

Example Scenario: A query estimated 100 rows from an index seek, but actually returned 10,000 rows likely needs updated statistics or improved indexing.

Key Operators and Their Costs

When comparing plans, pay attention to:

- **Index Seek/Scan**: Efficiency of Data Retrieval
- **Nested Loop/Hash/Merge Joins**: Optimal Join Strategies
- **Sorts and Spools**: Memory and I/O Consumption

Another important thing to remember is that high-cost operators in actual plans indicate potential areas for optimization.

Using Plan XML for Deep Analysis

For advanced analysis and automation, execution plans can be exported in XML format, as they allow for programmatic inspection and comparison across environments.

- Execution plans can be exported as XML for programmatic analysis.
- **Example**:

```
SELECT query_plan
FROM sys.dm_exec_query_stats AS qs
CROSS APPLY sys.dm_exec_query_plan(qs.plan_handle);
```

- They are useful for automation, or for comparing plans across environments.

Detecting Parameter Sniffing Issues

When queries run with different parameter values, the optimizer may generate vastly different execution plans. This may cause inconsistent performance due to parameter sniffing at some points.

- Compare actual plans with different parameter values.
- If the optimizer chooses very different plans for similar queries, parameter sniffing might have been occurring.
- Here are some mitigation strategies:
    - Use `OPTION (RECOMPILE)`.
    - Use `OPTIMIZE FOR UNKNOWN`.
    - Consider forcing plans in Query Store.

Using Execution Plan Warnings

Execution plans in SSMS may display yellow triangles, which indicate potential performance issues that need attention.

- Yellow triangles indicate warnings, such as:
    - Missing Statistics
    - Implicit Conversions
    - Memory Spills
- Therefore, you must address these to improve performance, and also align estimated plans closer to actual performance.

Best Practices for Execution Plan Analysis

Understanding query performance requires comparing estimated and actual execution plans to identify inefficiencies and wrong estimations. Therefore, you must implement the following best practices for execution plan analysis:

1. Always compare estimated and actual to understand discrepancies.
2. Focus on high-cost operators for optimization.
3. Check row counts and estimates to identify cardinality issues.
4. Use plan XML for automated analysis or tracking in DevOps pipelines.
5. Combine plan analysis with Query Store metrics for long-term monitoring.

Plan Cache and Reuse

Efficient query execution in SQL Server depends not only on well-written T-SQL, but also on how the execution plans are managed. The plan cache is a memory area where SQL Server stores compiled query execution plans for reuse. Therefore, understanding how plan caching works, when plans are reused, and when new plans are compiled is crucial for optimizing query performance, minimizing CPU overhead, and avoiding performance regressions.

Plan Cache

The plan cache is a portion of SQL Server's memory that is dedicated to storing compiled query plans. When a query is executed, SQL Server first checks the cache to see if a reusable plan already exists. If it does, SQL Server skips compilation, and then executes the cached plan. If not, a new plan is compiled and stored.

Benefits of Plan Caching:

- Reduces CPU usage by avoiding repeated compilation

- Speeds up query execution for frequently run queries
- Enables reuse of parameterized queries

Example Scenario:

```
-- Query executed multiple times
SELECT * FROM Orders WHERE CustomerID = 123;
```

- **First Execution**: The plan is compiled and stored in cache.
- **Subsequent Executions**: The cached plan is reused, which saves compilation time.

Plan Cache Structure

SQL Server organizes cached plans into several categories, which are:

1. **Ad Hoc Queries**: Single-use queries stored individually
2. **Prepared Statements**: Parameterized queries that use **`sp_executesql`**
3. **Stored Procedures**: Compiled plans for procedure execution
4. **Triggers and Functions**: Cached plans for reusable code objects

DMVs for Monitoring:

```
-- View cached plans
SELECT cp.objtype, cp.usecounts, qs.total_worker_time, qs.execution_count
FROM sys.dm_exec_cached_plans AS cp
CROSS APPLY sys.dm_exec_query_stats(cp.plan_handle) AS qs;
```

- **`usecounts`**: Indicates the number of times the plan has been reused
- **`total_worker_time`**: Indicates the cumulative CPU time used by the plan

Plan Reuse Mechanics

Understanding how SQL Server reuses execution plans helps you optimize query performance and reduce compilation overhead.

1. SQL Server normalizes the query (removes literals, applies parameterization).
2. It checks if an existing plan in cache matches the normalized query.
3. If a match is found, the plan is reused.
4. If no match is found, a new plan is compiled, and then stored.

Example with Parameterized Queries:

```
DECLARE @CustomerID INT = 123;
EXEC sp_executesql N'SELECT * FROM Orders WHERE CustomerID = @CustomerID', N'@
CustomerID INT', @CustomerID;
```

- Plan can be reused for different **`@CustomerID`** values.
- Mechanics avoid recompilation for each parameter variation.

Factors That Prevent Plan Reuse

Certain scenarios prevent SQL Server from reusing plans:

1. **Literal Values instead of Parameters**

```
-- Not reusable
SELECT * FROM Orders WHERE CustomerID = 123;
SELECT * FROM Orders WHERE CustomerID = 456;
```

- It creates separate plans for each literal value.

2. **Schema Changes**: Adding/removing columns or indexes invalidates plans.
3. **Statistics Updates**: Significant data changes can force recompilation.
4. **`OPTION (RECOMPILE)`**: Forces new plan generation at every execution.
5. **Temporary Tables**: Reuse may be limited if the table structure changes between executions.

Tip: *Use parameterization and **`sp_executesql`** to maximize plan reuse.*

Plan Cache Eviction

SQL Server may remove plans from cache when:

- Memory pressure occurs.
- Plans are unused for a long time.
- Database objects that are referenced by the plan are dropped or altered.

Monitoring Evictions:

```
SELECT TOP 50 *
FROM sys.dm_exec_cached_plans
ORDER BY usecounts ASC;
```

- Low **`usecounts`** can indicate that plans are not reused, or are evicted.

Parameter Sniffing and Plan Reuse

Parameter sniffing occurs when SQL Server compiles a plan using the first parameter value it sees. This can cause performance issues if the subsequent parameters are very different.

Example:

```
CREATE PROCEDURE GetOrdersByCustomer @CustomerID INT
AS
SELECT * FROM Orders WHERE CustomerID = @CustomerID;
```

- **First Execution**: **`CustomerID = 1`** → The plan is optimized for 1 order.
- **Later Execution**: **`CustomerID = 1,000`** → The plan may perform poorly.

Mitigation Strategies:

- Use **`OPTION (RECOMPILE)`** for volatile parameters.
- Use **`OPTIMIZE FOR UNKNOWN`** hint to generate neutral plans.
- Monitor plan reuse in DMVs for suboptimal performance.

Monitoring Plan Cache

Use Dynamic Management Views (DMVs) to monitor plan cache health and identify potential inefficiencies:

Common DMVs:

- **`sys.dm_exec_cached_plans`**: This reflects the cached plan metadata.

- **sys.dm_exec_query_stats**: This reflects the execution metrics for cached plans.
- **sys.dm_exec_sql_text(plan_handle)**: This retrieves SQL text from the plan handle.

Example Query:

```
SELECT TOP 20
    cp.cacheobjtype,
    cp.objtype,
    cp.usecounts,
    qs.total_worker_time,
    qs.total_elapsed_time,
    st.text AS sql_text
FROM sys.dm_exec_cached_plans AS cp
CROSS APPLY sys.dm_exec_query_stats(cp.plan_handle) AS qs
CROSS APPLY sys.dm_exec_sql_text(cp.plan_handle) AS st
ORDER BY cp.usecounts DESC;
```

Best Practices for Plan Reuse

Efficient query execution relies on plan reuse, which reduces CPU overhead and improves performance. Parameterization and careful plan management help SQL Server generate stable and reusable execution plans.

- **Parameterize Queries:** Always use parameters instead of literals to maximize plan reuse.

  ```
  DECLARE @CustomerID INT = 123;
  EXEC sp_executesql N'SELECT * FROM Orders WHERE CustomerID = @CustomerID', N'@
  CustomerID INT', @CustomerID;
  ```

- **Use sp_executesql for Dynamic Queries:** It allows passing parameters safely, and increases the chance of plan reuse.
- **Avoid Unnecessary Recompilation**: Use **OPTION (RECOMPILE)** only when needed, as frequent recompilations waste CPU.
- **Monitor Plan Cache Health**: Use DMVs like **sys.dm_exec_cached_plans** and **sys.dm_exec_query_stats** to monitor frequently compiled queries and memory usage.
- **Force Plan Reuse Strategically**: Use Query Store or plan guides to force stable plans for critical queries, if needed.
- **Reduce Ad Hoc Queries**: Excessive ad hoc queries can fragment plan cache. Consider using prepared statements or stored procedures.

Identifying Plan Reuse Issues

Understanding plan cache behavior helps identify inefficiencies in query execution and memory usage. High compilation rates, parameter sniffing, and ad hoc queries can all degrade performance if they are not managed properly.

- **High Compilation Rate**:

  ```
  SELECT objtype, usecounts, cacheobjtype
  FROM sys.dm_exec_cached_plans
  WHERE usecounts = 1;
  ```

  - It indicates rarely reused plans, and it may suggest excessive ad hoc queries.

- **Parameter Sniffing Problems**:
  - It occurs when a query performs well for initial parameter, but poorly for others.
  - Use **`OPTION (RECOMPILE)`** or **`OPTIMIZE FOR UNKNOWN`** to mitigate.
- **Inefficient Ad Hoc Queries**:
  - Queries with literals create multiple cached plans.
  - Convert to parameterized queries to reduce cache bloat.

Monitoring Plan Cache with DMVs

Dynamic Management Views provide insights into plan cache efficiency.

Example Query:

```
SELECT TOP 10
    cp.objtype,
    cp.usecounts,
    qs.execution_count,
    qs.total_worker_time,
    st.text AS sql_text
FROM sys.dm_exec_cached_plans AS cp
CROSS APPLY sys.dm_exec_query_stats(cp.plan_handle) AS qs
CROSS APPLY sys.dm_exec_sql_text(cp.plan_handle) AS st
ORDER BY cp.usecounts DESC;
```

- **`usecounts`**: Number of times the plan is reused
- **`execution_count`**: How often the query was executed
- **`total_worker_time`**: Total CPU consumed by this plan

Tip: *Focus optimization on queries with high execution count and high resource consumption.*

Handling Parameter Sniffing

Parameter sniffing happens when SQL Server creates an execution plan using the first supplied parameter value. While this plan may be optimal for that value, it can perform poorly for subsequent executions with different parameters.

- Parameter sniffing occurs when SQL Server generates a plan based on the first parameter value. As a result, the subsequent executions may perform poorly. Therefore, here are the mitigation strategies you can use to tackle them:
  1. **`OPTION (RECOMPILE)`**: Forces plan recompilation for each execution
  2. **`OPTIMIZE FOR UNKNOWN`**: Generates a plan suitable for generic parameters
  3. **`Dynamic SQL`**: Allows plan generation specific to parameter values

Example:

```
CREATE PROCEDURE GetOrdersByCustomer @CustomerID INT
AS
SELECT *
FROM Orders
WHERE CustomerID = @CustomerID
OPTION (OPTIMIZE FOR UNKNOWN);
```

Clearing Plan Cache

In certain troubleshooting or testing scenarios, it may be necessary to clear cached execution plans to force recompilation. This helps verify the impact of statistics, indexes, or query changes.

- Sometimes, it may be necessary to clear the plan cache for troubleshooting.

  Commands:

```
-- Clear entire plan cache (use with caution).
DBCC FREEPROCCACHE;

-- Clear cache for a single database.
ALTER DATABASE SCOPED CONFIGURATION CLEAR PROCEDURE CACHE;
```

Warning: Clearing the cache can temporarily degrade performance, as plans must be recompiled.

Monitoring Compilation and Recompilation Events

Frequent query recompilations can degrade performance, as they are often caused by schema changes, statistics updates, or hints. Hence, monitoring these events helps identify queries that put unnecessary CPU pressure on the server. Here are some strategies you can use to monitor them:

- Use Extended Events or SQL Trace to track compilation activity.
- Identify queries that frequently trigger recompilation due to schema changes, statistics updates, or hints.

Example Extended Event Query:

```
SELECT *
FROM sys.dm_xe_session_targets AS t
JOIN sys.dm_xe_sessions AS s ON t.event_session_address = s.address;
```

- Helps identify top queries that are causing CPU pressure due to recompilations.

Using Query Store for Plan Analysis

Query Store helps track plan reuse, detect regressions, and analyze historical execution statistics. It provides insights into plan changes, resource usage, and execution patterns, which makes it easier to maintain stable performance.

- Query Store can help analyze plan reuse and detect plan regressions.
- It captures historical execution statistics, including plan changes and resource usage.

Example:

```
SELECT qs.query_id, qs.plan_id, rs.avg_duration, rs.execution_count
FROM sys.query_store_query AS qs
JOIN sys.query_store_runtime_stats AS rs ON qs.query_id = rs.query_id;
```

- Identify high-cost queries, and also enforce plan stability, if needed.

Best Practices Recap for Plan Cache

Efficient plan reuse reduces CPU overhead and improves query performance. Therefore, following these practices helps maintain stable execution plans, and also minimizes unnecessary recompilations. These practices are:

1. Parameterize queries to maximize reuse.
2. Monitor plan cache health regularly.
3. Avoid excessive ad hoc queries.
4. Mitigate parameter sniffing with hints or dynamic SQL.
5. Use Query Store to detect plan regressions.
6. Force plans only when it is absolutely necessary.
7. Update statistics and indexes to reduce recompilation.

Best Practices for Plan Reuse

SQL Server performance benefits greatly when execution plans are reused effectively. Poorly managed queries or excessive ad hoc workloads can cause cache bloat and CPU overhead. Therefore, following these practices helps maintain a healthy and efficient plan cache:

1. Parameterize queries instead of using literals.
2. Use **`sp_executesql`** for dynamic queries.
3. Avoid unnecessary recompilations unless they are needed for correctness.
4. Monitor plan cache for high memory usage, or frequent recompilations.
5. Force plan reuse when beneficial using Query Store or plan guides.
6. Avoid excessive ad hoc queries; hence, consider prepared statements for repeated patterns.

Troubleshooting Plan Reuse Issues

Ensuring that SQL Server is reusing execution plans efficiently is crucial for reducing compilation overhead, as well as maintaining stable performance. Regular monitoring helps detect problems like excessive compilations or parameter sniffing issues before they degrade system efficiency. Therefore, you must:

- Check execution plan reuse count via **`usecounts`**.
- Investigate high compilation rates using **`sys.dm_exec_query_stats`**.
- Compare estimated and actual execution plans for frequently executed queries.
- Identify queries with parameter sniffing problems, and apply appropriate hints or dynamic SQL.

Identifying High-Frequency Ad Hoc Queries

High-frequency ad hoc queries can fragment the plan cache, reducing efficiency. Therefore, you must use the following DMV query to identify them:

```
SELECT TOP 10
    st.text AS sql_text,
    qs.execution_count,
    cp.usecounts,
    qs.total_worker_time
FROM sys.dm_exec_query_stats AS qs
CROSS APPLY sys.dm_exec_sql_text(qs.sql_handle) AS st
JOIN sys.dm_exec_cached_plans AS cp ON qs.plan_handle = cp.plan_handle
WHERE cp.objtype = 'Adhoc'
ORDER BY qs.execution_count DESC;
```

Action: Convert frequently executed ad hoc queries to parameterized queries or stored procedures to improve plan reuse.

Dealing with Ad Hoc Plan Cache Bloat

When SQL Server compiles too many single-use plans, the plan cache can become bloated. This will cause it to consume memory, and also reduce overall performance. Therefore, to address this, SQL Server provides the Optimize for Ad hoc Workloads option, which helps reduce cache pressure by storing only the lightweight stubs for first-time queries.

- SQL Server can run out of memory if too many single-use plans occupy the cache.
- Therefore, you must enable the "Optimize for Ad hoc Workloads" option to store only the plan stubs initially, as shown here:

  ```
  EXEC sp_configure 'show advanced options', 1;
  RECONFIGURE;
  EXEC sp_configure 'optimize for ad hoc workloads', 1;
  RECONFIGURE;
  ```

- This only fully compiles plans that are executed multiple times, and reduces cache pressure.

Monitoring Parameterized Query Reuse

Parameterized queries are essential for increasing plan reuse, and reducing compilation overhead. Therefore, by tracking query execution statistics in SQL Server, you can identify queries that execute frequently, but fail to reuse cached plans effectively.

- Parameterized queries increase plan reuse.
- Use **sys.dm_exec_query_stats** and **sys.dm_exec_cached_plans** to track reuse, as shown here:

  ```
  SELECT qs.execution_count, cp.usecounts, st.text AS query_text
  FROM sys.dm_exec_query_stats AS qs
  CROSS APPLY sys.dm_exec_sql_text(qs.sql_handle) AS st
  JOIN sys.dm_exec_cached_plans AS cp ON qs.plan_handle = cp.plan_handle
  WHERE cp.objtype = 'Prepared';
  ```

- Focus optimization on queries with high execution count, but low **usecounts** that indicate poor plan reuse.

Detecting Plan Eviction Issues

When SQL Server experiences low-memory pressure or frequent recompilations, cached plans may be evicted prematurely, and will lead to unnecessary recompilation overhead, as well as reflect degraded performance. Hence, monitoring and mitigating these evictions helps maintain stable query performance.

- Low-memory pressure or frequent recompilations can evict cached plans prematurely.
- Track plan eviction events using Extended Events or Performance Monitor counters, as shown here:

  ```
  SELECT *
  FROM sys.dm_os_memory_cache_counters
  WHERE type = 'CACHESTORE_SQLCP';
  ```

- **Solutions**: Increase memory for SQL Server, optimize ad hoc queries, or adjust the workload patterns.

Addressing Parameter Sniffing via Plan Reuse

Parameter sniffing occurs when SQL Server generates a query plan optimized for the first parameter value it encounters. While efficient for some inputs, this plan may perform poorly for others, especially when data distributions vary widely. Therefore, recognizing and mitigating parameter sniffing is essential for consistent query performance.

- Parameter sniffing occurs when a plan optimized for one parameter performs poorly for others.
- Therefore, here are some relevant mitigation techniques to tackle it:
    1. Use `OPTION (RECOMPILE)` for queries with highly variable parameters.
    2. Use `OPTIMIZE FOR UNKNOWN` to generate a generic plan.
    3. Force stable plans using Query Store, if necessary.

Using Query Store to Analyze Plan Reuse

SQL Server's Query Store provides valuable insight into execution plan behavior by capturing performance metrics over time. Hence, by analyzing execution counts and durations, you can identify queries that run frequently but consume excessive resources. This will help you to prioritize optimization efforts.

- Query Store captures execution count per plan over time, which allows you to monitor plan reuse trends.
- **Example DMV Query**:

```
SELECT qs.query_id, p.plan_id, rs.execution_count, rs.avg_duration
FROM sys.query_store_plan AS p
JOIN sys.query_store_runtime_stats AS rs ON p.plan_id = rs.plan_id
JOIN sys.query_store_query AS qs ON p.query_id = qs.query_id
ORDER BY rs.execution_count DESC;
```

- Focus on plans with high execution counts and high duration for optimization.

Best Practices for Plan Cache Management

Consistent plan reuse is critical for stable and efficient SQL Server performance. Hence, by parameterizing queries, reducing ad hoc compilations, and leveraging Query Store, you can minimize CPU overhead, reduce memory bloat, and ensure predictable query execution.

1. Parameterize queries wherever possible to maximize reuse.
2. Convert high-frequency ad hoc queries into stored procedures.
3. Monitor cache usage via DMVs and extended events.
4. Enable '`Optimize`' for ad hoc workloads to reduce memory bloat.
5. Update statistics regularly to maintain plan stability.
6. Use the Query Store to analyze plan performance and enforce optimal plans.
7. Address parameter sniffing proactively by using hints or plan forcing.

Operators and Cost Analysis

Execution plans in SQL Server are composed of operators the individual steps SQL Server takes to retrieve, join, filter, and aggregate data. Therefore, understanding these operators, their relative costs, and how they interact is critical for identifying performance bottlenecks, as well as for optimizing queries effectively.

Hence, this section explains the most common operators, their cost implications, and strategies for reducing their impact on query performance.

Understanding Execution Plan Operators

Operators represent the building blocks of a query execution plan. Each operator performs a specific action on data, such as reading from a table, filtering rows, or joining datasets. Therefore, operators can be broadly categorized as:

- **Data Access Operators**: They retrieve data from tables or indexes.
- **Join Operators**: They combine rows from two or more sources.
- **Aggregate and Compute Operators**: They perform calculations or summarizations.
- **Flow Control Operators**: They manage the order of data processing, such as sort or filter operators.
- **Parallelism Operators**: They manage execution across multiple threads for large datasets.

Data Access Operators

Understanding how SQL Server retrieves data is essential for query performance tuning. This is because the type of access, whether it is seek or scan, directly impacts I/O and CPU usage.

Index Seek

- Efficient retrieval using an index to locate specific rows
- Uses a range or exact match predicate
- **Example**:

  ```
  SELECT * FROM Orders WHERE OrderID = 1001;
  ```

- Ideal for selective queries with indexed columns

Index Scan

- Reads all rows in an index
- Less efficient for large tables if only a few rows are needed
- Can be caused by non-SARGable queries (for example, **`WHERE YEAR(OrderDate) = 2024`**)

Table Scan

- Reads all rows in a heap table
- Usually less efficient than an index scan
- Acceptable for small tables but should be avoided for large datasets

Join Operators

SQL Server uses different join strategies depending on table size, indexing, and query predicates. Therefore, choosing the right join method can significantly impact performance.

Nested Loop Join

- Executes an inner loop over one table for each row of the outer table
- Efficient for small datasets but can become slow for large tables
- **Optimization Tip**: Ensure that indexes exist on join keys.

Hash Join

- Builds a hash table from one input, and then probes it for matching rows from the other input
- Efficient for large, unsorted datasets
- It can be memory-intensive; it may spill to `tempdb` if there is insufficient memory.

Merge Join

- Requires sorted input (often via indexes)
- Efficient for pre-sorted datasets
- Can outperform hash joins if tables are already indexed and sorted

Aggregate and Compute Operators

These operators perform row ordering, calculations, and per-row computations. Therefore, understanding their behavior helps identify potential performance bottlenecks.

Sort

- Orders rows based on one or more columns
- Can consume memory; spills to `tempdb` if memory is insufficient
- Use indexed ordering where possible to avoid unnecessary sorts.

Aggregate

- Performs calculations like SUM, COUNT, AVG
- Can be optimized by pre-aggregating data, or using indexed views

Compute Scalar

- Performs scalar computations on each row
- Is usually low cost, but can accumulate if applied to large datasets

Flow Control Operators

Flow control operators manage how data moves and is processed within a query execution plan.

Filter: Filters remove rows that do not meet specific conditions.

- Applies `WHERE` clause predicates to remove rows
- Inefficient filters can cause scans instead of seeks.
- **Optimization Tip**: Ensure that predicates are SARGable (for example, avoid functions on columns).

Top/Row Number

- Used for limiting results or ranking
- Can be combined with indexes to improve efficiency

Spool Operators

- Temporarily stores intermediate results

- Types: Table Spool, Index Spool, and Eager Spool
- Can improve performance by reusing results, but may increase memory usage

Parallelism Operators

Parallelism operators distribute work across multiple threads to speed up queries.

- **Distribute Streams**: Split data across threads
- **Gather Streams**: Recombine parallelized data into a single stream
- **Repartition Streams**: Redistribute data for parallel operations

Optimization Tip: Excessive parallelism can lead to CXPACKET waits; hence, you should consider memory grants and query tuning to reduce overhead.

Operator Costs

Execution plans provide relative cost percentages for each operator.

- High-cost operators are the primary targets for optimization.
- **Examples**:
  - **Key Lookup**: 50% Cost → It may include missing columns in index.
  - **Nested Loop Join**: 10% Cost → It can optimize join order or indexing.
  - **Clustered Index Scan**: 40% Cost → You must consider filtered indexes, or rewriting predicates.

Tip: Operator cost percentages are relative within a plan; do not interpret them as absolute metrics. Therefore, you must combine them with actual execution statistics for better decisions.

Warnings and Bottlenecks

Warnings indicate potential performance problems in execution plans.

- Yellow warning triangles indicate potential problems such as:
  - Missing Statistics
  - Spills to `tempdb`
  - Implicit Conversions
  - High Memory Grants
- Therefore, to understand why operators are more expensive than expected, you must investigate warnings.

Best Practices for Operator Optimization

These practices help reduce query execution time and resource consumption. Therefore, you must:

1. Use indexes to support seek operations instead of scans.
2. Avoid non-SARGable predicates that prevent index usage.
3. Consider join order and indexing for nested loops and merge joins.
4. Reduce large sorts by leveraging indexed ordering or pre-aggregated data.
5. Monitor parallelism operators for excessive thread usage and memory spills.

6. Check for key lookups; consider covering indexes with **INCLUDE** columns.
7. Review aggregate operations; pre-aggregate them whenever possible, or use indexed views.

Advanced Operator Analysis

Detailed analysis of operators can uncover hidden inefficiencies. Therefore, to combat them, you must:

1. Combine the estimated and actual execution plans to detect discrepancies.
2. Examine row estimates and actual rows to spot cardinality estimation problems.
3. Identify operators with high cumulative costs across multiple queries for indexing, or query rewrite opportunities.
4. Use plan XML for detailed programmatic analysis and automation.

Identifying High-Cost Operators

Focusing on the most expensive operators maximizes optimization efforts. Therefore, you must remember that:

- Execution plans assign a relative cost percentage to each operator.
- You must focus optimization efforts on operators with the highest relative cost.
- Use this DMV query to identify expensive queries and operators:

```
SELECT TOP 10
    qs.total_worker_time / qs.execution_count AS avg_cpu_time,
    qs.total_logical_reads / qs.execution_count AS avg_logical_reads,
    st.text AS query_text
FROM sys.dm_exec_query_stats AS qs
CROSS APPLY sys.dm_exec_sql_text(qs.sql_handle) AS st
ORDER BY avg_cpu_time DESC;
```

- Examine execution plans of high-cost queries to optimize index usage, joins, and filters.

Detecting Missing Indexes via Operator Analysis

Missing indexes often cause scans that slow down queries. Therefore, you must remember to:

- Look for clustered index scans or table scans on large tables in the actual plan.
- SQL Server often provides 'Missing Index Recommendations' in execution plan properties.

Example DMV Query:

```
SELECT migs.avg_total_user_cost * migs.avg_user_impact AS improvement_measure,
       mid.statement AS table_column,
       migs.unique_compiles
FROM sys.dm_db_missing_index_groups AS mig
JOIN sys.dm_db_missing_index_group_stats AS migs ON mig.index_group_handle = migs.
group_handle
JOIN sys.dm_db_missing_index_details AS mid ON mig.index_handle = mid.index_handle
ORDER BY improvement_measure DESC;
```

- Use recommendations to create filtered or covering indexes, and reduce high-cost scan operators.

Detecting Inefficient Joins

Inefficient joins can drastically increase query runtime.

- Therefore, you must examine Nested Loop, Hash, and Merge Joins in the execution plan. These are explained as follows:
    - **Nested Loop**: Efficient for small datasets
    - **Hash Join**: Efficient for large datasets but memory-intensive
    - **Merge Join**: Efficient if the inputs are pre-sorted

Tip:

- Use appropriate indexes and join order to reduce the cost of join operators.
- Large Nested Loop Joins with millions of iterations often indicate missing indexes.

Analyzing Spool Operators

Spool operators store intermediate results to improve query reuse.

- Spool operators temporarily store intermediate results. Types include:
    - **Eager Spool:** Stores all rows immediately; can cause memory pressure
    - **Lazy Spool**: Stores rows as needed; is less memory intensive

Optimization Tip:

- Avoid unnecessary spools by rewriting queries, or adding covering indexes.

Investigating Sort Operators

Sort operators arrange rows, which can consume significant memory.

- Sort operators consume memory, and can spill to **`tempdb`** if insufficient memory is allocated.
- Look for memory grant warnings in execution plans.

Optimization Techniques:

1. Create indexes on ORDER BY columns.
2. Use TOP with ORDER BY to limit rows sorted.
3. Reduce unnecessary sorts in nested queries.

Compute Scalar and Expression Costs

Compute Scalar operators can calculate the expressions for each row.

- Compute Scalar operators perform calculations for each row.
- They are usually low cost, but repeated operations on large datasets can accumulate CPU usage.

Example:

```
SELECT OrderID, TotalAmount * 1.1 AS TotalWithTax
FROM Orders;
```

- Consider precomputing values, or using computed columns to reduce runtime calculation.

Evaluating Parallelism Operators

Parallelism operators can speed up queries, but also introduce waits.

- Distribute Streams, Gather Streams, Repartition Streams handle parallel execution.
- Monitor `CXPACKET` waits to detect excessive parallelism.

Optimization Tips:

- Adjust max degree of parallelism (`MAXDOP`), if necessary.
- Ensure memory grants are sufficient to avoid spills.
- Consider query rewrites for smaller datasets that do not require parallelism

Operator Warnings and Alerts

Warnings help identify potential issues before they become bottlenecks.

- Yellow warnings in execution plans indicate potential performance issues:
  - Missing Statistics
  - Implicit Conversions
  - Memory Spills

Action: Always investigate warnings to align estimated and actual plan costs.

Using Actual vs. Estimated Metrics for Operators

Comparing estimated and actual metrics highlights cardinality estimation problems.

- Compare estimated and actual rows for each operator.
  - Significant discrepancies indicate cardinality estimation problems.
  - You can address them by updating statistics or rewriting queries.

DMV Query Example:

```
SELECT plan_handle, objtype, est_rows, actual_rows
FROM sys.dm_exec_query_plan_stats;
```

Best Practices for Operator Cost Analysis

Prioritize operator analysis to maximize query performance. Therefore, you must:

1. Focus on high-cost operators first.
2. Use actual execution plans for real metrics.
3. Update statistics regularly to improve estimates.
4. Optimize indexing strategy to reduce scans and key lookups.
5. Monitor parallelism operators and memory grants.
6. Analyze joins and spools for possible rewrite or indexing.
7. Combine with Query Store metrics for historical insights.

☑ **Key Takeaway**: Operators are the building blocks of execution plans. Understanding their function, cost, and behavior allows developers to pinpoint bottlenecks and implement targeted optimizations. Therefore, by analyzing operator costs, warnings, and data flow, you can make informed decisions on indexing, query rewrites, and memory management to maximize SQL Server performance.

Query Store Setup and Usage

Query Store is a powerful SQL Server feature introduced in SQL Server 2016 to provide persistent monitoring of query performance over time. Unlike traditional execution plan analysis, which only captures current or recent queries, Query Store maintains historical performance metrics, such as execution statistics, execution plans, and runtime metrics. This enables developers and DBAs to proactively detect regressions, analyze trends, and even force optimal plans for critical queries.

Hence, this section covers Query Store setup, its key components, usage patterns, and the best practices for leveraging it to maintain SQL Server performance.

Query Store

Query Store is a built-in feature in SQL Server that continuously monitors query performance. It provides historical insight into execution patterns, while helping DBAs and developers maintain consistent performance. Query Store:

- Tracks query execution performance over time.
- Helps identify performance regressions due to plan changes.
- Simplifies root-cause analysis for slow queries.
- Enables plan forcing to maintain stable performance.
- Provides an alternative to ad-hoc plan cache inspection.

Example Use Case: A critical reporting query suddenly becomes slow after a statistics update. Query Store allows you to compare historical plans and execution metrics to pinpoint the regression, and force the previous plan, if it is necessary.

Enabling Query Store

Query Store is configured at the database level. You can enable it with the following T-SQL command:

```
ALTER DATABASE YourDatabase
SET QUERY_STORE = ON;
```

Additional options control Query Store behavior:

```
ALTER DATABASE YourDatabase
SET QUERY_STORE (
    OPERATION_MODE = READ_WRITE,      -- Enable read/write capture
    CLEANUP_POLICY = (STALE_QUERY_THRESHOLD_DAYS = 30), -- Remove old queries
    MAX_STORAGE_SIZE_MB = 100,        -- Limit size of Query Store
    INTERVAL_LENGTH_MINUTES = 15      -- Capture interval
);
```

Key Options:

- **`OPERATION_MODE: READ_WRITE or READ_ONLY`**
- **`CLEANUP_POLICY`**: Controls automatic removal of old queries
- **`MAX_STORAGE_SIZE_MB`**: Controls disk space for Query Store
- **`INTERVAL_LENGTH_MINUTES`**: Aggregation interval for runtime statistics

Query Store Components

Query Store consists of several key objects stored in system tables, which are

- **`sys.query_store_query`**: Contains unique queries captured
- **`sys.query_store_plan`**: Stores execution plans for each query
- **`sys.query_store_runtime_stats`**: Stores runtime metrics per plan
- **`sys.query_store_runtime_stats_interval`**: Maps runtime stats to time intervals

These DMVs allow querying Query Store programmatically, in addition to SSMS dashboards.

Example:

```
SELECT q.query_id, p.plan_id, rs.avg_duration, rs.execution_count
FROM sys.query_store_query AS q
JOIN sys.query_store_plan AS p ON q.query_id = p.query_id
JOIN sys.query_store_runtime_stats AS rs ON p.plan_id = rs.plan_id
ORDER BY rs.avg_duration DESC;
```

This shows queries ordered by average duration, which helps us identify high-cost queries.

Query Store in SSMS

SQL Server Management Studio provides a Query Store dashboard:

- **Top Resource Consuming Queries**: Shows queries using most CPU, I/O, or the duration
- **Tracked Queries**: Allows detailed investigation of query performance trends
- **Regressed Queries**: Identifies queries whose performance has worsened over time
- **Plan Comparison**: Comparing different execution plans and their runtime metrics

Benefits:

- It provides a visual interface for performance analysis.
- You can identify regressions without manual DMV queries.
- You can easily locate the most expensive queries for tuning or plan forcing.

Analyzing Performance Regressions

Query Store captures multiple execution plans for the same query. Therefore, you can analyze regressions using:

- **Historical Metrics**: Compare current plan and past plan.
- **Execution Statistics**: Includes duration, logical reads, and CPU usage.
- **Plan Differences**: Identify operator, or join changes cause slowdowns.

Example DMV Query:

```
SELECT q.query_id, p.plan_id, rs.avg_duration, rs.execution_count
FROM sys.query_store_query AS q
JOIN sys.query_store_plan AS p ON q.query_id = p.query_id
JOIN sys.query_store_runtime_stats AS rs ON p.plan_id = rs.plan_id
WHERE rs.avg_duration > 1000 -- Duration in milliseconds
ORDER BY rs.avg_duration DESC;
```

Tip: *Focus on queries with high execution count and high average duration to prioritize tuning.*

Forcing Plans in Query Store

One of Query Store's most valuable features is forcing a specific execution plan, which looks like:

1. Identify the query and the plan using Query Store DMVs or dashboard.
2. Compare historical performance to determine the best plan.
3. Force the plan with **`sp_query_store_force_plan`**.

```
EXEC sp_query_store_force_plan
    @query_id = 123,
    @plan_id = 456;
```

- This ensures consistent performance for critical queries.
- This forces SQL Server to ignore optimizer changes that may degrade performance.

Reverting Forced Plans:

```
EXEC sp_query_store_unforce_plan @query_id = 123, @plan_id = 456;
```

Best Practices:

- Force plans only when necessary.
- Monitor performance after forcing to ensure no unintended side effects.
- Document forced plans for future reference.

Query Store Metrics and Analysis

Query Store provides the following key metrics for analysis:

- **Execution Count**: It shows how often a plan is executed.
- **Average Duration**: It reflects the time taken per execution.
- **CPU / Logical Reads**: They reflect resource consumption.
- **Plan Changes**: Track optimizer-generated plan differences over time.

Example Analysis Query:

```
SELECT q.query_text_id, qs.plan_id, rs.avg_duration, rs.execution_count
FROM sys.query_store_query_text AS q
JOIN sys.query_store_plan AS qs ON q.query_text_id = qs.query_text_id
JOIN sys.query_store_runtime_stats AS rs ON qs.plan_id = rs.plan_id
ORDER BY rs.avg_duration DESC;
```

Best Practices for Query Store

To get the most benefit from Query Store, it should be configured thoughtfully and monitored regularly. A proper setup ensures reliable performance tracking without introducing overhead. Therefore, here are the best practices you must remember to implement:

1. Enable Query Store on critical production databases.
2. Set appropriate **`CLEANUP_POLICY`** to manage storage.
3. Monitor for plan regressions regularly.
4. Force plans sparingly and use them only for critical queries.
5. Combine Query Store insights with index tuning and query rewrites.
6. Avoid overloading Query Store by capturing only relevant queries and intervals.

Common Pitfalls

While Query Store is a powerful tool, it has constraints and potential pitfalls that should be managed carefully to avoid misleading insights or performance issues.

- **Excessive Forced Plans**: They can prevent the optimizer from improving queries after schema or index changes
- **Insufficient Storage**: It may cause Query Store to stop capturing data if the `MAX_STORAGE_SIZE_MB` is exceeded
- **Ignoring Intervals**: Too long aggregation intervals may hide short-term regressions.

Tip: *Regularly review Query Store metrics, and adjust the configuration for optimal insight.*

☑ **Key Takeaway**: Query Store is a powerful tool for tracking, analyzing, and stabilizing query performance. By enabling it, monitoring historical execution statistics, and forcing stable plans when necessary, you can gain proactive control over SQL Server performance, which prevents regressions. It also ensures consistent application responsiveness.

Forcing Plans and Analyzing Regressions

Query Store empowers SQL Server developers and DBAs to control execution plans, as well as proactively manage query performance. This section focuses on forcing specific execution plans, analyzing regressions, and using historical data to maintain stable and optimal query performance.

Overview

Even with a well-tuned query and optimized indexes, SQL Server's query optimizer may generate different execution plans over time. Changes in statistics, schema modifications, or varying parameter values can cause a plan regression, where the new plan performs worse than the previous one.

Therefore, Query Store provides a mechanism to:

- Compare historical execution plans.
- Identify regressions.
- Force the optimal plan to prevent performance degradation.

Identifying Plan Regressions

A plan regression occurs when a query's new execution plan performs worse than a previously observed plan. Common indicators include:

- Increased Duration or CPU Usage
- Higher Logical Reads or I/O
- Increased Execution Time Variance

DMV Example: Identify queries with multiple plans and performance variations:

```
SELECT qs.query_id, qs.plan_id, rs.avg_duration, rs.execution_count
FROM sys.query_store_plan AS qs
JOIN sys.query_store_runtime_stats AS rs
    ON qs.plan_id = rs.plan_id
JOIN sys.query_store_query AS q
    ON qs.query_id = q.query_id
```

```
WHERE rs.avg_duration > 1000
ORDER BY rs.avg_duration DESC;
```

Analysis Tip: *Look for high-cost plans with a significant performance gap compared to historical best-performing plans.*

Forcing an Execution Plan

Once the optimal plan is identified, SQL Server allows you to force it using Query Store. Forcing a plan ensures that SQL Server consistently uses the chosen plan for that query.

Example:

```
EXEC sp_query_store_force_plan
    @query_id = 123,
    @plan_id = 456;
```

- **`@query_id`**: The ID of the query in Query Store
- **`@plan_id`**: The ID of the plan you want to enforce

Key Notes:

- Forced plans persist until they are explicitly unforced.
- They help maintain performance stability after statistics updates, or the schema changes.

Reverting Forced Plans

If a forced plan becomes suboptimal due to changing data patterns or schema modifications, it can be unforced through:

```
EXEC sp_query_store_unforce_plan
    @query_id = 123,
    @plan_id = 456;
```

- SQL Server will then resume using the optimizer's chosen plan.
- It is essential to monitor performance after unforcing.

Comparing Plans

Query Store allows you to compare different plans for the same query to understand regressions. This can be done in the following ways:

- **Compare Execution Statistics**: Duration, CPU, and Logical Reads
- **Compare Plan Operators**: Join Types, Index Usage, and Operator Costs
- **Identify root causes for regression**; for example, if a nested loop join replaced a hash join, or a key lookup was introduced.

  Example DMV Query:

  ```
  SELECT p.plan_id, rs.avg_duration, rs.total_logical_reads
  FROM sys.query_store_plan AS p
  JOIN sys.query_store_runtime_stats AS rs ON p.plan_id = rs.plan_id
  WHERE p.query_id = 123
  ORDER BY rs.avg_duration ASC;
  ```

- Identify the execution plan that has the lowest duration and minimal I/O, and use it as a reference for optimizing query performance.

Best Practices for Forcing Plans

Forcing query plans can stabilize performance, but it should be applied judiciously and monitored closely to avoid long-term issues.

1. **Force Only High-Value Queries**: Forcing every plan can hinder optimizer improvements.
2. **Document Forced Plans**: Maintain a record of reasons for forcing each plan.
3. **Monitor Plan Performance Continuously**: Use Query Store metrics to ensure forced plans remain effective.
4. **Unforce If Data or Schema Changes Significantly**: A previously optimal plan may no longer be the best.
5. **Combine with Indexing and Query Rewrites**: Forcing plans alone is not a substitute for proper query tuning.

Plan Regression Scenarios

Plan regressions occur when a previously efficient execution plan suddenly performs poorly. Common causes include:

- **Statistics Update**: A query optimized for previous statistics may regress after new data distribution.
- **Parameter Sniffing**: Initial plan optimized for one parameter may perform poorly for others.
- **Index Changes**: Adding/Removing indexes can cause plan shifts.
- **SQL Server Upgrade**: Changes in the optimizer may introduce new plans with unexpected performance.

Analyzing Query Store Metrics

Query Store captures runtime statistics for each plan over intervals. The key metrics of Query Store thus include:

- **Average Duration**: Mean Execution Time
- **Execution Count**: Frequency of Plan Usage
- **Total Logical Reads**: I/O Consumption
- **CPU Time**: Resource Usage

Example:

```
SELECT q.query_id, p.plan_id, rs.avg_duration, rs.execution_count, rs.total_worker_
time
FROM sys.query_store_query AS q
JOIN sys.query_store_plan AS p ON q.query_id = p.query_id
JOIN sys.query_store_runtime_stats AS rs ON p.plan_id = rs.plan_id
WHERE rs.avg_duration > 1000
ORDER BY rs.avg_duration DESC;
```

- Prioritize high-duration plans for analysis and potential forcing.

Advanced Plan Forcing Techniques

Proper management of execution plans is essential for maintaining consistent query performance. The following strategies demonstrate how to use Query Store and related tools to enforce stable plans, as well as monitor workload behavior effectively.

- **Force Plan Per Query and Per Workload**: Use Query Store for individual critical queries.
- **Monitor Plan Drift**: Track if the optimizer changes require new forced plans.
- **Combine with Query Hints**: Sometimes, adding `OPTION (OPTIMIZE FOR UNKNOWN)` can reduce the need for forcing plans.
- **Use Query Store Dashboard**: Visualize regressions and performance trends in SSMS.

Key Takeaways

Managing query execution plans effectively is the key to ensuring consistent performance in SQL Server. The following points highlight how Query Store and forced plans can be used to maintain stability and prevent regressions:

- Query Store allows proactive plan management to prevent performance regressions.
- Forced plans are a valuable tool for critical queries, but they must be used judiciously.
- Historical metrics help identify regressions, understand root causes, and maintain stable performance.
- Always combine plan forcing with query optimization, indexing, and statistics management for maximum effect.

Conclusion

Chapter 9 has provided a deep dive into understanding and leveraging execution plans for performance tuning. You have learned the difference between estimated and actual execution plans, how to identify high-cost operators, and how SQL Server determines execution strategies. Moreover, key concepts such as plan cache reuse, parameter sniffing, and query recompilation were covered, which will help you recognize why queries may behave differently over time.

The chapter also introduced Query Store, a powerful tool to track historical query performance, monitor plan regressions, and enforce stable plans for critical workloads. Therefore, by learning how to configure and analyze Query Store metrics, you are now equipped to proactively manage query performance, detect regressions quickly, and make informed decisions about plan forcing and optimization.

Looking ahead, Chapter 10 will focus on transactions, concurrency, and isolation levels. You will explore how SQL Server ensures data integrity in multi-user environments, understand locking behaviors, and learn to choose appropriate isolation levels to balance consistency and performance.

CHAPTER 10

Transactions, Concurrency, and Isolation Levels

Introduction

In multi-user database systems, many users and applications can read, update, and delete data simultaneously. Without proper mechanisms to control concurrent access, databases would quickly become inconsistent and unreliable. Hence, SQL Server provides robust transaction management and concurrency control features to ensure that the operations remain consistent, reliable, and predictable even under heavy workloads.

This chapter explains the foundations of transactional consistency in SQL Server. We begin with the ACID principles, then move into transaction control commands that developers use every day (`BEGIN TRANSACTION`, `COMMIT`, `ROLLBACK`). We then explore locks, how they influence concurrency, and the common concurrency issues such as deadlocks, blocking, lost updates, and phantom reads. Finally, we analyze isolation levels and how SQL Server implements row versioning and snapshot isolation to balance performance with consistency.

Hence, by the end of this chapter, you will understand not just how transactions work, but also how to choose the right isolation level for your workload, detect and resolve deadlocks, and design applications that scale without sacrificing data integrity.

Structure

In this chapter, we will cover the following topics:

- ACID Principles
- Transaction Control Commands
- Lock Types and Behaviors
- Deadlocks and Blocking
- Isolation Levels and Their Trade-Offs
- Snapshot Isolation and Versioning

ACID Principles

When working with databases in multi-user environments, it is important that transactions behave in a predictable and reliable manner. SQL Server guarantees this reliability through the ACID properties—Atomicity, Consistency, Isolation, and Durability.

Therefore, every transaction, whether it is a simple bank transfer or a complex ETL pipeline, must honor these principles to ensure data integrity and system stability.

Think of ACID as the contract between you and the database engine. Thus, you must remember the following:

- You promise to define logical units of work correctly.
- SQL Server promises to handle failures, concurrency, and recovery, so that the data remains trustworthy.

Atomicity

A transaction is treated as a single unit of work. Here, either all the operations succeed, or none of them do.

Example: Suppose we transfer $100 from Account A to Account B. It will look like:

```
BEGIN TRANSACTION;
UPDATE Accounts SET Balance = Balance - 100 WHERE AccountID = 1; -- Debit
UPDATE Accounts SET Balance = Balance + 100 WHERE AccountID = 2; -- Credit
COMMIT;
```

- If both updates succeed, the transaction commits.
- If the first succeeds, but the second fails, SQL Server rolls back both. It also leaves the balances unchanged.

Here are the pitfalls you might encounter if atomicity fails:

- The money is debited, but not credited.
- Inventory is reduced, but is not shipped.
- There are serious integrity errors.

Diagram Idea:

The diagram should illustrate two linked operations, where both must either succeed (□) or fail (□), with no half-done state. Readers can create this diagram themselves to understand the concept.

Consistency

A transaction should bring the database from one valid state to another, and enforce rules, constraints, and business logic.

Example:

- A **CHECK** constraint ensures that the account balance does not go below 0.
- If a transaction tries to set a negative balance, SQL Server aborts it.

```
ALTER TABLE Accounts
ADD CONSTRAINT CK_Balance_Positive CHECK (Balance >= 0);
```

If someone attempts this:

```
UPDATE Accounts SET Balance = -500 WHERE AccountID = 1;
```

👉 The transaction fails because it violates consistency.

Here are the pitfalls you will encounter if consistency fails:

- The database holds impossible or corrupted values.

- The business logic breaks down (for example, negative stock, invalid dates, and duplicate primary keys).

Diagram Idea:

The diagram should depict a database state transition from **Valid State A → Valid State B**, making sure the system never enters an invalid state. Readers can create this diagram themselves to visualize safe state transitions.

Isolation

Concurrent transactions should not interfere with each other's operations. Hence, SQL Server uses locks and isolation levels to guarantee controlled visibility.

Example:

- Transaction 1 is updating a product price.
- Transaction 2 is reading the product price.

  Thus, depending on the isolation .level, Transaction 2 may see that:
- There is an old value (safe).
- There is a new uncommitted value (dirty read).
- The new uncommitted value might be blocked until Transaction 1 finishes.

```
SET TRANSACTION ISOLATION LEVEL READ COMMITTED;
```

Here are the pitfalls you might encounter if isolation is weak:

- **Dirty Reads**: Reading uncommitted data
- **Non-Repeatable Reads**: Getting different results in the same transaction
- **Phantom Reads**: New rows appearing mid-transaction

Durability

Once a transaction commits, its changes will be permanent, even if the system crashes immediately afterward.

SQL Server ensures durability through the transaction log (Write-Ahead Logging) in the following manner:

1. Changes are first written to the transaction log.
2. Then, they are applied to the data pages.
3. If a crash occurs, SQL Server replays the log on restart to restore committed transactions.

Example:

```
BEGIN TRANSACTION;
INSERT INTO Orders(CustomerID, OrderDate, Amount)
VALUES (1, GETDATE(), 250);
COMMIT;
```

- If power fails after **`COMMIT`**, **`SQL Server`** recovers the record from the log.

Here are the pitfalls of when durability fails:

- Confirmed sales/orders/payments may vanish after a crash.
- Users lose trust in the system.

Diagram Idea:

Transaction log → Disk → Recovery arrows showing committed transactions restored after crash

Real-Life Analogy

Imagine buying a plane ticket online. The ACID principles will correspond to the following analogies:

- **Atomicity**: Your card is charged *only if* your seat is reserved.
- **Consistency**: You cannot buy a ticket for a past date, or for a sold-out flight.
- **Isolation**: Two people cannot book the last seat at the same time.
- **Durability**: Even if the airline's website crashes after confirmation, your booking remains safe in their database.

Common Violations Prevented by SQL Server

Ensuring data integrity in SQL Server relies on understanding the ACID principles, which govern how transactions are executed and maintained reliably. Hence, this is how SQL Server deals with common violations:

- **Atomicity Violation**: Partial Update → SQL Server auto-rollbacks on failure.
- **Consistency Violation**: Bad Constraints → Use `CHECK`, `FOREIGN KEY`, triggers.
- **Isolation Violation**: Dirty Reads → Controlled with isolation levels.
- **Durability Violation**: Crashes → Transaction log ensures recovery.

Key Takeaways

Before exploring locks, concurrency, and isolation levels, it is essential to grasp the core principles that guarantee reliable transactions. Therefore, you must remember that:

- ACID is the foundation of transaction reliability.
- SQL Server enforces ACID through transaction log, locking, constraints, and recovery mechanisms.
- Understanding ACID is critical before diving into locks, concurrency, and isolation levels.

Transaction Control Commands

Transactions are the fundamental units of work in SQL Server. By grouping multiple statements together, you can ensure that either all succeed or none do (thanks to ACID).

Therefore, to manage transactions, SQL Server provides Transaction Control Commands that let you:

- Start a transaction.
- Save work at intermediate points.
- Commit successful work.
- Roll back errors.

The key commands are:

- `BEGIN TRANSACTION`
- `COMMIT TRANSACTION`
- `ROLLBACK TRANSACTION`

- `SAVE TRANSACTION`
- `@@TRANCOUNT` (System function to check nesting level)

BEGIN TRANSACTION

This marks the starting point of a transaction. Everything after this statement is part of the transaction, until it is explicitly committed or rolled back.

Syntax:

```
BEGIN TRANSACTION [transaction_name];
```

- transaction_name is optional, and is useful for readability, or nested transactions.

Example:

BEGIN TRANSACTION;

UPDATE Accounts SET Balance = Balance - 200 WHERE AccountID = 1;

UPDATE Accounts SET Balance = Balance + 200 WHERE AccountID = 2;

👉 At this point, the updates are pending. No one else can see them until COMMIT.

COMMIT TRANSACTION

This saves all changes since BEGIN TRANSACTION permanently.

Syntax:

```
COMMIT TRANSACTION [transaction_name];
```

Example:

```
BEGIN TRANSACTION;
UPDATE Products SET Stock = Stock - 1 WHERE ProductID = 100;
INSERT INTO Sales(ProductID, Quantity, SaleDate)
VALUES (100, 1, GETDATE());
COMMIT;
```

👉 Both updates are permanent. If SQL Server crashes now, the transaction log ensures recovery.

Pitfall: If you forget COMMIT, the changes remain uncommitted, and it may block other users.

ROLLBACK TRANSACTION

Definition:

Undoes all changes in the current transaction, and returns the database to its state before **`BEGIN TRANSACTION`**.

Syntax:

```
ROLLBACK TRANSACTION [transaction_name];
```

Example:

```
BEGIN TRANSACTION;
UPDATE Accounts SET Balance = Balance - 500 WHERE AccountID = 1;
-- Oops! Wrong AccountID, cancel it
ROLLBACK;
```

Nothing is changed, and there is a safe recovery from a mistake.

Important:

- A **ROLLBACK** cancels the entire transaction, unless a **SAVEPOINT** is used (see the next section).

SAVE TRANSACTION

This creates a **savepoint** within a transaction to roll back to a specific stage without undoing the entire transaction.

Syntax:

```
SAVE TRANSACTION savepoint_name;
ROLLBACK TRANSACTION savepoint_name;
```

Example:

```
BEGIN TRANSACTION;
UPDATE Accounts SET Balance = Balance - 100 WHERE AccountID = 1;
SAVE TRANSACTION BeforeCredit;

UPDATE Accounts SET Balance = Balance + 100 WHERE AccountID = 999; -- Invalid ID

-- Roll back only to savepoint, and not the entire transaction.
ROLLBACK TRANSACTION BeforeCredit;

-- Retry with correct account.
UPDATE Accounts SET Balance = Balance + 100 WHERE AccountID = 2;
COMMIT;
```

Here, the debit is preserved, the bad credit is undone, and the corrected credit succeeds.

@@TRANCOUNT

This is a system function that returns the nesting level of open transactions.

Example:

```
SELECT @@TRANCOUNT;  -- 0 if no open transactions
```

Nested Transactions Example:

```
BEGIN TRANSACTION;     -- @@TRANCOUNT = 1
BEGIN TRANSACTION;     -- @@TRANCOUNT = 2
ROLLBACK;              -- Rolls back all levels, @@TRANCOUNT = 0
```

In SQL Server, nested transactions do not behave like true independent transactions. A single **ROLLBACK** cancels them all.

Error Handling with TRY...CATCH

In production systems, you rarely commit blindly. Instead, you combine transactions with TRY... CATCH for safety.

Example:

```
BEGIN TRY
    BEGIN TRANSACTION;
```

```
    UPDATE Accounts SET Balance = Balance - 500 WHERE AccountID = 1;
    UPDATE Accounts SET Balance = Balance + 500 WHERE AccountID = 2;

    COMMIT;  -- success
END TRY
BEGIN CATCH
    ROLLBACK;  -- failure, undo all
    PRINT 'Transaction failed: ' + ERROR_MESSAGE();
END CATCH;
```

👉 This ensures that you do not leave half-finished operations in the database.

Hands-on Labs

Here are some exercises your readers can run to build intuition:

1. **Basic Transaction Control**

```
BEGIN TRANSACTION;
UPDATE Products SET Price = Price * 1.10;
ROLLBACK; -- Prices go back to original
```

2. **COMMIT vs. ROLLBACK**

```
BEGIN TRANSACTION;
UPDATE Products SET Price = Price * 0.90;
COMMIT; -- Permanent price reduction
```

3. **Using SAVEPOINT**

```
BEGIN TRANSACTION;
DELETE FROM Orders WHERE OrderDate < '2022-01-01';
SAVE TRANSACTION BeforeCleanup;

DELETE FROM Customers WHERE LastOrderDate < '2020-01-01';
ROLLBACK TRANSACTION BeforeCleanup; -- Undo customer deletion only

COMMIT;
```

4. **Checking Open Transactions**

```
BEGIN TRANSACTION;
SELECT @@TRANCOUNT; -- Should return 1
ROLLBACK;
```

Key Takeaways

Managing transactions properly ensures data integrity, and allows controlled error handling in multi-step operations. Therefore, you must remember that:

- `BEGIN TRANSACTION` marks the start of work.
- `COMMIT` makes all changes permanent.
- `ROLLBACK` undoes all changes (unless SAVEPOINT is used).
- `SAVE TRANSACTION` allows partial rollbacks.
- `@@TRANCOUNT` helps track nested transactions.
- Always wrap transactions in `TRY...CATCH` to prevent leaving uncommitted changes.

Lock Types and Behaviors

When multiple users access the database at the same time, SQL Server needs a way to coordinate access to data. Thus, locks are the mechanism used to ensure:

- Data Consistency (No Dirty Reads or Partial Updates).
- Isolation between Concurrent Transactions.
- Controlled Concurrency (Allows Multiple Readers, but Restricts Conflicting Writers).

SQL Server automatically manages locks, but understanding how they work allows developers to:

- Diagnose blocking issues.
- Avoid deadlocks.
- Improve query performance.
- Choose the right isolation level.

Lock Granularity

Locks can be taken at different levels of granularity, which means that SQL Server can lock just a row or the entire table, depending on the operation and contention.

- **Row-Level Lock**: It is the most fine-grained, and allows max concurrency.
- **Page-Level Lock**: It locks an 8 KB page (contains multiple rows).
- Table-Level Lock: The entire table is locked. Hence, it reduces concurrency, and may also improve efficiency.
- **Extent, Database, Key-Range Locks**: They are used in special cases.

Moreover, SQL Server dynamically chooses lock granularity using lock escalation.

Lock Modes

There are several types (modes) of locks in SQL Server:

1. **Shared (`S`) Lock**
    - Used for read operations (**`SELECT`**)
    - Allows multiple readers concurrently
    - Blocks writers (updates/inserts/deletes)

    Example:

    ```
    BEGIN TRANSACTION;
    SELECT * FROM Products WHERE ProductID = 1; -- S lock
    ```

2. **Exclusive (`X`) Lock**
    - Used for write operations (**`INSERT/UPDATE/DELETE`**)
    - Prevents all other access until the transaction commits or rolls back

    Example:

    ```
    BEGIN TRANSACTION;
    UPDATE Products SET Price = Price + 10 WHERE ProductID = 1; -- X lock
    ```

3. **Update (`U`) Lock**
    - A hybrid lock, which is used to prevent deadlocks during updates
    - Starts as an Update (`U`), and then converts to Exclusive (`X`) when modifying data

    Example:

    ```
    BEGIN TRANSACTION;
    SELECT * FROM Products WITH (UPDLOCK) WHERE ProductID = 1;
    -- SQL Server holds U lock, then converts to X on UPDATE
    UPDATE Products SET Price = Price - 5 WHERE ProductID = 1;
    ```

4. **Intent Locks (`IS`, `IX`, `SIX`)**
    - Do not block directly, but signal the intent to acquire lower-level locks
    - Used to manage hierarchy of locks
    - **`IS`** = Intent Shared (Planning to Read Rows)
    - **`IX`** = Intent Exclusive (Planning to Modify Rows)
    - **`SIX`** = Shared and Intent Exclusive

    👉 Moreover, without intent locks, SQL Server would not be able to manage table and row locks safely.

5. **Schema Locks (`Sch-S`, `Sch-M`)**
    - **`Sch-S` (Schema Stability)**: Allows reads while schema is stable
    - **`Sch-M` (Schema Modification)**: Exclusive schema changes (for example, **`ALTER TABLE`**)

    Example:

    ```
    ALTER TABLE Products ADD CategoryID INT; -- Sch-M lock
    ```

6. **Key-Range Locks**
    - Used in serializable isolation level to prevent phantom reads
    - Locks ranges of index keys, and not just existing rows

    Example:

    ```
    SET TRANSACTION ISOLATION LEVEL SERIALIZABLE;
    BEGIN TRANSACTION;
    SELECT * FROM Customers WHERE City = 'Denver';
    -- Prevents INSERT of new 'Denver' customers by locking range
    ```

Lock Escalation

SQL Server can escalate multiple fine-grained locks (like rows) to a coarser lock (like table) to reduce memory overhead.

- Therefore, lock escalation happens automatically when:
    - A transaction holds >5,000 row/page locks on a table.
    - SQL Server decides that escalation improves efficiency.

Example:

```
BEGIN TRANSACTION;
UPDATE Orders SET Status = 'Closed';  -- Likely escalates to table lock
```

👉 Therefore, lock escalation improves performance, but reduces concurrency.

Lock Compatibility

Not all locks block each other. SQL Server uses a compatibility matrix, which looks like:

Lock Mode	Compatible With
Shared (S)	Shared (S), Intent Shared (IS)
Exclusive (X)	None
Update (U)	Shared (S)
Intent Shared (IS)	Shared (S), Intent Shared (IS)
Intent Exclusive (IX)	None

Table 10.1: *SQL Server Lock Mode Compatibility*

👉 **Example**: Multiple SELECTs can run concurrently (as shared locks are compatible). However, a single UPDATE blocks them all (as the exclusive lock is incompatible).

Deadlocks

Locks can lead to deadlocks, where two transactions block each other.

Scenario:

- Transaction A locks Row 1, and wants Row 2.
- Transaction B locks Row 2, and wants Row 1.

Thereafter, SQL Server detects this pattern, and kills one transaction as a deadlock victim.

Example Simulation:

```
-- Session 1
BEGIN TRANSACTION;
UPDATE Accounts SET Balance = Balance - 10 WHERE AccountID = 1;

-- Session 2
BEGIN TRANSACTION;
UPDATE Accounts SET Balance = Balance - 20 WHERE AccountID = 2;

-- Now Session 1 tries:
UPDATE Accounts SET Balance = Balance - 10 WHERE AccountID = 2;

-- Session 2 tries:
UPDATE Accounts SET Balance = Balance - 20 WHERE AccountID = 1;
```

👉 SQL Server resolves by rolling back one transaction.

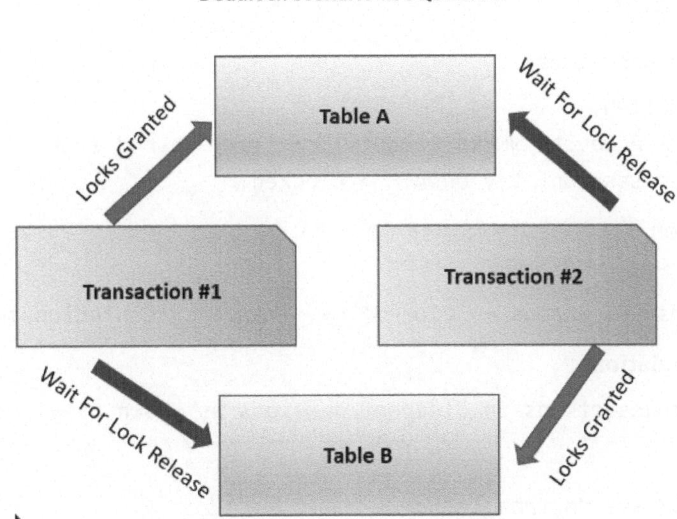

Figure 10.1: *Deadlock Diagram*

Lock Hints

Developers can override default locking using hints.

Examples:

```
SELECT * FROM Products WITH (NOLOCK); -- Dirty reads allowed (no S locks)
SELECT * FROM Products WITH (XLOCK);  -- Forces exclusive lock
SELECT * FROM Products WITH (ROWLOCK); -- Forces row-level lock
```

👉 Use hints with caution, as they can cause data inconsistencies if they are misused.

Monitoring Locks

To see locks in action, use this:

```
-- DMV query for active locks
SELECT
    request_session_id, resource_type, resource_description, request_mode, request_
status
FROM sys.dm_tran_locks;
```

👉 Essential for diagnosing blocking and deadlocks.

Best Practices

Proper transaction and locking strategies help maintain concurrency, while minimizing conflicts and performance bottlenecks. Therefore, you must follow these practices:

1. Keep transactions short to release locks quickly.
2. Access tables in the same order across transactions to reduce deadlocks.
3. Avoid user input while holding locks.
4. Use the lowest isolation level that meets requirements.
5. Monitor lock escalation, and then tune indexing accordingly.

Hands-on Labs

1. **Shared vs. Exclusive Locks**

```
BEGIN TRANSACTION;
SELECT * FROM Products WHERE ProductID = 1; -- Shared lock
-- In another session, try UPDATE → blocked.
```

2. **Lock Escalation**

```
BEGIN TRANSACTION;
UPDATE Orders SET Status = 'Closed'; -- Triggers escalation on large table.
```

3. **Deadlock Simulation**

```
-- Run two transactions in different sessions as shown previously.
```

4. **Check Locks**

```
SELECT * FROM sys.dm_tran_locks;
```

Key Takeaways

Understanding SQL Server's locking mechanisms is essential for balancing data consistency with concurrent access. Thus, remember the following takeaways:

- Locks ensure consistency and isolation.
- SQL Server uses multiple lock types (S, X, U, Intent, Schema, or Key-range).
- Lock escalation reduces overhead, but hurts concurrency.
- Deadlocks are inevitable in some cases, but they can be minimized with design.
- Use lock hints and isolation levels wisely.

Schema and Metadata Locks

- **Schema Modification Locks (`Sch-M`)**:
  - They are acquired when modifying table structures (**`ALTER TABLE`**, **`DROP COLUMN`**).
  - They prevent data modifications while the schema change occurs.
- **Schema Stability Locks (`Sch-S`)**:
  - They are acquired during queries that refer to the table structure.
  - They allow us to read the data, and also prevent schema modifications.

Tip: Long schema modifications can block concurrent queries; therefore, you should plan such operations during maintenance windows.

Application Locks (sp_getapplock)

- **Definition**: Logical locks controlled by the application instead of physical table/row locks
- Useful for custom concurrency control within stored procedures or business logic
- **Example**:

```
EXEC sp_getapplock @Resource='OrderProcessing', @LockMode='Exclusive';
-- Critical section code
EXEC sp_releaseapplock @Resource='OrderProcessing';
```

- Prevents multiple processes from entering a critical section concurrently

Escalation Thresholds and Lock Monitoring

SQL Server may escalate locks when many rows or pages are locked, which can impact concurrency.

- SQL Server automatically escalates locks when the row/page lock counts exceed thresholds.
- Use DMVs to monitor them, as shown here:

```
SELECT * FROM sys.dm_tran_locks;
SELECT request_session_id, resource_type, request_mode FROM sys.dm_exec_
requests;
```

- Proactively monitor high-concurrency tables to avoid blocking spikes due to escalation.

Lock Waits and Timeout Management

Managing lock waits and timeouts ensures that transactions do not hang indefinitely.

- Lock waits occur when a transaction requests a lock that is incompatible with an existing lock.
- Therefore, you should set **`LOCK_TIMEOUT`** to prevent indefinite waits:

```
SET LOCK_TIMEOUT 5000; -- Wait 5000ms, then fail
```

- This ensures that applications do not hang indefinitely during blocking situations.

Combining Locks with Isolation Levels

Locks and isolation levels work together to control data consistency and concurrency.

- Locks are the foundation of isolation level behavior, which can be:
    - **Read Committed**: Shares locks on reads
    - **Repeatable Read**: Holds shared locks until transaction ends
    - **Serializable**: Adds key-range locks to prevent phantoms
- Therefore, understanding this combination helps optimize concurrency while maintaining integrity.

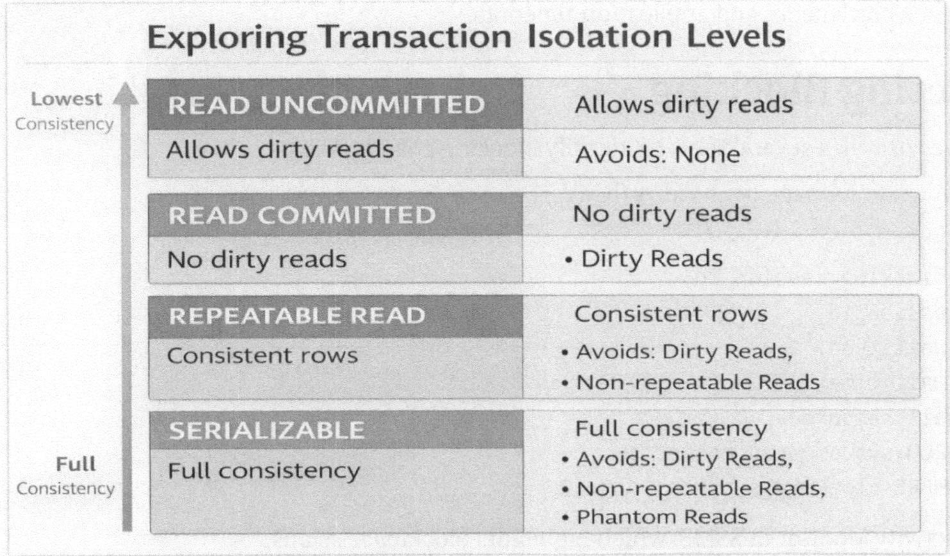

Figure 10.2: *Exploring Transaction Isolation Levels*

Locking Best Practices Summary

The mentioned best practices will help you maintain performance, and also reduce contention in multi-user environments:

1. Keep transactions short and targeted.
2. Optimize indexes to minimize locked rows/pages.
3. Use lock hints only when necessary and after testing.
4. Monitor lock waits, escalation, and blocking chains regularly.
5. Consider row versioning (RCSI or Snapshot) to reduce reader/writer conflicts.

Deadlocks and Blocking

Concurrency is inevitable in multi-user systems, and while SQL Server is designed to handle thousands of simultaneous queries, conflicts arise when multiple transactions compete for the same resources. The two most common issues are blocking and deadlocks. Therefore, understanding these phenomena, as well as how to detect, analyze, and prevent them, is crucial to writing scalable and robust T-SQL applications.

Blocking in SQL Server

Blocking occurs when one session holds a lock on a resource and another session attempts to acquire a conflicting lock on the same resource. Hence, the second session must wait until the first one completes (commits or rolls back) before it can proceed.

- **Example Scenario**:
  - Session A updates a row in the Orders table, but has not committed yet.
  - Session B tries to update the same row.
  - Session B is blocked until Session A commits or rolls back.

Blocking is not inherently a problem—it is a natural outcome of transaction isolation, and is also necessary to ensure data consistency. However, excessive or long-term blocking can cause performance bottlenecks and application timeouts.

Detecting Blocking

SQL Server provides several tools to identify blocking chains such as:

- Dynamic Management Views (DMVs)

```
SELECT
 blocking_session_id,
session_id,
 wait_type,
 wait_time,
wait_resource
FROM sys.dm_exec_requests
WHERE blocking_session_id <> 0;
```

- Activity Monitor in SSMS, which highlights blocking sessions.
- `sp_who2` command (legacy, but is still widely used):
- `EXEC sp_who2;`

Here, you can spot the sessions that are blocked by others.

Deadlocks in SQL Server

While blocking is temporary and resolves itself when the blocking transaction finishes, deadlocks represent a circular waiting condition that cannot be resolved without intervention.

- **Definition**: A deadlock occurs when two or more sessions are waiting for each other's resources. As a result, this creates a cycle of dependency. SQL Server automatically detects deadlocks, and resolves them by terminating one of the transactions, while raising Error 1205.
- **Example Scenario**:
  1. Session A locks row in Customers, and wants to update row in Orders.
  2. Session B locks row in Orders, and wants to update row in Customers.
  3. If neither can proceed, the situation is that of a deadlock.

Deadlock Detection and Resolution

SQL Server has a deadlock detection mechanism that periodically scans for circular locking dependencies. When it detects a deadlock, SQL Server chooses a deadlock victim, rolls it back, and releases its resources for the other transaction to continue.

You can also configure the deadlock priority by using:

`SET DEADLOCK_PRIORITY LOW;` : Makes this session more likely to be chosen as victim

`SET DEADLOCK_PRIORITY HIGH;` : Protects this session (unless conflict is unavoidable)

Capturing Deadlock Information

To troubleshoot deadlocks, SQL Server provides multiple tools such as:

1. **Extended Events**:

   ```
   CREATE EVENT SESSION DeadlockSession
   ON SERVER
   ADD EVENT sqlserver.deadlock_graph
   ADD TARGET package0.ring_buffer;
   ALTER EVENT SESSION DeadlockSession ON SERVER STATE = START;
   ```

2. **SQL Server Profiler**: Can capture deadlock graphs
3. **System Health Session (Runs By Default in SQL Server 2012+)**: Deadlock graphs are captured automatically, and can be queried from **`sys.fn_xe_file_target_read_file`**.

Thus, deadlock graphs help visualize the processes and resources involved, which makes troubleshooting easier.

Preventing Blocking and Deadlocks

To minimize blocking and avoid deadlocks:

- Keep transactions short, as long-running transactions increase the risk of blocking and deadlocks.
- Access resources in a consistent order. If all the transactions can access Customers before Orders, deadlock cycles become less likely.

- Use the right isolation level. This is because snapshot isolation can reduce blocking by allowing readers to access versioned data.
- Use indexes wisely. This is to prevent missing or non-optimal indexes, which can force SQL Server to scan large portions of a table, locking more rows than necessary.
- Avoid user interaction inside transactions. Always perform input validation *before* starting a transaction.

Deadlock Retry Logic

Since deadlocks are inevitable in highly concurrent systems, developers should implement retry logic in applications. This will look like:

```
DECLARE @retry INT = 3;

WHILE @retry > 0
BEGIN
    BEGIN TRY
        BEGIN TRANSACTION;
        -- Critical update logic
        COMMIT;
        BREAK;  -- Exit loop on success
    END TRY
    BEGIN CATCH
        IF ERROR_NUMBER() = 1205  -- Deadlock
        BEGIN
            SET @retry -= 1;
            IF @retry = 0 THROW;  -- Re-throw if retries exhausted
        END
        ELSE
        BEGIN
            THROW;  -- Re-throw other errors
        END
    END CATCH
END
```

Hence, this ensures that critical operations eventually succeed even in the presence of transient deadlocks.

Real-World Example

Imagine a high-traffic e-commerce system, where:

- Multiple users try to place orders (while updating the Orders table).
- A batch process simultaneously reconciles inventory (while updating the Products table).
- If both processes can access resources in inconsistent order, deadlocks will occur.

Solution:

- Apply indexing on Orders and Products foreign keys.
- Ensure consistent access order across stored procedures.
- Use snapshot isolation for read-heavy queries.

Key Takeaways

Understanding the difference between blocking and deadlocks is crucial for maintaining SQL Server concurrency and application reliability.

- **Blocking**: This refers to temporary waiting due to locks; it is normal, but should be minimized.
- **Deadlocks**: These are permanent cycles of waiting. SQL Server intervenes here by killing one session.
- Tools for troubleshooting include DMVs, Extended Events, Profiler, and deadlock graphs.
- Prevention strategies include short transactions, consistent access order, proper indexing, and setting up appropriate isolation levels.
- For application resilience, implement the retry logic for deadlock victims.

Common Deadlock Patterns

Recognizing typical deadlock scenarios helps developers design applications that avoid them. Therefore, here are some common deadlock patterns for you to consider:

- **`Update-Update` Deadlock**: Two transactions try to update the same rows in opposite order.
- **`Insert-Insert` Deadlock**: Two transactions insert into the same table with conflicting indexes.
- **`Select-Update` Deadlock**: A transaction reads rows, while another updates the same rows. This causes a conflict when the first transaction attempts to update.

Therefore, identifying these patterns helps developers anticipate and prevent deadlocks.

Deadlock Graph Analysis

SQL Server captures detailed information about deadlocks, which can be analyzed using graphs.

- SQL Server captures deadlocks as graph XML.
- Deadlock graphs show:
  - The sessions that were involved.
  - The resources that were contested.
  - The session that was chosen as the victim.

Example of Extended Events:

```
CREATE EVENT SESSION DeadlockSession
ON SERVER
ADD EVENT sqlserver.deadlock_graph
ADD TARGET package0.ring_buffer;
ALTER EVENT SESSION DeadlockSession ON SERVER STATE = START;
```

Minimizing Lock Escalation

Lock escalation can convert many row or page locks into a table lock, which can increase contention and deadlocks.

- Lock escalation occurs when SQL Server converts many row or page locks into a table lock.
- This causes blocking and deadlocks.
- Here are the best practices to minimize lock escalation:

- Use proper indexing to reduce scanned rows.
- Keep transactions short.
- Consider **ROWLOCK** hints for fine-grained control (use carefully).

Detecting Blocking Chains

Monitoring blocking chains helps identify queries or transactions that are causing performance bottlenecks.

- DMVs provide insight into blocked sessions. One of them may look like:

```
SELECT
    r.session_id AS blocked_session,
    r.blocking_session_id,
    r.wait_type,
    r.wait_time,
    t.text AS sql_text
FROM sys.dm_exec_requests r
JOIN sys.dm_exec_sql_text(r.sql_handle) t
ON r.sql_handle = t.sql_handle
WHERE r.blocking_session_id <> 0;
```

- Monitoring blocking chains helps identify problematic queries or transactions.

Preventing Deadlocks with Application Design

Good application design can significantly reduce deadlock occurrences. Therefore, here are some tips to make your application design better and deadlock-proof:

- Access tables in consistent order in all transactions.
- Avoid user input or delays during transactions.
- Use retry logic for deadlock victims.
- Keep batch updates small to reduce the chance of lock contention.

Tools for Deadlock Troubleshooting

Several SQL Server features help analyze and resolve deadlocks efficiently. Some of these tools are:

- **SQL Server Profiler**: Captures deadlock graphs
- **Extended Events**: Lightweight and is recommended for modern SQL Server versions
- **System Health Session**: Always-on default session that captures deadlocks
- **Query Store**: Can help identify queries involved in frequent deadlocks over time

Isolation Levels and Their Trade-offs

In SQL Server, the isolation level determines how transactions interact with each other when accessing the same data. Hence, choosing the right isolation level is to strike an effective balance between data consistency and system performance.

The ANSI SQL standard defines four classic isolation levels, and SQL Server extends them with two additional snapshot-based levels. Each level controls how locks are acquired, and determines whether a transaction can see the changes that are made by others before they commit.

Importance of Isolation Levels

Choosing the right isolation level is crucial for balancing data consistency and system performance in multi-user environments. This is important because:

- If the isolation is too strict, it will lead to scenarios where data consistency is guaranteed, but the concurrency suffers (queries will wait for longer).
- If the isolation is too loose, the performance will be great, but the data may be inconsistent (will result in dirty reads or phantom rows).

Thus, developers and DBAs must understand the trade-offs of each isolation level to choose the most suitable one for their workload.

The Phenomena of Concurrency

To evaluate isolation levels, we will look at the anomalies they prevent or allow:

1. **Dirty Read**: A transaction reads uncommitted changes from another transaction.
2. **Non-Repeatable Read**: A row read twice in the same transaction returns different results because another transaction updated it.
3. **Phantom Read**: A range query returns different sets of rows between two reads because another transaction inserted or deleted rows.
4. **Lost Update**: Two transactions update the same row, and one overwrites the other without awareness.

Isolation Levels in SQL Server

Understanding isolation levels is critical for balancing data consistency, concurrency, and performance in multi-user environments. Each level offers trade-offs between accuracy and system throughput. Therefore, you must have a look at each of them:

1. **Read Uncommitted**
   - **Description**: This is the lowest isolation level. Transactions can read uncommitted data (or as "dirty reads").
   - **Allowed Anomalies**: These include dirty reads, non-repeatable reads, and phantom reads.
   - **Performance**: It gives an excellent performance, along with minimal locking.
   - **Use Case**: Reporting queries where there is absolute accuracy is not critical, but performance is.

   ```
   SET TRANSACTION ISOLATION LEVEL READ UNCOMMITTED;
   SELECT * FROM Orders;   -- Might read uncommitted rows
   ```

2. **Read Committed (Default in SQL Server)**
   - **Description**: It prevents dirty reads by only allowing access to committed data. Still, it allows non-repeatable reads and phantom reads.
   - **Allowed Anomalies**: They allow for non-repeatable reads and phantom reads.
   - **Performance**: There is a good balance of consistency and concurrency.
   - **Use Case**: General OLTP workloads

   ```
   SET TRANSACTION ISOLATION LEVEL READ COMMITTED;

   SELECT * FROM Orders WHERE OrderID = 1001;
   ```

3. **Repeatable Read**
    - **Description**: This ensures that if a transaction reads a row, no other transaction will be able to modify it, until the first finishes. It also prevents dirty reads and non-repeatable reads. However, phantom rows may still appear.
    - **Allowed Anomalies**: It allows phantom reads.
    - **Performance**: It offers higher locking and potential blocking.
    - **Use Case**: Banking balances and inventory checks where consistency of row values matters.

```
SET TRANSACTION ISOLATION LEVEL REPEATABLE READ;

SELECT Balance FROM Accounts WHERE AccountID = 10;
```

4. **Serializable**
    - **Description**: This is the strictest ANSI level, as it prevents dirty reads, non-repeatable reads, and phantom reads by locking ranges.
    - **Allowed Anomalies**: None
    - **Performance**: It offers the lowest concurrency, and hence, a high blocking potential.
    - **Use Case**: Critical financial applications and end-of-month ledger calculations.

```
SET TRANSACTION ISOLATION LEVEL SERIALIZABLE;

SELECT * FROM Orders WHERE CustomerID = 5;
```

5. **Snapshot (SQL Server-Specific)**
    - **Description**: It provides consistency without locking by reading row versions from **`tempdb`**. Each transaction sees data as it existed when it began.
    - **Allowed Anomalies**: None of the classic anomalies (dirty, non-repeatable, or phantom) are found. However, update conflicts may occur.
    - **Performance**: This is excellent for read-heavy workloads, as it avoids blocking. However, it increases **`tempdb`** usage.
    - **Use Case**: Long-running reports on live transactional databases.

```
ALTER DATABASE MyDB SET ALLOW_SNAPSHOT_ISOLATION ON;

SET TRANSACTION ISOLATION LEVEL SNAPSHOT;

SELECT * FROM Orders;  -- Reads consistent snapshot
```

6. **Read Committed Snapshot Isolation (RCSI)**
    - **Description**: This is a variation of Read Committed, but instead of blocking readers, it uses row versioning in **`tempdb`**.
    - **Allowed Anomalies**: Non-repeatable reads and phantom reads are permissible.
    - **Performance**: This improves concurrency over Read Committed by avoiding shared locks.
    - **Use Case**: Mixed OLTP systems with heavy read/write concurrency.

```
ALTER DATABASE MyDB SET READ_COMMITTED_SNAPSHOT ON;
```

Comparing Isolation Levels

This table summarizes the behavior, concurrency, and consistency trade-offs for each isolation level in SQL Server. Hence, it will help developers and DBAs quickly understand which anomalies are allowed, as well as the expected performance impact.

Isolation Level	Dirty Reads	Non-Repeatable Reads	Phantom Reads	Concurrency	Consistency
Read Uncommitted	☑ Allowed	☑ Allowed	☑ Allowed	High	Low
Read Committed (Default)	✕ Prevented	☑ Allowed	☑ Allowed	Medium	Medium
Repeatable Read	✕ Prevented	✕ Prevented	☑ Allowed	Low-Medium	High
Serializable	✕ Prevented	✕ Prevented	✕ Prevented	Low	Very High
Snapshot	✕ Prevented	✕ Prevented	✕ Prevented	High	Very High
Read Committed Snapshot	✕ Prevented	☑ Allowed	☑ Allowed	High	Medium

Table 10.2: *Isolation Levels and Their Effects*

Choosing the Right Isolation Level

Selecting the appropriate isolation level balances consistency, concurrency, and performance depending on the workload. Therefore, you must understand when to do so. Here is list of the occurrences that demand that particular isolation levels be chosen for them:

- **Read Uncommitted**: This is best for *reporting queries* where performance is more critical than accuracy.
- **Read Committed (Default)**: This is for general purpose, and is a good balance for OLTP.
- **Repeatable Read**: This should be used when *row stability* is required (for example, checking balances).
- **Serializable**: This should be used for *absolute consistency* (for example, financial transfers, stock trades).
- **Snapshot/RCSI**: This should be used when *high concurrency and read consistency* is required (in reporting, or in mixed workloads).

Practical Considerations

Isolation levels interact with system resources and design; therefore, developing an awareness of these factors ensures reliable performance. Here are the practical considerations you must factor in:

- **Indexing Matters**: Poor indexing leads to large lock footprints under stricter isolation levels.
- **`tempdb` Overhead**: Snapshot-based isolation increases **`tempdb`** load; therefore, you must ensure that **`tempdb`** is properly sized.
- **Hybrid Strategies**: Developers often mix isolation levels according to the transaction type (for example, reporting queries in Snapshot, or financial updates in Serializable).
- **Testing is Critical**: Theoretical isolation guarantees may not match real-world performance until they are tested with concurrent workloads.

Practical Scenarios for Isolation Levels

Real-world use cases help illustrate the trade-offs of each isolation level. Hence, we are mentioning a few of them to strengthen your knowledge.

- **Scenario 1**: A banking system where balance calculations must be consistent
  - Use Repeatable Read or Serializable to ensure that no lost updates occur.
- **Scenario 2**: Reporting queries on a live OLTP system
  - Use Snapshot Isolation or RCSI to avoid blocking.
- **Scenario 3**: Inventory checks in an e-commerce system
  - Use Read Committed for most operations, and Serializable for critical stock updates.

Using Hints for Transaction-Level Control

Sometimes temporary overrides of the session or the database isolation level can improve concurrency without sacrificing integrity.

- SQL Server allows query hints to temporarily override the session or the database isolation level.
- **Example**:

```
SELECT * FROM Orders WITH (READPAST)
WHERE Status = 'Pending';
```

- Here, **READPAST** skips locked rows, which will help you avoid blocking in high-concurrency workloads.

Monitoring Isolation Level Effects

Proactive monitoring ensures that isolation choices do not introduce unexpected blocking or deadlocks.

- Use DMVs to see active transactions and isolation levels, as shown here:

```
SELECT session_id, transaction_id, transaction_state, transaction_status,
isolation_level
FROM sys.dm_tran_session_transactions AS st
JOIN sys.dm_tran_active_transactions AS at
ON st.transaction_id = at.transaction_id;
```

- This will help you identify the transactions that might be causing blocking or deadlocks due to isolation level choice.

Combining Isolation Levels and Locking Strategies

Understanding how isolation levels and lock hints interact allows fine-grained control over concurrency. Therefore, you must know that:

- Isolation levels control default locks, but you can also use locking hints such as:
  - **NOLOCK**, **ROWLOCK**, **UPDLOCK**, and **XLOCK**.
- A proper combination reduces contention, and maintains data integrity.

Guidelines for Choosing Isolation Levels

Practical rules help standardize isolation choices across applications. Therefore, you must remember the following guidelines:

1. Default to Read Committed for OLTP systems.
2. Use Repeatable Read or Serializable only when strict consistency is required.
3. Prefer Snapshot Isolation for reporting on live transactional systems.
4. Always test under real workloads, as isolation effects are context-dependent.

Isolation Level	Consistency	Concurrency	Blocking Risk	Suitable Use Case
Read Uncommitted	Low	High	None	Reporting, bulk reads
Read Committed	Medium	Medium	Some	General OLTP
Repeatable Read	High	Low-Medium	High	Account balances, inventory checks
Serializable	Very High	Low	Very High	Critical financial operations
Snapshot	Very High	High	Low	Reporting, long-running read queries
RCSI	Medium	High	Low	Mixed OLTP workloads

***Table 10.3**: Isolation Levels Overview*

Snapshot Isolation and Row Versioning

Traditional isolation levels rely on locking to maintain consistency. Therefore, transactions place shared (S), exclusive (X), or range locks to control access to data. While it is effective, locking may introduce blocking and deadlocks in high-concurrency systems.

To address this, SQL Server introduced row versioning-based isolation levels that reduce blocking by keeping older versions of rows in **`tempdb`**. Readers can then access a consistent view of data without having to wait for writers to release locks.

Snapshot Isolation (SI)

Snapshot Isolation provides a consistent, non-blocking view of the database for each transaction, which helps in balancing concurrency and consistency.

- **Definition**: Each transaction sees the database as it existed at the time the transaction began, regardless of concurrent modifications.
- **Mechanism**: When a row is modified, SQL Server stores a copy of the original version in **`tempdb`**. Readers use these versions instead of blocking writers.
- **Result**: Transactions operate on a transactionally consistent snapshot of the database, without being blocked by concurrent updates.

Think of SI as "time travel for transactions"—you always read data as it was when you started.

Read Committed Snapshot Isolation (RCSI)

RCSI is a practical variation of Snapshot Isolation, which is applied to the default Read Committed level. This improves concurrency for most OLTP workloads.

- **Variation of SI**: RCSI applies the same row versioning concept, but only for Read Committed isolation (which is SQL Server's default).
- **Behavior**: Instead of using locks for reads, it retrieves the latest committed row version.
- **Impact**:
    - Prevents blocking between readers and writers
    - Still allows non-repeatable reads and phantoms (since different versions may be retrieved in separate statements)
    - Improves concurrency for OLTP workloads

Internal Working of Row Versioning

When a transaction updates a row:

1. SQL Server copies the original row to version store in **tempdb**.
2. A 14-byte pointer (a row versioning tag) is added to the modified row in the main database.
3. Readers that started before the update will follow the pointer to the older version in **tempdb**.
4. Readers that started after the update will read the new value.

📌 The version store in **tempdb** is the key here—it holds all old versions until they are no longer needed by active transactions.

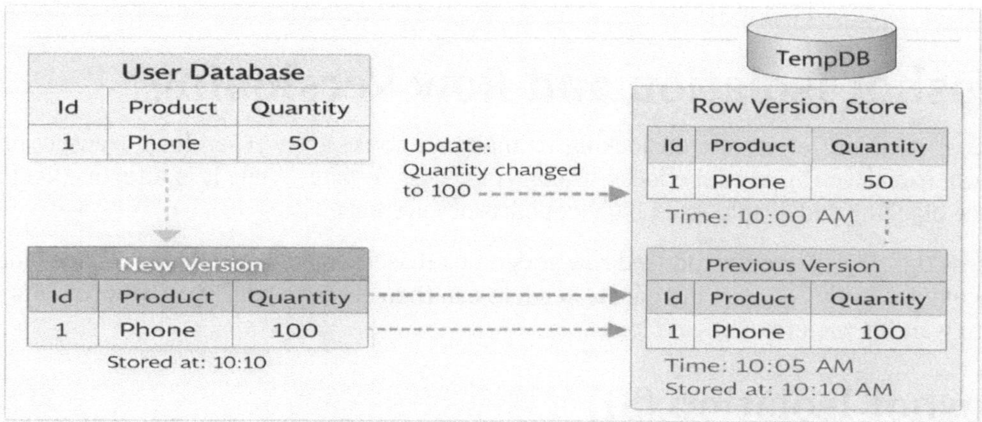

Figure 10.3: *Working with Row Versioning*

Enabling Snapshot and RCSI

Enabling Snapshot Isolation (Per-Transaction):

```
ALTER DATABASE MyDB SET ALLOW_SNAPSHOT_ISOLATION ON;

SET TRANSACTION ISOLATION LEVEL SNAPSHOT;

BEGIN TRANSACTION;
    SELECT * FROM Orders WHERE CustomerID = 5;
COMMIT;
Enabling RCSI (Database-Wide):
ALTER DATABASE MyDB SET READ_COMMITTED_SNAPSHOT ON;
```

⚠ Here, both features require ALTER DATABASE rights, and may cause schema modifications if active transactions exist.

Differences between SI and RCSI

The following table highlights the key differences between Snapshot Isolation (SI) and Read Committed Snapshot Isolation (RCSI), while focusing on scope, consistency, blocking behavior, and tempdb usage. This helps in choosing the appropriate isolation mechanism based on workload requirements.

Feature	Snapshot Isolation (SI)	Read Committed Snapshot Isolation (RCSI)
Scope	Per Transaction	Database-Wide Default for Read Committed
Consistency Model	Point-in-Time Snapshot	Latest Committed Version
Prevents Non-Repeatable Reads?	☑ Yes	✕ No
Prevents Phantom Reads?	☑ Yes	✕ No
Blocking Between Readers/Writers	✕ No	✕ No
tempdb Usage	High (Per Transaction)	High (All Read Committed Queries)

***Table 10.4:** Snapshot Isolation versus RCSI*

Trade-offs and Performance Implications

Understanding the advantages and disadvantages of Snapshot Isolation (SI) and Read Committed Snapshot Isolation (RCSI) is key to making informed concurrency decisions.

- **Advantages**:
  - Readers are never blocked by writers.
  - Writers are never blocked by readers.
  - Long-running reporting queries can run on live systems without blocking OLTP.
- **Disadvantages**:
  - **`tempdb` Overhead**: Heavy updates/Inserts can flood the version store.
  - **Update conflicts (SI only)**: if two concurrent transactions update the same row, the second one fails with an error at commit time:
    - Msg 3960, Level 16, State 2, Line 1
    - Snapshot isolation transaction is aborted due to update conflict.
  - **Storage Overhead**: Every updated row needs extra space for versioning.
  - **Maintenance Required**: **`tempdb`** must be sized and tuned (due to multiple data files, OR proper **`autogrowth`**).

Use Cases

Choosing between SI and RCSI depends on the workload requirements and concurrency patterns. Therefore, you must know about a few use cases for each of them:

- **Snapshot Isolation**
  - Analytical/Reporting queries on live OLTP data
  - Long transactions where you need a consistent snapshot
  - Financial reports that must reflect a specific point in time

- **RCSI**
    - High-concurrency OLTP environments with frequent contention between readers and writers
    - Systems where blocking between queries is a major bottleneck
    - Applications that cannot easily be modified to request Snapshot manually

Monitoring Row Versioning

Proactive monitoring of row versioning ensures that the performance is not degraded, and that **tempdb** does not fill unexpectedly.

Therefore, SQL Server exposes DMVs to track row versioning activity, which looks like this:

```
-- Check version store usage in tempdb.
SELECT
    version_store_reserved_page_count * 8 / 1024.0 AS VersionStoreMB
FROM sys.dm_db_file_space_usage;

-- Check active snapshot transactions.
SELECT *
FROM sys.dm_tran_active_snapshot_database_transactions;
```

Hence, it can be concluded that monitoring is essential, since excessive versioning can degrade performance, or fill **tempdb**.

Best Practices

Adhering to best practices ensures that SI and RCSI are delivering their respective benefits without introducing new performance problems. Therefore, make sure that you follow these practices:

1. Size **tempdb** Properly: Place it on fast storage (SSD/NVMe), pre-size, and use multiple files.
2. Monitor Version Store: Avoid long-running snapshot transactions that keep old versions alive.
3. Use SI Selectively: Prefer RCSI for OLTP, unless strict repeatability is required.
4. Test before Enabling: Concurrency issues may shift from *blocking* to *update conflicts*.

Conclusion

In this chapter, you gained a solid understanding of how SQL Server maintains data integrity and consistency in concurrent environments. The chapter covered ACID principles, transaction control commands, and different lock types, while explaining their effects on concurrency. You also learned about common concurrency challenges such as deadlocks, blocking, and phantom reads, along with strategies for mitigating them.

Additionally, isolation levels were explored in depth, which helped you make informed choices about consistency versus performance trade-offs. The chapter also introduced snapshot isolation and row versioning, demonstrating practical techniques to avoid blocking, as well as to reduce contention in OLTP systems.

Chapter 11 will build on these principles by showing how to automate database tasks using SQL Server Agent, SSIS, and PowerShell. You will learn how to streamline ETL processes, schedule jobs, and integrate automation into modern DevOps workflows.

CHAPTER 11

Automation with SSIS, SQL Agent, and PowerShell

Introduction

Database professionals deal with repetitive tasks every day. These include backups, maintenance, report generation, ETL (Extract, Transform, Load) operations, and monitoring. Manually performing these operations is not only inefficient, but is also prone to human error. Hence, automation is the key to ensuring reliability, consistency, and scalability in modern SQL Server environments.

In this chapter, we will explore the three most important automation tools for SQL Server professionals:

- **SQL Server Agent**: The built-in scheduling and job automation engine
- **SSIS (SQL Server Integration Services)**: A robust ETL and data workflow tool
- **PowerShell**: A flexible scripting language for automation, deployment, and integration with DevOps pipelines

Therefore, by the end of this chapter, you will have a practical understanding of how to set up, manage, and extend automation solutions for your SQL Server ecosystem.

Structure

In this chapter, we will cover the following topics:

- Creating and Scheduling SQL Agent Jobs
- SSIS Package Basics
- Error Handling in Automation
- PowerShell Scripting for SQL Server
- Integration with DevOps Pipelines

Creating and Scheduling SQL Agent jobs

SQL Server Agent is the cornerstone of automation in SQL Server. It allows database administrators and developers to schedule, monitor, and automate routine tasks without manual intervention. Therefore, this section explores its architecture, key components, and practical usage.

Architecture of SQL Server Agent

SQL Server Agent runs as a Windows service and interacts with the SQL Server Database Engine. Its main components include:

- **Jobs**: These are the units of work that can contain multiple steps.
- **Schedules**: These are the descriptions of when a job runs (daily, weekly, hourly, or on-demand)
- **Alerts**: They trigger notifications when specific conditions occur, such as SQL Server errors or performance thresholds.
- **Operators**: These are the database or system administrators who receive notifications via email, pager, or Net Send.
- **Proxies**: They allow jobs to execute under different security contexts, which gives controlled access to non-DBA users.

The combination of these components allows for centralized and automated task management.

Job Lifecycle

A job in SQL Server Agent follows a predictable lifecycle, which consists of the following phases:

1. **Creation**: Define the job and its steps.
2. **Scheduling**: Assign one or more schedules to determine when it runs.
3. **Execution**: SQL Server Agent executes each step in sequence.
4. **Completion**: The job reports success, failure, or retry attempts.
5. **Monitoring**: Job history and logs are maintained for troubleshooting and auditing.

Creating Jobs

A job consists of one or more steps, each of which can run different types of commands:

- **T-SQL Scripts**: For queries, data modifications, or maintenance tasks
- **SSIS Packages**: For executing ETL workflows
- **PowerShell Scripts**: For advanced automation and system integration
- **Operating System Commands**: File manipulation, batch scripts, or third-party utilities

Example: Creating a Job for Daily Database Maintenance

```
USE msdb;
GO
EXEC sp_add_job
    @job_name = N'Daily Maintenance Job';

EXEC sp_add_jobstep
    @job_name = N'Daily Maintenance Job',
    @step_name = N'Rebuild Indexes',
    @subsystem = N'TSQL',
    @command = N'ALTER INDEX ALL ON dbo.Orders REBUILD;',
    @retry_attempts = 3,
    @retry_interval = 5;

EXEC sp_add_schedule
    @schedule_name = N'Daily at 2AM',
    @freq_type = 4,  -- Daily
    @active_start_time = 020000;  -- 2:00 AM

EXEC sp_attach_schedule
    @job_name = N'Daily Maintenance Job',
```

```
    @schedule_name = N'Daily at 2AM';

EXEC sp_add_jobserver
    @job_name = N'Daily Maintenance Job';
```

Job Steps and Error Handling

While creating SQL Server Agent jobs, each step can be configured to handle errors intelligently and control execution flow. Job steps determine how SQL Server responds when an issue occurs, including retry logic and conditional continuation options.

- Job Steps can be configured with retry attempts and error handling options, which are:
    - Continue on error.
    - Quit the job reporting success.
    - Quit the job reporting failure.
- Job step types include:
    - T-SQL
    - **`CmdExec`** (OS Commands)
    - PowerShell
    - SSIS Package Execution

Example: T-SQL Step with Retry

```
EXEC sp_add_jobstep
    @job_name = N'Daily Backup',
    @step_name = N'Full Backup Step',
    @subsystem = N'TSQL',
    @command = N'BACKUP DATABASE AdventureWorks TO DISK=''C:\Backups\AW.bak'' WITH
INIT;',
    @retry_attempts = 3,
    @retry_interval = 10;
```

Scheduling Jobs

Job scheduling defines *when and how often* SQL Server Agent jobs execute. Schedules can be one-time, recurring, or can be triggered on demand, which allows for flexible automation for administrative tasks.

- SQL Server Agent supports multiple schedule types:
    - Recurring (Daily, Weekly, or Monthly)
    - One-Time
    - On-Demand (Manual Execution)
- Jobs can have multiple schedules.
- Example: Daily job runs at 2 AM and 2 PM.

```
EXEC sp_add_schedule
    @schedule_name = N'Dual Daily Schedule',
    @freq_type = 4, -- Daily
    @active_start_time = 020000; -- 2:00 AM

EXEC sp_add_schedule
```

```
    @schedule_name = N'Dual Daily Schedule',
    @freq_type = 4,
    @active_start_time = 140000; -- 2:00 PM
```

Alerts and Operators

SQL Server Agent can automatically notify administrators of important events or errors through *alerts* and *operators*. Alerts detect specific SQL Server conditions, while operators define how notifications are sent.

- Operators are recipients of notifications such as email, pager, or net send.
- Alerts are triggered based on:
    - SQL Server Errors (By Severity or Error Number)
    - Performance Conditions (CPU Usage, Blocking, Deadlocks)

Example: Alert for SQL Severity 16 Errors

```
EXEC sp_add_alert
    @name = N'Critical Error Alert',
    @severity = 16,
    @notification_message = N'Critical error occurred!';

EXEC sp_add_notification
    @alert_name = N'Critical Error Alert',
    @operator_name = N'DBA Team',
    @notification_method = 1; -- Email
```

Security and Proxy Accounts

Not all job steps should run with the same credentials. Therefore, SQL Server Agent uses *proxy accounts* to provide controlled access for tasks that need higher privileges, while enhancing their flexibility and security.

- Jobs usually run under SQL Server Agent Service Account, but some tasks require elevated privileges.
- Proxies allow jobs to execute with different credentials, controlling access to:
    - **`CmdExec`** Steps
    - PowerShell Steps
    - SSIS Packages

Example: Assigning Proxy for PowerShell Job Step

```
EXEC msdb.dbo.sp_grant_proxy_to_subsystem
    @proxy_name = N'DBAdminProxy',
    @subsystem_id = 12; -- PowerShell subsystem
```

Job Monitoring and Logging

Monitoring SQL Server Agent jobs ensures that automation processes run reliably. Therefore, job history and logs help DBAs quickly diagnose failures, track performance, and confirm job completion.

- SQL Server Agent maintains job history, including:
    - Job Start and End Times

 - Step Success or Failure
 - Retry Attempts

- Querying job history can look like:

```
SELECT job_id, step_id, step_name, run_status, run_date, run_time
FROM msdb.dbo.sysjobhistory
WHERE job_id = 'YOUR_JOB_ID';
```

- **Best Practice**: Configure logging to tables or files for auditing and troubleshooting.

Best Practices

Following best practices helps maintain reliable and efficient SQL Server Agent operations. Consistency in job configuration, monitoring, and security ensures stable and predictable automation. Therefore, you must keep in mind to follow these practices:

1. Keep jobs short to reduce the risk of blocking and deadlocks.
2. Centralize logging to help with troubleshooting.
3. Use the retry logic for transient failures.
4. Use alerts and operators for proactive monitoring.
5. Use proxies carefully, and follow the principle of least privilege.
6. Test in non-production first to avoid accidental data loss or overloading.

SQL Server Integration Services (SSIS)

SQL SSIS is a powerful ETL (Extract, Transform, Load) tool that allows you to move, transform, and clean data between sources and destinations. SSIS provides a graphical interface, advanced control flow features, and robust error handling, all of which makes it a cornerstone of SQL Server automation.

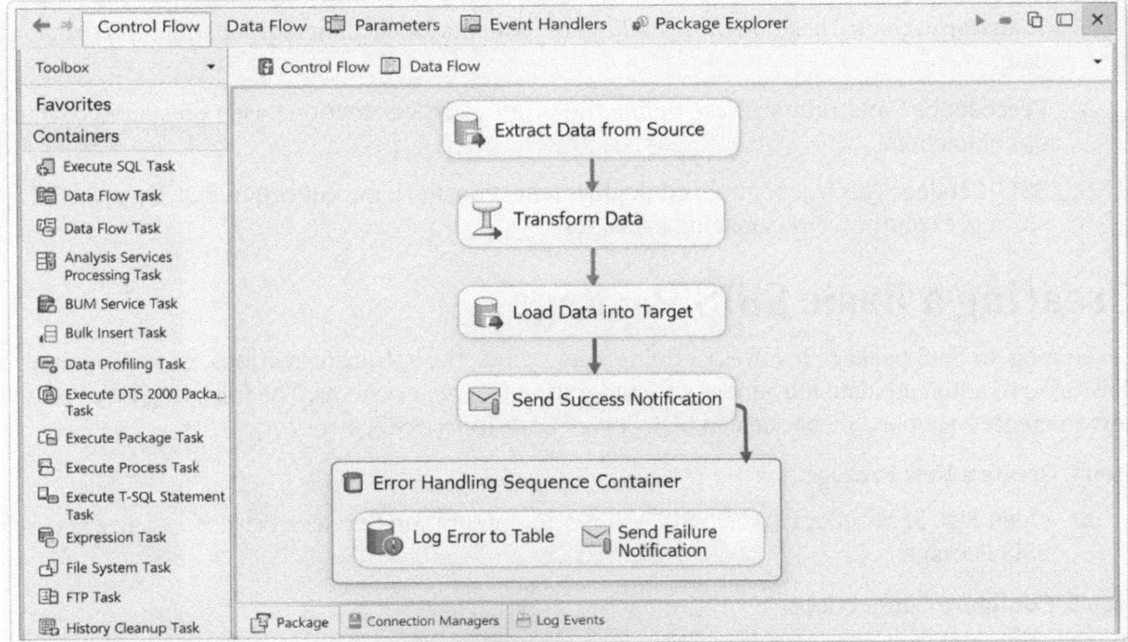

***Figure 11.1**: Automating Database Tasks with SSIS*

Introduction to SSIS

SSIS is used for:

- **Data Integration:** This refers to data from one database to another, from flat files and other sources.
- **Data Transformation**: This refers to cleansing, aggregating, and reshaping data for analytics or reporting.
- **Workflow Automation**: This refers to scheduling ETL processes, file transfers, as well as other repetitive database tasks.
- **Error Handling and Logging**: This refers to capturing failed records, logging errors, and alerting administrators.

Key components:

- **Control Flow**: Manages task execution order, looping, and conditional logic
- **Data Flow**: Handles data extraction, transformation, and loading
- **Event Handlers**: Respond to runtime events, such as errors or warnings
- **Variables**: Store values that can be reused across tasks and packages
- **Connections**: Define the sources and the destinations for your data

SSIS Architecture

SSIS architecture consists of:

1. **SSIS Packages**: This is the primary unit of work, which contains control flow, data flow, and event handlers.
2. **Tasks**: These are the units of work in the control flow, for example, Execute SQL Task and File System Task.
3. **Transformations**: These are the Dataflow components for cleaning, aggregating, and reshaping data.
4. **Precedence Constraints**: These define the order of task execution based on success, failure, or completion.
5. **SSIS Catalog**: This is a centralized deployment repository introduced in SQL Server 2012 for storing, executing, and managing packages.

Creating a Basic SSIS Package

Developing an SSIS package involves defining data connections, transformations, as well as control flow tasks to automate data movement and integration between systems. The following steps outline how to create a simple SSIS package in SQL Server Data Tools (SSDT):

Step 1: Create a New Package.

a. Open SQL Server Data Tools (SSDT) → Go to 'Integration Services Project' → Click on 'New SSIS Package'.

Step 2: Configure Connections.

a. Add OLE DB Source for the source database.
b. Add OLE DB Destination for the target database.

Step 3: Design Data Flow.

a. Drag a Data Flow Task into the Control Flow.

b. Inside Data Flow: Add Source → Add Transformations (if needed) → Go to Destination.

Step 4: Execute the Package.

a. Press F5, or execute via SSIS catalog for deployment.

Data Flow Transformations

Transformations lie at the core of SSIS ETL logic. They are of the following types:

- **Derived Column**: Used to create new columns or transform existing ones.
- **Lookup**: Used to join data from reference tables.
- **Conditional Split**: Used to route data based on conditions.
- **Aggregate**: Used to perform sums, counts, or other calculations.
- **Data Conversion**: Used to change data types to match target schema

Example: Clean Customer Data

- **Conditional Split**: Used to separate valid and invalid email addresses
- **Derived Column**: Used to format phone numbers
- **Aggregate**: Used to calculate total sales per customer.

Control Flow Tasks

Control flow defines the order and logic of execution. The tasks that come under this umbrella are:

- **Execute SQL Task**: Used to run SQL queries or stored procedures
- **File System Task**: Used to move, copy, or delete files
- **Script Task**: Used to implement custom logic using C# or VB.NET
- **For Loop/Foreach Loop Containers**: Used to iterate over files, records, or other objects
- **Sequence Container**: Used to group tasks for better organization

Example: Daily ETL Workflow

1. **File System Task**: Used to move yesterday's CSV file to staging folder
2. **Data Flow Task**: Used to load and transform data
3. **Execute SQL Task**: Used to update summary tables
4. **Send Mail Task**: Used to notify users of completion

Event Handlers

Event handlers allow reactive error handling in the following ways:

- `OnError`: Used to capture errors at task or package level
- `OnWarning`: Used to respond to warnings without stopping execution
- `OnPostExecute`: Used to run logic after task completion

Example: You can log SSIS package errors to a table using `OnError` event handler.

Variables and Parameters

Variables store temporary values for use across tasks and transformations:

- **Scope**: Package, container, or task level
- **Usage**: Dynamic file paths, counters, and status flags

Parameters:

- Allow external values to be passed at runtime.
- Enable reusability of packages across environments.

Example: Use a parameter `SourceFilePath` to dynamically load different CSV files in production and staging phases.

Logging and Auditing

Logging is critical for automated ETL processes. Logging and auditing can thus be performed via the following instruments:

- SSIS supports multiple log providers like SQL Server, text files, XML, Windows Event Log.
- **Log Events**: `OnError`, `OnWarning`, `OnPreExecute`, and `OnPostExecute`
- You can track row counts, execution times, and errors.

Example: You can store package execution logs in `dbo.SSISExecutionLog` with details like:

- Package Name
- Start and End Time
- Rows Processed
- Error Descriptions

Error Handling Strategies in SSIS

Effective error handling in SSIS ensures that data integration processes remain resilient, reliable, and recoverable even when unexpected issues occur. To tackle them, SSIS provides multiple mechanisms that can capture, log, and respond to runtime errors, all without halting the entire package.

Key Strategies:

- **Redirect Rows**: Move failing rows to an error table instead of stopping the package.
- **Retry Logic**: Use For Loop Containers or Script Tasks for transient failures.
- **Event-Based Alerts**: Trigger email notifications for critical failures.

Example: Redirect invalid customer rows to `CustomerErrorLog` for later review.

Deployment and Execution

SSIS packages can be deployed using:

1. **SSIS Catalog (Integration Services Catalog)**: Used for centralized deployment with environment support
2. **File System Deployment**: Used to deploy `.dtsx` files to a shared folder
3. **Command-Line Execution**: Involves using `DTExec.exe` or `DTExecUI.exe` for automated execution

4. **SQL Agent Jobs**: Used to schedule SSIS packages as steps for daily, hourly, or ad-hoc execution

Example: SQL Agent Job Step for SSIS:

- **Subsystem**: SSIS
- **Package Source**: SSIS Catalog
- **Schedule**: Daily at 2 A.M.

Advanced SSIS Concepts

SSIS provides many advanced features that allow developers to build resilient, scalable, and flexible ETL pipelines. These include:

Parent-Child Packages

Breaking down large ETL processes into smaller, modular packages improves manageability and reusability. In SSIS, a parent package can orchestrate multiple child packages, which creates a flexible and scalable architecture.

- **Concept**: Modularize ETL processes by breaking large packages into smaller reusable child packages.
- **Benefit**: It is easier to maintain and reuse, and also provides better error isolation.
- **Example**:
    - `ParentPackage.dtsx` orchestrates workflow.
    - `ChildPackage_Extract.dtsx`, `ChildPackage_Transform.dtsx`, and `ChildPackage_Load.dtsx` handle individual tasks.
- The parent can execute child packages using the `Execute Package Task`.

Checkpoints

Checkpoints in SSIS improve recovery from package failures by allowing execution to resume from the last successful task. This feature saves time during long-running ETL jobs.

- **Concept**: Allow the package to restart from the last successful task after a failure.
- **Implementation**: Enable Checkpoints in package properties, and then define a Checkpoint File path.
- **Benefit**: It saves time for long-running ETL processes.
- **Example**:
    - CheckpointFile.chk stores progress.
    - If the package fails at the Data Load task, it restarts from this task instead of rerunning the full package.

Event Handling

Event handlers enable proactive error response and detailed monitoring within SSIS packages. They help automate alerts, logging, or recovery actions based on events.

- **Advanced Event Handlers**: Combine multiple event types (`OnError`, `OnWarning`, `OnTaskFailed`) to trigger alerts, log data, or start compensating tasks.
- **Scenario**: Send email only if a critical package fails while logging all warnings for review.

Configurations and Environment Variables

SSIS configurations allow packages to adapt to multiple environments (Development, Test, Production), that too without any modification.

- **Concept**: Parameterize packages for multiple environments (Dev, Test, or Prod).
- **Implementation**: Use SSIS Environment Variables in the SSIS Catalog to dynamically assign values for:
    - Connection Strings
    - File Paths
    - Thresholds or Constants
- **Benefit**: Packages become portable and environment-independent.

Expressions

SSIS Expressions enable dynamic assignment of property values at runtime, which improves flexibility and reduces hardcoded values.

- Dynamically set property values using SSIS Expressions.
- **Examples**:
    - **File Path**: `@[User::FolderPath] + "\\Sales_" + (DT_WSTR, 8)YEAR(GETDATE()) + ".csv"`
    - **Conditional Logic for Derived Columns**: `ISNULL([SalesAmount]) ? 0 : [SalesAmount]`

Logging and Auditing

Logging provides visibility into package execution, and also helps in diagnosing issues during runtime.

- **Advanced Logging**: You can customize logs to capture:
    - Package Execution Times
    - Row Counts Processed per Task
    - Errors, Warnings, and Messages
- Use SQL Server logging provider for centralization, flat file logs for archiving, and XML logs for package portability.

Error Handling Strategies

Robust error handling ensures that SSIS packages can continue, or they can gracefully fail based on business needs.

- **Redirect Row**: Capture invalid or non-conforming rows for further review.
- **Retry Logic**: Loop tasks with For Loop Container for transient errors (network, locks).
- **Event-Based Alerts**: Email or API notification for failures.
- **Fail-Fast vs. Continue**: Decide whether tasks should fail the package immediately, or continue downstream tasks.

Deployment and Execution Options

SSIS provides flexible deployment models to suit various operational needs, from development to enterprise environments. These models are:

- **SSIS Catalog Deployment**: Central repository, parameters, and environment integration.
- **File System Deployment**: Store .dtsx files on shared folders.
- **Command Line Execution**: DTExec.exe and DTExecUI.exe for scheduled or ad-hoc runs.
- **SQL Agent Jobs**: Orchestrate package execution, handle dependencies, and set alerts.

Performance Optimization Techniques

Optimizing SSIS performance ensures efficient ETL operations and resource utilization. Hence, you must be aware about the following optimization techniques that help you get the best performance:

1. **Minimize Blocking Transformations**: Avoid sorts, aggregates, or lookups that block data flow.
2. **Use Fast Load Options**: For large data inserts, use OLE DB Destination with Fast Load.
3. **Batch Processing**: Process rows in batches to improve memory efficiency.
4. **Reduce Data Movement**: Filter or transform as early as possible in the data flow.
5. **Parallel Execution**: Use multiple Data Flow tasks or `MaxConcurrentExecutables` property to process tasks in parallel.

Version Control and CI/CD

Integrating SSIS with modern version control and deployment pipelines ensures reliability and traceability.

- Store SSIS packages in Git, Azure Repos, or TFS.
- Use DevOps pipelines to automate deployment across environments.
- **Benefits**:
  - Track changes.
  - Enable rollbacks.
  - Ensure consistency across development, testing, and production environments.

Monitoring and Maintenance

Regular monitoring helps maintain package health and optimize performance over time.

- Monitor package execution via SSISDB or custom logging tables.
- Schedule maintenance tasks for logs (archive old entries) and package validation.
- Periodically review performance metrics and execution history to optimize packages.

Real-World Use Case: Multi-Source ETL

Scenario: A retail company integrates sales data from stores, e-commerce, and suppliers.

Implementation:

1. Extract data from multiple sources using SSIS Data Flow tasks.
2. Apply transformations: clean, normalize, calculate totals.
3. Load into staging and production tables.
4. Handle errors with redirect rows and event handlers.
5. Schedule daily execution with SQL Agent and send notifications on completion.
6. Parameterize package to switch between Dev, Test, and Prod environments.

Outcome:

- Centralized, automated ETL process
- Reduced manual intervention
- Real-time monitoring and alerting
- High data quality and integrity

Best Practices

A well-designed SSIS architecture ensures reliability, maintainability, and scalability of ETL workflows. Hence, following these best practices helps maintain consistent performance and reduces operational risks:

- Create a modular design with parent/child packages.
- Parameterize for environment independence.
- Implement robust error handling and event logging.
- Optimize data flows for performance.
- Use version control and CI/CD for deployments.
- Schedule and monitor via SQL Agent or external orchestration tools.

Best Practices for SSIS Packages

Strong SSIS design principles improve data quality, simplify maintenance, and enhance scalability. Therefore, the following guidelines summarize the proven approaches for developing production-ready packages:

1. **Modular Design**: Separate extraction, transformation, and load tasks.
2. **Parameterize Everything**: This includes file paths, connection strings, and thresholds.
3. **Centralized Logging**: Store logs in a table or dashboard.
4. **Error Handling**: Redirect errors, and use event handlers.
5. **Version Control**: Keep packages in Git or TFS.
6. **Optimize Performance**: Minimize blocking transformations, and use batch operations.

Case Study: Daily Sales ETL Workflow

Scenario: A retail company wants to automate daily sales imports:

1. **Extract**: Read CSV files from the sales directory.
2. **Transform**: Clean and validate data (format phone numbers, and calculate totals).
3. **Load**: Insert them into staging tables, and then aggregate them to production tables.
4. **Error Handling**: Redirect invalid rows to `ErrorLog`.
5. **Automation**: Schedule SSIS package via SQL Agent job, send notification emails on completion.

Outcome:

- A fully automated and auditable workflow
- Centralized logging and error handling
- Scalable for future daily imports

Error Handling in Automation

Automation is only effective if it handles errors gracefully. Without proper error handling, failed jobs, ETL packages, or scripts can go unnoticed, which can lead to data inconsistencies, missed reports, or operational downtime. Thus, this section explains error detection, logging, retries, and recovery strategies for SQL Server automation using SQL Agent, SSIS, and PowerShell.

Importance of Error Handling

Proper error handling provides:

1. **Reliability**: Automation continues running even when transient errors occur.
2. **Auditability**: Logs provide a history of failures and successes.
3. **Proactive Alerts**: Alerts notify operators or administrators immediately.
4. **Data Integrity**: It prevents corrupted or incomplete data from being committed.

Error Handling in SQL Server Agent

Step-Level Error Handling

Each SQL Agent job step can be configured to respond differently if it fails in the following ways:

- Quit the job that reports the failure.
- Quit the job that reports success.
- Continue to the next step.

Example: Configuring Retries for a Backup Step

```
EXEC sp_add_jobstep
    @job_name = N'Daily Backup',
    @step_name = N'Full Backup',
    @subsystem = N'TSQL',
    @command = N'BACKUP DATABASE AdventureWorks TO DISK = ''C:\Backups\AW.bak'' WITH
INIT;',
    @retry_attempts = 3,
    @retry_interval = 5;
```

- **`@retry_attempts`**: Number of retries before reporting failure
- **`@retry_interval`**: Wait time in minutes between retries

Using Alerts and Operators

Alerts detect critical errors automatically, as shown here:

```
EXEC msdb.dbo.sp_add_alert
    @name = N'Database Error Alert',
    @severity = 16,
    @notification_message = N'Critical database error occurred.';

EXEC msdb.dbo.sp_add_notification
    @alert_name = N'Database Error Alert',
    @operator_name = N'DBA Team',
    @notification_method = 1; -- Email
```

***Tip**: Combine retries with alerts to ensure that transient errors are automatically retried, while serious errors trigger notifications.*

Error Handling in SSIS

Error handling in SQL Server Integration Services (SSIS) is a critical aspect of building robust, reliable, and maintainable ETL workflows. SSIS provides multiple mechanisms to detect, capture, and manage errors that occur during package execution. It therefore allows developers to maintain data integrity and minimize disruptions in production environments. Proper error handling ensures that failures are logged, problematic data is isolated, and processes can either recover or fail gracefully without impacting downstream systems.

Data Flow Error Outputs

In SSIS, error handling within data flows is crucial for maintaining data quality and preventing package failures. When data issues, such as type mismatches or constraint violations occur, SSIS allows developers to redirect problematic rows instead of halting the entire process.

- Each transformation or source can redirect error rows to an error output.
- It can capture information such as error code, error column, and row data.

Example: Redirecting Failing Rows

- Flat File Source → Conditional Split → `ErrorOutput`
- **Destination**: `dbo.SSIS_ErrorLog`

Logging Columns for SSIS and PowerShell Automation

Centralized logging is essential for tracking errors, auditing execution, and troubleshooting automation workflows. The table provided here lists the common columns that are captured in logs for SSIS packages and PowerShell scripts.

Column	Description
`RowData`	Raw row causing error
`ErrorCode`	SSIS error code
`ErrorColumn`	Column causing the error
`Timestamp`	Execution time

***Table 11.1**: Logging Columns for Automation*

Event Handlers

Event handlers respond to runtime events in the following ways:

- `OnError`: Executes when a task fails
- `OnWarning`: Captures non-critical warnings
- `OnPostExecute`: Runs after task completion to check results

Example: Logging Errors to SQL Table

1. Create an `OnError` event handler in SSIS.
2. Use Execute SQL Task to insert details into `PackageErrorLog`.
3. Include variables such as `System::ErrorDescription` and `System::SourceName`.

Retry Logic in SSIS

Transient failures such as network timeouts or temporary database locks can occasionally cause SSIS packages to fail. Therefore, instead of stopping the entire process immediately, you can implement retry logic to automatically attempt the operation again before escalating the issue.

Use For Loop containers to control the number of retries for a given task. This allows SSIS to reattempt the operation several times. To prevent infinite looping, configure the `MaximumErrorCount` property appropriately.

- Use For Loop containers to retry tasks multiple times.
- Configure `MaximumErrorCount` property to prevent infinite loops.

Example: Retry a data load 3 times before sending an alert.

Error Handling in PowerShell

PowerShell provides structured error handling using `try...catch...finally` blocks.

Example: Backup Database with Retry and Logging

```
try {
    $server = New-Object Microsoft.SqlServer.Management.Smo.Server "localhost"
    $backup = New-Object Microsoft.SqlServer.Management.Smo.Backup
    $backup.Action = "Database"
    $backup.Database = "AdventureWorks"
    $backup.Devices.AddDevice("C:\Backups\AW.bak","File")
    $backup.SqlBackup($server)
    Write-Host "Backup completed successfully"
}
catch {
    Write-Host "Backup failed: $_"
    Add-Content -Path "C:\Logs\BackupErrors.txt" -Value "$(Get-Date): $_"
}
finally {
    Write-Host "Backup attempt finished"
}
```

Here,

- `try`: Executes the primary operation
- `catch`: Captures any errors
- `finally`: Runs cleanup or logging regardless of success/failure

Combined Automation Strategy

Modern data environments require seamless coordination across multiple automation tools to ensure reliability and maintainability. Therefore, by combining SQL Agent, SSIS, and PowerShell, organizations can achieve a resilient and self-recovering automation framework.

1. SQL Agent jobs handle scheduling and alerts.
2. SSIS packages handle ETL data flow and transformation with error redirection.
3. PowerShell scripts handle complex logic, deployments, and logging.

Workflow Example:

1. SQL Agent triggers SSIS package.
2. The package logs errors to the table, and then redirects failing rows.
3. SQL Agent email alert is sent if the package fails.
4. PowerShell script collects logs, and then sends consolidated reports to admins.

Logging Best Practices

Consistent and structured logging is crucial for troubleshooting, auditing, and process optimization in automated systems. Logs provide transparency into package execution and help identify performance bottlenecks or data quality issues.

- Therefore, you must always log:
  - Start and End Times
  - Number of Rows Processed
  - Failed Row details
  - Error Codes and Messages
- Centralize logs in SQL Server tables or network locations for auditing.
- Use structured log formats (JSON or CSV) for easier automation reporting.

Monitoring and Recovery

Effective monitoring and timely recovery ensure that data pipelines and automated jobs remain stable, even when they are under failure conditions. Therefore, regularly inspecting the job history and error patterns can prevent recurring problems.

- Monitor job history regularly via `msdb.dbo.sysjobhistory.`
- Identify repeated failures to prevent recurring issues.
- Implement automated retry mechanisms for transient network or database failures.
- Schedule notification alerts for critical jobs to prevent downtime.

Best Practices for Error Handling in Automation

Error handling must be consistent across SQL Agent, SSIS, and PowerShell to ensure system stability and predictable recovery behavior. Properly structured error management reduces downtime and improves maintainability. Hence, you must be aware about the following error handling practices:

1. Keep transactions small and atomic to simplify recovery.
2. Use the retry policies for transient errors (network or locked resources).
3. Log errors centrally for historical tracking.
4. Send alerts for only critical failures to avoid alert fatigue.
5. Test automation scripts and packages in development environments before production.
6. Combine SQL Agent, SSIS, and PowerShell for a robust automation framework.

Case Study: Automated ETL Error Handling

Scenario: A retail company automates daily sales ETL through the following steps:

1. The SSIS package loads sales CSV into staging tables.

2. PowerShell performs database backups.
3. SQL Agent schedules tasks and monitors workflow.

Error Handling Implementation:

- Redirect invalid rows in SSIS to ErrorLog.
- Log package start, end, and error messages in `AutomationLog`.
- PowerShell backup includes try/catch/finally for error logging.
- SQL Agent sends email if and when a step fails.

Outcome:

- Reliable and auditable automation
- Immediate notifications for failures
- Easy troubleshooting via centralized logs

Centralized Error Logging across Systems

A best practice in automation is to centralize error logs from SQL Agent, SSIS, and PowerShell into a single repository. Hence, you should pay attention to the following:

- **SQL Server Table**: Create a table `AutomationErrorLog` to capture errors from all automation processes.
- **Columns**: They include `TaskName`, `PackageName`, `JobStep`, `ErrorCode`, `ErrorMessage`, `ExecutionTime`, and `User`.
- **Benefits**: It provides for easier monitoring, historical analysis, and troubleshooting across multiple systems.

Example: Insert SSIS `OnError` events into `AutomationErrorLog` using an Execute SQL Task in the event handler.

Categorizing Errors

Not all errors are equal; categorize them for better handling. These errors can be:

- **Critical Errors**: They cause job or package failure (for example, database connection loss).
- **Non-Critical Errors**: They can be logged and ignored without stopping execution (for example, missing optional files).
- **Warning Events**: They monitor performance or minor anomalies.

Implementation: Use precedence constraints in SSIS or conditional steps in SQL Agent to handle different error types appropriately.

Automated Recovery and Retry Strategies

In any automated ETL or data pipeline, temporary disruptions such as network outages, deadlocks, or server timeouts are inevitable. A well-designed retry and recovery mechanism ensures minimal downtime and smooth continuation of workflows without manual intervention.

Key Techniques:

- **Retry on Transient Errors**: Implement retry logic for temporary failures such as network interruptions or deadlocks.
- **Exponential Backoff**: Wait progressively longer between retries to reduce system stress.

- **Fallback Mechanisms**: Redirect data to a backup location if primary processing fails.

Example in SSIS: Use a For Loop Container to retry a Data Flow Task up to three times with a 5-minute delay between attempts.

Notification Strategies

Timely and targeted notifications allow operators to act quickly on system failures, while ensuring that minor issues do not escalate into production outages. Therefore, combining multiple alerting channels increases visibility and accountability.

- **Email Alerts**: Notify operators immediately when critical errors occur.
- **Dashboard Alerts**: Integrate logs with Power BI or monitoring dashboards.
- **SMS or Teams Integration**: Use PowerShell or APIs to send instant alerts to teams.

Example:

```
Send-MailMessage -To "dba@example.com" -Subject "ETL Failure" -Body "Package ETL_
Sales failed at $(Get-Date)" -SmtpServer "smtp.example.com"
```

Error Handling in Looped or Batch Processes

Batch or loop-based automation (such as file imports or iterative ETL tasks) must isolate and manage errors at the iteration level. This allows the process to continue even if individual items fail. Therefore, you must be aware about the following error handling practices to boost efficiency:

- When you are processing multiple files or batches, isolate errors per iteration.
- Continue processing other files even if one fails, and log the failed iteration for further review.
- Use Loop Containers in SSIS or foreach loops in PowerShell with try/catch inside the loop.

Example: Process 10 CSV files; thereafter, you can log failures, but continue processing remaining files.

Integrating Error Handling with DevOps

Integrating error management into CI/CD pipelines improves transparency and traceability across deployment environments. DevOps integration ensures that each version of your ETL or automation process has corresponding error context. Therefore, you should take the following steps to integrate the two:

- **CI/CD Pipelines**: Capture errors from automated ETL runs, and then integrate with deployment dashboards.
- **Versioned Logging**: Keep logs associated with the exact version of the ETL package or script.
- **Automated Rollback**: Trigger rollback scripts when critical errors occur in production.

Benefit: Streamlined operational monitoring and reduced downtime

Testing and Simulation of Errors

Before deploying automation solutions into production, simulate error conditions to ensure reliability under real-world stress. Proactive failure testing helps confirm that recovery, logging, and alerting mechanisms work as intended. Therefore, you should implement the following practices:

- Simulate failures during development to validate error handling.

- **Examples**:
  - Disconnect source database during ETL.
  - Corrupt or rename input files.
  - Trigger intentional script errors in PowerShell.
- Ensure that packages handle failures gracefully, and that they also notify the operators.

Continuous Monitoring and Review

Error handling is not a one-time configuration—it requires continuous observation, analysis, and refinement. Therefore, by reviewing and trending error data, teams can proactively resolve root causes and improve system reliability. For efficient error handling, you must:

- Regularly review error logs and notifications.
- Identify recurring errors, and then implement permanent fixes.
- Use aggregated logs to optimize ETL performance, and to reduce future failures.

Tip: *Combine SQL queries on* **`AutomationErrorLog`** *with dashboards for trend analysis.*

Case Study: Enterprise ETL Error Handling

Scenario: A multinational retailer automates daily sales ETL across 50 stores:

- **SSIS Packages**: They extract sales data, transform, and load into a centralized database.
- **PowerShell Scripts**: They automate backups and send status reports.
- **SQL Agent Jobs**: They schedule ETL and monitoring tasks.

Error Handling Implementation:

1. Redirect invalid data rows in SSIS to **`ErrorLog`**.
2. Log execution details to **`AutomationErrorLog`** table.
3. Retry failed tasks for transient errors using For Loop Container.
4. Notify DBA via email and Teams for critical failures.
5. Monitor daily execution with dashboards in Power BI.

Outcome:

- High reliability of ETL workflows
- Rapid error identification and resolution
- Reduced downtime and improved operational efficiency

Best Practices

Effective automation requires not only building processes, but also ensuring reliability, observability, and resilience. Implementing structured error handling, monitoring, and recovery strategies improves uptime, reduces manual intervention, and ensures data integrity across ETL, SQL Agent, and PowerShell workflows. Therefore, you must be aware about the following practices:

- Centralize logging for all automation tools.
- Categorize errors into critical, non-critical, and warnings.
- Implement retries and fallback mechanisms for transient failures.

- Notify relevant stakeholders immediately.
- Test and simulate errors during development.
- Integrate error handling with CI/CD and DevOps pipelines.
- Continuously monitor logs and trends to optimize workflows.

PowerShell Scripting for SQL Server

PowerShell is a versatile automation and scripting language that allows SQL Server administrators and developers to automate tasks, deploy solutions, and integrate with modern DevOps pipelines. With the SqlServer module and SQL Server Management Objects (SMO), PowerShell provides full access to SQL Server management, querying, and maintenance capabilities.

Using PowerShell for SQL Server

Automation using PowerShell offers several advantages:

1. **Consistency**: Standardized scripts ensure that repeated tasks run the same way.
2. **Flexibility**: Scripts can interact with the OS, SQL Server, and other applications.
3. **Integration**: It works well with CI/CD pipelines, DevOps tools, and task schedulers.
4. **Error Handling**: Built-in try...catch...finally blocks provide robust error management.
5. **Reporting and Logging**: You can easily capture execution details to files, databases, or dashboards.

Connecting to SQL Server

PowerShell can connect to SQL Server using:

- **`Invoke-Sqlcmd`**: Executes T-SQL scripts
- **SMO Objects**: Provides full management capabilities

Example: Using `Invoke-Sqlcmd`

```
Invoke-Sqlcmd -ServerInstance "localhost" -Database "AdventureWorks" -Query "SELECT
COUNT(*) AS TotalOrders FROM Sales.SalesOrderHeader"
```

Example: Using SMO

```
Import-Module SqlServer
$server = New-Object Microsoft.SqlServer.Management.Smo.Server "localhost"
$databases = $server.Databases
$databases | ForEach-Object { Write-Host $_.Name }
```

Automating Backups

Backups are one of the most critical administrative tasks. PowerShell allows automated, repeatable, and configurable backup routines.

Example: Full Database Backup

```
$server = New-Object Microsoft.SqlServer.Management.Smo.Server "localhost"
$backup = New-Object Microsoft.SqlServer.Management.Smo.Backup
$backup.Action = "Database"
$backup.Database = "AdventureWorks"
```

```
$backup.Devices.AddDevice("C:\Backups\AW.bak","File")
$backup.SqlBackup($server)
Write-Host "Backup completed successfully"
```

Enhancements:

- Add error handling with try...catch.
- Use timestamped backup file names for versioning.
- Schedule with SQL Agent or Windows Task Scheduler.

Automating Deployments

PowerShell simplifies deployments for database projects:

- Deploy DACPAC files to SQL Server.
- Apply schema changes and updates across multiple environments.

Example: Deploying DACPAC

```
Import-Module SqlServer
$DacServices = New-Object Microsoft.SqlServer.Dac.DacServices "Data
Source=localhost;Initial Catalog=master;Integrated Security=True"
$DacPackage = "C:\Deploy\MyDatabase.dacpac"
$DacServices.Deploy($DacPackage, "MyDatabase", $true) # True = upgrade if exists
Write-Host "DACPAC deployment completed"
```

Monitoring SQL Server with PowerShell

PowerShell can be used to monitor server health, performance, and resource usage.

Example: Check Database Status

```
$server = New-Object Microsoft.SqlServer.Management.Smo.Server "localhost"
foreach ($db in $server.Databases) {
    Write-Host "Database: $($db.Name), Status: $($db.Status)"
}
```

Example: Monitor Long-Running Queries

```
Invoke-Sqlcmd -ServerInstance "localhost" -Database "master" -Query "
SELECT session_id, status, start_time, command
FROM sys.dm_exec_requests
WHERE status = 'running' AND command <> 'SELECT'"
```

Automating Maintenance Tasks

PowerShell allows you to automate tasks like:

- Index Rebuilds
- Statistics Updates
- Shrinking Files (If Required)
- Purging Old Backup Files

Example: Rebuild Indexes

```
$server = New-Object Microsoft.SqlServer.Management.Smo.Server "localhost"
$db = $server.Databases["AdventureWorks"]

foreach ($table in $db.Tables) {
    foreach ($index in $table.Indexes) {
        if ($index.IsClustered -or $index.IsUnique) {
            Write-Host "Rebuilding index $($index.Name) on table $($table.Name)"
            $index.Rebuild()
        }
    }
}
```

Error Handling in PowerShell Scripts

PowerShell supports structured error handling through:

- `try`: Attempts execution
- `catch`: Handles errors
- `finally`: For cleanup or logging

Example: Retry on Backup Failure

```
$attempts = 0
$maxAttempts = 3
do {
    try {
        $backup.SqlBackup($server)
        Write-Host "Backup successful"
        $success = $true
    } catch {
        Write-Host "Backup failed: $_"
        Start-Sleep -Seconds 10
        $attempts++
    }
} while (-not $success -and $attempts -lt $maxAttempts)
```

Integrating PowerShell with SQL Agent

PowerShell scripts can be seamlessly integrated into SQL Server Agent jobs, and can enable fully automated workflows that combine scheduling, alerts, and notifications.

- PowerShell scripts can be executed as job steps in SQL Server Agent.
- You may combine them with schedules, alerts, and notifications for fully automated workflows.

Example: SQL Agent Job Step

- **Subsystem**: PowerShell
- **Command**: `C:\Scripts\DailyBackup.ps1`

Logging and Reporting

Centralized logging ensures visibility, auditing, and troubleshooting for PowerShell automation tasks. You can:

- Capture execution logs to text files, CSV, or database tables.
- Include timestamps, error codes, and status messages.
- Use logs for audit, compliance, or troubleshooting.

Example: Log to CSV

```
$log = @{
    Time = Get-Date
    Task = "Daily Backup"
    Status = "Success"
}
$log | Export-Csv -Path "C:\Logs\AutomationLog.csv" -Append -NoTypeInformation
```

Best Practices for PowerShell Automation

PowerShell provides a powerful way to automate database and system tasks, and integrating it with SQL Server Agent enables fully scheduled, monitored, and automated workflows.

1. Use modules (**`SqlServer`**, **`dbatools`**) for robust functions.
2. Parameterize scripts for environment flexibility.
3. Implement error handling and retry logic.
4. Maintain centralized logging for audit and monitoring.
5. Test scripts thoroughly in non-production environments.
6. Secure credentials using Windows Credential Manager or Azure Key Vault.

Case Study: Automating ETL and Backup Workflow

Scenario: A retail company wants to:

1. Import daily sales CSV files into the staging database.
2. Transform and load data into production tables.
3. Backup the database nightly.
4. Send email notifications on success/failure.

Implementation:

- SSIS package handles ETL and transformation.
- SQL Agent job schedules SSIS package and PowerShell scripts.
- PowerShell script performs database backup and logs execution.
- Alerts notify DBAs if any step fails.

Outcome: Fully automated, auditable, and reliable daily data pipeline.

Integration with DevOps Pipelines

Automation is critical in modern software delivery, and integrating SQL Server tasks into DevOps pipelines ensures repeatable, reliable, and auditable database operations. Therefore, DevOps practices such as CI/CD (Continuous Integration/Continuous Deployment), version control, and automated testing can be applied to database workflows using SSIS, SQL Server Agent, and PowerShell.

Error Handling in the DevOps Pipeline

Error handling is an essential aspect of a reliable DevOps pipeline. Database deployments and automated SQL Server tasks must fail deterministically when an error occurs to prevent partial executions and inconsistent states.

When integrating SQL Server operations, such as SSIS package execution, schema deployments, or PowerShell-based automation, pipelines should explicitly detect failures, halt subsequent stages, and log meaningful error details. This ensures that issues are immediately visible and traceable during Continuous Integration and Continuous Deployment (CI/CD) processes.

Effective DevOps error handling typically includes validating return codes, enforcing fail-fast behavior, capturing detailed logs, and surfacing SQL Server error messages that are generated during execution. Therefore, these practices improve deployment reliability, simplify troubleshooting, and support repeatable, auditable database operations.

Error Handling Considerations:

1. **Transaction Management:**
    - Wrap critical SQL scripts or SSIS packages in transactions to ensure atomicity.
    - Use `TRY...CATCH` blocks in T-SQL to catch and log errors without failing silently.
2. **Logging and Notifications:**
    - Configure logging in SSIS packages or PowerShell scripts to write detailed error messages to tables or log files.
    - Integrate with DevOps tools (for example, Azure DevOps, Jenkins) to send alerts via email or Teams/Slack when errors occur.
3. **Retry Mechanisms:**
    - Implement retries for transient errors (like network issues or deadlocks) in SQL scripts or pipeline tasks.
    - Use exponential backoff strategies to avoid overwhelming the database.
4. **Pipeline Failures and Rollbacks:**
    - Ensure that a failed SQL task triggers a pipeline rollback if part of a deployment.
    - Maintain database snapshots or backups for automatic recovery when critical failures occur.
5. **Validation and Testing:**
    - Include automated validation steps in your pipeline to check that SQL deployments succeeded, and that schema/data changes do not break functionality.
    - Use unit testing frameworks like **`tSQLt`** to validate stored procedures and functions before promotion to production.

Therefore, by adding structured error handling into your DevOps pipeline, SQL Server tasks become more resilient, predictable, and maintainable, which reduces downtime and ensures data integrity.

Benefits of Integrating SQL Server Automation with DevOps

Here are the benefits of integrating SQL Server automation with DevOps pipelines:

1. **Consistency**: Database deployments and ETL processes follow standardized workflows.

2. **Reliability**: Automated testing and error handling reduce failures.
3. **Auditability**: Versioned deployments ensure traceability of schema changes.
4. **Rapid Deployment**: Continuous deployment reduces manual intervention and deployment time.
5. **Collaboration**: Database developers, DBAs, and application developers can work in a unified workflow.

Version Control for Database Projects

Before integrating automation into pipelines:

- Use source control (Git, Azure DevOps Repos) to track:
    - T-SQL Scripts
    - SSIS Packages
    - PowerShell Scripts
    - Configuration Files

Best Practices:

- Store environment-specific settings in configuration files, and not hard-coded values.
- Commit incremental changes with meaningful messages.
- Use branching strategies (feature, release, or hotfix) for safe deployments.

Continuous Integration (CI) for SQL Server

Continuous Integration ensures that database changes are validated automatically whenever the code is checked in.

Steps:

1. **Build the Database Project**. Compile T-SQL scripts using SQL Server Data Tools (SSDT) or DACPAC.
2. **Run Unit Tests**.
    a. Use `tSQLt` framework for T-SQL unit testing.
    b. Execute tests automatically using PowerShell scripts.
3. **Package Artifacts**. Generate deployable packages (DACPAC, SSIS project, PowerShell scripts).

Example: CI Workflow with Azure DevOps

- **Trigger**: Commit to the main branch.
- **Steps**:
    1. **Build SQL Server Database Project**: Generate DACPAC.
    2. **Execute tSQLt Tests**: Output the pass/fail report.
    3. **Generate Artifact**: The DACPAC is stored for deployment.

Continuous Deployment (CD) for SQL Server

Continuous Deployment automates delivery of database changes to target environments. You can implement it via the following steps:

1. Deploy DACPAC to Test/Staging Environment. **`Use SqlPackage.exe or`** PowerShell **`DacServices`** object.
2. Execute SSIS Packages. Use ETL packages for populating test data or migrating existing data.
3. Run Post-Deployment Scripts. This involves seed data, cleanup, or index optimization.
4. Set Approval Gates (Optional). They require human approval before production deployment.

Example: PowerShell Deployment Script

```
# Deploy DACPAC
$DacServices = New-Object Microsoft.SqlServer.Dac.DacServices "Data
Source=localhost;Initial Catalog=TestDB;Integrated Security=True"
$DacPackage = "C:\Artifacts\TestDB.dacpac"
$DacServices.Deploy($DacPackage, "TestDB", $true) # Upgrade if exists

# Execute ETL
Invoke-ProcessSSISPackage -PackagePath "C:\SSIS\ETL.dtsx" -Environment "Test"

# Send notification
Send-MailMessage -To "dba@example.com" -Subject "Deployment Complete" -Body "TestDB
deployed successfully" -SmtpServer "smtp.example.com"
```

Integrating SQL Agent Jobs in DevOps

Automating SQL Agent jobs within DevOps pipelines ensures repeatable, consistent, and auditable deployment across environments.

- SQL Agent jobs can be created or updated as part of deployment pipelines using PowerShell to:
    - Create new jobs.
    - Update job schedules.
    - Attach SSIS packages as steps.

Example: Automate Job Creation in CI/CD

```
$server = New-Object Microsoft.SqlServer.Management.Smo.Server "localhost"
$job = New-Object Microsoft.SqlServer.Management.Smo.Agent.Job($server.JobServer,
"Nightly ETL Job")
$job.Create()
# Add steps, schedule, and notifications programmatically
```

- This ensures repeatable job setup across environments (development, testing, and production).

Logging and Monitoring in Pipelines

Centralized logging and monitoring provide visibility into the execution of SQL Agent jobs, SSIS packages, and PowerShell scripts.

- Therefore, pipeline execution logs should capture:
    - Build Results (Success/Failure)
    - Test Results
    - Deployment Details (Scripts Run, Packages Executed)
    - ETL Success/Failure and Row Counts

- Centralized logging allows auditing, debugging, and rollback.

Tools: Azure DevOps, GitHub Actions, Jenkins, Octopus Deploy, or TeamCity

Error Handling in DevOps Pipelines

Integrating error handling into DevOps pipelines prevents failures from cascading and allows proactive alerts. Therefore, you must:

- Implement retry logic for transient errors (network, locks, or deadlocks).
- Use conditional execution for tasks; only proceed if previous tasks succeed.
- Send alerts on failures using email, Teams, or Slack notifications.

Example: Conditional Deployment in Azure DevOps YAML

```
- task: PowerShell@2
  displayName: 'Deploy DACPAC'
  condition: succeeded()
  inputs:
    filePath: 'DeployDatabase.ps1'
```

Best Practices for DevOps Integration

Following best practices ensures reliable, maintainable, and repeatable automated workflows. Therefore, you must:

1. Use parameterized scripts and packages for environment flexibility.
2. Automate database testing before deployment.
3. Maintain version-controlled artifacts (DACPAC, SSIS, PowerShell).
4. Use separate environments for development, testing, and production.
5. Automate backup and rollback procedures.
6. Include monitoring, logging, and alerts in every pipeline stage.

Version-Controlled Deployment

Storing scripts and packages in version control ensures traceability, rollback, and environment consistency. Therefore, you must be aware of the following:

- **Concept**: Store SSIS packages, PowerShell scripts, and SQL scripts in version control systems (Git, Azure Repos, TFS).
- **Benefit**: Track changes, enable rollbacks, and maintain environment consistency.
- **Implementation**:
    - Organize packages and scripts into repositories per environment (Dev, Test, Prod).
    - Tag releases for production deployments.
    - Integrate CI/CD pipelines to automatically deploy new versions to target environments.

CI/CD Pipeline Automation

CI/CD pipelines automate validation, deployment, and testing to reduce errors and speed up delivery.

- **Continuous Integration (CI)**: Automatically build and validate packages/scripts whenever changes are committed.

- **Continuous Deployment (CD)**: Automatically deploy approved packages to staging or production environments.
- **Example**:
  - The developer pushes SSIS package changes to Git.
  - CI pipeline validates package syntax, runs unit tests, and generates artifacts.
  - CD pipeline deploys packages to SSIS Catalog with environment-specific parameters.

Automated Testing in Pipelines

Automated testing ensures reliability of ETL, scripts, and deployments before production rollout.

- **Unit Testing**: Validate small ETL tasks or PowerShell scripts independently.
- **Integration Testing**: Validate end-to-end workflow in staging environment.
- **Regression Testing**: Run previously executed scenarios to ensure that changes do not break existing workflows.
- **Benefit**: This detects errors early, and reduces production failures.

Environment-Specific Parameterization

Parameterization enables safe execution across multiple environments without modifying code. Additionally, you must be aware about the following:

- **Concept**: Use environment variables, SSIS parameters, or configuration files for Dev, Test, and Prod.
- **Benefit**: Enables the same package or script to run safely in multiple environments without hard-coded values.
- **Example**:
  - Database connection strings, file paths, or thresholds are parameterized.
  - CI/CD pipeline injects appropriate values during deployment.

Monitoring and Logging in Pipelines

Centralized monitoring and logging enable rapid detection of failures and performance issues.

- **Centralized Monitoring**: Capture logs from SSIS, PowerShell, and SQL Agent within pipeline dashboards (Azure DevOps, Jenkins, and GitLab CI/CD).
- **Alerting**: Notify teams immediately if pipelines fail, or when data quality issues occur.
- **Example**: Pipeline triggers Teams or email notification on failure, including detailed logs from SSIS Execution, PowerShell scripts, and SQL jobs.

Automated Rollback Strategies

Automated rollback prevents partial deployments from causing data inconsistencies.

- **Concept**: Rollback changes automatically if critical failures occur during deployments or ETL executions.
- **Implementation**:
  - Use SQL scripts to revert database schema changes.
  - Use SSIS checkpoint files or staging tables to revert partial ETL loads.
  - Integrate rollback tasks in CI/CD pipeline steps.

Containerization and Infrastructure as Code

Containerization and IaC provide consistent, reproducible environments for automated deployments.

- **Containerization:** Package ETL packages or scripts in Docker containers to ensure environment consistency.
- **Infrastructure as Code (IaC):** Automate creation and configuration of SQL Server instances, SSIS servers, and supporting resources.
- **Benefit:** This ensures reproducible deployments, reduces environment drift, simplifies scaling, and integrates smoothly into DevOps pipelines.

Data Quality and Validation in Pipelines

Automated validation ensures the integrity of data after ETL or deployments.

- **Automated Validation Tasks**: Validate data integrity after ETL or deployment.
- **Checks include**:
    - Row Counts Matching Expected Values
    - Null or Duplicate Data Detection
    - Referential Integrity Checks
- **Example:** Include a Data Quality task in pipeline to automatically fail deployment if validation fails.

Integration with Scheduling and Orchestration Tools

Pipelines integrate with schedulers for unified ETL orchestration and dependency management.

- Modern DevOps pipelines can integrate with schedulers like SQL Agent, Airflow, or Jenkins to coordinate ETL execution.
- **Benefits**:
    - Unified Orchestration of ETL, Testing, and Deployment
    - Dependency Management across Tasks
    - Reduced Manual Intervention

Real-World Case Study: DevOps for Retail ETL

Scenario: A multinational retailer automates daily ETL for sales and inventory data across multiple regions:

1. **Version Control**: All SSIS packages and PowerShell scripts are stored in Git.
2. **CI Pipeline**: On commit, validate packages, run unit tests, and generate artifacts.
3. **CD Pipeline**: Deploy packages to staging and production SSIS catalogs with environment-specific parameters.
4. **Monitoring**: The logs are aggregated in the central dashboard; the notifications are sent on failure.
5. **Data Validation**: This includes automated checks for row counts, duplicates, and missing data.
6. **Rollback**: On critical failure, pipeline triggers rollback scripts for staging tables.

Outcome:

- A fully automated and auditable ETL process
- Faster deployment with minimal downtime
- Improved reliability and error transparency

Best Practices for DevOps Integration

Effective DevOps integration requires standardized, automated, and auditable workflows to ensure reliable deployment, maintainability, and rapid recovery from failures. Thus, you must implement these best practices:

1. Maintain version control for all ETL packages, scripts, and configuration files.
2. Parameterize all environment-specific values.
3. Automate testing, validation, and deployment through CI/CD pipelines.
4. Integrate monitoring and alerting into pipelines for immediate action.
5. Implement rollback strategies for safe deployments.
6. Leverage containerization and IaC for consistent environments.
7. Continuously review pipelines for optimization and error reduction.

Case Study: End-to-End DevOps Pipeline for SQL Server

Scenario: A company wants to automate database deployments, ETL, and backups as part of CI/CD:

Pipeline Steps:

1. The developer commits the T-SQL scripts to the Git repository.
2. **CI Pipeline**:
    a. Build DACPAC.
    b. Run tSQLt tests.
    c. Package SSIS and PowerShell scripts.
3. **CD Pipeline**:
    a. Deploy DACPAC to the test environment.
    b. Execute SSIS ETL packages.
    c. Run nightly backup using PowerShell.
    d. Send success/failure notifications.

Outcome: A fully automated, auditable, and repeatable pipeline that reduces manual effort and errors.

Best Practices in Automation

Automation is critical to modern database management and ETL workflows. However, poorly designed automation can lead to failures, data inconsistencies, or system downtime. Hence, this section outlines best practices for designing, implementing, and maintaining robust automation in SQL Server using SQL Agent, SSIS, PowerShell, and DevOps pipelines.

Plan and Document Automation Workflows

Before implementing automation, it is crucial to document the workflow to ensure clarity, accountability, and maintainability. Therefore, you must:

- Document workflows before implementation; map each task, dependencies, and failure handling.
- Include step-by-step flow diagrams for SQL Agent jobs, SSIS packages, and PowerShell scripts.
- Identify critical tasks that require alerting or human intervention.
- Use version control to track workflow changes and maintain historical context.

Example: Maintain a workflow document showing:

1. The SSIS package for ETL
2. The PowerShell script for backup
3. The SQL Agent job scheduling sequence
4. The notifications and alerting points

Standardize Configuration and Parameters

Automation is more robust and portable when configurations are parameterized rather than hard-coded. Therefore, you must:

- Avoid hard-coding paths, connection strings, or credentials.
- Use variables, parameters, or environment configurations for flexibility.
- Maintain separate configuration files for Dev, Test, and Production environments.

Example: Using SSIS Environment Variables

- Define `FilePath` and `ConnectionString` variables in SSIS environment.
- Reference these variables in all packages to ensure portability across environments.

PowerShell Tip: Store sensitive information securely using Windows Credential Manager or Azure Key Vault instead of plaintext.

Implement Robust Error Handling

Proactive error handling ensures workflows continue reliably and failures are captured for troubleshooting.

- Always use `try...catch...finally` blocks in PowerShell scripts.
- Use error outputs and event handlers in SSIS packages.
- Configure SQL Agent steps with retry attempts and alerts.
- Log every error to centralized tables, files, or dashboards for auditing.

Example: Retry Failed Tasks in SSIS

- Use a For Loop Container to attempt a Data Flow task 3 times before failing.
- Capture failed rows and errors in a `PackageErrorLog` table.

Centralized Logging and Monitoring

Structured logging provides visibility into automation workflows and enables auditing, trend analysis, and rapid issue resolution. Therefore, you must:

- Maintain logs in structured, centralized locations for analysis and reporting.
- **Include**:
  - Start and End Times
  - Row Counts Processed
  - Error Codes and Messages
  - Script/Package Names
- Enable monitoring via dashboards or alerting systems.

Example: PowerShell Script Logs

```
$log = @{
    Timestamp = Get-Date
    Task = "ETL Load"
    Status = "Success"
    RowsProcessed = 1523
}
$log | Export-Csv -Path "C:\Logs\AutomationLog.csv" -Append -NoTypeInformation
```

Modular Design for Reusability

Breaking workflows into reusable components improves maintainability, testing, and readability. Hence, you must:

- Design modular SSIS packages and PowerShell scripts that can be reused in multiple workflows.
- Use child packages in SSIS to separate tasks (for example, ETL extraction, transformation, and load).
- Break complex PowerShell scripts into functions to improve maintainability.

Example: SSIS Modular Design

- `Extract_Customers.dtsx`
- `Transform_Customers.dtsx`
- `Load_Customers.dtsx`

Testing and Validation

Testing ensures automation workflows behave as expected, maintain data integrity, and perform efficiently. Therefore, you must:

- Always test automation workflows in a development or staging environment.
- **Validate**:
  - Data Accuracy
  - Error Handling
  - Performance under Load
- Include unit tests for T-SQL scripts using tSQLt.
- Test PowerShell scripts with sample data and dry-run options before production.

Security Best Practices

Proper security practices protect sensitive data and prevent unauthorized access to automation workflows. Therefore, you must:

- Limit permissions for automated accounts.
- Avoid using high-privilege accounts such as sa or admin for automation tasks.
- Secure credentials using credential managers or encrypted files.
- Audit automated tasks regularly to ensure no unauthorized access.

Example: SQL Agent job uses a dedicated SQL login with minimum required privileges.

Scheduling and Dependency Management

Efficient scheduling and dependency management prevent conflicts, resource contention, and ensure proper execution order. Therefore, you must:

- Schedule jobs considering system load and peak hours.
- Use job dependencies to ensure tasks run in the correct order.
- Avoid overlapping tasks that might lock resources or cause conflicts.

Example: SQL Agent Schedules

1. **2 A.M.**: Load staging tables via SSIS.
2. **3 A.M.**: Transform and load production tables.
3. **4 A.M.**: Backup database

Notifications and Alerts

Alerts ensure that stakeholders are immediately aware of failures and can take corrective action. Thus, you must:

- Configure alerts for:
  - Job Failures
  - SSIS Package Errors
  - Critical PowerShell Exceptions
- Send notifications via email, Teams, Slack, or dashboards.
- Include sufficient details in notifications to facilitate troubleshooting.

Versioning and Deployment

Maintaining version control and structured deployment reduces risk, and also ensures repeatability across environments. Therefore, you must:

- Track all automation scripts and packages using version control.
- Maintain separate artifacts for development, testing, and production environments.
- Use CI/CD pipelines for controlled deployment of database changes, ETL packages, and scripts.

Example: Store SSIS .dtsx files and PowerShell scripts in GitHub or Azure Repos; deploy them using Azure DevOps pipeline.

Performance Considerations

Optimizing performance ensures workflows run efficiently and reduce resource impact. Therefore, you must:

- Avoid unnecessary data transformations or any looping inside SSIS Data Flow tasks.
- Optimize PowerShell scripts by minimizing database calls, and also for using bulk operations.
- Monitor job duration and resource usage, while adjusting schedules or workflows as needed.

Regular Maintenance and Review

Ongoing review and maintenance prevent workflow degradation and keep automation reliable. Therefore, you must

- Regularly review logs, failed tasks, and pipeline execution history.
- Archive old logs to maintain performance.
- Periodically update scripts and packages for efficiency, security, and maintainability.

Case Study: End-to-End Automation Best Practices

Scenario: A retail company uses SQL Agent, SSIS, and PowerShell for daily sales ETL, database backups, and reporting.

Implementation:

1. Modular SSIS packages separate extract, transform, and load steps.
2. PowerShell scripts handle database backups and monitoring.
3. SQL Agent orchestrates workflows with retries and notifications.
4. DevOps pipeline deploys DACPACs and SSIS packages with CI/CD.
5. Centralized logging captures execution, errors, and performance metrics.

Outcome:

- Reliable automation
- Improved monitoring and error detection
- Reduced manual intervention
- Secure and auditable workflows

Conclusion

This chapter highlighted the importance of automation for efficient and reliable database management. You learned to create and schedule SQL Server Agent jobs, handle errors, and automate backups and maintenance tasks. SSIS was introduced as a tool for building ETL pipelines, with practical examples of data import/export workflows.

PowerShell scripting was also covered for automating deployment, monitoring, and administrative tasks, helping bridge database operations with DevOps practices. Therefore, by combining SQL Agent, SSIS, and PowerShell, you now have the skills to design robust, automated workflows that reduce manual intervention and improve operational efficiency.

The next chapter will introduce cloud-native development using Azure SQL and Synapse Analytics, while teaching you how to migrate workloads, manage security, and optimize performance in cloud environments.

CHAPTER 12
Azure SQL and Synapse Integration

Introduction

This chapter will introduce you to the concept of implementing cloud-native SQL development using Azure SQL Database and Synapse Analytics. Hence, we will explore the differences between service models, the fundamentals of Azure SQL Database, and how to configure and scale resources with elastic pools. You will also learn the essentials of Synapse Analytics for large-scale data warehousing and analytics, as well as PolyBase and external tables for integrating external data sources. Finally, the chapter will address the critical aspects of cloud-based security and cost management, which will equip you to build resilient and efficient SQL solutions in the cloud.

Structure

In this chapter, the following topics will be covered:

- Azure SQL Database Fundamentals
- Elastic Pools and Scaling Options
- Synapse Analytics Overview
- PolyBase and External Tables
- Security and Cost Management in Cloud

Azure SQL Database Fundamentals

Azure SQL Database is Microsoft's cloud-native, fully managed relational database service built on the same SQL Server engine. It removes the burden of managing physical servers, patching, upgrades, and backups, and still offers the full T-SQL language and advanced features that SQL professionals are familiar with.

Therefore, this section explains the architecture, deployment models, performance tiers, high availability, disaster recovery, and monitoring fundamentals.

Deployment Models

Azure SQL Database provides several deployment options that are tailored to address different application and business needs. These models are of the following types:

- **Single Database**
    - It represents a fully managed, isolated database.

    - It is best for modern applications that need a dedicated and predictable performance environment.
- **Elastic Pool**
    - In an elastic pool, many databases share a single pool of resources.
    - It is ideal for multi-tenant SaaS applications where each customer has their own database, but workloads vary.
- **Managed Instance (Though It is Closer to SQL Server Lift-and-Shift, and is Worth Distinguishing)**
    - It offers almost cent-percent SQL Server compatibility.
    - It is best for migrating on-premises workloads with minimal code changes.
- **SQL on Azure Virtual Machines**
    - It refers to a full SQL Server that runs on IaaS.
    - It is used when applications require OS-level access, or when SQL Server features are not supported in PaaS.

Service Tiers and Compute Models

Azure SQL Database provides multiple ways to allocate compute and storage resources, which can be:

- **DTU-Based Model (Database Transaction Unit):** It simplifies resource measurement by combining CPU, memory, and I/O into one metric. Hence, it is good for small to medium workloads.
- **vCore-Based Model**: It offers transparency by letting you choose CPU cores, memory, and storage. Additionally, it allows customers to align performance with on-premises specs.
- **Provisioned Compute**: It features fixed performance levels that are billed hourly.
- **Serverless Compute**: It automatically scales CPU and pauses during inactivity. It is also rather cost-effective for intermittent or unpredictable workloads.

Storage and Backup Management

Azure SQL Database uses Azure Storage for data files and logs, with the following features:

- **Automatic Backups**:
    - They retain information for 7–35 days, depending on the service tier.
    - They come with Long-Term Retention (LTR), which can store backups for up to 10 years.
- **Geo-Redundant Storage (GRS):** It ensures resilience by replicating backups to paired Azure regions.
- **Point-in-Time Restore**: It restores a database to any second within the retention period.

High Availability (HA) Architecture

Azure SQL Database provides built-in HA without user intervention, via the following features:

- **Always-On Technology**: It is built on quorum-based replicas across fault domains.
- **Zone Redundancy**: It is used for premium and business-critical tiers. Additionally, it features replicas that span multiple availability zones.
- **Automatic Failover**: It is transparent to applications, and also ensures continuity.

Thus, the HA eliminates the need for configuring failover clusters, or mirroring manually.

Security Features

Security is a first-class citizen in Azure SQL Database. Therefore, you must know about the following features in Azure SQL Database:

- **Authentication and Identity**:
  - SQL Authentication (Username/Password)
  - Azure Active Directory (AAD) integration for centralized identity
- **Encryption**:
  - TDE (Transparent Data Encryption) for data at rest
  - Always Encrypted for sensitive columns, as it ensures that data remains encrypted end-to-end
  - TLS for data in transit
- **Network Security**:
  - Built-in firewall rules
  - Private endpoints (VNet integration)
- **Advanced Threat Protection (ATP)**: Real-time monitoring of anomalies like SQL injection or unusual logins

Monitoring and Performance Management

Azure provides tools to optimize workloads, which are:

- Query Performance Insight: Identifies resource-hungry queries
- Intelligent Insights: Uses AI to detect performance bottlenecks automatically
- Automatic Tuning: Applies and reverts query plan changes automatically
- Azure Monitor and Log Analytics: Centralized logging and alerting

Integration with Azure Ecosystem

Azure SQL Database seamlessly integrates with other Azure services such as:

- **Azure Data Factory (ADF)**: For ETL pipelines
- **Power BI**: For visualization and reporting
- **Azure Synapse Analytics**: For large-scale warehousing
- **Azure Functions/Logic Apps**: To trigger events or workflows on database changes

Thus, this ecosystem makes Azure SQL a natural fit for both OLTP and hybrid analytics architectures.

Common Use Cases

- **OLTP Applications**: It includes dealing with transactional workloads such as e-commerce or finance.
- **Multi-Tenant SaaS Apps**: Elastic pools provide resource efficiency.
- **Hybrid Analytics**: These analytics come with Synapse and Power BI integration.
- **Dev/Test Environments**: You may spin them up and down easily without CAPEX.

Limitations and Considerations

While powerful, Azure SQL Database has limitations like:

- Some SQL Server features are not supported (for example, SQL Agent jobs, and certain cross-database queries in single DBs).
- The performance depends on choosing tiers correctly.
- Network latency can impact workloads if applications are not in the same region.

Automatic Tuning in Azure SQL Database

Azure SQL Database includes automatic tuning features such as automatic index creation, index dropping, and query plan correction. These features use AI-driven telemetry to detect performance regressions, and then fix them without manual intervention.

- Automatic Indexing ensures that missing indexes are created to improve query performance.
- Plan Correction detects suboptimal plans (like parameter sniffing issues), and forces SQL Server to revert to a previously better-performing plan. This greatly reduces DBA workload, and thus ensures performance consistency in mission-critical applications.

Service Tiers: General Purpose vs. Business Critical vs. Hyperscale

Azure SQL offers three main service tiers, which are:

- **General Purpose**: It is used for balanced compute and storage; it is the best for most workloads.
- **Business Critical**: It uses SSD-based storage, and has a high availability with Always On replicas. Additionally, it is suitable for OLTP workloads that require low latency.
- **Hyperscale**: It is designed for massive databases (up to 100TB, and beyond). It supports instant scaling, fast backups, and rapid restores. As you can see, each tier supports different SLAs, performance guarantees, and resiliency features. Therefore, choosing the right one ensures cost efficiency and performance alignment.

Geo-Replication and Failover Groups

High availability in the cloud is critical. To support it, Azure SQL provides the following features:

- **Active Geo-Replication**: It provides up to 4 readable secondary replicas across regions for DR (Disaster Recovery).
- **Auto-Failover Groups**: They display automatic failover between paired regions with minimal downtime.

  Hence, these features and groups ensure global availability and business continuity in case of regional outages.

Monitoring with Azure Metrics and Alerts

Azure SQL provides built-in monitoring and diagnostic logs such as:

- Azure Monitor Metrics track DTU/CPU usage, storage, I/O, and deadlocks.
- Diagnostic Settings export logs to Log Analytics, Event Hubs, or Storage.
- Alerts can notify teams when thresholds (for example, CPU > 90%) are exceeded. This enables proactive performance and security management.

Integration with Azure Data Factory (ADF)

Although not part of core Azure SQL itself, most enterprise use cases require integrating Azure SQL with ADF pipelines. ADF enables the following:

- ETL/ELT processes with Azure SQL as a source/destination
- Data ingestion from on-premises SQL Servers into Azure SQL
- Scheduled automation for batch data loads

  Hence, all these features allow Azure SQL to function as both an operational data store (ODS), as well as a staging layer for analytics.

Backup and Restore in Azure SQL

Backups in Azure SQL are automated and continuous. Hence, here are a few characteristics of backups in Azure SQL that you should be aware of:

- Point-in-time restore (PITR) can show you records of up to 35 days.
- Geo-redundant backups are stored across multiple regions for disaster recovery.
- Long-term retention (LTR) policies allow backups to be kept for up to 10 years. Unlike on-premises SQL Server, DBAs do not need to manually manage backups. This ultimately reduces administrative overhead.

Azure SQL vs. SQL Server on VMs (IaaS vs. PaaS)

Key distinctions:

- **Azure SQL Database (PaaS)**: Microsoft manages patching, backups, and scaling.
- **SQL Server on VM (IaaS)**: It gives you full control over OS and SQL configuration, but it requires manual management.
- **Managed Instance (MI)**: It is a hybrid option that offers almost full SQL Server compatibility with less overhead than IaaS.

  Hence, this helps enterprises choose the right deployment model based on compatibility, control, and migration complexity.

Cost Models: DTU vs. vCore

Azure SQL pricing is based on two models, which are:

- **DTU-Based (Database Transaction Units)**: It is a simplified model combining CPU, memory, and I/O.
- **vCore-Based**: It is a flexible model that allows for independent selection of compute, storage, and memory.

  Hence, understanding these models is essential for cost optimization. This is also important as many enterprises are moving to vCore for better transparency and scalability.

Hybrid Connectivity: VPN and ExpressRoute

For enterprises running hybrid cloud solutions, the following options are available:

- **Site-to-Site VPN**: It securely connects on-premises SQL Server apps to Azure SQL over the internet.

- `ExpressRoute`: It is a dedicated, private fiber connection for mission-critical workloads that require low latency.

  Hence, using either of these options ensures secure, reliable connectivity between on-premises data centers and Azure SQL.

Use Cases of Azure SQL Database

Azure SQL Database provides a flexible, fully managed relational platform that is suitable for a wide range of scenarios, from transactional workloads to analytics staging.

- **OLTP Applications**: High-throughput transactional apps
- **Multi-Tenant SaaS Apps**: Isolated databases for each customer, and is scalable with elastic pools
- **Disaster Recovery Platform**: Geo-replicated backup of on-prem SQL Server
- **Analytics Staging Layer**: Occurs before data flows into Synapse Analytics

Best Practices

When designing and managing Azure SQL databases, following best practices ensure optimal performance, security, and cost efficiency. Therefore, you must:

- Choose serverless for unpredictable workloads, and provisioned for steady workloads.
- Use geo-replication for mission-critical data.
- Leverage AAD authentication instead of SQL logins.
- Regularly review Azure Advisor recommendations for optimization.
- Enable automatic tuning to reduce DBA overhead.

Elastic Pools and Scaling Options

Azure SQL Database Elastic Pools are designed for cost efficiency and performance optimization in scenarios where multiple databases have unpredictable or fluctuating workloads. Instead of provisioning dedicated resources for each database, elastic pools allow a group of databases to share compute and storage resources, which ensures better utilization and reduces costs.

Therefore, this section explores pool design, scaling strategies, workload management, cost implications, monitoring, and real-world best practices.

Concept of Elastic Pools

Elastic pools in Azure SQL provide a cost-effective way to manage multiple databases with varying and unpredictable usage patterns such as:

- **Shared Resource Model**
  - Multiple databases (called *pooled databases*) run on a single set of resources (CPU, memory, I/O).
  - The pool guarantees an overall budget of performance that can be consumed dynamically by any database.
- **Use Case Example**: A SaaS application hosts 1,000 customer databases. Some customers are active only during business hours, others during evenings, while some remain mostly idle. Hence, instead of paying for 1,000 isolated DTU/vCore databases, elastic pools ensure only active ones consume resources, which reduces cost drastically.

Resource Allocation (DTUs vs. vCores)

Elastic pools support both compute models, as explained here:

- **DTU-Based Elastic Pools**
  - Databases share a defined number of DTUs (Database Transaction Units).
  - This is easier for organizations without deep infrastructure knowledge.
  - These pools are ideal for small to medium workloads.
- **vCore-Based Elastic Pools**
  - You get more transparency with CPU cores, memory, and storage.
  - These pools are better suited for enterprises needing predictable scaling and hybrid pricing models (including Azure Hybrid Benefit for SQL licensing).
  - They allow you to scale up and down flexibly.

Scaling Options in Elastic Pools

Elastic pools can scale both vertically and horizontally. These options are explained in detail here:

- **Vertical Scaling (Scale Up/Scale Down)**
  - Adjust the pool's total compute and storage capacity.
  - Example: Moving from a 50 vCore pool to a 100 vCore pool
  - It is useful when workloads consistently exceed the pool limits.
- **Horizontal Scaling (Adding/Removing Databases)**
  - You can increase or decrease the number of databases within a pool.
  - Example: A SaaS provider may add new customer databases daily.
- **Dynamic Workload Distribution**
  - Databases within a pool dynamically consume resources, depending on the demand.
  - This ensures that no single database is "starved", while unused capacity is shared.

Auto-Scaling vs. Manual Scaling

Elastic pools can be scaled manually or via automated strategies to match workload demands efficiently. They include:

- **Manual Scaling**
  - Admins explicitly configure pool size and max/min resources per database.
  - This provides full control, but requires monitoring.
- **Auto-Scaling (Serverless for Single DB vs. Pool Flexibility)**
  - Pools do not yet have "serverless" mode, but admins can implement Azure Monitor alerts and automation to resize pools automatically.
  - This is useful for seasonal spikes (for example, holiday traffic for retail apps).

Workload Patterns Suited for Elastic Pools

Elastic pools are best used when:

- Multiple small-to-medium databases exist with varied utilization.

- Peak usage of databases occurs at different times.
- Individual database workloads are unpredictable, but aggregate demand is predictable.
- Applications use multi-tenant architecture, such as:
    - SaaS Platforms (Each customer gets a database)
    - Financial or Healthcare Systems (Branch-Specific Databases)

However, they are not ideal when:

- A single database consumes most of the pool resources consistently; therefore, it is better to provision dedicated compute.

Cost Management and Optimization

Elastic pools provide cost-effective resource management for multiple databases by sharing compute and storage resources. Some of these features are:

- **Cost Efficiency**
    - Elastic pools are cheaper than provisioning isolated databases with similar peak capacity.
    - Microsoft estimates savings of up to 74% for SaaS multi-tenant workloads.
- **Azure Hybrid Benefit**
    - Organizations with on-premises SQL Server licenses can reuse them in vCore pools to lower costs.
- **Right-Sizing Pools**
    - Start small, monitor usage, and scale pool resources gradually.
    - Use min/max per-database limits to prevent one tenant from monopolizing resources.

Monitoring Elastic Pools

Here are some tools to monitor usage:

- **Azure Portal Metrics**: CPU, DTU %, Storage utilization, and I/O metrics
- **Query Performance Insight**: Identifies the top consuming queries across databases
- **Intelligent Insights**: Detects anomalies and recommends scaling actions
- **Custom Alerts**
    - **Example**: "Send alert when pool utilization > 80% for 15 minutes."

Limitations of Elastic Pools

While elastic pools offer cost and performance benefits, there are certain limitations to consider before implementing them, which are:

- **Single Region Deployment**: Pools reside in one region; therefore, cross-region workloads require geo-replication.
- **No Serverless Model Yet**: Unlike single database deployments, pools cannot auto-pause.
- **Overcommitment Risks:**
    - If too many databases spike simultaneously, workloads may experience throttling.
    - Therefore, it requires you to carefully set the max limits per database.

Real-World Use Cases

Elastic pools are ideal for workloads with varying and unpredictable activity patterns:

- **SaaS Applications**
  - **Example**: A learning management platform hosts 5,000 student databases. During exams, different students' databases peak at different times, which makes elastic pools an ideal choice.
- **Retail and E-commerce:** Regional store databases have activity spikes only during business hours.
- **Healthcare:** Each clinic maintains a separate patient database, but usage fluctuates based on appointment schedules.

Best Practices

To maximize the benefits of elastic pools, follow these guidelines:

- Use Elastic Pools for Multi-Tenant Models, instead of putting all tenants in one database.
- Set min/max limits per database to avoid resource hogging.
- Monitor and resize regularly using Azure Advisor recommendations.
- Consider splitting pools if a subset of databases is consistently overconsuming.
- Automate scaling with Azure Automation or Functions.

Advanced Scaling Scenarios

For applications with high growth or fluctuating workloads, elastic pools can be combined with additional strategies to maintain performance and availability. These strategies are:

- **Sharding with Elastic Pools**: When the customer count grows beyond pool limits, create multiple pools and distribute databases.
- **Burst Scaling**: During seasonal traffic, temporarily increase pool resources and scale them down later.
- **Geo-Replication and Elastic Pools**: Combine pools with Active Geo-Replication for high availability and global workloads.

Intelligent Performance Insights for Elastic Pools

Azure SQL Elastic Pools provide performance telemetry that identifies underutilized or overutilized databases within the pool. Using Intelligent Insights, administrators can:

1. Detect long-running queries impacting other databases.
2. Identify "noisy neighbor" scenarios where one database hogs resources.
3. Recommend index creation, query plan corrections, and tuning strategies. This ensures fair resource distribution across all pooled databases.

Scaling Strategies: Horizontal vs. Vertical

Elastic pools support two scaling strategies:

- **Vertical Scaling**: Increase compute or storage at the pool level (for example, moving from 100 eDTUs to 400 eDTUs).

- **Horizontal Scaling**: Spread workloads across multiple pools or shard databases. Enterprises often combine both, while ensuring that mission-critical databases scale vertically, and lightweight tenants scale horizontally.

Cost Optimization with Elastic Pools

Elastic pools are designed for cost savings when:

- Multiple databases have variable workloads—peak usage differs across time zones/customers.
- Idle databases do not need dedicated compute.
- SaaS providers host thousands of customer databases with varying activity patterns. Therefore, by aggregating resources, enterprises can reduce overprovisioning costs while maintaining performance.

Workload Management with Resource Governance

Azure allows fine-tuning of individual database limits inside a pool in the following ways:

- **Minimum eDTU/vCore per DB**: Guarantees a baseline performance
- **Maximum eDTU/vCore per DB**: Prevents one database from consuming all the pool resources
- **Per-DB Storage Limits**: Enforces quota-based allocation. Therefore, this governance ensures a fair distribution of resources across tenants.

Monitoring Elastic Pools with Azure Monitor

Elastic pools integrate seamlessly with Azure Monitor and Log Analytics using the following resources:

- Metrics such as CPU usage, DTU utilization, and storage per database
- Alerts for thresholds (for example, if a tenant DB consumes >80% of pool resources)
- Workload analytics via Query Store per database to identify heavy queries. Therefore, using these resources helps DBAs ensure balanced performance across all pooled workloads.

Business Continuity in Elastic Pools

Elastic pools also support HA/DR features like:

- Zone Redundant Configuration for regional availability
- Active Geo-Replication across regions
- Auto-Failover Groups to replicate entire pools, and not just individual databases Hence, using these features allows SaaS providers and enterprises achieve global business continuity without complex manual replication.

Elastic Pools in Multi-Tenant SaaS Architectures

A primary use case of elastic pools is in Software-as-a-Service (SaaS), which plays out as:

- Each customer gets their own database for data isolation.
- All customer databases are placed into one or more elastic pools.
- Databases scale dynamically based on tenant activity, while ensuring cost predictability.

  As a result, this model is widely adopted in industries like fintech, healthcare, and e-commerce, which are domains where tenant isolation and compliance are critical considerations.

Elastic Jobs for Management at Scale

Elastic jobs allow you to:

1. Run scheduled queries or maintenance tasks across all the databases in a pool.
2. Apply schema changes, collect statistics, and update data uniformly.
3. Automate administrative tasks (for example, reindexing, or data cleanup) without connecting to each database individually.

   Hence, this feature is essential for SaaS solutions managing a large volume of tenant databases.

Best Practices for Elastic Pool Design

- **Baseline Sizing**: Start small and scale up based on telemetry.
- **Group by Workload Similarity**: Place databases with similar patterns in the same pool.
- **Set Min/Max Limits**: Avoid noisy neighbor effects.
- **Leverage Query Store**: Monitor query performance per database.
- **Use Multiple Pools**: Separate heavy workloads from lightweight tenants.

Future Trends in Elastic Pool Scaling

Microsoft continues evolving elastic pools with:

- Serverless pools where compute scales to zero during inactivity.
- AI-driven scaling that predicts usage spikes (seasonal, time-zone driven).
- Integration with Hyperscale architecture for extreme scalability (beyond 100 TB).

  Hence, these innovations will make elastic pools even more cost-efficient and resilient.

Synapse Analytics Overview

Azure Synapse Analytics (formerly known as Azure SQL Data Warehouse) is Microsoft's cloud-based analytics service that brings together enterprise data warehousing and big data analytics into a single unified platform. Synapse allows organizations to ingest, prepare, manage, and analyze large volumes of data using familiar SQL-based tools, while also integrating seamlessly with other Azure services such as Power BI, Azure Data Lake, and Azure Machine Learning.

Hence, this section provides a comprehensive overview of Synapse Analytics, including its architecture, core features, workload types, performance tuning, integration capabilities, cost management, and real-world use cases.

Azure Synapse Analytics

- **Definition**
  - Azure Synapse is a cloud-native analytics platform that combines data warehousing, data integration, and big data analytics.
  - It permits users to query structured, semi-structured, and unstructured data using T-SQL or Apache Spark.
- **Key Idea:** Instead of moving data into different specialized systems, Synapse allows you to run analytical queries across data lakes, relational stores, and streaming pipelines, all in one place.

- **Positioning in Azure Ecosystem:** It acts as the analytics layer in a given modern data architecture, and sits between the data storage (Data Lake or SQL DB) and reporting/AI layers (Power BI or Azure ML).

Core Components of Synapse Analytics

Azure Synapse Analytics provides multiple compute and orchestration options to handle structured, semi-structured, and unstructured data at scale. Its key components include:

- **Dedicated SQL Pools**
  - It was formerly known as Azure SQL Data Warehouse.
  - It is a Massively Parallel Processing (MPP) system designed for high-performance queries over petabyte-scale structured data.
  - Here, the data is distributed across multiple compute nodes.
- **Serverless SQL Pools**
  - It is a pay-per-query model.
  - It enables querying of files in Azure Data Lake (CSV, Parquet, JSON, and so on), without the need for pre-provisioned compute.
  - It is great for exploratory analysis and ad-hoc queries.
- **Apache Spark Pools**
  - It allows for Big Data processing using Apache Spark.
  - It is ideal for data transformation, AI/ML model training, and working with unstructured data.
- **Synapse Pipelines**
  - They provide built-in data integration and ETL/ELT orchestration based on Azure Data Factory.
  - They can ingest data from over 90 connectors (SQL, Oracle, Salesforce, SAP, Blob Storage, and so on).
- **Synapse Studio**
  - It is a web-based unified management workspace.
  - It allows you to build queries, create pipelines, monitor jobs, and integrate with Power BI all in one place.

Data Architecture in Synapse

Synapse separates storage and compute to provide scalable analytics. The architecture consists of:

- **Storage Layer**
  - It relies heavily on Azure Data Lake Storage (ADLS Gen2) for raw/semi-structured data.
  - Dedicated SQL pools handle relational/structured data.
- **Compute Layer**
  - It consists of query engines (Dedicated SQL, Serverless SQL, Spark).
  - Resources can be scaled independently of storage.
- **Integration Layer**
  - It includes pipelines for ingesting and transforming data.

- **Analytics and Visualization Layer**
  - Tight integration with Power BI for interactive dashboards.
  - It can be integrated with ML for predictive analytics.

Workload Types Supported

Synapse supports diverse analytics workloads such as:

- **Data Warehousing Workloads**
  - Reporting, dashboards, and aggregations over large relational datasets
  - **Example**: Monthly financial reports, customer purchase history
- **Big Data Analytics**
  - Analyze raw/semi-structured logs, clickstream, and IoT telemetry.
  - **Example**: Retail analyzing web clickstream logs
- **Data Science and AI Integration**
  - Prepare features for Machine Learning (ML), or run Spark ML models.
  - **Example**: Fraud detection using historical transaction data
- **Real-Time or Near Real-Time Analytics**
  - Synapse can be combined with Event Hubs and Stream Analytics to support low-latency queries.
  - **Example**: Monitoring airline flight operations in near real time

Performance and Scalability

Synapse is designed for large-scale, high-performance workloads. You can further ensure scalability and performance via implementing the following strategies:

- **Massively Parallel Processing (MPP)**
  - Data is distributed across nodes for faster queries.
  - Large joins, aggregations, and scans are parallelized.
- **Scaling Compute**
  - Dedicated SQL pools allow scaling from DWU (Data Warehousing Units) up/down.
  - Serverless pools scale automatically per query.
- **Materialized Views and Result Set Caching:** Improve performance by precomputing common aggregations.
- **Data Partitioning and Distribution:** Key to avoiding data movement across nodes (which is important in performance tuning).

Integration with Other Azure Services

Synapse tightly integrates with various services in the Azure ecosystem to extend capabilities such as:

- **Power BI**: For direct integration for visualization
- **Azure Data Lake**: For native storage and query integration
- **Azure Machine Learning**: Training and deploying models using Synapse data

- **Azure Purview**: For data governance and lineage
- **Event Hubs/IoT Hub**: Streaming real-time data into Synapse

Security and Compliance

Synapse provides enterprise-grade security features like:

- **Authentication**: For integration with Azure AD
- **Encryption**: To encrypt data at rest and in transit
- **Row-Level and Column-Level Security**: To control access at a granular level
- **Dynamic Data Masking**: To protect sensitive fields like SSNs
- **Compliance**: Certified by HIPAA, ISO, SOC, and GDPR

Cost Model

Synapse offers flexible pricing models such as:

- **Dedicated SQL Pools**
    - Pay for reserved compute resources (DWUs).
    - It can be paused/resumed to save costs.
- **Serverless SQL Pools**
    - Pay only per TB of data processed.
    - There is no upfront provisioning required.
- **Apache Spark Pools**
    - Pay for vCores and execution time.
- **Optimization Strategy**
    - Use dedicated pools for predictable workloads.
    - Use serverless pools for exploratory/occasional queries.
    - Use auto-pause/resume to minimize costs.

Real-World Use Cases

Synapse is used across industries for analytics and reporting. Some of these applications are in:

- **Retail and E-commerce**: Customer behavior analytics, recommendation engines, and sales dashboards
- **Healthcare**: Population health management and predictive models for patient readmission
- **Financial Services**: Fraud detection and portfolio risk analytics
- **Airlines and Aerospace**: Predictive maintenance and flight operations analysis
- **Government and Public Sector**: Large-scale census and policy data analysis

Advantages of Synapse Analytics

Azure Synapse Analytics provides a unified platform that combines data warehousing, big data, and data lake capabilities. Additionally, it offers flexibility, scalability, and integration for modern analytics workloads. We have discussed more advantages, such as:

- A unified data warehouse, a data lake, and a Big Data platform
- Supports structured, semi-structured, and unstructured data
- Availability of on-demand and provisioned models
- Deep Azure ecosystem integration (Power BI, ML, and Data Factory)
- Enterprise-grade security and compliance

Limitations and Challenges

While Azure Synapse Analytics is a powerful platform, users must be aware of its limitations and challenges to design effective solutions, which can be:

- **Latency in Real-Time Analytics**: This is not as low-latency as it is while streaming-first tools.
- **Learning Curve**: It requires a strong understanding of both SQL MPP and Big Data tools.
- **Storage Costs**: ADLS costs can grow rapidly with large uncompressed datasets.
- **Performance Tuning Required**: Distribution/partition strategies are critical.

Best Practices

To maximize performance, reduce costs, and ensure scalability, consider implementing the following best practices:

1. Use dedicated SQL pools for structured, repeatable reporting workloads.
2. Use serverless pools for raw lake data exploration.
3. Store data in Parquet/Delta formats for faster query performance.
4. Optimize table distribution (hash/round-robin/replicated) to reduce data movement.
5. Combine Power BI with Synapse for near real-time dashboards.
6. Set up cost alerts and auto-pause to prevent runaway bills.

PolyBase Integration in Synapse Analytics

Synapse Analytics uses PolyBase to query external data sources directly from the data warehouse without ETL. Therefore, here are some points that you should remember about PolyBase integration in Synapse Analytics:

- It supports querying Azure Blob Storage, Data Lake Storage, Hadoop, as well as external relational databases.
- It eliminates the need to move large datasets physically into Synapse before analysis.
- **Example**: A finance team can query transaction logs in blob storage directly, as shown here:

  ```
  CREATE EXTERNAL TABLE Sales_External
  WITH (DATA_SOURCE = AzureBlobStorage, LOCATION = 'transactions/')
  AS SELECT * FROM Sales_External;
  ```

- This reduces storage duplication, and hence accelerates data integration.

Serverless SQL Pools for Ad Hoc Analysis

Synapse offers serverless SQL pools, which offer the following features:

- Query the data stored in data lakes, without having to provision dedicated compute.
- It is a pay-per-query model, and is thus ideal for ad hoc analytics.

- Example: A data analyst can run exploratory queries on CSV, Parquet, or JSON files directly from Synapse.

Best Practice: Use serverless pools for occasional analytics workloads and dedicated pools for high-performance, production-grade ETL pipelines.

Dedicated SQL Pools

Dedicated SQL pools provide provisioned compute for:

- Large-scale analytics workloads
- High concurrency queries for OLAP scenarios
- Massively Parallel Processing (MPP) across multiple nodes for faster aggregations and joins

Example:

- A retail company analyzing 1 billion sales records can partition the data across compute nodes, and thus enable sub-second aggregation queries.

Best Practice: Align the DWUs (Data Warehouse Units) with expected workloads, and remember to monitor usage with Workload Management.

Data Lake Integration

Synapse integrates tightly with Azure Data Lake Storage Gen2, which allows for:

- Direct querying of raw, semi-structured, or structured files
- Building a data lake + warehouse hybrid architecture
- Combining batch and streaming data sources for analytics

Example: Combining CSV sales data and JSON IoT logs in the same query for cross-analysis

Security and Compliance in Synapse

Synapse provides the following features for security and compliance:

- Row-Level Security (RLS) for user-specific data access
- Dynamic Data Masking (DDM) to obscure sensitive fields
- TDE (Transparent Data Encryption) and encryption in transit (TLS)
- Auditing and integration with Azure AD for identity management
- Additionally, compliance with GDPR, HIPAA, and PCI-DSS makes Synapse suitable for enterprise workloads.

Workload Management and Resource Classes

Synapse allows resource class configuration to optimize query concurrency as follows:

- Small, medium, and large resource classes can allocate different memory/compute per query.
- It enables balancing concurrent small queries with large ETL batch jobs.
- It helps in preventing a single heavy query from monopolizing resources.

Monitoring and Performance Tuning

Synapse provides tools like:

- **Query Performance Insights**: To visualize slow queries and resource bottlenecks
- **Workload Management**: To assign priorities to different query types
- **Dynamic Management Views (DMVs)**: To inspect execution stats, node usage, and queue waits

Example: Identifying a long-running join between fact and dimension tables and adjusting partitioning accordingly.

Data Movement Optimization

Synapse minimizes data movement across nodes with the following distribution strategies:

- Hash-Distributed Tables: Efficient for large fact tables with join operations
- Round-Robin Tables: Simple distribution without key-based partitioning
- Replicated Tables: Smaller dimension tables that are replicated across nodes for faster joins

Choosing the right distribution type reduces shuffle operations, improving performance.

Integration with Power BI and Machine Learning (ML)

Azure Synapse Analytics enables seamless integration with Power BI and Azure Machine Learning, while providing a complete end-to-end analytics workflow. Data can flow from ingestion to transformation, visualization, and predictive modeling without moving between platforms. Moreover:

- Synapse integrates natively with Power BI for dashboards.
- Data can be exported for Azure Machine Learning to run predictive models.
- This enables end-to-end analytics workflows from ingestion to transformation to visualization, and finally, to ML insights.

Best Practices for Synapse Analytics

To optimize performance, security, and cost-efficiency in Synapse Analytics, follow these guidelines:

- Partition large fact tables using hash or round-robin strategies.
- Use serverless SQL pools for exploration and dedicated pools for production ETL/analytics.
- Enable monitoring and alerts for workload bottlenecks.
- Apply row-level security and dynamic data masking for sensitive data.
- Archive historical data in data lakes to optimize storage costs.

PolyBase and External Tables

One of the most powerful capabilities within Azure Synapse Analytics and Azure SQL Database is the ability to seamlessly query external data sources without physically moving data into the database. This is made possible through PolyBase and external tables. Together, they enable developers and analysts to integrate heterogeneous data sources (structured, semi-structured, and unstructured) into a unified SQL query experience.

Therefore section explains PolyBase, how it works, the role of external tables, and the best practices to implement for performance and security.

PolyBase

PolyBase is a data virtualization technology that allows SQL Server, Azure SQL Database, and Azure Synapse to query data stored outside the database as if it were inside a native table. Moreover:

- It supports structured data (relational databases), semi-structured data (CSV, JSON, ORC, Parquet), and unstructured files stored in Azure Blob Storage, Azure Data Lake Storage (ADLS), or Hadoop Distributed File System (HDFS).
- Users do not need to build complex ETL pipelines for every scenario. Instead, they can access data "in place", which reduces duplication and storage costs.

Key Benefit: Query big data platforms (Hadoop, Spark, cloud object storage) and traditional databases using T-SQL, all without requiring specialized connectors or programming.

External Tables

External tables act as metadata objects that define the schema of external data, so that SQL queries can reference it like a regular table. Unlike internal tables, they do not store data within the database. Instead, they provide a logical mapping to the underlying external data source.

Example Use Case:

- Finance team queries CSV files stored in ADLS without importing them into Synapse.
- Marketing analysts combine relational customer data from Azure SQL Database with unstructured clickstream logs in blob storage.

PolyBase Workflow

The general workflow for using PolyBase and external tables involves four main steps, which are:

1. **Create a Database Scoped Credential**. Securely define the authentication mechanism to access external data (for example, SAS token, Managed Identity, or Service Principal).
2. **Create an External Data Source**. Define the location of the external storage system (for example, an Azure Blob container, an ADLS Gen2 path, or a Hadoop cluster).
3. **Create an External File Format (Optional)**. Specify the file type (CSV, Parquet, ORC, and so on), encoding, field terminators, and compression type.
4. **Create an External Table**. Define the schema that maps external data to a relational structure, and eventually makes it queryable via T-SQL.

Supported Data Sources

PolyBase supports a wide range of external data sources such as:

- **Cloud Storage Services**:
    - Azure Blob Storage
    - Azure Data Lake Storage (Gen1 and Gen2)
    - Amazon S3 (via Connectors)
- **Big Data Platforms**:
    - Hadoop Clusters
    - Spark Environments

- **Relational Databases**:
    - Oracle
    - Teradata
    - MongoDB (via ODBC Connectors)
- **File-Based Data**:
    - CSV, TSV
    - Parquet
    - ORC
    - Avro
    - JSON

Example: Querying Data in Azure Blob Storage

The following is an example of how you can query external CSV files that are stored in Azure Blob Storage:

```
-- Step 1: Create a database scoped credential.
CREATE DATABASE SCOPED CREDENTIAL BlobCred
WITH IDENTITY = 'SHARED ACCESS SIGNATURE',
SECRET = 'sv=2025-01-01&ss=bfqt&srt=sco&sp=rlx...';

-- Step 2: Define the external data source.
CREATE EXTERNAL DATA SOURCE BlobStorage
WITH (
    TYPE = HADOOP,
    LOCATION = 'abfss://data@mydatalake.dfs.core.windows.net/',
    CREDENTIAL = BlobCred
);

-- Step 3: Define the file format.
CREATE EXTERNAL FILE FORMAT CsvFormat
WITH (
    FORMAT_TYPE = DELIMITEDTEXT,
    FORMAT_OPTIONS (FIELD_TERMINATOR = ',', STRING_DELIMITER = '"', FIRST_ROW = 2)
);

-- Step 4: Create the external table.
CREATE EXTERNAL TABLE ExternalSalesData (
    SaleID INT,
    ProductName NVARCHAR(100),
    SaleAmount DECIMAL(10,2),
    SaleDate DATETIME
)
WITH (
    LOCATION = '/sales/2025/',
    DATA_SOURCE = BlobStorage,
    FILE_FORMAT = CsvFormat
);
```

```
-- Step 5: Query the external table.
SELECT TOP 10 * FROM ExternalSalesData;
```

With this setup, you can query sales data directly from Blob storage without importing it into Synapse or SQL Server.

Performance Considerations

While PolyBase makes querying external data easy, performance tuning is critical. Therefore, you must consider the following:

- **Pushdown Computation**: PolyBase can push filtering and projection operations closer to the data source, which reduces the amount of data transferred.
- **Partition Pruning**: Use partitioned external tables to query subsets of large datasets.
- **File Format Optimization**: Prefer Parquet or ORC over CSV for faster reads and better compression.
- **Indexing Strategy**: Since external tables cannot have indexes, consider staging frequently used data into internal tables for repeated queries.

Security in PolyBase and External Tables

Security is a key consideration when integrating external data. Therefore, to maintain it, you must:

- Use Azure AD authentication or Managed Identity, and you should not embed secrets.
- Restrict access to external storage via firewall rules and private endpoints.
- Encrypt data in transit (TLS) and at rest (Azure Storage Encryption).
- Use role-based access control (RBAC) to manage external data source access.

Advantages of PolyBase and External Tables

PolyBase and external tables allow seamless access to data across relational and big data sources. This eventually reduces the ETL complexity and enables hybrid architectures. We have mentioned a few more advantages here:

- Seamless integration of big data and relational data
- Reduces ETL complexity by enabling "schema-on-read"
- Cost savings by avoiding unnecessary data duplication
- Enables hybrid architectures across on-prem, cloud, and third-party sources

Limitations

While PolyBase and external tables are powerful, there are performance and functional constraints, which are explained as follows:

- The performance may lag compared to querying internal tables.
- External tables cannot be indexed or enforced with constraints.
- Write operations are limited, and are primarily used for read-only querying (even though PolyBase supports some data movement with `CREATE EXTERNAL TABLE AS SELECT` in Synapse).

Best Practices

To maximize performance and reliability when using PolyBase and external tables:

1. Use Parquet format for analytical workloads due to compression and columnar storage.
2. Avoid querying extremely small files, which can cause performance overhead due to file fragmentation; consolidate them when possible to improve efficiency.
3. For repeated queries, stage the data into internal tables for performance.
4. Secure external connections using Azure Key Vault to manage credentials.
5. Use external tables for exploratory analysis, and internal tables for production workloads.

Performance Considerations with PolyBase

PolyBase allows querying external data directly, but its performance depends on:

- The network throughput that exists between SQL and the external source.
- File Format: Parquet and ORC formats are optimized for columnar storage; therefore, CSV/JSON may be slower.
- Predicate Pushdown: The filters that are applied in SQL query should be pushed down to the external source to reduce data movement.
- Partitioning: Large datasets benefit from partitioned external tables to parallelize queries.

Best Practice: Use Parquet files with partitioning and push filters to minimize data transfer for faster query performance.

Security and Authentication

When using PolyBase, remember to use the following in the stipulated ways:

- **Azure Blob Storage/Data Lake**: Use Managed Identity or SAS tokens for authentication.
- **External RDBMS**: Use SQL Auth or Active Directory credentials.
- **Encryption in Transit**: TLS is supported for secure connections.

Example:

```
CREATE EXTERNAL DATA SOURCE MyBlob
WITH (
    TYPE = HADOOP,
    LOCATION = 'abfss://container@account.dfs.core.windows.net/',
    CREDENTIAL = MyManagedIdentity
);
```

Best Practice: Always use least-privilege credentials, and also make sure to secure the access methods to external data.

Using External Tables for ETL Simplification

PolyBase external tables reduce the need for intermediate ETL steps in the following manner:

1. By querying the raw data directly from Azure Data Lake
2. By joining multiple external sources with internal tables for analysis
3. Example: Consolidating sales CSV files from multiple regions without importing each file

Benefit: This reduces storage redundancy and ETL overhead.

Integration with Synapse Analytics

PolyBase enables seamless integration of external data into Synapse Analytics, and allows you to query and combine diverse data sources for analytics. The integration is further realized by the following facts:

- PolyBase allows direct querying of external data from Synapse SQL pools.
- External tables can act as a staging layer before transforming the data into dedicated SQL tables.
- This is ideal for big data pipelines that combine structured and semi-structured data for analytics.

Data Virtualization across Heterogeneous Sources

PolyBase supports multiple source types like:

- Relational Databases (SQL Server, Oracle, or Teradata)
- Hadoop and HDFS Clusters
- Azure Blob Storage, Data Lake
- Cosmos DB

Use Case: Run a query joining on-premises SQL Server transactional data and Azure Data Lake logs, without moving the data physically.

Limitations and Workarounds

While external tables in PolyBase enable flexible data access, they have performance and feature constraints that must be managed. These constraints are thus mentioned as follows:

- The joins between the external tables may be slower than the ones between internal tables; therefore, you should consider importing hot datasets.
- In some sources, unsupported data types might require mapping.
- Query hints and indexing are limited on external tables.

Workaround: Use CTEs or staging tables for frequently joined external data to improve performance.

Monitoring PolyBase Queries

Tracking external query execution helps identify bottlenecks and optimize performance. You can do so via:

- Using Dynamic Management Views (DMVs) like `sys.dm_pdw_exec_requests` in Synapse or `sys.dm_exec_requests` in SQL Database
- Tracking external query duration, row counts, and resource consumption
- Identifying slow queries or external bottlenecks

Best Practices for External Tables

Following best practices ensure efficient and reliable querying of external data. These practices are:

- Using columnar formats (Parquet/ORC) instead of row-based (CSV/JSON) formats
- Partitioning large external tables to parallelize scans
- Pushing filters and projections to external sources

- Regularly monitoring query performance and external source health
- Combining external tables with internal staging tables for frequent analysis

Hybrid Cloud Architectures

PolyBase enables integration between on-premises and cloud data sources. This is achieved through the following features:

- PolyBase enables on-premises and cloud integration.
- Example: Keep historical transaction data in Data Lake, transactional OLTP in Azure SQL, and query both via external tables.
- It is thus useful for gradual cloud migrations, as it avoids completely replicating the full data upfront.

Cost Optimization Strategies

Efficient use of external tables can reduce query costs and resource consumption. You can implement this by:

- Querying only the required columns and rows to minimize data transfer
- Using serverless SQL pools for ad hoc queries to avoid provisioning dedicated compute
- Archiving rarely accessed external data in cold storage
- Monitoring query metrics to identify cost-heavy queries

Future Enhancements and Trends

PolyBase continues to evolve, and is now offering better integration, performance, and hybrid capabilities. These new enhancements are:

- Integration with Delta Lake for transactional data on external sources
- Improved predicate pushdown and query optimization
- Better tooling for monitoring and alerts on external data queries
- Continued focus on hybrid architectures with on-prem and multi-cloud support

Security and Cost Management in Cloud

When you are working with Azure SQL Database and Azure Synapse Analytics, security and cost management will surface as two of the most critical considerations. Unlike traditional on-premises SQL Server deployments, cloud services introduce shared responsibility models for security and a pay-as-you-go pricing structure. Therefore, it means that DBAs, developers, and architects must adapt to new paradigms, and also ensure that the data remains secure, compliant, and cost-efficient. Moreover, it should still deliver the required performance.

Hence, this section explores the security frameworks, the authentication methods, encryption, compliance standards, monitoring, and the strategies for cloud cost optimization in SQL workloads.

Error Handling, Cost Management, and Network Security in a DevOps Pipeline

A well-designed DevOps pipeline must address not only automation and reliability, but also error handling, cost management, and network security. These considerations are especially important when deploying and operating SQL Server workloads in cloud or hybrid environments. Some of these considerations are discussed here:

- **Error handling** ensures that database deployments and automated SQL Server tasks fail deterministically whenever an issue occurs. Therefore, pipelines should validate execution results, enforce fail-fast behavior, and capture detailed logs and SQL Server error messages. This prevents partial deployments, and also simplifies troubleshooting during CI/CD processes.
- **Cost management** is a critical aspect of pipeline design, particularly in environments that provision cloud-based database resources on demand. Therefore, pipelines should avoid unnecessary resource usage by shutting down idle services, limiting execution time, and monitoring resource consumption during builds and deployments. Moreover, incorporating cost-awareness into DevOps workflows helps prevent unexpected expenses, and also supports the efficient use of infrastructure.
- **Network security** must also be enforced throughout the pipeline. Database connections should be restricted using secure authentication, encrypted communication, and network-level controls such as firewalls, private endpoints, or virtual networks. Additionally, sensitive credentials should be stored securely, and should never be embedded directly in pipeline scripts or configuration files.

Therefore, by incorporating structured error handling, cost management controls, and network security practices, DevOps pipelines can deliver reliable, secure, and cost-effective SQL Server deployments, and also maintain operational transparency and governance.

Azure Security Framework for SQL

Microsoft Azure follows a shared responsibility model, which is realized in the following ways:

- Microsoft secures the infrastructure, physical hardware, and platform services.
- Customers are responsible for securing data, identities, applications, and access policies.

For Azure SQL and Synapse, this means that:

- Microsoft ensures the physical security, network segmentation, and automatic updates.
- You must configure firewalls, authentication, encryption, and access governance.

Authentication and Identity Management

Azure SQL supports multiple authentication methods, each suitable for different scenarios. These are:

- **SQL Authentication**
  - It is a traditional login method with a username and password.
  - It is easy to configure, but it is also less secure if it is not managed with complex passwords and rotation policies.
- **Azure Active Directory (Azure AD) Authentication**
  - It integrates SQL access with corporate identity and Role-Based Access Control (RBAC).
  - It enables Single Sign-On (SSO) and Multi-Factor Authentication (MFA).
  - It is recommended for enterprise workloads for central identity governance.
- **Managed Identity Authentication**
  - It allows applications running in Azure (App Service, Functions, and Logic Apps) to authenticate without storing credentials.

- It reduces the risk of credential leaks in configuration files or connection strings.

Network Security and Firewalls

Azure SQL provides layered network protection to minimize attack surfaces, which are:

- **Server-Level Firewall Rules**: They control the IP ranges that can connect to your SQL Server.
- **VNet Service Endpoints**: They restrict access to only specific Azure Virtual Networks (AVNs).
- **Private Endpoints**: They allow SQL connections only over private IPs, and can completely isolate from public internet.
- **Advanced Threat Protection**: It monitors for unusual logins, brute-force attempts, and SQL injection attacks.

Best Practice: Always prefer private endpoints, and make sure that you deny public internet access to production SQL databases.

Encryption and Data Protection

Azure SQL provides multiple encryption features to protect data at rest and in transit, which are:

- **Encryption in Transit**: Secures all connections with TLS/SSL
- **Transparent Data Encryption (TDE)**: Encrypts entire databases at rest using AES encryption
- **Always Encrypted**: Protects sensitive columns (for example, SSN, credit card numbers) to the extent that even Microsoft cannot read them
- **Dynamic Data Masking (DDM)**: Obscures sensitive data in query results for non-privileged users
- **Row-Level Security (RLS)**: Restricts access to rows based on user identity

Example: With RLS, a sales manager can query the same Sales table as other managers, but they can only see rows for their respective region.

Compliance and Auditing

Organizations running SQL workloads in the cloud often face regulatory requirements such as:

- GDPR (Europe)
- HIPAA (Healthcare)
- PCI-DSS (Payment Systems)
- SOX (Financial Reporting)

Azure SQL and Synapse provide tools for compliance, which can be:

- **SQL Auditing**: Logs database events for monitoring and forensic analysis
- **Azure Defender for SQL**: Detects SQL injection, brute-force attacks, and misconfigurations
- **Data Classification**: Labels sensitive data for reporting and auditing

Cost Management in Azure SQL and Synapse

While Azure provides flexibility and scalability, costs can grow quickly without governance. Therefore, managing cloud costs requires strategic planning, which can be done through:

1. **Pricing Models**
    - **DTU-Based (Database Transaction Units)**: A simple, fixed performance model
    - **vCore-Based**: Provides more control with separate compute, memory, and storage costs
    - **Serverless Tier**: Auto-scales compute based on workload, and pauses during inactivity to save costs
    - **Hyperscale Tier**: Allows massive scaling, but can be costly if it is over-provisioned
2. **Cost Optimization Techniques**
    - **Elastic Pools**: They share resources across multiple databases with fluctuating workloads.
    - **Auto-Pause (Serverless)**: They are ideal for development/testing databases.
    - **Reserved Instances (1-3 Years)**: They result in significant savings for predictable workloads.
    - **Scaling Compute Only during Peak Hours**: Use automation scripts or Azure Automation Runbooks to scale up and down.
3. **Synapse-Specific Cost Controls**
    - **Dedicated SQL Pools (Provisioned Model)**: They charge by compute size, even when they are idle.
    - **Serverless SQL Pools**: These are pay-per-query models, and are great for ad-hoc analysis.
    - **Pause/Resume Compute**: They are critical for reducing costs when you are not querying.

Monitoring and Alerts for Security and Cost

Effective governance requires continuous monitoring. This can be done through:

- **Azure Monitor and Log Analytics**: Track query performance, CPU usage, and failed login attempts.
- **Cost Alerts**: Set thresholds to detect unexpected cost spikes.
- **Resource Tags**: Assign costs to departments, projects, or environments for accountability.
- **Security Alerts**: Detect SQL injection, abnormal logins, and excessive privilege usage.

Best Practices for Security and Cost Management

Implementing strong security controls while optimizing costs ensures both compliance and budget efficiency in Azure SQL and Synapse environments. Therefore, you must:

- Use Azure AD with MFA instead of SQL authentication.
- Always enable TDE and auditing.
- Apply the least privilege principle with RBAC.
- Use elastic pools or serverless tier for unpredictable workloads.
- Leverage reserved instances for production workloads with predictable usage.
- Configure alerts for cost overruns and security anomalies.

Azure Role-Based Access Control (RBAC) Best Practices

Azure SQL and Synapse use RBAC to manage permissions at scale by/through:

- Assigning roles at resource, resource group, or subscription level
- Built-in Roles: SQL DB Contributor, Synapse Admin, or Reader
- Creating custom roles for fine-grained access control

Best Practice: Use the least privilege principle to grant only the permissions that are required for the job; avoid assigning high-level roles unnecessarily.

Managed Identity Authentication

Azure services support Managed Identity (MI) for secure authentication in the following manner:

- It eliminates storing credentials in code or configuration files.
- **Example**: Azure SQL can authenticate automatically to Azure Key Vault or Blob Storage using MI.

  ```
  CREATE DATABASE SCOPED CREDENTIAL MyCredential
  WITH IDENTITY = 'Managed Identity';
  ```

- It improves security posture, besides simplifying credential rotation.

Transparent Data Encryption (TDE) and Always Encrypted

Protecting sensitive data both at rest and in use is essential for compliance and security in modern database environments. Therefore, you must be aware of the following TDE features:

- TDE encrypts data at rest automatically using the AES 256-bit encryption.
- Always Encrypted protects sensitive data at the column level, while ensuring client-side encryption.
- TDE is ideal for PII, financial, or healthcare data, as it ensures that it is meeting the compliance requirements (such as GDPR or HIPAA).

Example: Protecting a `CreditCardNumber` column using Always Encrypted can be done via:

```
CREATE COLUMN MASTER KEY MyCMK
WITH KEY_STORE_PROVIDER_NAME = 'AZURE_KEY_VAULT';
```

Auditing and Threat Detection

Azure SQL includes built-in auditing and threat detection mechanisms. Therefore, you must:

- Audit actions like logins, schema changes, and failed attempts.
- Enable Advanced Threat Protection (ATP) to detect SQL injection attempts, anomalous access patterns, and brute-force attacks.
- Audits can be exported to Log Analytics, Storage, or Event Hub for compliance reporting.

Network Security and Firewalls

Securing database access at the network level is critical to prevent unauthorized connections and data breaches. Therefore, you must:

- Configure server-level and database-level firewall rules.
- Use Virtual Network Service Endpoints (VNSEs) to restrict traffic to trusted networks.
- Enable private endpoints for secure connectivity to Azure SQL or Synapse from within the VNet.

Best Practice: Avoid exposing databases to the public internet whenever possible.

Cost Management with Azure Advisor

Azure Advisor provides the following recommendations for cost optimization:

- Identify underutilized databases or pools.
- Suggest compute scaling down during low-demand periods.
- Highlight opportunities for Reserved Instance Purchase (RIP) to reduce long-term costs.

Example: A elastic pool with many idle databases can be scaled down to save eDTUs, without compromising performance.

Monitoring and Alerts for Cost Control

Keeping track of usage and cost is essential to prevent budget overruns and optimize resource allocation. Therefore, you must:

- Use the Azure Monitor and Cost Management and the Billing dashboards.
- Set budget alerts for unexpected spikes in DTU/vCore usage.
- Integrate with Power BI to track historical cost trends per workload or department.

Automated Scaling for Cost Efficiency

Dynamic scaling ensures performance during peak workloads, while minimizing costs during idle periods. Therefore, you must employ the following strategies to automate scaling:

- Use elastic pools and serverless compute options for workloads that have fluctuating usage.
- Enable auto-pause for serverless pools to suspend compute when they are inactive to save costs.
- Scale compute dynamically based on workload peaks using automation scripts or Azure Automation.

Backup and Retention Cost Optimization

Efficient backup strategies reduce storage costs while ensuring data availability and compliance. Hence, you must be mindful of a few of them:

- Configure LTR policies judiciously, and avoid keeping rarely accessed backups at high-performance tiers.
- Use geo-redundant storage selectively for mission-critical data.
- Archive historical data in Blob Storage Cool/Archive tiers to reduce storage costs.

Compliance and Governance

Maintaining regulatory compliance protects your organization and ensures responsible resource use. Therefore, you must:

- Maintain a centralized security policy using Azure Policy.
- Enforce data classification to identify sensitive columns and tables.
- Audit resource usage and access logs regularly to ensure regulatory compliance.

Cost Allocation and Chargeback

Proper allocation helps track expenses, assign accountability, and optimize budgets. Therefore, to ensure it, you must:

- Tag resources with department, project, or workload identifiers.
- Allocate costs to business units that are using Azure Cost Management for accountability.
- Additionally, proper allocation allows enterprises to optimize budget planning and identify high-cost workloads.

Best Practices Summary for Security and Cost Management

Combining security with cost control ensures both safe and efficient operations. Therefore, you must remember the following best practices:

- Implement RBAC and Managed Identity for secure access.
- Encrypt sensitive data using TDE and Always Encrypted.
- Monitor usage with Azure Monitor and Cost Management dashboards.
- Automate scaling and backup retention to control costs.
- Apply firewall rules and VNet integration to enhance network security.
- Regularly review threat detection alerts and audit logs.

Key Takeaways

Security and cost management are the two sides of the same coin in cloud SQL deployments. Strong security ensures data integrity and compliance, while cost management ensures the maintenance of financial sustainability. Therefore, by leveraging features like Azure AD, encryption, auditing, monitoring, elastic pools, and reserved instances, organizations can balance security, performance, and cost-efficiency in Azure SQL Database and Synapse Analytics.

Conclusion

In this chapter, you explored cloud-based SQL solutions and modern data warehousing with Azure services. You also learned about the differences between Azure SQL Database, Managed Instances, and SQL Server on VMs, and how to configure elastic pools, firewall rules, and Azure Active Directory authentication.

Further, this chapter explored Synapse Analytics and PolyBase, while demonstrating how to query external data and handle large-scale analytics workloads. Topics like cost management, security best practices, and performance optimization techniques were covered, so that you are able to deploy resilient and scalable cloud-native SQL solutions.

The next chapter will shift focus to security, permissions, and auditing, while teaching you how to protect sensitive data, enforce fine-grained access control, and implement compliance strategies.

CHAPTER 13
Security, Permissions, and Auditing

Introduction

Security is a foundational concern for database administrators and developers alike. This is because protecting sensitive data, controlling access, and ensuring compliance with regulations are important considerations that help organizations maintain trust and minimize risks. Therefore, in this chapter, we will focus on SQL Server security best practices, and will cover authentication, authorization, advanced access control techniques, encryption, as well as some auditing strategies.

Structure

In this chapter, we will cover the following topics:

- User Authentication and Authorization
- Role-Based Security and Permissions
- Row-Level Security and Data Masking
- Encryption (TDE, Always Encrypted)
- Auditing and Compliance

User Authentication and Authorization

Authentication and authorization are the foundations of database security. Authentication ensures that a user or process is who they claim to be, while authorization controls the actions that they are allowed to perform once they are authenticated. SQL Server provides multiple authentication methods and flexible mechanisms to manage user access. Therefore, understanding these mechanisms is critical for building secure and compliant database applications.

SQL Server Authentication

SQL Server Authentication is the traditional login method where users provide a username and password to connect to the database.

Features:

- Credentials are stored inside SQL Server.
- It is independent of Windows domain accounts.
- It is useful for applications that require database access without domain trust.

Example: Creating a SQL Server Login

```
CREATE LOGIN SalesUser WITH PASSWORD = 'StrongP@ssw0rd!';
```

Best Practices:

- Enforce strong password policies that include complexity, expiration, and history.
- Disable SQL authentication for servers that can rely on Windows Authentication for centralized security.
- Monitor failed login attempts for security auditing.

Windows Authentication

Windows Authentication leverages Active Directory (AD) to validate users. This method is considered more secure because it relies on domain credentials, besides integrating with organizational identity policies.

Features:

- It supports Kerberos authentication for secure and single-sign-on (SSO) experiences.
- It allows centralized management of users and groups.
- It works well with domain-controlled environments.

Example: Creating a Windows Login

```
CREATE LOGIN [DOMAIN\JohnDoe] FROM WINDOWS;
```

Best Practices:

- Prefer Windows Authentication over SQL Server Authentication whenever possible.
- Use Active Directory groups instead of individual accounts to simplify role management.
- Enable Kerberos to avoid "double-hop" issues in multi-tier applications.

Azure Active Directory Authentication

For cloud-hosted SQL databases, Azure AD provides the following identity management capabilities:

- It supports multi-factor authentication (MFA).
- It enables centralized control for both on-premises and cloud users.
- It integrates with Azure Role-Based Access Control (RBAC) for granular permissions.

Example: Creating a Database User Mapped to an Azure AD Account

```
CREATE USER [aaduser@domain.com] FROM EXTERNAL PROVIDER;
ALTER ROLE db_datareader ADD MEMBER [aaduser@domain.com];
```

Best Practices:

- Leverage Azure AD for hybrid environments to maintain centralized identity.
- Use conditional access policies to enforce compliance with organizational security standards.
- Integrate MFA and passwordless authentication methods for enhanced security.

Contained Database Users

Contained users allow authentication at the database level, independent of server-level logins. Therefore, using contained users is especially useful for cloud or multi-tenant databases.

Benefits:

- Contained users simplify the migration of databases between servers.
- They reduce dependency on server-level logins.
- They support both SQL and Azure AD authentication.

Example: Creating a Contained SQL User

```
CREATE USER SalesUser WITH PASSWORD = 'StrongP@ssw0rd!';
```

Best Practices:

- Enable containment only for databases that require portability.
- Use contained users with least privilege permissions.

External Authentication Providers

SQL Server can integrate with external identity providers via OAuth 2.0, SAML, or Azure AD B2C in the following ways:

- They provide authentication for applications that connect to SQL Server, without needing you to manage local credentials.
- They support modern Single Sign-on (SSO) experiences.
- They enhance security by leveraging enterprise identity policies.

Best Practices:

- Use external providers for web and mobile applications to avoid storing credentials in the database.
- Combine them with token-based authentication for temporary access.

Multi-Factor Authentication (MFA) Integration

Multi-Factor Authentication (MFA) adds an extra layer of security beyond usernames and passwords. In MFA, users must provide:

- Something that they know (a password)
- Something that they have (a mobile authenticator, or a token)
- Optionally, something that indicates their identity (biometric verification)

Implementation:

- For Azure SQL Database, you can enable MFA via Azure AD policies.
- For on-prem SQL, you can integrate MFA with Active Directory Federation Services (ADFS).

Benefits:

- MFA significantly reduces the risk of compromised credentials.
- MFA enforces corporate security policies for sensitive databases.

Login Auditing

Auditing login events helps detect unauthorized access attempts, besides ensuring compliance.

Example: Capturing Failed Login Attempts

```
SELECT login_name, COUNT(*) AS FailedAttempts
FROM sys.fn_get_audit_file('C:\AuditLogs\*', DEFAULT, DEFAULT)
```

```
WHERE action_id = 'LGIF' -- Login failed
GROUP BY login_name;
```

Best Practices:

- It helps us configure alerts for repeated failed logins.
- It can be integrated with SIEM tools for enterprise-level monitoring.

Authorization and Permission Management

Authorization defines what a user can do after authentication. It includes the following components:

- **Explicit Permissions**: Granted directly to users
- **Schema-Based Permissions**: Applied at the schema level
- **Ownership Chaining**: Reduces the need for redundant grants

Example: Granting `SELECT` Permission on a Table

```
GRANT SELECT ON dbo.Customers TO SalesUser;
```

Best Practices:

- Always apply the least privilege principle.
- Use roles to simplify permission management.
- Regularly audit permissions to prevent privilege creep.

Impersonation and `EXECUTE AS`

SQL Server supports impersonation to test and execute the actions that occur in another user's context.

Example:

```
EXECUTE AS USER = 'SalesUser';
SELECT * FROM dbo.Sales;
REVERT;
```

Use Cases:

- Testing permissions
- Safely running stored procedures with elevated privileges
- Debugging security-related issues

Best Practices Summary

Ensuring secure access to Azure SQL databases requires a combination of strong authentication methods, role-based access control, and regular auditing. Therefore, you must be familiar with the following best practices to facilitate secure access to Azure SQL databases:

1. Prefer Windows or Azure AD Authentication over SQL authentication wherever possible.
2. Use contained users for portable databases.
3. Implement multi-factor authentication to secure sensitive databases.
4. Apply the least privilege principle while granting permissions.
5. Regularly audit login activity and permissions for compliance.
6. Use roles and groups to centralize and simplify access control.
7. Combine authentication strategies with encryption and auditing for a defense-in-depth security model.

Multi-Factor Authentication (MFA) and Conditional Access (Azure AD)

MFA and Azure AD Conditional Access require a second factor (app prompt, SMS, or FIDO2 key) for Azure AD-backed logins to Azure SQL/Managed Instance.

They matter because they can greatly reduce any risk that may come from stolen passwords; additionally, they can implement a policy like *block legacy auth, require compliant device, or enforce location/time.*

Here is how you can use MFA and Conditional Access:

- You can enforce MFA via Azure AD Conditional Access on users/groups that are used for Azure SQL.
- You must prefer the passwordless (FIDO2/Authenticator) setting wherever possible.

  Tips:

  - *You should pair MFA only with Azure AD-only authentication (disable SQL logins wherever feasible).*
  - *You must exclude automation principals; use Managed Identity instead.*

Login Auditing and Alerting

Goal: Detect brute force, anomalous locations, or disabled accounts that might try to connect

Server Audit (Example):

```
-- Create and enable an audit to file.
CREATE SERVER AUDIT Audit_Logins
TO FILE (FILEPATH = 'D:\Audits\', MAXSIZE = 1 GB, ROLLOVER_ON_SHUTDOWN = ON);
ALTER SERVER AUDIT Audit_Logins WITH (STATE = ON);

-- Capture failed/successful logins.
CREATE SERVER AUDIT SPECIFICATION Audit_LoginActivity
FOR SERVER AUDIT Audit_Logins
ADD (SUCCESSFUL_LOGIN_GROUP),
ADD (FAILED_LOGIN_GROUP)
WITH (STATE = ON);
```

Here, you must operationalize the following:

- Stream to SIEM (Sentinel/Splunk); send alerts on spikes.
- Correlate with firewall and OS logs.

Contained Database Users (Deep Dive)

Contained database users can authenticate directly at the database level without requiring a server-level login. This design simplifies database migrations and provides better isolation for tenants in multi-tenant environments.

Create:

```
ALTER DATABASE SalesDb SET CONTAINMENT = PARTIAL;
USE SalesDb;
CREATE USER app_user WITH PASSWORD = 'Str0ngP@ss!';
```

Observations:

- Differences in **tempdb** collation are observed; cross-DB access is limited.
- Password policies for contained users depend on DB settings (therefore, consider enforcing them wherever possible).

  You may prefer these approaches when working with per-database portability, SaaS tenants, or Azure SQL single databases.

External Identity and Service Principals

External identities in Azure SQL are used to manage access for both human users and applications. Typically, **Azure AD users and groups** are employed for interactive access by administrators and analysts, while **service principals or managed identities** are used for applications, jobs, and automated processes.

Example: Create an AAD User in Azure SQL

```
CREATE USER [app-spn-name] FROM EXTERNAL PROVIDER;
ALTER ROLE db_datareader ADD MEMBER [app-spn-name];
```

Best Practice: Use Managed Identity for running code in Azure; avoid embedded secrets.

Principals, Securables, and Permissions Hierarchy

In SQL Server, security is organized into a hierarchy that defines who can access what and at which level. This hierarchy consists of principals, which represent the entities that request access; securables, which are the resources being protected; and permissions, which determine the allowed actions on those resources.

Principals: Logins, users, roles, application roles, and certificates, keys

Securables: Server, database, schema, object (table/view/proc), column, and endpoint

Permissions: **GRANT/REVOKE/DENY** with inheritance and scopes

Here are some effective permissions:

```
SELECT * FROM fn_my_permissions(NULL, 'DATABASE');
SELECT * FROM fn_my_permissions('dbo.Sales', 'OBJECT');
```

Rule of Thumb: **DENY** trumps **GRANT**; therefore, you must use it sparingly to avoid any surprises.

Ownership Chaining and Cross-DB Chaining

Ownership chaining refers to the occurrences when permission checks skip intermediate objects if their owner is the same.

- **Benefits**: You need fewer grants, which result in simpler code paths.
- **Drawbacks**: Ownership chaining can unintentionally expose the data if a caller executes a module that can reach protected objects.

Controls:

-- Disable cross-database chaining at server or database level (recommended **default**).

```
EXEC sp_configure 'cross db ownership chaining', 0; RECONFIGURE;
ALTER DATABASE FinanceDb SET DB_CHAINING OFF;
```

Guidance: Keep chaining **OFF**; instead, use module signing or **EXECUTE AS** for targeted elevation.

Module Signing (Certificates) for Safe Privilege Elevation

Signing a module allows a stored procedure to execute with additional permissions without granting those permissions to the calling users. This approach is safer than assigning broad roles, as it limits elevated privileges to the specific module only.

Pattern: Sign a proc with a certificate; map cert to a user; and then grant permissions to the certificate-user.

Example:

```
-- 1) Create a helper proc that needs elevated rights.
CREATE PROC dbo.usp_RebuildIndex @tbl sysname
AS
    DECLARE @sql nvarchar(4000) = N'ALTER INDEX ALL ON '
                                + QUOTENAME(@tbl) + N' REBUILD';
    EXEC (@sql);

-- 2) Create a certificate and sign the proc.
USE YourDb;
CREATE CERTIFICATE MaintCert ENCRYPTION BY PASSWORD='X!'
WITH SUBJECT='Elevate index maintenance';
ADD SIGNATURE TO OBJECT::dbo.usp_RebuildIndex BY CERTIFICATE MaintCert WITH
PASSWORD='X!';

-- 3) Create a user from the certificate and grant needed permissions.
CREATE USER MaintCertUser FROM CERTIFICATE MaintCert;
GRANT ALTER ON SCHEMA::dbo TO MaintCertUser;  -- narrowly scoped
```

Result: Callers can execute the stored procedure, but only the procedure itself has ALTER permissions; the callers do not receive these elevated rights.

EXECUTE AS and Impersonation (When and How)

Use Cases: Testing permissions; encapsulating code that needs higher privilege

Scoping: `EXECUTE AS CALLER | SELF | OWNER | 'user'`

Example:

```
CREATE PROC dbo.usp_SecureTask
WITH EXECUTE AS OWNER
AS
    -- runs with the owner's token
    EXEC dbo.usp_InternalWork;
GO
```

Good Practice: Prefer module signing for long-lived elevation, and use **EXECUTE AS** for narrow, auditable needs. Always **REVERT** in sessions after **EXECUTE AS USER**.

Endpoint and Server-Level Permissions

Examples: Database mirroring, Availability Groups (HADR), Service Broker, and custom TDS endpoints
Example of Granting CONNECT on Endpoint:

```
GRANT CONNECT ON ENDPOINT::Hadr_endpoint TO [DOMAIN\SqlSvc];
```

Admin Tip: Limit who can **`CREATE ANY ENDPOINT`**, as well as the ones who can **`CONNECT ON ENDPOINT`**.

SQL Agent Proxies and Credentials (Authorization for Jobs)

SQL Agent Proxies and Credentials matter as they run job steps (PowerShell, SSIS, **`CmdExec`**) under least-privilege principals.

Pattern:

1. Create a Credential (this should map to a domain account).
2. Create a Proxy, and then tie the job steps to it.

   Example:

```
EXEC msdb.dbo.sp_add_credential
     @credential_name='AgentFileCred',
     @identity='DOMAIN\AgentFileAcct',
     @secret='StrongSecret!';

EXEC msdb.dbo.sp_add_proxy
     @proxy_name='FileOpsProxy',
     @credential_name='AgentFileCred';

EXEC msdb.dbo.sp_grant_login_to_proxy
     @proxy_name='FileOpsProxy', @login_name='DOMAIN\JobRunner';

EXEC msdb.dbo.sp_grant_proxy_to_subsystem
     @proxy_name='FileOpsProxy', @subsystem_id=3; -- CmdExec
```

Outcome: Jobs will be able to access files/network shares without any intervention from over-privileged SQL Agent service accounts.

Connection String Hardening and TLS

The major goals of connection string hardening and TLS are to prevent MITM, enforce encryption, and remove the trust on self-signed certificates.

ADO.NET Sample:

```
Server=tcp:myserver.database.windows.net,1433; Authentication=Active Directory
Integrated; Encrypt=True; TrustServerCertificate=False;
Server side: Use modern TLS (1.2/1.3), valid certificates, and disable legacy
protocols/ciphers.
Azure SQL: Encryption enforced by default; set client to Encrypt=True &
TrustServerCertificate=False.
```

Kerberos, SPNs, and Delegation (The "Double-Hop")

The problem that you might confront here is that the user's identity is lost when they connect to the app and the app connects to SQL. This can happen because the Kerberos delegation has not been configured.

Fix: *Register SPN for SQL service account, and then configure the constrained delegation.*

SPN Examples:

- **Default Instance**: `MSSQLSvc/myhost.contoso.com:1433`

- **Named Instance**: `MSSQLSvc/myhost.contoso.com:INSTANCENAME`

  Admin Note: Use **`setspn -S`**, and make sure that you confirm it with **`klist`**. Additionally, you should use gMSA for auto-managed passwords/SPNs.

Role-Based Security and Permissions

After authentication determines *the users who* can connect to SQL Server, authorization and role-based security determine *what* they can do. Here, instead of granting permissions directly to individual users—which can become unmanageable at scale—SQL Server offers a role-based model. This is because roles simplify the security administration by grouping permissions, and then assigning them to multiple users or groups.

Introduction to Roles in SQL Server

Roles are containers for permissions. Therefore, by assigning users to roles, administrators can enforce the principle of least privilege while avoiding complex, error-prone direct permissions.

Types of Roles:

- **Fixed Server Roles**: They control server-level administration.
- **Fixed Database Roles**: They provide predefined sets of database permissions.
- **User-Defined Roles**: They are custom roles that are designed for specific applications or business logic.
- **Application Roles**: They are special roles that can be activated by applications with a password.

Best Practice: Always prefer roles over direct permissions for easier management, auditing, and scalability.

Server-Level Roles

Server-level roles control access to instance-wide functionality. Hence, SQL Server comes with several fixed server roles, such as:

- **`sysadmin`**: For full control of the SQL Server instance
- **`Serveradmin`**: To configure server-wide settings
- **`Securityadmin`**: To manage logins, passwords, and permissions
- **`dbcreator`**: To create, alter, drop, and restore databases
- **`bulkadmin`**: To run bulk insert operations
- **`diskadmin`**: To manage disk files
- **`processadmin`**: To process running on SQL Server

Example: Adding a Login to a **`sysadmin`** Role

```
ALTER SERVER ROLE sysadmin ADD MEMBER [DOMAIN\JohnDoe];
```

Best Practices:

- Grant **`sysadmin`** privileges only to a limited number of trusted administrators.
- Use separation of duties (SoD) by assigning specific server roles, and do not provide broad permissions.

Database-Level Roles

Database roles exist within a specific database. Therefore, SQL Server provides fixed database roles for common access needs, which are:

- **db_owner**: For full control of the database
- **db_datareader**: Can read all tables/views
- **db_datawriter**: Can modify all tables/views
- **db_ddladmin**: Can create/modify schema objects
- **db_securityadmin**: To manage role membership and permissions
- **db_backupoperator**: Can back up the database
- **db_denydatareader**: Explicitly denies read access
- **db_denydatawriter**: Explicitly denies write access

Example: Adding a User to db_datareader

```
ALTER ROLE db_datareader ADD MEMBER SalesUser;
```

Best Practices:

- Avoid using **db_owner** unless it is absolutely necessary.
- Use deny roles to block access when the inheritance gives unintended permissions.

User-Defined Database Roles

When predefined roles seem too broad or too restrictive, you can create custom roles tailored to business needs.

Example: Creating a Custom Role

```
CREATE ROLE SalesReportRole;
GRANT SELECT ON dbo.Sales TO SalesReportRole;
ALTER ROLE SalesReportRole ADD MEMBER SalesUser;
```

Benefits:

- Provides flexibility in fine-tuned security
- Keeps permissions organized and reusable
- Reduces administrative overhead as compared to granting individual permissions

Application Roles

Application roles allow applications to assume a database identity using a shared password. Unlike user roles, they are not tied to logins.

Example: Creating an Application Role

```
CREATE APPLICATION ROLE SalesAppRole
WITH PASSWORD = 'Str0ngAppP@ss!';
```

Usage:

```
EXEC sp_setapprole 'SalesAppRole', 'Str0ngAppP@ss!';
```

Best Practices:

- Use application roles sparingly, as password-based access can be harder to manage securely.
- Prefer contained users + app authentication wherever possible.

Schema-Based Permissions

Permissions can also be granted at the schema level. This approach ensures consistency across objects within the schema.

Example: Granting Schema-Level `SELECT`

```
GRANT SELECT ON SCHEMA::Sales TO SalesReportRole;
```

Advantages:

- Simplifies security administration by grouping objects
- Useful in multi-tenant and modular database designs

Role Membership Management

Managing role memberships is critical to ensure effective access control.

Example: Adding/Removing Members

```
ALTER ROLE db_datareader ADD MEMBER JohnDoe;
ALTER ROLE db_datareader DROP MEMBER JohnDoe;
```

Best Practices:

- Review role memberships periodically to prevent instances of "privilege creep".
- Use Active Directory groups wherever possible for centralized management.

Fine-Grained Permissions

SQL Server supports granular permissions beyond fixed roles. Therefore, permissions can be applied to:

- Objects (Tables, Views, or Stored Procedures)
- Columns (Column-Level Security)
- Rows (Row-Level Security Policies)
- Schemas and Databases

Example: Column-Level Permission

```
GRANT SELECT (CustomerName, Email) ON dbo.Customers TO SalesUser;
```

Example: Row-Level Security

```
CREATE SECURITY POLICY SalesFilter
ADD FILTER PREDICATE dbo.fn_SalesPredicate(SalesPersonID) ON dbo.Sales;
```

Combining Roles with Permissions

Roles can be layered for flexibility in the following manner:

- Assign base permissions to general roles.
- Add specialized roles for exceptions.

Example:

- **`SalesReportRole`**: For read-only access
- **`SalesManagerRole`**: For read, write, and DDL

As you can see here, the users can inherit the right set of permissions without excessive duplication when roles are layered with permissions.

Auditing Role and Permission Usage

Auditing ensures compliance, besides detecting unauthorized privilege escalation.

Example: Querying Permissions

```
SELECT dp1.name AS Grantee, dp2.name AS Grantor, perm.permission_name, obj.name AS ObjectName
FROM sys.database_permissions perm
JOIN sys.database_principals dp1 ON perm.grantee_principal_id = dp1.principal_id
JOIN sys.database_principals dp2 ON perm.grantor_principal_id = dp2.principal_id
LEFT JOIN sys.objects obj ON perm.major_id = obj.object_id;
```

Best Practices:

- Enable SQL Audit or Extended Events to track permission changes.
- Log role membership changes for forensic analysis.

Best Practices for Role-Based Security

Implementing effective role-based security ensures that users have the right level of access, and that centralized control is maintained alongside risk minimization. Hence, you must follow the provided best practices for role-based security:

1. Always apply the principle of least privilege.
2. Use roles instead of direct permissions for scalability.
3. Separate administrative roles (DDL) from data access roles (DML).
4. Prefer schema-level grants over object-level grants to maintain consistency.
5. Use Active Directory groups for enterprise-wide access control.
6. Regularly review and audit role memberships.
7. Minimize the use of application roles; instead, consider Azure AD or contained users.

Row-Level Security and Data Masking

Row-Level Security (RLS) and Data Masking are advanced features in SQL Server that provide fine-grained access control and data protection beyond traditional role-based permissions. While authentication and authorization decide *who can access* a database, RLS and masking determine *what subset of data they can see*, as well as *how much of it is visible*. Therefore, this section explores these two key security pillars in detail, with practical design patterns, performance considerations, and real-world use cases.

Introduction to Row-Level Security

Row-Level Security (RLS) allows administrators to restrict data visibility at the row level based on the user's identity, role, or context.

- For example, a sales representative should only see their own customers, while a regional manager might see all customers in their region.
- RLS is transparent to applications; therefore, there is no need to add WHERE clauses manually in queries. Moreover, SQL Server enforces the restrictions automatically.

Key Benefits:

- Centralized security logic at the database layer
- Reduced reliance on application code to enforce filtering
- Consistency across all access methods (T-SQL queries, reports, and APIs)

Security Predicates in RLS

SQL Server implements RLS using security predicates attached to a table. These are user-defined inline table-valued functions that return conditions for access.

Types of Predicates:

- **Filter Predicate:** Excludes rows that a user should not see
  - Example: `WHERE SalesRepID = USER_ID()`
- **Block Predicate:** Prevents unauthorized inserts, updates, or deletes
  - Example: A user cannot update rows that belong to another department.

Hence, this approach ensures both read and write security at the row level.

Implementing RLS in Practice

Here are the steps to configure Row-Level Security:

1. Create a predicate function to encapsulate the filter logic.

```
CREATE FUNCTION dbo.fn_RLS_Predicate(@UserID INT)
RETURNS TABLE
WITH SCHEMABINDING
AS
RETURN SELECT 1 AS fn_result WHERE @UserID = USER_ID();
```

2. Apply security policy to bind the function to a table.

```
CREATE SECURITY POLICY SalesRLS
ADD FILTER PREDICATE dbo.fn_RLS_Predicate(UserID)
ON dbo.Sales;
```

3. Test the policy to validate that users are only seeing the permitted rows.

Real-World Scenarios for RLS

Row-Level Security (RLS) enables fine-grained access control by restricting the rows a user can see, based on their identity or role. RLS is used in plenty of real-world scenarios. We have mentioned some of them for you here:

- **Multi-Tenant Applications:** Isolate customer data per tenant in SaaS platforms.
- **HR Systems:** Employees can view their own HR records but not others.
- **Healthcare Databases:** Doctors access only their patients' records.
- **Government/Defence:** Restrict classified records by clearance level.

Challenges and Performance Considerations with RLS

Although RLS is powerful, it comes with the following challenges and performance considerations:

- **Complex Predicate Functions:** Overly complex logic can hurt performance.

- **Indexing Impact**: Ensure that indexes align with filtering columns.
- **Debugging Complexity**: Developers may be surprised by "missing rows."
- **Security Risks**: Poorly written predicates may unintentionally expose data.

Best Practice: Keep predicate logic simple and well-indexed.

Introduction to Dynamic Data Masking (DDM)

Dynamic Data Masking (DDM) obfuscates sensitive data in query results, which ensures that users without special privileges are not able to view the actual values.

- **Example**: Show credit card numbers as XXXX-XXXX-XXXX-1234, and not as full digits.
- Unlike encryption, data masking does not alter data at rest; it only affects the result set that is returned.

Masking Functions in SQL Server

SQL Server supports multiple masking rules such as:

1. **Default Masking**: Replaces the full value with a standard mask
2. **Email Masking**: Exposes only the first character and domain. **Example**: `jXXX@XXXXX.com`
3. **Partial Masking**: Shows part of the string while masking the rest. **Example**: Social `Security Number` → `XXX-XX-6789`.
4. Random Masking (for Numbers): Replaces numeric values with a random number within a specified range

Implementing Dynamic Data Masking

Follow these steps to configure DDM:

1. Add a `Masked` Column

```
CREATE TABLE Customers (
CustomerID INT PRIMARY KEY,
Email NVARCHAR(100) MASKED WITH (FUNCTION = 'email()'),
SSN CHAR(11) MASKED WITH (FUNCTION = 'partial(0,"XXX-XX-",4)')
);
```

2. Assign privileges such that:
   - Users with `UNMASK` permission can see the data completely.
   - Without it, only masked results should be visible.

Use Cases for Data Masking

Data masking helps protect sensitive information by obfuscating it for non-production environments or users who do not require full access. It is used in several domains, some of which we have mentioned here:

- **Development Environments**: Developers can test with masked production data without violating compliance.
- **Business Reporting**: Analysts may see aggregated data but not sensitive PII.
- **Customer Support**: Support staff can identify a customer with partial details without accessing sensitive information.

Combining RLS and DDM

RLS and DDM complement each other in the following manner:

- RLS restricts *which rows* users can see.
- DDM controls *how much information* users can see within those rows.

Example:

- A sales rep sees only their customers' rows (RLS).
- Within those rows, credit card numbers are masked (DDM).

Limitations and Considerations

While Row-Level Security (RLS) and Dynamic Data Masking (DDM) enhance data protection, they have inherent limitations such as:

- DDM does not protect data from administrators or users with UNMASK rights.
- RLS does not encrypt data; it only restricts visibility.
- Both features must be combined with encryption, auditing, and strong authentication for a complete security strategy.

Best Practices for RLS and DDM

To maximize effectiveness and maintain compliance, you should follow these best practices:

- Keep security logic at the database layer for consistency.
- Use the least privilege principle; grant UNMASK only when it is required.
- Monitor query performance under RLS, especially with large datasets.
- Regularly audit masking rules to align with compliance policies (HIPAA, GDPR, or PCI-DSS).

Encryption (TDE and Always Encrypted)

Encryption is one of the most critical aspects of database security. It ensures that even if unauthorized parties gain access to the database files or intercept communications, they would not be able to make sense of the data without proper keys. Therefore, SQL Server provides multiple encryption mechanisms. The two that are the most widely used out of them are Transparent Data Encryption (TDE) and Always Encrypted.

While TDE protects data "at rest", Always Encrypted ensures that data remains protected not only at rest, but also "in transit" and "in use". Hence, understanding the differences, use cases, and best practices for each is essential to build robust security in T-SQL environments.

The Importance of Encryption in SQL Server

Encryption plays a critical role in protecting the sensitive data that is stored and processed by SQL Server. As databases support mission critical applications, besides handling personally identifiable information (PII), financial records, and regulated data, encryption ensures confidentiality even in the event of unauthorized access. Therefore, by rendering data unreadable without the appropriate keys or certificates, encryption reduces the risk of data exposure, and also strengthens an organization's overall security posture across on-premises, cloud, and hybrid environments.

- Data Protection in Compliance: Regulations like HIPAA, GDPR, PCI-DSS, and SOX mandate strong encryption of the sensitive data.

- Defense in Depth: Even if other security layers fail (like weak passwords or misconfigured firewalls), encryption keeps raw data unreadable.
- Safeguarding Data at Multiple Layers: Encryption should protect:
    - **At Rest**: Database files, backups, logs
    - **In Transit**: Data traveling over the network
    - **In Use**: Data being queried, stored in memory, or returned to applications

Transparent Data Encryption (TDE)

Transparent Data Encryption (TDE) encrypts the entire database at the storage level. It protects database files, transaction logs, and backups, all without requiring you to make changes to the application layer.

Functioning of TDE

TDE encrypts SQL Server and Azure SQL databases at rest to protect sensitive data, including backups and transaction logs. It does not require application changes. Furthermore:

- TDE uses a Database Encryption Key (DEK) that is stored in the database boot record.
- DEK is protected by a certificate stored in the master database.
- The certificate is protected by the Database Master Key (DMK), which in turn is secured by the Service Master Key (SMK).
- Encryption and decryption happen transparently. Therefore, queries and applications do not need modification.

Steps to Enable TDE

Transparent Data Encryption (TDE) protects SQL Server and Azure SQL databases at rest by encrypting data, backups, and transaction logs without requiring application changes.

1. **Create a Master Key in the master database**.

   ```
   CREATE MASTER KEY ENCRYPTION BY PASSWORD = 'StrongPassword!';
   ```

2. **Create a Certificate**.

   ```
   CREATE CERTIFICATE TDECert WITH SUBJECT = 'TDE Certificate';
   ```

3. **Create a Database Encryption Key (DEK) in the target database**.

   ```
   USE MyDatabase;
   CREATE DATABASE ENCRYPTION KEY
   WITH ALGORITHM = AES_256
   ENCRYPTION BY SERVER CERTIFICATE TDECert;
   ```

4. **Enable encryption on the database**.

   ```
   ALTER DATABASE MyDatabase SET ENCRYPTION ON;
   ```

Benefits of TDE

The following are the key advantages of using Transparent Data Encryption (TDE) to secure your database at rest and maintain application transparency:

- It is simple to configure.

- No application code changes are required.
- TDE protects backups and log files automatically.

Limitations of TDE

While TDE provides strong at-rest encryption, it has certain limitations and considerations that should be understood before implementation. Have a look at some of them:

- TDE does not encrypt data in transit (you must use SSL/TLS for that).
- TDE comes with a performance overhead (usually 3-5%).
- The keys must be backed up properly—losing them means losing access to all the data.

Always Encrypted

Always Encrypted is designed for protecting sensitive data in use. Unlike TDE, which is transparent to the application, Always Encrypted requires application involvement in encryption and decryption.

Functioning of Always Encrypted

Always Encrypted ensures sensitive data remains protected even from database administrators by performing encryption and decryption on the client side.

- Data is encrypted client-side using a column encryption key before being sent to SQL Server.
- SQL Server stores only encrypted values, while decryption occurs only in the client application with the right key.
- SQL Server itself never sees plaintext data—not even DBAs or administrators despite having direct access.

Steps to Enable Always Encrypted

The following steps demonstrate how to configure Always Encrypted in SQL Server, including creating the master and column encryption keys, as well as applying encryption to sensitive columns to ensure data confidentiality:

1. **Create a Column Master Key (CMK) (stored in Windows Certificate Store or Azure Key Vault).**

```
CREATE COLUMN MASTER KEY CMK_Auto
WITH (
    KEY_STORE_PROVIDER_NAME = N'MSSQL_CERTIFICATE_STORE',
    KEY_PATH = N'CurrentUser/My/6A0A43...'
);
Create a Column Encryption Key (CEK).
CREATE COLUMN ENCRYPTION KEY CEK_1
WITH VALUES (
    COLUMN_MASTER_KEY = CMK_Auto,
    ALGORITHM = 'RSA_OAEP',
    ENCRYPTED_VALUE = 0x123456...
);
```

Encrypt a column.

```
CREATE TABLE Customers (
```

```
        CustomerID INT PRIMARY KEY,
        SSN NVARCHAR(11) COLLATE Latin1_General_BIN2 ENCRYPTED WITH
        (
            COLUMN_ENCRYPTION_KEY = CEK_1,
            ENCRYPTION_TYPE = DETERMINISTIC,
            ALGORITHM = 'AEAD_AES_256_CBC_HMAC_SHA_256'
        )
    );
```

Benefits of Always Encrypted

Always Encrypted provides column-level encryption to protect sensitive data, while ensuring that it remains confidential even from database administrators. It also allows authorized applications to access it securely. Additionally, Always Encrypted:

- Protects data at rest, in transit, and in use.
- Ensures that DBAs cannot see sensitive data like credit card numbers or social security numbers.
- Supports integration with Azure Key Vault for centralized key management.

Limitations of Always Encrypted

While Always Encrypted secures sensitive columns, it has operational constraints and may require application modifications. Therefore, it is important to understand its limitations before implementation.

- Limited set of operations supported (for example, no LIKE, and no range queries with randomized encryption)
- Requires application changes to support the Always Encrypted driver
- Slight overhead due to encryption/decryption at client side

Choosing between TDE and Always Encrypted

Selecting the right encryption strategy depends on your security requirements. This is because TDE protects entire databases at rest, while Always Encrypted secures specific sensitive columns, including during transit and use.

Therefore, SQL Server auditing helps track and monitor database activities to ensure compliance and detect unauthorized access, but it should be implemented thoughtfully to balance security and performance.

Feature	TDE	Always Encrypted
Protects at Rrest	☑	☑
Protects in Transit	✗ (use TLS)	☑
Protects in Use	✗	☑
Requires App Changes	✗	☑
Protects Backups/Logs	☑	☑
Prevents DBA Data Access	✗	☑

Table 13.1: *Feature Comparison of TDE and Always Encrypted*

Best Practice: Use TDE for broad database-level encryption and Always Encrypted for highly sensitive columns.

Key Management in SQL Server Encryption

Proper key management is critical to maintain access to encrypted data, as keys should be securely stored, backed up, and rotated periodically to ensure compliance and prevent data loss. Therefore, here are a few tips to manage them in SQL Server:

- Creating Backups of Keys is Mandatory: Losing a certificate or CMK renders data inaccessible.
- Store keys in secure stores like Azure Key Vault or Hardware Security Modules (HSMs).
- Rotate encryption keys periodically for compliance.

Real-World Use Cases

Different encryption technologies are suited for distinct scenarios: TDE is ideal for database-wide compliance; Always Encrypted protects highly sensitive columns; while many organizations combine both for layered security. Therefore, here are some use cases for you to consider more scenarios where encryption technologies are used:

- **TDE**: Banks encrypt entire databases to comply with PCI-DSS for credit card storage.
- **Always Encrypted**: Healthcare applications encrypt patient SSNs and medical records to meet HIPAA.
- **Combination**: Many enterprises use TDE for general compliance, and Always Encrypted for ultra-sensitive columns.

Best Practices

Follow the proven best practices for encryption, including backing up keys, using strong algorithms, testing application compatibility, and monitoring performance to ensure secure and efficient database operations. Here are some of them:

- Always backup certificates and keys after setup.
- Use `AES_256` as the preferred encryption algorithm.
- Test application compatibility with Always Encrypted before enabling it.
- Use `TLS 1.2/1.3` for in-transit protection alongside TDE.
- Monitor encryption performance impacts, and scale accordingly.

Auditing and Compliance

Auditing and compliance are critical components of database security. While authentication, authorization, and encryption protect against unauthorized access, auditing ensures accountability by recording who did what, when, and how within the database. Compliance frameworks (such as GDPR, HIPAA, SOX, and PCI-DSS) often mandate database-level auditing to ensure transparency, traceability, and adherence to regulatory standards.

In SQL Server, multiple native tools and third-party solutions can be used to implement comprehensive auditing strategies. These solutions not only capture user activity, but also provide mechanisms for reporting, monitoring, and alerting whenever suspicious or unauthorized actions occur.

Therefore, this section elaborates on key auditing and compliance features, best practices, and implementation guidelines.

Importance of Auditing in SQL Server

Auditing serves multiple business and technical purposes such as:

- **Accountability**: Auditing tracks who accessed the data and performed operations (for example, `SELECT`, `INSERT`, or `DELETE`).
- **Forensics**: Auditing helps investigate security breaches and anomalies.
- **Compliance**: Auditing meets regulatory requirements (for example, GDPR mandates that you log personal data access).
- **Change Tracking**: Auditing identifies unauthorized schema or configuration changes.
- **Monitoring Insider Threats**: Auditing detects misuse of privileges by DBAs or developers.

Examples of Auditing:

- A bank must track all queries made against the Customer table for PCI-DSS.
- A healthcare provider must log access to `PatientRecords` for HIPAA.

SQL Server Audit Framework

SQL Server provides a built-in Audit Framework, which was first featured in SQL Server 2008 Enterprise Edition (which was available in the Standard Edition later).

Key Components:

- **Audit Object**: Defines where the audit log will be stored (for example, file, Windows Security log, or Windows Application log)
- **Server Audit Specification**: Tracks server-level events (for example, logins, and role changes)
- **Database Audit Specification**: Tracks database-level events (for example, `SELECT` on a sensitive table)

Example:

```
-- Step 1: Create Audit Object (Store Logs in a File).
CREATE SERVER AUDIT Audit_SensitiveData
TO FILE (FILEPATH = 'C:\AuditLogs\')
WITH (ON_FAILURE = CONTINUE);

-- Step 2: Enable Audit.
ALTER SERVER AUDIT Audit_SensitiveData
WITH (STATE = ON);

-- Step 3: Create Database Audit Specification.
CREATE DATABASE AUDIT SPECIFICATION Audit_CustomerTable
FOR SERVER AUDIT Audit_SensitiveData
ADD (SELECT ON dbo.Customer BY public)
WITH (STATE = ON);
```

Hence, this configuration logs every `SELECT` on the `Customer` table made by any user.

SQL Server Audit vs. SQL Trace vs. Extended Events

SQL Server provides multiple logging mechanisms. Thus, choosing the right one depends on granularity, performance, and compliance needs.

- **SQL Server Audit**
  - Best for compliance and regulatory logging
  - Structured, tamper-evident logs
  - Supports fine-grained control
- **SQL Trace (Deprecated)**
  - Legacy method; was later replaced by Extended Events
  - Still used in older systems
- **Extended Events**
  - Lightweight, flexible monitoring
  - Useful for performance tuning, but not compliance

👉 **Best Practice**: Use SQL Server Audit for compliance, Extended Events for diagnostics, and avoid SQL Trace for new systems.

Common Audit Scenarios

Some widely implemented audit scenarios include:

- **Login/Logout Activity**: Track successful and failed login attempts.
- Privilege Escalation: Monitor role membership changes (for example, adding user to sysadmin).
- **Data Access**: Log **`SELECT`** queries on sensitive tables (for example, **`Salary`**, **`CreditCard`**, **`PatientData`**).
- **Schema Changes**: Detect unauthorized **`DROP TABLE`**, **`ALTER TABLE`**, and so on.
- **Configuration Changes**: Capture changes in settings like encryption keys or linked servers.

Example of Auditing Failed Logins:

```
CREATE SERVER AUDIT SPECIFICATION Audit_LoginActivity
FOR SERVER AUDIT Audit_SensitiveData
ADD (FAILED_LOGIN_GROUP)
WITH (STATE = ON);
```

Audit Log Management and Retention

Audit logs must be handled carefully to remain useful in compliance investigations. Therefore, here are a few tips you must remember about audit log management and retention:

- **Retention Policies**: Define how long logs should be kept (for example, 7 years for financial data under SOX).
- **Archival**: Store old logs in secure, encrypted storage (Azure Blob, S3, or cold storage).
- **Tamper-Proofing**: Store logs in Windows Security Log or write-only storage to prevent DBA manipulation.
- **Log Rotation**: Implement automatic rollover for large files.

Integration with Compliance Frameworks

Different industries require specific audit controls such as:

- **HIPAA (Healthcare)**: Must track access to patient data

- **GDPR (Europe)**: Requires you to log all access to Personally Identifiable Information (PII)
- **SOX (Financial)**: Enforces traceability of changes to financial systems
- **PCI-DSS (Payment Card Data)**: Requires you to monitor all activity on credit card-related tables

☞ Moreover, SQL Server Audit specifications should be mapped directly to regulatory controls to prove compliance during audits.

Third-Party Auditing Tools

While SQL Server Audit is powerful, many enterprises use third-party tools for:

- **Advanced Reporting**: Visual dashboards and compliance-ready templates
- **Centralized Auditing**: For collecting logs across multiple servers and databases
- **Alerting**: Real-time alerts on suspicious activity
- **Machine Learning Detection**: For identifying unusual access patterns

Popular Tools:

- ApexSQL Audit
- Quest Change Auditor
- Redgate SQL Monitor (with Audit Add-ons)

Best Practices in SQL Server Auditing

SQL Server auditing helps track and monitor database activities to ensure compliance and detect unauthorized access. However, it should be implemented thoughtfully to balance security and performance. Therefore, you must remember these best practices:

- Audit only sensitive objects to avoid performance overhead.
- Store logs in centralized, secure storage.
- Encrypt logs at rest.
- Monitor and alert on failed logins and privilege escalations.
- Review audit reports regularly (monthly or quarterly).
- Automate compliance reporting for regulators.

Monitoring, Alerts, and Incident Response

Auditing is not just about logging, but about responding as well. Hence, you must implement the following tips for efficient logging and monitoring:

- **Real-Time Alerts**: Set up SQL Agent jobs or PowerShell scripts to email alerts for critical events (for example, schema drop or failed logins).
- **SIEM Integration**: Forward logs to Splunk, Azure Sentinel, or ELK stack for enterprise-wide monitoring.
- **Incident Response Playbooks**: Define the steps for DBAs and security teams to tackle suspicious activities.

Example: Sending Alert for Failed Logins

```
EXEC msdb.dbo.sp_send_dbmail
    @profile_name = 'DBMailProfile',
```

```
    @recipients = 'securityteam@company.com',
    @subject = 'SQL Server Security Alert',
    @body = 'Multiple failed login attempts detected on SQL Server!';
```

Future of Auditing in Cloud and Hybrid Environments

As more organizations move to Azure SQL Database or Azure Synapse, auditing is evolving at every turn of time. Therefore, you should be aware of the innovations in the domain to understand their utility for cloud and hybrid environments:

- **Azure SQL Auditing**: Logs that are stored directly in Azure Blob Storage or Log Analytics
- **Integration with Microsoft Sentinel**: Advanced threat detection using Machine Learning (ML)
- **Cross-Platform Auditing**: Single-pane auditing across on-premises SQL Server, Azure SQL, PostgreSQL, and MySQL
- **Automated Compliance Checks**: Cloud-native policies that automatically flag non-compliant servers

Conclusion

This chapter emphasized the critical role of security in SQL Server environments. You gained practical knowledge of authentication, role-based security, and permission hierarchies. Advanced features such as Row-Level Security, Dynamic Data Masking, and encryption techniques like TDE and Always Encrypted were also covered in depth.

Additionally, auditing strategies and compliance requirements were explored, including SQL Server Audit and third-party tools. Hence, by understanding these concepts, you are now equipped to build secure, compliant, and trustworthy database applications.

The next chapter will introduce unit testing with tSQLt, and will teach you how to ensure code reliability, as well as how to integrate testing into modern development workflows.

CHAPTER 14
Unit Testing T-SQL with tSQLt

Introduction

Testing is critical for ensuring the reliability and maintainability of SQL Server development. Unlike application code, database code has historically lacked robust testing practices, leading to production bugs, performance regressions, and untested logic in stored procedures and functions. The tSQLt framework changes that by enabling database developers to apply modern testing practices such as unit testing, mocking, and Test-Driven Development (TDD) directly inside SQL Server. In this chapter, you will learn how to install and configure tSQLt, write and run unit tests for stored procedures and functions, and use mocking and faking techniques to isolate code under test from production data. We will also cover naming conventions, best practices, and TDD workflows that help keep test suites maintainable. Finally, we will see how tSQLt integrates into CI/CD pipelines with Azure DevOps and GitHub Actions, ensuring automated quality gates for SQL development teams.

Structure

In this chapter, we will cover the following topics:

- Installing tSQLt framework
- Writing and running unit tests
- Mocking and faking database objects
- Test-driven development best practices
- Integration with CI/CD

Installing tSQLt Framework

The first step in adopting unit testing for SQL Server development is installing the tSQLt framework, an open-source testing framework designed specifically for T-SQL. Installing tSQLt is relatively straightforward, but it requires careful preparation of the database environment and permissions. This section explains each step in detail, including prerequisites, installation, configuration, and troubleshooting.

Prerequisites for Installing tSQLt

Before you can install tSQLt, several conditions must be met:

- **SQL Server Version:** tSQLt supports SQL Server 2005 and later, but it is the most effective on SQL Server 2016 and higher, where newer features (such as **TRY...CATCH** error handling) are more reliable.
- **CLR Integration:** tSQLt depends on the SQL CLR (Common Language Runtime) for certain features. This must be enabled in the database server.

  ```
  EXEC sp_configure 'clr enabled', 1;
  RECONFIGURE;
  ```

- **Dedicated Test Database:** Best practice is to install tSQLt into a separate test database, rather than in production databases. This ensures test isolation, and avoids unnecessary risks.
- **Permissions:** You need sysadmin or at least sufficient rights to:
  - Create schemas
  - Create assemblies
  - Enable CLR
  - Create stored procedures and functions

Downloading the tSQLt Framework

tSQLt is distributed as a SQL script file (`tSQLt.class.sql`). To obtain it:

1. Navigate to the official site: https://tsqlt.org.
2. Download the latest release package.
3. Extract the zip file, which contains:
   - **`tSQLt.class.sql`** → main installer script
   - Example test files and documentation

Tip: *Always download the latest stable release to ensure compatibility with modern SQL Server versions.*

Creating a Dedicated Test Database

To keep production and testing separate:

```
CREATE DATABASE MyTestDB;
GO

USE MyTestDB;
GO
```

This new database will house the tSQLt framework and test classes.

Enabling CLR Integration

As mentioned, tSQLt requires CLR:

```
EXEC sp_configure 'show advanced options', 1;
RECONFIGURE;

EXEC sp_configure 'clr enabled', 1;
RECONFIGURE;
```

This step must be performed before running the installation script.

Installing the Framework Script

Run the installation script against your test database:

```
USE MyTestDB;
GO
:r "C:\path\to\tSQLt.class.sql"
```

Or paste the contents of **`tSQLt.class.sql`** into SSMS, and execute.

Verifying the Installation

After installation, verify that tSQLt objects are created:

- Schemas created: tSQLt
- Procedures created:
  - **`tSQLt.NewTestClass`**
  - **`tSQLt.NewTest`**
  - **`tSQLt.RunAll`**

Test with:

```
EXEC tSQLt.RunAll;
```

If no tests exist, the result will simply indicate success with no tests executed.

Configuring the Test Environment

tSQLt is schema-based. You create test classes (schemas) to organize tests. Example:

```
EXEC tSQLt.NewTestClass 'TestSales';
```

This creates a schema **`TestSales`** for storing test procedures.

Every test procedure is a stored procedure within this schema.

Handling Common Installation Errors

During installation of tSQLt, certain common errors may occur. Hence, understanding their causes and solutions helps ensure a smooth setup in your test environment.

- **`Error: CLR not enabled.`**
  → Ensure that you ran sp_configure 'clr enabled', 1;.
- **`Error: Assembly permission denied.`**
  → Requires appropriate permissions (often **`ALTER ASSEMBLY`** rights). Run with sysadmin, if necessary.
- **`Error: Objects already exist.`**
  → May occur, if reinstalling. Drop the test database and create it fresh, or manually drop the existing tSQLt schema.

Best Practices for Installing tSQLt

Following the best practices ensures that tSQLt has been installed safely, and consistently across the test environments.

- Always use a dedicated test database.
- Never install tSQLt into production environments.
- Automate installation via scripts so that CI/CD pipelines can recreate the environment easily.
- Use source control to version the tSQLt.class.sql file in case updates are needed.

Automating Installation for DevOps Pipelines

In modern development pipelines, tSQLt installation is often automated:

1. Include tSQLt.class.sql in your repository.
2. Add a pipeline step (Azure DevOps, GitHub Actions, Jenkins, and so on.) to:
    a. Deploy a test database
    b. Run the installation script
    c. Run tests

Example (PowerShell):

```
sqlcmd -S . -d MyTestDB -i "tSQLt.class.sql"
```

This makes sure your testing environment can be consistently rebuilt.

Uninstalling or Resetting tSQLt

If you need to remove tSQLt:

1. Drop the test database entirely:
    ```
    DROP DATABASE MyTestDB;
    ```
2. Or, drop the schema and associated objects manually (not recommended, unless necessary).

This is often useful when starting fresh in CI/CD pipelines.

Security Considerations

When using tSQLt, it is essential to consider security implications to prevent unauthorized access, and ensure realistic test results.

- **CLR Security**: Enabling CLR has security implications. Only install in environments where CLR is approved.
- **Testing Permissions**: Ensure that tests run with the same permissions as application code where possible, so that results are realistic.
- **Separation**: Keep testing environments isolated from production data and accounts.

Writing and Running Unit Tests

Once the tSQLt framework is installed, the next step is to write and execute unit tests against your database objects. Unlike traditional SQL development (which often relies on manual verification), tSQLt provides a structured, repeatable, and automated way to validate logic.

This section explains the core workflow of writing tests with tSQLt: creating test classes, writing test procedures, using assertions, and running tests individually or in groups.

Understanding the Structure of tSQLt Tests

In tSQLt:

- Test Classes → Schemas that group related tests.
- Test Procedures → Stored procedures inside test classes. Each procedure represents one-unit test.
- Assertions → Helper procedures provided by tSQLt to validate results (for example, compare expected vs actual).

Analogy: Think of test classes as "**`folders`**," test procedures as "**`files`**," and assertions as the "**`checks`**" inside each file.

Creating a Test Class

A test class is a schema that organizes tests logically (by feature, module, or object).

```
EXEC tSQLt.NewTestClass 'TestSales';
```

- This creates a schema named **`TestSales`**.
- All test procedures for validating the Sales module will live here.

Tip: *Use naming conventions for clarity, for example:*

- **`TestHR`** → *Tests for HR module*
- **`TestFinance`** → *Tests for Finance module*

Writing Your First Test

A test is simply a stored procedure in the test class schema.

Example:

```
CREATE PROCEDURE TestSales.[test that 1 equals 1]
AS
BEGIN
    -- Assertion: checks if values are equal
    EXEC tSQLt.AssertEquals 1, 1;
END;
```

- Naming convention: test that <condition> makes it clear what is being tested.
- Running this test will pass, since 1 = 1.

This "trivial test" confirms that the framework works correctly.

Running Tests

tSQLt provides several ways to run tests:

- Run all tests in the database:

  ```
  EXEC tSQLt.RunAll;
  ```

Run all tests in a specific class:

```
EXEC tSQLt.Run 'TestSales';
```

Run a single test:

```
EXEC tSQLt.Run 'TestSales.[test that 1 equals 1]';
```

The results are returned as a standard result set showing success/failure and error messages.

Assertions: Validating Results

Assertions are the heart of tSQLt. They check whether expected results match actual results. Some commonly used assertions are as follows:

1. **`AssertEquals`** → Compares two scalar values

   ```
   EXEC tSQLt.AssertEquals 100, 100; -- Pass
   ```

2. **`AssertEqualsString`** → Compares strings

   ```
   EXEC tSQLt.AssertEqualsString 'Hello', 'Hello';
   ```

3. **`AssertEmptyTable`** → Verifies a table has no rows

   ```
   EXEC tSQLt.AssertEmptyTable 'dbo.TempTable';
   ```

4. **`AssertEqualsTable`** → Compares contents of two tables

   ```
   EXEC tSQLt.AssertEqualsTable 'ExpectedResults', 'ActualResults';
   ```

5. **`AssertObjectExists`** → Ensures an object exists

   ```
   EXEC tSQLt.AssertObjectExists 'dbo.Customers';
   ```

These assertions provide granular, testable checks for SQL logic.

Example: Testing a Stored Procedure

Suppose we want to test a stored procedure:

```
CREATE PROCEDURE dbo.GetCustomerById
    @CustomerId INT
AS
BEGIN
    SELECT CustomerId, Name
    FROM dbo.Customers
    WHERE CustomerId = @CustomerId;
END;
Step 1: Create Test Class
EXEC tSQLt.NewTestClass 'TestCustomers';
Step 2: Write a Test
CREATE PROCEDURE TestCustomers.[test GetCustomerById returns expected record]
AS
BEGIN
    -- Arrange: Fake table and insert sample data
  EXEC tSQLt.FakeTable 'dbo.Customers';

    INSERT INTO dbo.Customers (CustomerId, Name) VALUES (1, 'John Doe');

    -- Act: Execute stored procedure
```

```
    CREATE TABLE #Actual (CustomerId INT, Name NVARCHAR(100));
    INSERT INTO #Actual
    EXEC dbo.GetCustomerById @CustomerId = 1;

    -- Expected results
    CREATE TABLE #Expected (CustomerId INT, Name NVARCHAR(100));
    INSERT INTO #Expected VALUES (1, 'John Doe');

    -- Assert: Compare tables
  EXEC tSQLt.AssertEqualsTable '#Expected', '#Actual';
END;
```

Here:

- **Arrange** → Set up test data using **FakeTable**.
- **Act** → Run the procedure.
- **Assert** → Compare expected vs actual results.

Using FakeTable and Spy Procedures

tSQLt provides advanced helpers for isolating tests:

- **FakeTable** → Creates a lightweight version of a table without constraints (useful for testing without real data).

  ```
  EXEC tSQLt.FakeTable 'dbo.Orders';
  ```

- **SpyProcedure** → Tracks calls to a procedure (for example, logging, auditing) to confirm it was executed.

  ```
  EXEC tSQLt.SpyProcedure 'dbo.LogOrder';
  ```

These tools enable isolation, and prevent tests from being affected by unrelated dependencies.

Running Multiple Tests and Test Suites

Tests can be grouped into suites for batch execution.

- To run all tests for Sales and Customers:

  ```
  EXEC tSQLt.Run 'TestSales';
  EXEC tSQLt.Run 'TestCustomers';
  ```

- In CI/CD pipelines, **tSQLt.RunAll** is typically executed automatically after deployment.

Handling Expected Failures

Sometimes, you want to test error conditions. tSQLt provides **ExpectException**.

Example:

```
CREATE PROCEDURE TestCustomers.[test GetCustomerById throws error for invalid id]
AS
BEGIN
    EXEC tSQLt.ExpectException;
    EXEC dbo.GetCustomerById @CustomerId = -1;
END;
```

If the procedure raises an error, the test passes.

Best Practices for Writing Tests

Following the best practices when writing tSQLt tests ensure maintainable, reliable, and automated database testing.

1. One Assertion per Test → Keep tests focused and simple.
2. Use Meaningful Names → For example, test inserting duplicate throws error.
3. Isolate Tests → Use FakeTable so that tests do not depend on production data.
4. Repeatable Tests → Each run should produce the same result.
5. Automate Execution → Integrate with DevOps pipelines.

Advanced Example: Testing Business Logic

Suppose you have a rule:

- "Customers under 18 cannot place orders."

You can test it with:

```
CREATE PROCEDURE TestOrders.[test underage customer cannot place order]
AS
BEGIN
    EXEC tSQLt.FakeTable 'dbo.Customers';
    EXEC tSQLt.FakeTable 'dbo.Orders';

    INSERT INTO dbo.Customers (CustomerId, Name, Age) VALUES (1, 'Alice', 15);

    EXEC tSQLt.ExpectException;

    INSERT INTO dbo.Orders (OrderId, CustomerId, Amount) VALUES (101, 1, 500);
END;
```

This validates business rules automatically with every deployment.

Viewing and Analyzing Test Results

When you run tests, results are displayed like this:

TestCase	Result	Msg
TestCustomers.[test GetCustomerById returns expected record]	Success	
TestOrders.[test underage customer cannot place order]	Success	

***Table 14.1**: Test Results*

- `Success` → Test passed.
- `Failure` → Error details displayed (for example, mismatched values, missing rows).

This immediate feedback loop ensures early bug detection.

Benefits of tSQLt Unit Tests

tSQLt unit tests provide a structured framework to validate database code, ensuring reliability and accelerating development.

- Ensures stored procedures, functions, and triggers behave as expected.

- Reduces reliance on manual QA queries.
- Provides living documentation of system behavior.
- Enhances agility by catching regressions quickly.

Mocking and Faking Database Objects

One of the most powerful features of tSQLt is its ability to isolate database objects for testing by using mocking and faking techniques. In traditional software development, mocking allows you to replace dependencies with test-specific substitutes. Similarly, tSQLt provides the ability to replace tables, views, and procedures with controlled versions, ensuring that tests run in isolation without side effects on production data.

This capability is critical in T-SQL development, where database objects are tightly coupled. Without isolation, testing would require preparing production-like data or risking unwanted data changes. Mocking and faking provide a safe and predictable testing environment.

The Need for Mocking in SQL Testing

SQL code often depends on multiple tables, procedures, or external systems. For example, testing a stored procedure that calculates monthly revenue might require joins across several large tables. Running tests directly on production tables has drawbacks:

- Risk of modifying real data
- Complex data setup
- Unpredictable dependencies

By mocking tables or faking procedures, you can:

- Control the dataset with minimal rows.
- Eliminate dependencies on unrelated objects.
- Focus the test only on the logic being validated.

Mocking Tables with `tSQLt.FakeTable`

The most frequently used feature in tSQLt mocking is the **`tSQLt.FakeTable`** procedure. This allows you to replace a real table with a "fake" version during a test.

How it works:

- tSQLt drops the real table temporarily (in the test schema's context).
- A fake table with the same schema is created.
- All constraints, triggers, and foreign keys are removed unless explicitly included.

Syntax:

```
EXEC tSQLt.FakeTable @TableName = 'SchemaName.TableName';
```

Example:

```
-- Fake the Sales.Orders table for isolated testing
EXEC tSQLt.FakeTable 'Sales.Orders';

-- Insert test-specific data
INSERT INTO Sales.Orders (OrderID, CustomerID, OrderDate, TotalAmount)
VALUES (1, 'CUST01', '2025-01-01', 500.00);
```

```
-- Run the procedure under test
EXEC Sales.CalculateMonthlyRevenue '2025-01';

-- Assert the expected result
EXEC tSQLt.AssertEquals @Expected = 500.00, @Actual = (SELECT Revenue FROM Sales.
MonthlyRevenue WHERE Month = '2025-01');
```

Here, the test executes entirely on the fake version of **Sales.Orders**, leaving the real table unaffected.

Benefits of Fake Tables

Fake tables in tSQLt allow tests to run in complete isolation from production data, improving reliability and performance.

- **Isolation**: Each test runs with its own clean table.
- **Performance**: Small test datasets speed up execution.
- **Predictability**: The test outcome is independent of production data.
- **Repeatability**: Tests can be re-run consistently.

Mocking Stored Procedures

Sometimes, you need to mock stored procedures rather than tables. This is useful when:

- A procedure calls external services (for example, APIs).
- A procedure performs heavy writes not relevant to the current test.

tSQLt provides **tSQLt.SpyProcedure**, which replaces the target procedure with a spy version that:

- Captures input parameters.
- Records execution calls.
- Does not execute the original logic (unless explicitly configured).

Example:

```
EXEC tSQLt.SpyProcedure 'HR.SendEmailNotification';

-- Call the procedure under test
EXEC HR.OnboardNewEmployee 'EMP01', 'John Doe';

-- Verify the notification was attempted
EXEC tSQLt.AssertObjectExists 'HR.SendEmailNotification_SpyProcedureLog';
```

Here, we check that the onboarding procedure attempted to send a notification without actually sending an email.

Mocking Functions

Functions are more challenging to mock because SQL Server does not allow function overriding directly. However, you can simulate mocking by:

- Encapsulating function calls into stored procedures and mocking those.
- Using fake tables that serve as input to functions.

Some teams restructure their design to avoid direct reliance on functions in test scenarios, ensuring better testability.

Handling Foreign Keys in Fake Tables

When using **FakeTable**, foreign key constraints are dropped by default to simplify test setup. If constraints are required for validation logic, you can re-add them after faking.

Example:

```
EXEC tSQLt.FakeTable 'Sales.Orders';

-- Add back a foreign key for validation tests
ALTER TABLE Sales.Orders
ADD CONSTRAINT FK_Orders_Customers FOREIGN KEY (CustomerID)
REFERENCES Sales.Customers(CustomerID);
```

This allows controlled enforcement of referential integrity during specific tests.

Seeding Test Data

Mocked tables require custom test data. You should:

- Insert only the minimal required rows.
- Use descriptive values for readability (for example, '**CUST_TEST**' instead of 'A1').
- Avoid unnecessary fields unless required by logic.

Best practice: Each test should fully define its dataset, ensuring that it can run independently without hidden dependencies.

Combining Fake Tables and Assertions

A common pattern is:

1. Fake the required table(s).
2. Insert the known test data.
3. Execute the procedure/function under test.
4. Use tSQLt assertions (**AssertEquals**, **AssertEmptyTable**, and so on.) to validate.

This isolates the test from unrelated objects, and ensures precise control.

Mocking Complex Dependencies

For stored procedures that touch multiple layers, combine mocking techniques such as:

- Fake tables for data input/output.
- Spy procedures for service calls.
- Predefined stubs for reference lookups.

This modular approach allows testing business logic in isolation without spinning up the entire system.

Debugging with Mocking

When a test fails:

- Verify whether the fake table schema matches expectations.
- Ensure that the test data was inserted correctly.
- Check the spy log tables created by tSQLt to confirm procedure calls.

Thus, Mocking makes debugging easier since you can eliminate external noise, and focus on the core logic.

Best Practices for Mocking and Faking

Mocking and faking in tSQLt help simulate real-world behavior, while keeping tests isolated, fast, and predictable.

- Always reset test environments using **`tSQLt.NewTestClass`** to avoid cross-test contamination.
- Keep faked tables lean, and do not insert the unnecessary data.
- Name tests descriptively (for example, **`test_CalculateRevenue_HandlesEmptyOrders`**).
- Prefer fake tables over real data imports for speed and consistency.
- Use spy procedures only when side effects (like emails or service calls) must be avoided.

Common Pitfalls

Even when following the best practices, certain pitfalls can undermine test reliability and realism, if not carefully managed.

- **Over-mocking:** Excessive mocking can result in unrealistic tests that do not reflect production.
- **Forgetting constraints:** Without re-adding constraints, some logic may not behave as in production.
- **Test leakage:** If fake tables are not properly scoped, they may affect other tests.

Real-World Use Case

Imagine testing an inventory reorder system:

- Procedure **`ReorderStock`** pulls from Inventory and calls **`SendPurchaseOrder`**.
- Fake the Inventory table with minimal rows.
- Spy on **`SendPurchaseOrder`** to confirm that the correct vendor is notified.
- Assert that **`PurchaseOrder`** was inserted with expected values.

This isolates the business logic (when to reorder) without touching vendor APIs or full warehouse datasets.

Test-Driven Development Best Practices

Test-Driven Development (TDD) is a software development methodology where tests are written before the actual code. In T-SQL, TDD ensures that stored procedures, functions, and triggers are correct, maintainable, and resilient from the outset. Using the tSQLt framework, developers can implement TDD principles effectively in SQL Server environments.

This section explores the best practices, workflows, and strategies for TDD in T-SQL.

Understanding TDD in SQL Development

TDD is built around a simple cycle often called Red-Green-Refactor:

1. **Red**: Write a test that fails because the functionality is not yet implemented.
2. **Green**: Write the minimal code required to make the test pass.
3. **Refactor**: Optimize the code, while ensuring all tests continue to pass.

Benefits in SQL:

- Early detection of logical errors.
- Documentation of business rules through tests.
- Easier maintenance and refactoring.
- Reduced regression risk during changes.

Organizing Test Classes

Proper organization of test classes ensures maintainability:

- **Create a separate schema per module**:

  ```
  EXEC tSQLt.NewTestClass 'TestInventory';
  EXEC tSQLt.NewTestClass 'TestSales';
  ```

- **Naming conventions**:
  - Prefix test classes with Test for clarity.
  - Name procedures descriptively, for example,

    `test_ReorderStock_WhenInventoryLow`.

- **Grouping by business functionality improves readability and reporting.**

Writing Focused Unit Tests

Each test should validate one specific behavior:

- Test one stored procedure or function at a time.
- Avoid testing multiple outcomes in a single test.
- Use minimal datasets to keep tests fast and isolated.

Example:

```
CREATE PROCEDURE TestInventory.[test ReorderStock triggers when quantity below
threshold]
AS
BEGIN
    EXEC tSQLt.FakeTable 'Inventory';
    INSERT INTO Inventory(ItemID, Quantity, ReorderLevel) VALUES (101, 5, 10);

    EXEC tSQLt.SpyProcedure 'SendPurchaseOrder';
    EXEC ReorderStock;

    EXEC tSQLt.AssertEquals 1, (SELECT COUNT(*) FROM PurchaseOrders WHERE ItemID =
101);
END;
```

This single test validates the core behavior of the **`ReorderStock`** procedure.

Writing Tests before Code (Red Phase)

In TDD, the first step is writing a test for functionality that does not exist yet:

- Forces developers to think about expected behavior and edge cases.
- Ensures that all requirements are captured in executable tests.

- **Example**: Write a test for a stored procedure that calculates discounts before implementing the procedure.

```
CREATE PROCEDURE TestSales.[test ApplyDiscount handles over 100 orders]
AS
BEGIN
    EXEC tSQLt.FakeTable 'Orders';
    INSERT INTO Orders(OrderID, Total) VALUES (1, 1200);

    EXEC ApplyDiscount @OrderID = 1;

    EXEC tSQLt.AssertEquals 1000, (SELECT Total FROM Orders WHERE OrderID = 1);
END;
```

The test fails initially because **`ApplyDiscount`** is not implemented as this is the Red phase.

Implementing Minimal Code (Green Phase)

Once a failing test exists:

- Write only the minimal T-SQL code required to pass the test.
- Avoid over-engineering at this stage.
- Run the test frequently to confirm correctness.

Example: Minimal procedure implementation to pass the discount test

```
CREATE PROCEDURE ApplyDiscount @OrderID INT
AS
BEGIN
    UPDATE Orders
    SET Total = 1000
    WHERE OrderID = @OrderID;
END;
```

Run the test again, as it should now pass (the Green phase).

Refactoring SQL Code

After tests pass:

- Refactor T-SQL for readability, performance, or maintainability.
- Tests act as a safety net, ensuring existing functionality is not broken.
- Examples of refactoring:
    - Simplify joins or subqueries.
    - Replace temporary tables with CTEs.
    - Optimize indexes or queries.

Example: Replace a temporary table with a CTE without affecting the test outcome

```
WITH OrderCTE AS (
    SELECT * FROM Orders WHERE OrderID = @OrderID
)
UPDATE OrderCTE
SET Total = 1000;
```

Thus, tests continue passing after refactoring.

Handling Edge Cases

TDD encourages you to anticipate the edge cases:

- Null inputs
- Zero or negative values
- Maximum lengths of strings or numbers
- Invalid foreign keys

Example test for a null input:

```
CREATE PROCEDURE TestSales.[test ApplyDiscount handles null order ID]
AS
BEGIN
    EXEC tSQLt.ExpectException;
    EXEC ApplyDiscount @OrderID = NULL;
END;
```

This ensures that the procedure gracefully handles unexpected inputs.

Automating Test Execution

Integrate TDD with CI/CD pipelines:

- Run all tests automatically after code deployment.
- Fail the build if any test fails.
- Example using PowerShell and sqlcmd:
  `sqlcmd -S . -d TestDB -Q "EXEC tSQLt.RunAll"`

Automated execution ensures continuous verification of SQL logic.

Version Control Integration

Integrating tSQLt tests with version control ensures that tests evolve alongside your database code, and provides traceability for changes.

- Store tSQLt tests in the same repository as T-SQL code.
- Commit tests alongside procedures/functions.
- This ensures traceability and easy rollback if code changes break tests.

Naming Conventions for Clarity

Adopt consistent naming conventions:

- `Test class → Test<Module>`
- `Test procedure → test_<Procedure>_<Condition>`
- **Examples**:
  - `test_ReorderStock_WhenInventoryLow`
  - `test_ApplyDiscount_WhenOver100Orders`

Thus, descriptive names improve readability and simplify reporting.

Benefits of TDD in SQL

Test-Driven Development (TDD) in SQL promotes writing tests before codes, ensuring reliability, maintainability, and alignment with business rules.

- Early detection of errors
- Documented business logic
- Safe refactoring
- Automation-friendly
- Confidence during production deployment

Common Pitfalls and Solutions

Awareness of common TDD pitfalls helps teams implement SQL tests effectively, and avoid errors or unrealistic test coverage (refer to the following table).

Pitfall	Solution
Writing tests after coding	Adopt TDD mindset tests first, code second
Overcomplicated tests	Keep tests small and focused
Ignoring edge cases	Explicitly test for nulls, empty tables, and invalid inputs
Not isolating dependencies	Use `FakeTable` and `SpyProcedure` for mocks

Table 14.2: *Common Pitfalls and Solutions*

Real-World Example: Sales Discount Module

A practical example demonstrates how TDD ensures correctness, performance, and maintainability in SQL development.

Step 1: Write failing tests for each discount scenario.

Step 2: Implement minimal codes to pass tests.

Step 3: Refactor for performance (indexes, joins).

Step 4: Re-run all tests automatically via CI/CD.

Outcome: Fully tested, maintainable, and reliable SQL code aligned with business rules.

Integration with CI/CD

Continuous Integration and Continuous Deployment (CI/CD) are crucial in modern database development. Integrating tSQLt unit tests with CI/CD pipelines ensures that every code change is automatically verified, reducing the risk of errors and enabling faster, reliable deployments. This section explores how to integrate T-SQL testing into CI/CD pipelines, and provides practical guidance.

CI/CD Pipeline Integration

Hence, CI/CD pipeline integration can seem complex at first, especially for database systems. To make it easier, it is best to focus on a small number of core ideas, rather than specific tools or platforms.

At a basic level, CI/CD integration means storing SQL scripts in version control, automatically validating them when changes are made, and deploying them in a consistent order across environments. Database changes should be incremental, repeatable, and designed to fail safely, if an error occurs.

Readers should begin with simple automation, such as executing validated SQL scripts during a build or release stage. As confidence grows, additional steps such as automated testing, approval gates, and environment-specific configurations can be added gradually. This step-by-step approach reduces risks, while improving reliability.

By treating database changes as code and automating them incrementally, CI/CD pipelines become manageable, predictable, and easier to maintain.

Understanding CI/CD in SQL Development

Continuous Integration (CI) involves automatically building and testing database code whenever changes are committed to version control.

Continuous Deployment (CD) takes this further by automatically deploying validated code to development, staging, or production environments.

Benefits for T-SQL projects:

- Immediate feedback on code changes.
- Reduced risk of breaking production.
- Automated validation of business rules.
- Traceable history of changes and test results.

Preparing T-SQL Projects for CI/CD

Before integrating tSQLt tests into CI/CD, ensure that your project is structured properly:

- Store T-SQL scripts in version control (Git, Azure Repos, or GitHub).
- Separate schema creation, stored procedures/functions, and tSQLt test scripts.
- Use scripts for deploying test databases to ensure a clean environment.

Example structure:

```
/DatabaseProject
    /Schema
        Tables.sql
        Views.sql
    /Procedures
        ReorderStock.sql
        ApplyDiscount.sql
    /Tests
        TestInventory.sql
        TestSales.sql
```

Automating Test Execution with CI Tools

Popular CI/CD platforms include:

- Azure DevOps Pipelines
- GitHub Actions
- Jenkins
- TeamCity

To run tSQLt tests:

1. Provision a test database.
2. Deploy the latest T-SQL scripts.
3. Execute **tSQLt.RunAll** or specific test classes.
4. Collect results, and report success/failure.

Azure DevOps YAML Example:

```
trigger:
- main

pool:
  vmImage: 'windows-latest'

steps:
- task: SqlAzureDacpacDeployment@1
  inputs:
    azureSubscription: 'MyAzureSubscription'
    ServerName: 'myserver.database.windows.net'
    DatabaseName: 'TestDB'
    SqlUsername: '$(sqlUser)'
    SqlPassword: '$(sqlPassword)'
    DacpacFile: '$(Build.ArtifactStagingDirectory)/Database.dacpac'
    DeployType: 'DacpacTask'

- script: |
    sqlcmd -S myserver.database.windows.net -d TestDB -U $(sqlUser) -P $(sqlPassword)
-Q "EXEC tSQLt.RunAll"
  displayName: 'Run tSQLt Unit Tests'
```

Test Reporting and Feedback

CI/CD platforms provide real-time feedback on test execution:

- Pass/Fail indicators: Fail the pipeline if any test fails.
- Detailed logs: Inspect error messages from tSQLt assertions.
- Historical tracking: Analyze trends in test failures to detect regressions.

Best practice: Fail the build immediately, if a unit test fails, preventing broken codes from progressing through the pipeline.

Handling Test Data in CI/CD

Proper handling of test data ensures that automated pipelines run reliably, consistently, and without impacting production environments.

- Use **FakeTables**, and mock data to isolate tests.
- Avoid using production data in pipelines.
- Seed databases with minimal datasets for speed.
- Reset the database state, before each pipeline run to ensure repeatability.

Example:

```
EXEC tSQLt.FakeTable 'Inventory';
INSERT INTO Inventory(ItemID, Quantity, ReorderLevel) VALUES (101, 5, 10);
```

Deploying to Multiple Environments

CI/CD workflows typically involve:

1. **Development Environment**: Frequent deployments, run all unit tests.
2. **Staging Environment**: Integration tests, full database refresh.
3. **Production Environment**: Only tested, approved code is deployed.

Thus, automate database deployments using DACPACs, SQL scripts, or migration tools, while ensuring that tSQLt tests pass, before moving the code forward.

Integrating with Test Coverage Tools

Track code coverage to ensure that critical business logic is tested:

- Combine tSQLt with SQL code coverage tools.
- Identify untested stored procedures or functions.
- Improve test coverage incrementally.

Benefit: Ensures that new code additions are always accompanied by tests.

Notifications and Alerts

Configure your CI/CD pipeline to notify the team on:

- Failed test executions
- Code deployment errors
- Regression warnings

Example: Email, Slack, or Teams notifications, when a test fails in Azure DevOps.

Handling Parallel Test Execution in CI/CD

In large databases with hundreds of tests, running them sequentially can be time-consuming. Therefore, modern CI/CD pipelines allow parallel test execution to speed up feedback cycles:

- **tSQLt supports independent tests**: Since each test is isolated using fake tables and test classes, multiple tests can run simultaneously without interfering with each other.
- **Implementation in pipelines**: Most CI/CD tools like Azure DevOps and GitHub Actions support parallel jobs. You can partition tests by test class or module.

Example: Azure DevOps parallel jobs

```
jobs:
- job: TestInventory
  steps:
    - script: sqlcmd -S $(server) -d TestDB -Q "EXEC tSQLt.Run 'TestInventory'"
      displayName: 'Run Inventory Tests'

- job: TestSales
```

```
steps:
  - script: sqlcmd -S $(server) -d TestDB -Q "EXEC tSQLt.Run 'TestSales'"
    displayName: 'Run Sales Tests'
```

Benefits:

- Significant reduction in overall test execution time.
- Faster feedback for developers.
- Efficient utilization of CI/CD resources.

Best Practices:

- Ensure that each test class is independent and self-contained.
- Avoid shared state across classes, when running tests in parallel.
- Use consistent seeding and cleanup strategies.

Versioning and Rollback Strategies

Integrating tSQLt tests in CI/CD also requires careful versioning and rollback planning:

- **Database versioning:** Track schema changes, stored procedures, and tSQLt test scripts in source control. Each pipeline build corresponds to a specific version of the database.
- **Automated rollback:** In case tests fail or deployment errors occur, CI/CD pipelines can roll back to the last successful deployment using:
  - DACPAC deployment with rollback
  - Transaction-based scripts
  - Database snapshots in SQL Server

Example using DACPAC rollback:

```
# Deploy DACPAC
Invoke-Sqlcmd -ServerInstance "myserver" -Database "TestDB" -InputFile "Database.
dacpac"

# If tests fail
Invoke-Sqlcmd -ServerInstance "myserver" -Database "TestDB" -InputFile
"PreviousVersion.dacpac"
```

Benefits:

- Maintains production stability even when tests fail.
- Provides a safe way to validate experimental changes.
- Ensures compliance with DevOps best practices for version control.

Best Practices:

- Always tag CI/CD builds with version numbers or Git commit hashes.
- Maintain baseline snapshots of critical databases.
- Combine rollback strategies with automated tSQLt test validation.

Best Practices for CI/CD Integration

Integrating tSQLt unit tests into CI/CD pipelines ensures reliable, automated, and consistent database deployments, while catching regressions early.

1. **Automate everything**: Deploy database schema, objects, and run tSQLt tests automatically.
2. **Isolate environments**: Never run CI/CD tests on production databases.
3. **Use version control**: All scripts and tests should be under source control.
4. **Fail fast**: Pipeline should stop on test failures to prevent faulty code from progressing.
5. **Keep tests small and fast**: Optimize test execution time to maintain a responsive CI/CD workflow.
6. **Log everything**: Capture test outputs and errors for audit and debugging purposes.
7. **Review pipelines regularly**: Adjust to accommodate schema changes or new tests.

Real-World Example

Scenario: Deploying a sales discount module.

Step 1: Developer commits stored procedures and tSQLt tests to GitHub.

Step 2: GitHub Actions triggers pipeline:

a. Deploys the schema and procedures to a test database.

b. Runs all tSQLt tests (**`tSQLt.RunAll`**).

Step 3: If tests pass, pipeline deploys code to staging for integration testing.

Step 4: Alerts the team, if any test fails.

Outcome: Fast feedback loop, confidence in changes, and reliable deployments.

Conclusion

This chapter highlighted the importance of testing for reliable SQL development. You learned to install and configure the tSQLt framework, write unit tests for stored procedures and functions, and use mocking to isolate tests from production data.

Best practices for test organization, naming conventions, and execution were presented, along with integration into Test-Driven Development (TDD) workflows. The chapter also showed how to incorporate CI/CD pipelines for automated testing, ensuring that database changes are validated continuously.

The next chapter will focus on real-world case studies and the future of T-SQL, demonstrating practical applications, cloud migration scenarios, and emerging trends.

CHAPTER 15

Case Studies and the Future of T-SQL

Introduction

This chapter brings together all the concepts, best practices, and advanced techniques discussed throughout the book. It focuses on real-world case studies, practical solutions, and a forward-looking perspective on T-SQL development. The aim is to help readers apply T-SQL knowledge strategically, while preparing for emerging technologies and trends.

Structure

In this chapter, we will cover the following topics:

- Migrating Legacy SQL to Modern Platforms
- Performance Tuning Case Studies
- Cloud Migration Challenges
- Temporal Tables and System-Versioned Data
- AI and Machine Learning Integration
- Future Directions of T-SQL Development

Migrating Legacy SQL to Modern Platforms

Legacy SQL systems, especially those running older versions of SQL Server often contain outdated design patterns, deprecated features, and inefficient queries. Migrating these systems to modern platforms such as SQL Server 2022, Azure SQL Database, or Azure SQL Managed Instance requires careful planning and execution. This section provides a detailed guide for performing successful migrations.

Understanding Legacy SQL Systems

Before migration, it is crucial to analyze and understand the existing database environment:

- **Database version:** SQL Server 2005, 2008, or older may have features not supported in modern SQL Server versions.
- **Schema design:** Identify tables, indexes, constraints, and relationships.
- **Stored procedures and functions:** Review complex procedural logic, loops, and cursors.
- **Dependencies:** Map inter-object dependencies, including views, triggers, and user-defined functions.

- **Data volume and growth patterns:** Assess historical and projected data size for scalability planning.

Example: A manufacturing company running SQL Server 2008 had hundreds of stored procedures using cursors and dynamic SQL. Direct migration to Azure SQL required refactoring and modernizing queries.

Challenges in Migrating Legacy SQL

Migration is rarely straightforward due to several common issues:

1. **Deprecated features:** Certain SQL Server constructs, such as old join syntax or system functions, may not be supported.
2. **Performance issues:** Legacy code often relies on inefficient queries or cursors, causing bottlenecks in modern environments.
3. **Lack of testing:** Many legacy databases have no automated unit tests, making validation difficult.
4. **Integration complexity:** Legacy databases are often tied to multiple applications and reporting systems.
5. **Compliance requirements:** Data migration may require adherence to regulatory standards, especially in finance or healthcare.

Planning a Migration Strategy

A well-defined migration strategy reduces risks, and ensures a smooth transition:

- **Inventory of all objects:** Document tables, procedures, functions, views, triggers, and dependencies.
- **Select the target platform:** Decide between on-premises SQL Server upgrades or cloud migration (Azure SQL Database, Managed Instance, and so on).
- **Define migration phases:** Use incremental migration or a lift-and-shift approach depending on complexity.
- **Establish test environments:** Ensure that a staging environment mirrors production for validation.

Tip: *Use tools like Azure Database Migration Assistant (DMA) to identify compatibility issues and estimate effort.*

Refactoring Legacy Code

Refactoring is critical to modernize SQL and improve maintainability:

1. **Replace cursors with set-based operations:** Cursors are often slower and resource-intensive.
2. **Use CTEs and MERGE statements:** Simplify complex logic and enable efficient data operations.
3. **Modularize code:** Break monolithic procedures into reusable stored procedures and user-defined functions.
4. **Standardize naming conventions:** Ensure consistency for long-term maintainability.

Example:

```
Original cursor-based code:
DECLARE @EmpID INT
DECLARE cur CURSOR FOR SELECT EmployeeID FROM Employee
OPEN cur
FETCH NEXT FROM cur INTO @EmpID
WHILE @@FETCH_STATUS = 0
BEGIN
    UPDATE Employee SET Status = 'Active' WHERE EmployeeID = @EmpID
    FETCH NEXT FROM cur INTO @EmpID
END
CLOSE cur
DEALLOCATE cur
Refactored set-based code:
UPDATE Employee
SET Status = 'Active'
WHERE EmployeeID IN (SELECT EmployeeID FROM Employee)
```

Benefits: Improved performance, readability, and easier future maintenance.

Implementing Automated Testing

Automated testing ensures that migrated databases behave as expected:

- Use tSQLt framework to create unit tests for stored procedures, functions, and triggers.
- Test data transformations, business logic, and constraints in the new environment.
- Validate data integrity after each migration phase.

Example: Test inventory procedure

```
EXEC tSQLt.NewTestClass 'InventoryTests';
EXEC tSQLt.NewTest 'TestReorderLevelCalculation';
```

Data Migration and Validation

Ensuring accurate and reliable data migration requires structured extraction, transformation, and rigorous validation to maintain data integrity across environments.

- **Data extraction:** Use tools such as SSIS or Azure Data Factory for ETL processes.
- **Data transformation:** Apply necessary transformations for new schemas or cloud compatibility.
- **Validation:** Compare row counts, checksums, and business rule outputs between legacy and modern databases.

Example: Validate row counts

```
SELECT COUNT(*) AS OldDB_Count FROM LegacyDB.dbo.Inventory;
SELECT COUNT(*) AS NewDB_Count FROM ModernDB.dbo.Inventory;
```

Leveraging Modern Platform Features

Once migrated, modern SQL platforms provide opportunities to enhance functionality:

- **Temporal tables:** Track historical changes automatically.

- **Columnstore indexes:** Improve analytical query performance.
- **Dynamic data masking and encryption:** Improve security and compliance.
- **Query Store:** Monitors performance regressions post-migration.

Example:

```
Enabling system-versioned temporal table for audit purposes:
ALTER TABLE Employee
SET (SYSTEM_VERSIONING = ON (HISTORY_TABLE = dbo.EmployeeHistory));
```

Migration Best Practices

A structured and carefully monitored approach to database migration ensures minimal disruption, maintains data integrity, and optimizes performance in the target environment.

1. **Plan in phases:** Start with low-risk databases.
2. **Validate at each stage:** Ensure schema, logic, and data integrity.
3. **Monitor performance:** Use Query Store and DMVs to detect slow queries.
4. **Document changes:** Maintain detailed records of schema modifications and refactored procedures.
5. **Train team members:** Ensure that development and operations teams understand new platform features.

Real-World Example

A logistics company migrated from SQL Server 2005 to Azure SQL Managed Instance:

- Refactored over 300 stored procedures into modular, set-based operations.
- Automated testing with tSQLt caught 20 critical issues before deployment.
- Leveraged elastic pools to scale for fluctuating workloads.
- Reduced monthly operational costs by 35%, while improving query performance by 50%.

Key Takeaways

Successful database modernization combines careful planning, thorough testing, and adoption of modern features to ensure optimum performance, security, and maintainability.

- Legacy SQL systems require careful analysis, refactoring, and testing before migration.
- Modern T-SQL constructs and cloud platforms provide better performance, scalability, and maintainability.
- Automated testing, version control, and monitoring are critical for successful migration.
- Post-migration, organizations can leverage temporal tables, encryption, and cloud-native features for future-ready databases.

Performance Tuning Case Study

Performance tuning is a crucial skill for database developers and administrators. Real-world systems often face slow query execution, high CPU usage, and inefficient data access patterns. This case study walks through a systematic approach to analyzing, optimizing, and validating database performance.

Understanding the Performance Problem

A financial services firm was experiencing slow reporting queries on a 500 GB transaction table, with some reports taking over 2 hours to complete. The first step in tuning is understanding the problem:

- Identify affected queries and stored procedures.
- Measure query execution times and frequency.
- Collect system metrics (CPU, memory, I/O usage) during query execution.
- Interview users to understand critical business requirements.

Example:

```
SELECT TOP 10 query_text, total_elapsed_time, execution_count
FROM sys.dm_exec_query_stats AS qs
CROSS APPLY sys.dm_exec_sql_text(qs.sql_handle) AS st
ORDER BY total_elapsed_time DESC;
```

This query identifies the most expensive queries in the system, providing a starting point for optimization.

Analyzing Execution Plans

Execution plans reveal how SQL Server processes queries and where bottlenecks occur:

- **Estimated execution plan:** Shows the optimizer's plan before execution.
- **Actual execution plan:** Captures the plan after execution with actual row counts.
- **Identify expensive operators** such as table scans, nested loops, and key lookups.

Example:

```
SET STATISTICS IO ON;
SET STATISTICS TIME ON;
GO
SELECT * FROM Transactions WHERE TransactionDate >= '2025-01-01';
GO
```

This helps to determine if indexes are being utilized and whether queries are SARGable.

Index Design and Optimization

Indexes are fundamental to improving query performance. Strategies include:

- **Clustered versus Non-clustered indexes:** Use clustered for primary key and frequently filtered columns, non-clustered for secondary queries.
- **Covering indexes:** Include all columns needed for a query to eliminate lookups.
- **Filtered indexes:** Apply to a subset of data for selective queries.

Example:

```
Original query without index:
SELECT * FROM Transactions WHERE CustomerID = 12345;
Optimized with non-clustered index:
CREATE NONCLUSTERED INDEX IX_Transactions_CustomerID
ON Transactions(CustomerID);
```

Result: Reduced query execution from 120 seconds to 5 seconds.

Query Refactoring

Inefficient queries are common in legacy systems. Refactoring includes:

- Rewriting cursors to set-based queries.
- Eliminating unnecessary subqueries and nested **SELECTs**.
- Using CTEs to simplify complex joins.

Example: Cursor replacement

```
-- Original cursor-based query
DECLARE cur CURSOR FOR SELECT TransactionID FROM Transactions;
OPEN cur
FETCH NEXT FROM cur INTO @TransID
WHILE @@FETCH_STATUS = 0
BEGIN
    UPDATE Transactions SET Status = 'Processed' WHERE TransactionID = @TransID;
    FETCH NEXT FROM cur INTO @TransID
END
CLOSE cur
DEALLOCATE cur;
Refactored set-based query:
UPDATE Transactions
SET Status = 'Processed'
WHERE TransactionDate < GETDATE();
```

Result: Dramatic reduction in CPU usage and execution time.

Statistics Management

Outdated statistics can cause the query optimizer to make poor decisions:

- Regularly update statistics on large tables using **UPDATE STATISTICS**.
- Enable **AUTO_UPDATE_STATISTICS** for dynamic optimization.
- Monitor column distribution statistics to ensure accurate cardinality estimation.

Example:

```
UPDATE STATISTICS Transactions WITH FULLSCAN;
```

Benefits: Improved execution plan choices and query performance.

Partitioning Large Tables

Partitioning is effective for large, historical datasets:

- Divide a table into smaller, manageable partitions by date or category.
- Improves query performance and maintenance tasks.
- Enables partition-level switching and archiving.

Example:

```
CREATE PARTITION FUNCTION pf_TransactionsDateRange (DATE)
AS RANGE LEFT FOR VALUES ('2024-01-01', '2024-06-30', '2024-12-31');
```

Benefits: Queries targeting specific ranges scan fewer rows, improving efficiency.

Implementing Query Hints

Sometimes, the query optimizer requires guidance:

- Use **`OPTION (RECOMPILE)`** to avoid parameter sniffing issues.
- Apply **`FORCESEEK`** to enforce index usage.
- Use **`MAXDOP`** to control parallelism for expensive queries.

Example:

```
SELECT * FROM Transactions
WHERE CustomerID = 12345
OPTION (RECOMPILE);
```

Monitoring and Validation

After optimizations, monitor performance to ensure improvements:

- Use Query Store to compare before-and-after execution times.
- Check DMVs for wait stats, blocking, and long-running queries.
- Validate correctness using tSQLt tests or sample data validation.

Example:

```
SELECT TOP 50 *
FROM sys.dm_exec_query_stats qs
CROSS APPLY sys.dm_exec_sql_text(qs.sql_handle) AS st
ORDER BY total_elapsed_time DESC;
```

Real-World Results

After implementing the above steps:

- Average query execution time reduced from 2 hours to 15 minutes.
- CPU usage dropped by 70%, reducing hardware costs.
- Users experienced faster reporting, improving business decision-making.
- Maintenance became easier with modular, well-indexed, and optimized the T-SQL code.

Lessons Learned

Effective database modernization and optimization rely on continuous analysis, iterative improvements, and leveraging modern T-SQL capabilities.

- **Always start with data-driven analysis:** execution plans, DMVs, Query Store.
- **Combine indexing, query refactoring, and statistics management** for maximum impact.
- **Leverage modern T-SQL features** like CTEs, MERGE, and partitioning.

- **Validate changes with automated testing** to maintain correctness.
- **Performance tuning is an iterative process**, not a one-time task.

Cloud Migration Challenges

Migrating on-premises SQL Server databases to cloud platforms like Azure SQL Database, Azure SQL Managed Instance, or Azure Synapse Analytics is increasingly common. While cloud platforms offer scalability, high availability, and cost savings, migration comes with unique challenges. This section details these challenges, and provides strategies for successful cloud adoption.

Understanding Cloud Platforms

Before migration, it is critical to understand the available options:

- **Azure SQL Database:** Fully managed, single-database or elastic pool model. Ideal for SaaS and transactional workloads.
- **Azure SQL Managed Instance:** Near 100% compatibility with on-prem SQL Server, supports legacy features.
- **SQL Server on Azure VMs:** Full control over SQL Server, including unsupported legacy features, but requires VM management.
- **Azure Synapse Analytics:** Designed for analytics workloads, large-scale data processing, and reporting.

Key Consideration: Selecting the right target platform depends on workload type, required features, and desired maintenance responsibilities.

Connectivity and Network Latency

Cloud databases require robust network connectivity:

- Ensure low-latency, and high-bandwidth connections to support transactional workloads.
- Use Azure ExpressRoute or VPNs for secure private connections.
- Consider geo-replication and multi-region deployment to optimize access for distributed users.

Example: A multinational firm migrating ERP databases implemented ExpressRoute to reduce latency from 120ms to under 10ms for critical operations.

Security and Compliance Challenges

Cloud migration must maintain data security and regulatory compliance:

- **Firewall and network security:** Configure Azure SQL firewall rules and private endpoints.
- **Authentication:** Migrate to Azure Active Directory (AAD) for centralized identity management.
- **Encryption:** Ensure that the data is protected in transit (TLS) and at rest (TDE or Always Encrypted).
- **Regulatory compliance:** HIPAA, GDPR, and PCI DSS may impose additional constraints.

Best Practice: Perform a security audit prior to migration to identify gaps, and implement the required policies.

Compatibility and Feature Gaps

Not all legacy SQL Server features are supported in the cloud:

- **Unsupported features:** SQL Server Agent jobs, certain CLR assemblies, or extended stored procedures may require refactoring.
- **T-SQL compatibility:** Review the deprecated functions and syntax that may break in modern SQL versions.
- **Third-party integrations:** Ensure that all applications can connect to cloud endpoints without disruption.

Strategy: Use Azure Database Migration Assistant (DMA) to analyze compatibility issues, and generate reports with recommended changes.

Performance and Resource Scaling

Cloud performance management differs from on-premises:

- **Elastic pools:** Share resources among multiple databases to optimize cost and performance.
- **Service tiers:** Select appropriate DTUs or vCores based on workload demands.
- **Monitoring:** Use Query Store, Azure Monitor, and Metrics Explorer to track query performance and resource usage.

Example: A financial services client migrated 20 reporting databases into an elastic pool to handle unpredictable monthly reporting spikes efficiently, avoiding over-provisioning.

Data Migration Strategies

Choosing the right migration method is critical:

- **Lift-and-shift (offline):** Backup and restore databases to the cloud. Fast, but requires downtime.
- **Online migration (minimal downtime):** Use Azure Database Migration Service (DMS) for continuous replication, while cutover occurs.
- **ETL-based migration:** Use SSIS or Azure Data Factory to transform and load data into new schemas.

Best Practice: Perform a pilot migration to validate data integrity, performance, and application compatibility before full production cutover.

Cost Management Challenges

Cloud adoption can incur unexpected costs:

- Pay-per-use billing models require careful capacity planning.
- Long-running queries or high DTU/vCore usage may spike costs.
- Storage costs for historical or large datasets can accumulate.

Strategy:

- Use Azure Cost Management + Billing for budgeting and alerts.
- Implement tiered storage and data archiving for cost optimization.
- Optimize queries and indexing to reduce resource consumption.

Real-World Example

A healthcare organization migrated 15 on-premises databases to Azure SQL Managed Instance:

- Identified incompatible features with DMA, and refactored stored procedures.
- Leveraged temporal tables for auditing patient data.
- Implemented Query Store to monitor performance, and detect regressions post-migration.
- Reduced monthly infrastructure costs by 35%, while improving scalability and resilience.

Lessons Learned

Successful database migration and modernization require careful planning, testing, and continuous monitoring to balance performance, security, and cost.

1. **Thorough assessment:** Identify compatibility, security, and performance requirements before migration.
2. **Pilot first:** Validate critical workloads in a staging environment.
3. **Monitor continuously:** Use Query Store, DMVs, and cloud monitoring tools.
4. **Refactor intelligently:** Remove deprecated features, optimize queries, and adopt cloud-native practices.
5. **Cost-aware planning:** Consider elastic pools, auto-scaling, and storage optimization to control expenses.

Temporal Tables and System-Versioned Data

Temporal tables, introduced in SQL Server 2016, are a powerful feature for automatically tracking historical changes to data. They allow developers and administrators to query data as it existed at any point in time without writing complex triggers or audit logic. This section provides a detailed guide on designing, implementing, and leveraging temporal tables in modern T-SQL development.

Understanding Temporal Tables

A temporal table consists of two components:

1. **Current table (system-versioned):** Holds the latest version of the data.
2. **History table:** Automatically stores previous versions of rows whenever they are updated or deleted.

Key Benefits:

- **Automated change tracking:** No need for manual triggers or audit columns.
- **Historical queries:** Retrieve past states of data for reporting or compliance.
- **Data recovery:** Easily restore accidentally modified or deleted data.

Example:

```
CREATE TABLE Employee
(
    EmployeeID INT PRIMARY KEY,
    Name NVARCHAR(100),
    Position NVARCHAR(50),
```

```
    Salary DECIMAL(10,2),
    ValidFrom DATETIME2 GENERATED ALWAYS AS ROW START NOT NULL,
    ValidTo DATETIME2 GENERATED ALWAYS AS ROW END NOT NULL,
    PERIOD FOR SYSTEM_TIME (ValidFrom, ValidTo)
)
WITH (SYSTEM_VERSIONING = ON (HISTORY_TABLE = dbo.EmployeeHistory));
```

Here, Employee is the current table, and EmployeeHistory stores all the previous versions of rows automatically.

System-Versioned Data Mechanics

System-versioned temporal tables maintain the historical data without manual intervention:

- **`UPDATE` operations:** Previous row version is moved to the history table.
- **`DELETE` operations:** Deleted rows are moved to the history table.
- **Automatic timestamping:** ValidFrom and ValidTo columns track the period each row version was valid.

Example of history table content:

Employee ID	Name	Position	Salary	ValidFrom	ValidTo
1	Alice	Analyst	70000	2024-01-01 00:00	2024-06-01 12:00
1	Alice	Senior Analyst	80000	2024-06-01 12:00	9999-12-31 00:00

Table 15.1: *Employee Table*

Querying Temporal Data

Temporal tables provide powerful querying capabilities:

- **As of a Specific Time:** Retrieve data as it existed at a particular timestamp.

  ```
  SELECT * FROM Employee
  FOR SYSTEM_TIME AS OF '2024-05-01 09:00';
  ```

- **Between Two Points in Time:** Get historical changes within a date range.

  ```
  SELECT * FROM Employee
  FOR SYSTEM_TIME BETWEEN '2024-01-01' AND '2024-06-01';
  ```

- **All Historical Versions:** Access the full history of a row.

  ```
  SELECT * FROM Employee
  FOR SYSTEM_TIME ALL
  WHERE EmployeeID = 1;
  ```

Use Cases for Temporal Tables

Temporal tables provide built-in versioning of data, enabling organizations to track historical changes, and simplify auditing, recovery, and analysis.

1. **Auditing and Compliance:** Maintain a complete record of changes for regulatory requirements.
2. **Data Recovery:** Restore accidentally deleted or updated rows.

3. **Business Reporting:** Track trends over time, such as salary changes, promotions, or stock levels.
4. **Debugging:** Identify when and how data changes occurred in production systems.

Integrating with ETL and Reporting

Temporal tables integrate well with modern reporting and ETL processes:

- **ETL pipelines:** Use temporal queries to extract historical snapshots for data warehouses.
- **Power BI reporting:** Analyze trends over time without complex transformations.
- **Version comparison:** Compare the current and past data directly in SQL without manual joins.

Example:

```
SELECT t1.EmployeeID, t1.Salary AS CurrentSalary, t2.Salary AS PreviousSalary
FROM Employee FOR SYSTEM_TIME AS OF '2024-06-01' t1
JOIN EmployeeHistory t2 ON t1.EmployeeID = t2.EmployeeID;
```

Best Practices for Temporal Tables

To maximize the benefits of temporal tables, while maintaining performance and accuracy, follow these recommended practices.

1. **Indexing:** Create indexes on commonly queried columns for improved performance.
2. **Partitioning:** Partition large temporal tables by date to improve query performance.
3. **Storage management:** Monitor history table growth, and archive old data, if necessary.
4. **Schema changes:** Use ALTER TABLE carefully, ensuring that system-versioning is temporarily disabled, if required.
5. **Consistency checks:** Regularly validate that the history table accurately reflects changes in the main table.

Limitations and Considerations

To maximize the benefits of temporal tables, while maintaining performance and accuracy, follow these recommended practices.

- Temporal tables may increase storage usage due to retained historical versions.
- Some operations (for example, dropping columns or altering data types) require temporarily disabling system versioning.
- Querying very large history tables may require filtered or partitioned indexes to maintain performance.

Real-World Example

A retail company implemented temporal tables for their Orders table:

- Enabled system-versioning to track all order status changes.
- Automated reports were generated showing orders processed per month and historical trends.
- Recovered accidentally deleted records using the history table, saving significant operational effort.

- Integrated temporal data with Power BI for visual trend analysis without modifying ETL pipelines.

Outcome: Streamlined auditing, improved historical reporting, and reduced manual intervention for data recovery.

Key Takeaways

Temporal tables offer powerful time-based data tracking, but their effectiveness depends on proper implementation and maintenance.

- Temporal tables provide automatic historical tracking, and simplify audit requirements.
- System-versioned data allows queries as-of, between, or all versions of a row.
- They are highly effective for auditing, compliance, reporting, and debugging.
- Proper indexing, storage management, and partitioning are essential for optimum performance.

AI and Machine Learning Integration

Integrating AI and Machine Learning (ML) into SQL Server environments allows organizations to unlock predictive insights, automate decision-making, and enhance data-driven applications. SQL Server, along with Azure services, provides built-in support for executing R and Python scripts, training models, and scoring data directly in the database.

Understanding AI and ML in SQL Server

SQL Server supports in-database AI/ML using:

- **SQL Server Machine Learning Services (MLS):** Enables running Python or R scripts directly in the database.
- **Stored Procedures for ML:** Allows embedding model training and scoring within T-SQL stored procedures.
- **Azure ML Integration:** Use SQL Server to access and score models deployed in Azure Machine Learning.

Benefits:

- Reduce data movement between systems.
- Improve performance by processing data directly where it resides.
- Enable real-time predictions and analytics in applications.

Training Models in SQL Server

You can train ML models directly on SQL Server data:

1. **Prepare Data:** Clean and normalize datasets using T-SQL queries.
2. **Train Model:** Use Python or R scripts with built-in SQL Server procedures.
3. **Evaluate Accuracy:** Test models using historical data within the database.

Example: Train a regression model in SQL Server using Python

```
EXEC sp_execute_external_script
  @language = N'Python',
  @script = N'
```

```
import pandas as pd
from sklearn.linear_model import LinearRegression

model = LinearRegression()
model.fit(InputDataSet[["Feature1","Feature2"]], InputDataSet["Target"])
OutputDataSet = pd.DataFrame({"Prediction": model.
predict(InputDataSet[["Feature1","Feature2"]])})
',
  @input_data_1 = N'SELECT Feature1, Feature2, Target FROM SalesData;',
  @output_data_1_name = N'OutputDataSet';
```

This trains a linear regression model on historical sales data, and outputs predictions.

Scoring Models in SQL Server

Once a model is trained, scoring new data can be done within T-SQL:

- Use stored procedures or **sp_execute_external_script** to apply the model.
- Integrate scoring into ETL pipelines or real-time applications.

Example: Score new customer data for churn prediction

```
EXEC sp_execute_external_script
  @language = N'Python',
  @script = N'
OutputDataSet = model.predict(InputDataSet)
',
  @input_data_1 = N'SELECT CustomerFeatures FROM NewCustomerData;',
  @params = N'@model varbinary(max)',
  @model = @trainedModel;
```

Integration with Azure Machine Learning

SQL Server can leverage Azure ML for cloud-based model deployment:

- **Deploy models in Azure ML:** Centralized management of models.
- **Score from SQL Server:** Use T-SQL with REST APIs or integration packages to call cloud models.
- **Pipeline automation:** Trigger scoring jobs as part of ETL or reporting workflows.

Example: Using T-SQL to call Azure ML endpoint

```
EXEC sp_invoke_external_rest_api
  @url = 'https://<azureml-endpoint>/score',
  @method = 'POST',
  @body = @jsonInput;
```

Use Cases

Machine learning (ML) in SQL enables organizations to leverage historical and real-time data for predictive, analytical, and AI-driven insights.

- **Predictive Analytics:** Forecast sales, inventory, or customer churn using historical data.
- **Anomaly Detection:** Detect fraud, unusual transactions, or system anomalies in real-time.

- **Recommendation Systems:** Provide product recommendations by analyzing user behavior.
- **Natural Language Processing (NLP):** Sentiment analysis or text classification for customer feedback.

Best Practices

To maximize effectiveness and reliability, machine learning workflows in SQL should follow structured preparation, management, and monitoring practices.

- **Data Preparation:** Clean, normalize, and aggregate data in SQL before ML processing.
- **Model Lifecycle Management:** Maintain version control for models, track accuracy over time.
- **Security:** Ensure that external scripts and cloud endpoints are secure.
- **Performance Optimization:** Use batch scoring and indexes to avoid performance bottlenecks.
- **Monitoring:** Continuously monitor model performance and retrain periodically.

Real-World Example

A retail chain implemented SQL Server ML Services for predictive inventory management:

- Trained models using historical sales and seasonality data.
- Scored incoming orders in real-time to predict stockouts.
- Integrated with Power BI dashboards for actionable insights.
- Achieved a 20% reduction in lost sales due to improved forecasting.

Lessons Learned

Implementing machine learning directly within SQL environments offers significant benefits, but also highlights key considerations for success.

- In-database ML reduces data movement, and improves query performance.
- Proper data cleaning and transformation are critical for accurate predictions.
- Combining T-SQL with Python or R provides flexible and powerful analytics.
- Cloud integration enables scalable, enterprise-grade AI solutions.
- Monitoring and retraining models ensure long-term accuracy and reliability.

Future Directions of T-SQL Development

T-SQL continues to evolve to meet modern data challenges, cloud adoption, and advanced analytics needs. This section explores emerging trends, upcoming features, and best practices that developers and DBAs should consider for future-proofing their SQL Server skills and applications.

Cloud-Native T-SQL Development

As organizations increasingly migrate workloads to Azure SQL Database, Managed Instances, and Synapse Analytics, T-SQL development is shifting toward cloud-native patterns:

- **Serverless computing:** Pay-per-query models reduce costs for sporadic workloads.
- **Elastic pools:** Multi-database resource sharing allows scalable and cost-efficient architectures.

- **Managed services:** Reduced operational overhead lets developers focus on logic and performance, rather than infrastructure.

Example: Developing T-SQL stored procedures that automatically scale with Azure SQL Database elastic pools to handle seasonal traffic spikes.

Integration with AI and Machine Learning

T-SQL will increasingly serve as a platform for in-database AI and ML:

- Running Python or R scripts directly in SQL Server.
- Leveraging SQL Server ML Services for model training, scoring, and deployment.
- Cloud ML services integration for scalable AI applications.

Trend: Organizations are embedding predictive analytics, recommendation engines, and anomaly detection directly into the database layer for real-time decision-making.

Real-Time Analytics and Streaming Data

Modern applications require real-time insights:

- Temporal tables and system-versioned data will be increasingly used for historical tracking and auditing.
- Streaming data integration with T-SQL via Azure Stream Analytics, Event Hubs, and real-time ETL pipelines.
- Materialized views and in-memory tables will improve real-time query performance.

Example: IoT sensors feeding data into Azure SQL Managed Instance for real-time monitoring and alerting.

Graph and JSON Data Handling

T-SQL is evolving to handle semi-structured and graph data:

- **Graph tables:** Represent complex relationships like social networks, recommendation systems, and supply chains.
- **JSON support:** `OPENJSON`, `JSON_VALUE`, and `FOR JSON` allow flexible integration with modern applications.
- **XML enhancements:** Continued support for hybrid applications that still rely on XML.

Example: Storing customer interactions in JSON format for analytics and visualization in Power BI.

Serverless and Edge Computing Trends

T-SQL is adapting to serverless architectures and edge computing:

- Query execution on-demand in serverless databases reduces idle costs.
- Integration with edge devices for low-latency data processing in industrial and IoT applications.
- Pushdown computation to the database layer minimizes network traffic, and speeds analytics.

Best Practice: Design queries that are cloud-optimized, and can take advantage of serverless execution without changing core business logic.

Automation, DevOps, and CI/CD

The future of T-SQL development will increasingly focus on automation and integration with DevOps pipelines:

- **tSQLt and unit testing:** Automated testing for reliability and regression prevention.
- **PowerShell and Azure DevOps integration:** Automate deployments, backups, and monitoring.
- **Infrastructure as Code (IaC):** Manage database schemas, permissions, and jobs programmatically.

Example: Continuous integration pipelines automatically deploy T-SQL stored procedures, run unit tests, and update production databases with minimal manual intervention.

Enhanced Security and Compliance

Security will remain a top priority in future T-SQL development:

- Row-level security and dynamic data masking will continue evolving to support multi-tenant and regulated applications.
- Always Encrypted and TDE enhancements for stricter data protection.
- Compliance automation using auditing frameworks and AI-assisted monitoring for unusual activity.

Trend: Security baked into T-SQL workflows, reducing the need for separate compliance monitoring tools.

Emerging AI-Assisted Development

Future T-SQL developers will leverage AI-assisted coding and optimization such as:

- AI-powered query recommendations to improve performance.
- Automated index and statistics optimization.
- Predictive analysis of execution plans to prevent bottlenecks.

Example: AI analyzing historical query patterns and suggesting query rewrites or indexing strategies to optimize performance.

Real-World Outlook

Professionals interviewed in this book predict that:

- T-SQL will become more cloud-centric, AI-integrated, and real-time capable.
- Automation and CI/CD adoption will become standard for enterprise SQL Server environments.
- Developers will need to embrace hybrid data models, including structured, semi-structured, and graph data.
- Security and compliance will be built into the database layer, making auditing and encryption seamless.

Key Takeaways

Modern SQL development emphasizes cloud integration, automation, and advanced analytics to build secure, efficient, and future-ready database solutions.

- **Cloud-first development:** Optimize T-SQL for Azure SQL Database and Managed Instances.
- **In-database AI/ML:** Integrate predictive analytics and automation into SQL workflows.
- **Real-time and hybrid data:** Use temporal tables, graph tables, and JSON for modern analytics.
- **DevOps and automation**: Implement testing, CI/CD, and automated deployments for reliability.
- **Security by design:** Incorporate encryption, row-level security, and auditing in all database development.
- **Future-ready skills:** Embrace AI-assisted optimization, serverless patterns, and edge computing.

Conclusion

This chapter tied together practical insights from previous chapters with real-world case studies. You explored performance tuning, legacy modernization, and cloud migration projects. Temporal tables and system-versioned data were highlighted for auditability and historical tracking.

This chapter also examined future directions in T-SQL development, including AI integration, serverless patterns, and new SQL Server features. Interviews and industry perspectives offered guidance on long-term database strategy and innovation, inspiring readers to think beyond immediate technical solutions.

The next chapter will conclude the book with best practices for T-SQL development and database design, distilling practical experience into actionable guidelines for writing maintainable, high-performance, and secure SQL codes.

Chapter 16
Best Practices for T-SQL Development and Database Design

Introduction

This chapter distills years of experience and practical insights into a set of proven best practices for T-SQL development and relational database design. Readers will learn how to write clean, consistent, and efficient T-SQL code, while also making architectural decisions that ensure long-term scalability, performance, and maintainability. Hence, whether you are building new systems or refactoring legacy ones, these principles will serve as a blueprint for high-quality SQL development in real-world environments.

Structure

In this chapter, we will cover the following topics:

- T-SQL Coding Standards and Conventions
- Query Design Best Practices
- User-Defined Objects
- Performance-Oriented Design
- Transaction and Concurrency Management
- Maintainability and Refactoring
- Security and Auditing Practices
- Tooling and Modern Development Workflows
- Common Anti-Patterns to Avoid in T-SQL
- Design for Portability and Cloud Readiness

T-SQL Coding Standards and Conventions

Coding standards and conventions form the backbone of any professional development practice. In T-SQL, well-structured and consistent code not only improves readability and collaboration but also reduces bugs, eases maintenance, and enhances performance tuning efforts. A SQL environment is often shared by many developers, DBAs, and analysts, so consistency becomes vital to avoid confusion and ensure scalability.

This section presents a set of standards and conventions to follow when writing T-SQL code, covering naming practices, formatting, commenting, error handling, and style guidelines.

Importance of Coding Standards

Adhering to coding standards ensures that the SQL code is consistent, efficient, and maintainable across teams and projects.

- **Readability:** Developers across teams should be able to read and understand each other's code quickly.
- **Maintainability:** Clear structure makes debugging and refactoring easier.
- **Performance:** Standardized practices help avoid costly anti-patterns like unnecessary cursors or improper indexing.
- **Collaboration:** New developers can onboard faster when a standard convention exists.
- **Compliance:** Standards help in regulated industries where auditability is required.

Naming Conventions

Naming is one of the most critical aspects of T-SQL development. Consistent naming makes schema objects self-describing.

- **General Guidelines:**
  - Use PascalCase for schema objects (for example, `CustomerOrders`, `InvoiceDetails`).
  - Use `snake_case` or lowercase for variables (for example, `@order_id`, `@max_value`).
  - Avoid spaces or special characters in names.
  - Always use meaningful names (`CustomerPhoneNumber`, instead of `CustPh`).
- **Tables**:
  - Singular names are often preferred (`Customer`, not Customers) since rows represent an entity.
  - Prefixing schema for grouping (`Sales.Customer`, `HR.Employee`).
- **Columns**:
  - Name columns descriptively (`FirstName`, `LastName`, `OrderDate`).
  - Use suffixes like _id for primary keys (`CustomerID`).
- **Stored Procedures**:
  - Prefix with `usp_` for clarity (for example, `usp_GetCustomerByID`).
  - Avoid `sp_` as it is reserved for system procedures.
- **Constraints**:
  - `PK_TableName` for primary keys.
  - `FK_TableName_ReferencedTable` for foreign keys.
  - `CHK_TableName_Column` for check constraints.
- **Indexes**:
  - `IX_TableName_ColumnName` (for example, `IX_Customer_LastName`).

Formatting Conventions

Consistent formatting makes queries easier to read.

- **Keywords in UPPERCASE**:

```
SELECT FirstName, LastName
FROM Customer
WHERE Country = 'USA';
```

- **Indentation**:
  - Align **JOIN**s and **WHERE** conditions properly.
  - Use new lines for each clause.
- **JOIN Formatting**:

```
SELECT c.CustomerName, o.OrderDate
FROM Customer AS c
INNER JOIN Orders AS o ON c.CustomerID = o.CustomerID
WHERE o.OrderDate >= '2023-01-01';
```

- **Column Lists**:
  - Avoid **SELECT *;** always list columns explicitly.

Commenting Standards

Documentation within SQL is often overlooked but essential.

- **Inline Comments: For single-line explanations.**

```
-- Exclude inactive customers
WHERE IsActive = 1;
```

- **Block Comments: For larger descriptions.**

```
/*
  This stored procedure retrieves customers who placed
  orders in the last 30 days. It uses an index on OrderDate.
*/
```

- **Header Comments in Procedures**:

```
/*
 Procedure: usp_GetActiveCustomers
  Author: John Doe
  Date: 2025-05-01
  Description: Retrieves active customers in the last 6 months
*/
```

Consistent Use of Aliases

Applying consistent conventions in SQL queries and schema design improves readability, reduces errors, and ensures maintainable codes.

- Always alias tables in queries for clarity:

```
SELECT c.CustomerName, o.OrderID
```

```
FROM Customer AS c
JOIN Orders AS o ON c.CustomerID = o.CustomerID;
```

- Use short but meaningful aliases (`c` for `Customer`, not `x1`).

Error Handling Conventions

Structured error handling ensures that failures are captured consistently, making debugging and auditing easier.

- Use `TRY...CATCH` for structured error handling.
- Log errors into a standard error table.
- Return appropriate error codes or messages.

Example:

```
BEGIN TRY
    INSERT INTO Orders (CustomerID, OrderDate)
    VALUES (@CustomerID, GETDATE());
END TRY
BEGIN CATCH
    INSERT INTO ErrorLog (ErrorMessage, ErrorTime)
    VALUES (ERROR_MESSAGE(), GETDATE());
END CATCH;
```

Consistency in Data Types

Maintaining consistent data types across tables ensures data integrity, simplifies joins, and prevents unexpected conversion errors.

- Use consistent data types across related tables.
  Example: if `CustomerID` is `INT` in `Customer`, it should be `INT` in `Orders`.
- Avoid unnecessary use of large data types (`NVARCHAR(MAX)` unless required).
- Standardize use of `DATETIME2` over `DATETIME` for precision.

Example of a Well-Structured Procedure

```
/*
  Procedure: usp_GetOrdersByCustomer
  Author: Meron
  Date: 2025-08-30
  Purpose: Returns all orders for a given customer with optional date filters
*/
CREATE PROCEDURE dbo.usp_GetOrdersByCustomer
    @CustomerID INT,
    @StartDate DATE = NULL,
    @EndDate DATE = NULL
AS
BEGIN
    SET NOCOUNT ON;

    SELECT o.OrderID, o.OrderDate, o.TotalAmount
    FROM dbo.Orders AS o
```

```
    WHERE o.CustomerID = @CustomerID
      AND (@StartDate IS NULL OR o.OrderDate >= @StartDate)
      AND (@EndDate IS NULL OR o.OrderDate <= @EndDate);
END;
```

Thus, by enforcing these T-SQL coding standards and conventions, teams create a consistent development culture that ensures scalability, maintainability, and security across all database environments. Over time, these practices reduce technical debt, and make onboarding new developers significantly easier.

Query Design Best Practices

Designing efficient and maintainable queries is at the heart of T-SQL development. Queries that are poorly written can lead to performance bottlenecks, incorrect results, and higher operational costs in both on-premises and cloud environments. Query design is not only about producing the right answer but producing it fast, consistently, and at scale.

This section provides a comprehensive set of best practices for query design, organized into clear principles with detailed explanations, examples, and use cases.

Write for Clarity First, Optimize Second

A common mistake is writing cryptic queries that are difficult for others (or even your future self) to understand. Always prioritize readability and correctness before premature optimization.

- **Bad Practice (unclear):**

  ```
  SELECT c.id, c.n, o.amt
  FROM c, o
  WHERE c.i = o.i AND o.s = 'A'
  ```

- **Good Practice (clear, maintainable):**

  ```
  SELECT
      c.CustomerID,
      c.CustomerName,
      o.OrderAmount
  FROM Customers AS c
  INNER JOIN Orders AS o
      ON c.CustomerID = o.CustomerID
  WHERE o.Status = 'Active';
  ```

- Use meaningful aliases, descriptive column names, and indentation.
- Focus on making queries self-explanatory.

Avoid `SELECT *`

Using **`SELECT *`** retrieves all columns, which:

- Increases I/O and memory usage.
- Breaks applications, if schema changes.
- Prevents index optimization since unused columns are retrieved.

- Bad Practice:

```
SELECT * FROM Orders;
```

- Good Practice:

```
SELECT OrderID, OrderDate, CustomerID, TotalAmount
FROM Orders;
```

- Always list the exact columns required.
- Helps performance, and makes intent clear.

Use Proper Joins Instead of Subqueries Where Appropriate

Subqueries can be useful, but improper use leads to poor performance. Often, a join is more efficient and clearer.

- **Subquery Example**:

```
SELECT CustomerName
FROM Customers
WHERE CustomerID IN (SELECT CustomerID FROM Orders WHERE Status = 'Active');
```

- **Better with `Join`**:

```
SELECT DISTINCT c.CustomerName
FROM Customers AS c
INNER JOIN Orders AS o
    ON c.CustomerID = o.CustomerID
WHERE o.Status = 'Active';
```

- Joins are usually more optimizer-friendly than correlated subqueries.
- Use subqueries only when they make logic more intuitive.

Use Set-Based Logic, Avoid RBAR (Row-By-Agonizing-Row)

T-SQL is optimized for set-based operations, not row-by-row processing.

Avoid loops and cursors unless absolutely necessary.

- **Inefficient Cursor Example**:

```
DECLARE cur CURSOR FOR SELECT OrderID FROM Orders;
OPEN cur;
FETCH NEXT FROM cur INTO @OrderID;
WHILE @@FETCH_STATUS = 0
BEGIN
   UPDATE Orders SET Status = 'Processed' WHERE OrderID = @OrderID;
   FETCH NEXT FROM cur INTO @OrderID;
END
CLOSE cur;
DEALLOCATE cur;
```

- **Efficient Set-Based Query**:

  ```
  UPDATE Orders
  SET Status = 'Processed'
  WHERE Status = 'Pending';
  ```

  One set-based query can replace thousands of row-based updates.

Use Sargable Queries (Search-ARGument-Able)

A sargable query allows SQL Server to use indexes efficiently. Non-sargable queries force full scans.

- **Non-Sargable (bad)**:

  ```
  SELECT *
  FROM Orders
  WHERE YEAR(OrderDate) = 2025;
  ```

- **Sargable (good)**:

  ```
  SELECT *
  FROM Orders
  WHERE OrderDate >= '2025-01-01'
    AND OrderDate < '2026-01-01';
  ```

Always avoid wrapping columns in functions.

Rewrite predicates to maximize the index usage.

Be Careful with `NULLs` and Three-Valued Logic

`NULL` handling in SQL follows three-valued logic (**`TRUE`**, **`FALSE`**, **`UNKNOWN`**). This often leads to unexpected results.

- **Potential Issue**:

  ```
  SELECT * FROM Employees WHERE ManagerID <> 5;
  ```

  This query excludes rows where **`ManagerID IS NULL`** because **`NULL <> 5`** is **`UNKNOWN`**, not **`TRUE`**.

- **Correct Handling**:

  ```
  SELECT * FROM Employees
  WHERE ManagerID <> 5 OR ManagerID IS NULL;
  ```

  Always test queries with **`NULL`** values. Use **`IS NULL`** and **`IS NOT NULL`** explicitly.

Use CTEs and Window Functions Wisely

Common Table Expressions (CTEs) and window functions make queries more readable and powerful.

- **Example with CTE + Window Function**:

```
WITH OrderTotals AS (
    SELECT
        CustomerID,
        SUM(TotalAmount) AS TotalSpent
    FROM Orders
    GROUP BY CustomerID
)
```

```
SELECT
    CustomerID,
    TotalSpent,
    RANK() OVER (ORDER BY TotalSpent DESC) AS RankBySpending
FROM OrderTotals;
```

Use CTEs for modular query design. Use window functions for analytics without joins or subqueries.

Minimize Use of DISTINCT

DISTINCT often hides bad query design. It forces deduplication, which is costly.

- **Bad Practice:**

```
SELECT DISTINCT c.CustomerName, o.OrderAmount
FROM Customers c
JOIN Orders o ON c.CustomerID = o.CustomerID;
```

- **Better: Fix joins or use proper filtering.**

  Use **DISTINCT** only when logically required.

Summary

- Prioritize clarity and correctness.
- Avoid bad habits (**SELECT ***, non-sargable queries, and **DISTINCT** abuse).
- Favor set-based, sargable, and well-structured queries.
- Design for scalability and maintainability, not just short-term fixes.
- Benchmark and document every critical query.

User-Defined Objects

In SQL Server, user-defined objects are database objects created by developers to encapsulate business logic, extend SQL Server functionality, or improve maintainability and reusability. These objects include:

- User-Defined Data Types (UDTs)
- User-Defined Functions (UDFs)
- User-Defined Stored Procedures
- User-Defined Tables and Table Types
- User-Defined Schemas

When designed well, these objects promote consistency, enforce business rules, and improve productivity. However, misuse can result in performance bottlenecks, over-abstraction, or maintenance challenges. This section outlines the best practices for designing and managing user-defined objects.

User-Defined Data Types (UDTs)

UDTs allow developers to define custom data types based on existing system types. They enforce consistency in column definitions across tables.

Example:

```
-- Creating a UDT for Email
CREATE TYPE dbo.EmailAddress FROM NVARCHAR(320) NOT NULL;
```

Benefits:

- Consistency across tables and stored procedures.
- Centralized control of business rules.
- Improved readability in schema design.

Best Practices:

- Use UDTs for widely reused attributes (for example, Email, PhoneNumber).
- Avoid over-engineering (do not create a UDT for every column).
- Document the purpose of each UDT.

User-Defined Functions (UDFs)

UDFs encapsulate reusable logic that can be applied in queries, similar to functions in traditional programming.

Types:

1. **Scalar UDFs – return a single value.**

```
CREATE FUNCTION dbo.fnGetFullName(@FirstName NVARCHAR(50), @LastName
NVARCHAR(50))
RETURNS NVARCHAR(100)
AS
BEGIN
    RETURN RTRIM(@FirstName) + ' ' + RTRIM(@LastName);
END;
```

2. **Inline Table-Valued Functions (iTVFs) – return a table using a single `SELECT`.**

```
CREATE FUNCTION dbo.fnActiveCustomers()
RETURNS TABLE
AS
RETURN
    SELECT CustomerID, Name FROM dbo.Customers WHERE IsActive = 1;
```

3. **Multi-Statement Table-Valued Functions (mTVFs)** – return a table constructed through multiple statements.

Benefits:

- Promote reusability and modularity.
- Improve query readability.
- Centralize business logic.

Risks and Best Practices:

- Avoid scalar UDFs in **`SELECT`** statements – they can cause row-by-row execution and hurt performance. Prefer inline TVFs.
- Use iTVFs over mTVFs whenever possible.
- Test performance impacts before applying UDFs in production workloads.

User-Defined Stored Procedures

Stored procedures are compiled units of T-SQL that encapsulate logic for data manipulation, validation, and workflows.

Example:

```
CREATE PROCEDURE dbo.uspAddOrder
    @CustomerID INT,
    @OrderDate DATETIME,
    @TotalAmount DECIMAL(10,2)
AS
BEGIN
    SET NOCOUNT ON;

    INSERT INTO dbo.Orders(CustomerID, OrderDate, TotalAmount)
    VALUES (@CustomerID, @OrderDate, @TotalAmount);
END;
```

Benefits:

- Encapsulation of complex logic.
- Improved security (permissions can be applied to procedures instead of tables).
- Parameterization improves performance and reusability.

Best Practices:

- Use naming conventions (**`usp_ prefix`** or schema-based grouping).
- Keep procedures focused and modular.
- Avoid returning multiple unrelated result sets unless necessary.
- Use **`TRY...CATCH`** blocks for error handling.
- Favor parameterized stored procedures over dynamic SQL to prevent SQL injection.

User-Defined Tables and Table Types

SQL Server allows defining custom table types for structured parameters and temporary storage.

Example - Table Type:

```
CREATE TYPE dbo.OrderItemType AS TABLE
(
    ProductID INT,
    Quantity INT,
    Price DECIMAL(10,2)
);
```

Example - Using Table-Valued Parameter:

```
CREATE PROCEDURE dbo.uspInsertOrderItems
    @OrderItems dbo.OrderItemType READONLY
AS
BEGIN
    INSERT INTO dbo.OrderItems(ProductID, Quantity, Price)
    SELECT ProductID, Quantity, Price FROM @OrderItems;
END;
```

Benefits:

- Efficiently pass multiple rows as a parameter.
- Great for batch inserts or updates.

- Enforce structured data across procedures.

Best Practices:

- Use table-valued parameters instead of passing CSV strings.
- Define primary keys or unique constraints on table types when needed.
- Avoid excessive use in performance-critical loops.

User-Defined Schemas

Schemas are logical containers for database objects. They provide organizational clarity, and enable security boundaries.

Example:

```
CREATE SCHEMA Sales AUTHORIZATION dbo;
CREATE TABLE Sales.Orders(OrderID INT PRIMARY KEY, CustomerID INT);
```

Benefits:

- Logical grouping of objects (for example, Sales, HR, and Finance).
- Improved security – grant permissions at the schema level.
- Easier deployment and modularity.

Best Practices:

- Use schemas to group by business domain or functional area.
- Avoid dumping all objects in the dbo schema.
- Apply schema-based security for role management.

Common Pitfalls with User-Defined Objects

User-defined objects can improve modularity and code reuse, but improper usage can lead to performance and maintenance challenges.

- **Over-abstraction**: Creating too many objects for trivial tasks.
- **Performance bottlenecks**: Scalar UDF misuse or procedural-heavy stored procs.
- **Maintenance overhead**: Undocumented or inconsistently used objects.

Best Practices Summary

Following these guidelines ensure efficient, maintainable, and secure use of user-defined objects such as:

- Use UDTs sparingly for consistency.
- Prefer inline TVFs over scalar/multi-statement UDFs.
- Keep stored procedures modular and secured.
- Use table-valued parameters for batch operations.
- Organize objects with schemas for clarity and security.
- Always document and version-control user-defined objects.

Performance-Oriented Design

Designing databases and writing T-SQL code with performance in mind is critical to building scalable, reliable systems. Poorly designed queries or schema structures may function correctly, but they often become bottlenecks under heavy workloads, leading to slow response times, resource contention, and increased maintenance costs.

Performance-oriented design is not just about "making queries run faster"; it is about building databases and queries that scale, remain maintainable, and handle growth gracefully. This section focuses on best practices, techniques, and considerations for designing high-performance T-SQL solutions.

Indexing Strategy

Indexes are the backbone of performance tuning in SQL Server. They accelerate query execution by reducing the amount of data scanned. However, indexes also introduce overhead for data modifications (**INSERT**, **UPDATE**, **DELETE**).

Types of Indexes:

- **Clustered Indexes**: Organize data physically on disk. Each table can have one.
- **Non-Clustered Indexes**: Logical copies of data that speed up read operations.
- **Filtered Indexes**: Cover a subset of data for queries with predictable filters.
- **Columnstore Indexes**: Optimized for analytics and large aggregations.

Example:

```
-- Creating a non-clustered index for faster lookups
CREATE NONCLUSTERED INDEX IX_Customers_Email
ON dbo.Customers (EmailAddress)
INCLUDE (FirstName, LastName);
```

Best Practices:

- Design indexes based on query patterns, not guesses.
- Use covering indexes (INCLUDE columns) to reduce lookups.
- Avoid over-indexing; balance read and write performance.
- Regularly monitor fragmentation and unused indexes.

Query Optimization

Well-designed queries minimize resource consumption, while returning the correct results.

Techniques:

1. **Avoid `SELECT *`**: Fetch only needed columns.

   ```
   SELECT CustomerID, FirstName FROM dbo.Customers WHERE IsActive = 1;
   ```

2. **Use Proper Joins**: Choose **INNER JOIN**, **LEFT JOIN**, or **EXISTS** based on logic.
3. **Filter Early**: Apply restrictive **WHERE** clauses before aggregation.
4. **Leverage Set-Based Operations**: Replace row-by-row logic with set-based queries.

Example – Poor vs. Optimized:

✗ Row-by-row update

```
DECLARE cur CURSOR FOR SELECT OrderID FROM dbo.Orders;
-- Updates executed one row at a time (very slow)
  Set-based update
```

```
UPDATE dbo.Orders
SET Status = 'Shipped'
WHERE ShipDate <= GETDATE();
```

Data Modeling for Performance

The physical design of tables and relationships significantly impacts query performance.

Key Considerations:

- **Normalization vs. Denormalization**
  - Normalize to reduce redundancy and anomalies.
  - Denormalize selectively for reporting or high-read workloads.
- **Data Types**
  - Use the smallest possible data type (`TINYINT` vs `INT`, `CHAR(2)` vs `VARCHAR(50)`).
  - Avoid overusing `NVARCHAR(MAX)` unless necessary.
- **Partitioning**
  - Split large tables into partitions for faster query access.
- **Constraints**
  - Use primary keys, foreign keys, and check constraints to enforce integrity and assist the optimizer.

TempDB and Intermediate Storage

Temporary storage (TempDB, table variables, temp tables) often affects performance.

Best Practices:

- Use temp tables (`#TempTable`) for large intermediate datasets.
- Use table variables only for small, lightweight sets.
- Index temporary structures if used in joins.
- Monitor TempDB contention with multiple data files.

Execution Plans and Statistics

SQL Server uses statistics and execution plans to decide the most efficient query path.

Best Practices:

- Always review execution plans for slow queries.
- Keep statistics up-to-date using `AUTO UPDATE STATISTICS`.
- Identify missing indexes and expensive operators.
- Use query hints only as a last resort.

Concurrency and Locking

High concurrency environments require careful handling of locks and isolation levels.

Techniques:

- Use appropriate isolation levels (`READ COMMITTED`, `SNAPSHOT`).

- Keep transactions short and narrow to minimize blocking.
- Use optimistic concurrency when possible.

Example:

```
SET TRANSACTION ISOLATION LEVEL SNAPSHOT;
BEGIN TRAN;
-- Business logic here
COMMIT;
```

Transaction and Concurrency Management

One of the most critical aspects of designing robust T-SQL solutions is the proper management of transactions and concurrent access. Transactions ensure data consistency and integrity, while concurrency control balances multiple users accessing the same resources simultaneously, without creating blocking, deadlocks, or dirty reads.

In enterprise systems where thousands of queries execute concurrently, poor transaction design can lead to severe bottlenecks, application errors, and even data corruption. This section explores the principles, isolation levels, patterns, and best practices for effective transaction and concurrency management.

Fundamentals of Transactions

A transaction is a logical unit of work that must follow the ACID properties:

- **Atomicity**: All statements within a transaction succeed or none do.
- **Consistency**: The database transitions from one valid state to another.
- **Isolation**: Transactions do not interfere with each other.
- **Durability**: Once committed, changes are permanent, even in case of failure.

Example:

```
BEGIN TRANSACTION;

UPDATE dbo.Accounts
SET Balance = Balance - 500
WHERE AccountID = 1001;

UPDATE dbo.Accounts
SET Balance = Balance + 500
WHERE AccountID = 1002;

COMMIT TRANSACTION;  -- Ensures both succeed or both fail
```

If either statement fails, a `ROLLBACK` restores data to its original state.

Explicit versus Implicit Transactions

- **Implicit Transactions**: SQL Server automatically starts a new transaction after each commit/rollback.
- **Explicit Transactions**: Controlled by the developer using `BEGIN TRAN`, `COMMIT`, `ROLLBACK`.

☞ **Best Practice:** Always use explicit transactions for multi-statement operations to avoid ambiguity.

Transaction Scope and Lifetime

Key Guidelines:

- Keep transactions short: Long transactions hold locks longer, causing blocking.
- Avoid user interaction inside a transaction (for example, waiting for input).
- Access objects in a consistent order across transactions to reduce deadlocks.
- Use savepoints for partial rollbacks:

```
BEGIN TRANSACTION;

UPDATE dbo.Orders SET Status = 'Processing' WHERE OrderID = 101;
SAVE TRANSACTION BeforeInventory;

UPDATE dbo.Inventory SET Quantity = Quantity - 1 WHERE ItemID = 500;

IF @@ERROR <> 0
    ROLLBACK TRANSACTION BeforeInventory;

COMMIT TRANSACTION;
```

Concurrency Control and Isolation Levels

SQL Server provides several transaction isolation levels to balance consistency and concurrency:

1. **READ UNCOMMITTED** – Allows dirty reads (fastest, least safe).
2. **READ COMMITTED (default)** – Prevents dirty reads but allows non-repeatable reads.
3. **REPEATABLE READ** – Prevents dirty and non-repeatable reads but not phantom rows.
4. **SERIALIZABLE** – Strictest; prevents all anomalies but reduces concurrency.
5. **SNAPSHOT** – Uses row versioning to eliminate locks and blocking (requires tempdb version store).

Example:

```
SET TRANSACTION ISOLATION LEVEL SNAPSHOT;

BEGIN TRANSACTION;
SELECT * FROM dbo.Customers WHERE Country = 'USA';
COMMIT;
```

Best Practice: Choose the lowest isolation level that still guarantees correctness.

Deadlocks and Blocking

Understanding blocking and deadlocks is critical for ensuring smooth SQL Server transaction processing, and avoiding performance bottlenecks.

- Blocking occurs when one transaction holds a lock needed by another.
- Deadlocks occur when two transactions block each other cyclically.

Preventing Deadlocks:

- Access tables in the same order across transactions.
- Keep transactions short and simple.
- Use appropriate indexes to reduce locking overhead.
- Monitor with SQL Server Profiler or Extended Events.

Example of Deadlock-Prone Access:

- Transaction A updates Customers then Orders.
- Transaction B updates Orders then Customers.

☞ This inconsistent order creates a potential deadlock.

Optimistic versus Pessimistic Concurrency

Choosing the right concurrency control strategy helps maintain data integrity, while optimizing performance in multi-user environments.

- **Pessimistic Concurrency**: Assumes conflicts will occur → uses locks to prevent them.
- **Optimistic Concurrency**: Assumes conflicts are rare → checks row versions before committing.

Example - Optimistic Check:

```
UPDATE dbo.Products
SET Price = 50, RowVersion = RowVersion + 1
WHERE ProductID = 200 AND RowVersion = @CurrentRowVersion;

IF @@ROWCOUNT = 0
    PRINT 'Concurrency conflict detected!';
```

- **Best Practice:** Use optimistic concurrency in high-read environments (like OLTP web apps).

Maintainability and Refactoring

As database systems evolve, queries, stored procedures, and other T-SQL code often undergo numerous changes. A design that may work today can become inefficient, unreadable, or fragile tomorrow if not written with maintainability and adaptability in mind. Poorly structured T-SQL leads to technical debt, making enhancements, debugging, and optimization costly.

Maintainability and refactoring practices ensure that T-SQL solutions remain readable, consistent, testable, and adaptable in the long term. This section provides strategies, patterns, and best practices for sustainable database development.

Principles of Maintainable T-SQL

Writing maintainable T-SQL ensures long-term readability, reduces errors, and simplifies future enhancements.

- **Readability**: Queries should be self-explanatory with proper formatting, indentation, and naming.
- **Consistency**: Follow coding standards and conventions across teams.
- **Modularity**: Break complex logic into smaller stored procedures, functions, or views.
- **Testability**: Code should be easily testable with predictable outputs.
- **Flexibility**: Queries should anticipate schema changes, and be adaptable.

☞ Think of T-SQL not only as code for machines but as documentation for future developers.

Refactoring Strategies

"Refactoring" means improving internal code structure without changing its external behavior. Common refactoring activities in T-SQL include:

- **Eliminating duplicate logic**: For example, replace repeated filtering logic across queries with a view or inline table-valued function.
- **Breaking down monolithic queries**: A single 200-line stored procedure should be split into smaller, reusable units.
- **Replacing procedural loops with set-based logic**: Replace `WHILE` loops with set operations for efficiency and readability.
- **Simplifying joins and subqueries**: Remove unnecessary subqueries and replace with CTEs or window functions.
- **Parameterization**: Refactor hardcoded values into parameters for reusability.

Documentation and Commenting

Maintainability is strongly tied to documentation quality.

- **Use header comments in stored procedures/functions**:

```
/* Procedure: usp_GetActiveOrders
   Author: A. Developer
   Created: 2025-08-31
   Purpose: Returns all active orders with customer info.
   Notes: Optimized for orders placed in the last 12 months. */
```

- Add inline comments only where the logic is not obvious.
- Keep comments updated during refactoring—outdated comments create confusion.

Version Control for T-SQL

SQL code should be managed in a Version Control System (VCS) like Git.

- Store schema objects, procedures, functions, and scripts in a repository.
- Use branching strategies (for example, GitFlow) for collaborative work.
- Tag and label releases to match database deployments.
- Refactor code in feature branches, test, and merge only after validation.

☞ **Treat T-SQL like application code:** It should always be under version control.

Modularization and Reuse

Well-structured, modular code is easier to maintain such as:

- Use views to encapsulate common queries.
- Use inline table-valued functions for reusable result sets.
- Use stored procedures for repeatable business logic.
- Apply schema separation (Sales, H.R., Finance, and so on) for logical grouping.

Example:

```
Instead of repeating a join across 10 queries:
SELECT o.OrderID, c.CustomerName
FROM dbo.Orders o
JOIN dbo.Customers c ON o.CustomerID = c.CustomerID;
```

Refactor into a view:

```
CREATE VIEW dbo.vw_OrderCustomers AS
SELECT o.OrderID, c.CustomerName
FROM dbo.Orders o
JOIN dbo.Customers c ON o.CustomerID = c.CustomerID;
```

Now, simply query:

```
SELECT * FROM dbo.vw_OrderCustomers WHERE CustomerName LIKE 'A%';
```

Testing and Validation

Maintainable codes must be easy to test such as:

- Write unit tests for stored procedures and functions.
- Use test databases with representative data sets.
- Automate testing for performance regressions after refactoring.
- Implement error handling consistently with TRY...CATCH blocks.

☞ **Example:** Before refactoring a complex query, capture the baseline execution time, and compare after changes.

Security and Auditing Practices

Security and auditing in SQL Server environments go beyond merely controlling access. They form the backbone of trustworthy database systems, ensuring data confidentiality, integrity, and availability, while also providing mechanisms for accountability and compliance.

Thus, as regulations like GDPR, HIPAA, SOX, and PCI DSS tighten, organizations are held to high standards regarding data handling. A secure database environment not only protects sensitive information but also ensures that all access and modifications are monitored, auditable, and traceable.

In this section, we explore the best practices for implementing robust security, and auditing strategies in T-SQL development.

Principles of Database Security

Before diving into technical practices, it is essential to understand the three security pillars:

- **Confidentiality**: Protecting data from unauthorized access.
- **Integrity**: Preventing unauthorized changes or corruption.
- **Availability**: Ensuring that the data is accessible to authorized users when needed.

A good security design always balances usability vs. control – overly strict controls may hinder productivity, while weak controls expose data to risks.

Authentication Best Practices

Authentication verifies who the user is. In SQL Server, two main modes exist:

- Windows Authentication (Preferred) – Integrates with Active Directory; offers Kerberos support, password policies, and stronger security.
- SQL Server Authentication – Uses SQL logins with passwords stored in SQL Server; typically used when Windows Auth is not possible.

Best Practices:

- Always prefer Windows Authentication for enterprise systems.
- Enforce strong password policies if SQL Authentication is used.
- Use Azure Active Directory authentication for hybrid/cloud workloads.
- Minimize shared logins; instead, assign individual accounts for traceability.

Authorization and Principle of Least Privilege

"**Authorization**" defines what the user can do. SQL Server provides granular permission control at the object and database level.

Best Practices:

- Adopt Principle of Least Privilege (POLP) – users should only have the minimum permissions required to perform their jobs.
- Use roles rather than granting permissions directly to users.
- Separate read-only, read-write, and administrative roles.
- Periodically review and revoke unused permissions.

Example: Instead of **granting db_datawriter**, create a custom role with only the necessary **INSERT** or **UPDATE** permissions.

Securing Sensitive Data

Databases often contain Personally Identifiable Information (PII) or financial records. Protecting such data is critical.

Techniques:

- **Row-Level Security (RLS)**: Limit rows returned to users based on policies.
- **Dynamic Data Masking (DDM)**: Mask sensitive fields (for example, show XXXX-1234 instead of full credit card).
- **Column Encryption**: Encrypt sensitive columns like SSNs or credit card numbers.
- **Transparent Data Encryption (TDE)**: Encrypts entire database files at rest.

💡 Combine RLS + DDM + Encryption for multi-layered protection.

SQL Injection Prevention

SQL injection remains one of the most common attack vectors.

Best Practices:

- Always use parameterized queries instead of dynamic SQL.
- Avoid string concatenation in queries.
- Use stored procedures with strict input validation.
- Enable SQL injection detection in Web Application Firewalls (WAF).

Example:

❌ **Vulnerable**:

```
EXEC('SELECT * FROM Users WHERE Username = ''' + @username + '''');
 Safe:
```

```
EXEC sp_executesql N'SELECT * FROM Users WHERE Username = @Username', N'@Username
NVARCHAR(50)', @Username;
```

Auditing Database Activities

"`Auditing`" provides traceability, and helps to satisfy compliance requirements.

Options in SQL Server:

- SQL Server Audit: Logs events like logins, schema changes, permission changes.
- Change Data Capture (CDC): Captures data changes for replication or auditing.
- Temporal Tables: Maintain historical versions of records automatically.
- Custom Triggers: Capture specific DML operations.

💡 Always store audit logs in tamper-proof storage (for example, WORM storage, SIEM integration, and so on).

Tooling and Modern Development Workflows

Modern T-SQL development no longer happens in isolation. Developers and database administrators (DBAs) increasingly rely on specialized tooling, automation, and collaborative workflows to accelerate delivery, reduce human error, and enforce quality standards. In this section, we explore the key tools and practices that modern SQL professionals should adopt, along with strategies for integrating T-SQL development into broader DevOps pipelines.

Integrated Development Environments (IDEs)

Choosing the right IDE enhances productivity, collaboration, and the efficiency of T-SQL development and administration.

- **SQL Server Management Studio (SSMS):** The classic environment for managing SQL Server instances, debugging queries, and administering databases. Still the go-to for DBAs.
- **Azure Data Studio (ADS):** A lightweight, cross-platform IDE for T-SQL development, offering extensions, source control integration, and Jupyter notebook support.
- **Third-Party IDEs (for example, `DataGrip`, `DBeaver`, and `SentryOne` Plan Explorer):** Provide additional capabilities such as query profiling, visual explain plans, and database comparison tools.

Best practice: Choose an IDE that balances productivity features with compatibility for your team's workflows. Thus, ADS is preferred in DevOps and cross-platform environments, while SSMS remains strong for administration-heavy tasks.

Source Control for Database Code

Just as application code belongs to source control, so does T-SQL code:

- **Version Control Systems (VCS):** GitHub, Azure Repos, or GitLab ensure that scripts, stored procedures, and schema definitions are tracked over time.
- **Schema-as-Code:** Tools like Redgate SQL Source Control or SSDT (SQL Server Data Tools) allow database schema changes to be versioned alongside the application code.
- **Benefits:**
  - Enables team collaboration.

  - Supports rollback and history tracking.
  - Provides traceability for compliance.

Continuous Integration (CI) for Databases

CI ensures that database changes are automatically validated, before being merged into production.

- **Build Pipelines:** Tools such as Azure DevOps, Jenkins, or GitHub Actions can build and validate SQL scripts.
- **Unit Testing**: Frameworks like tSQLt are integrated into pipelines to automatically run regression tests.
- **Static Code Analysis:** Automated tools check T-SQL code for performance issues, deprecated features, or security flaws.

Continuous Delivery (CD) and Deployment

CD automates the deployment of schema and data changes across environments (dev → test → staging → production).

- **Schema Migration Tools:** Flyway, Liquibase, or Redgate SQL Change Automation track incremental changes.
- **State-Based vs. Migration-Based Deployment:**
  - **State-based** (for example, SSDT): Compares target database to a model and applies differences.
  - **Migration-based** (for example, Flyway): Applies step-by-step change scripts, offering fine-grained control.
- **Rollback Strategies**: Always design deployments with safe rollback scripts or backup plans.

Infrastructure as Code (IaC) for Databases

Databases are increasingly managed via IaC tools:

- ARM Templates, Terraform, or Bicep can provision SQL Server or Azure SQL Databases.
- **Benefits:**
  - Ensures repeatable, consistent environments.
  - Speeds up onboarding and disaster recovery.
  - Reduces manual configuration errors.

Error Handling, Cost Management, Network Security, Cloud Readiness, and CI/CD Automation

Modern DevOps pipelines for SQL Server workloads must be designed with cloud readiness and continuous delivery in mind. In addition to automation, pipelines should account for reliability, security, scalability, and operational efficiency across cloud and hybrid environments.

- **Error handling** is essential to ensure deterministic pipeline behavior. Database deployments, SSIS executions, and automated SQL scripts should immediately fail when errors occur, with detailed logs and SQL Server error messages captured for troubleshooting. This prevents partial executions and inconsistent database states.

- **Cost management** is particularly important in cloud environments where database resources may be provisioned dynamically. Pipelines should minimize unnecessary resource usage by controlling execution time, scaling resources appropriately, and deallocating or pausing services when they are no longer required. Monitoring resource consumption during CI/CD execution helps prevent unexpected operational costs.
- **Network security** must be enforced at every stage of the pipeline. Secure authentication, encrypted connections, and restricted network access should be used when connecting to SQL Server instances. Secrets and credentials should be stored securely using managed identity services or secret vaults, rather than embedded directly in pipeline definitions.
- **Cloud readiness** requires database solutions to be designed for elasticity, resilience, and automation. Pipelines should support infrastructure-as-code, environment-specific configurations, and repeatable deployments across development, testing, and production environments. Database scripts and SSIS packages should be cloud-compatible and capable of operating in scalable and distributed environments.
- **CI/CD automation** enables consistent and repeatable database delivery. Version-controlled database objects, automated testing, and environment-specific deployment stages ensure that changes are validated before reaching production. Integrating SQL Server tasks into CI/CD workflows reduces manual intervention, improves release reliability, and supports rapid iteration.

Thus, by addressing error handling, cost management, network security, cloud readiness, and CI/CD automation together, DevOps pipelines can deliver secure, scalable, and cost-efficient SQL Server deployments that align with modern cloud-first architectures.

Best Practices Summary

Therefore, following the structured best practices ensures reliable, maintainable, and high-quality SQL development and deployment.

- Keep all SQL code in source control.
- Automate testing and deployments through CI/CD.
- Use database migration tools to minimize risks.
- Adopt Infrastructure as Code for consistent environments.
- Enforce quality gates (linting, testing, and peer review).
- Use monitoring tools to create feedback loops for continuous improvement.

Common Anti-Patterns to Avoid in TSQL

Even highly skilled developers can fall into certain T-SQL pitfalls that degrade performance, increase maintenance costs, or even compromise security. Identifying these anti-patterns is as important as learning best practices because avoiding them often provides immediate improvements in query speed, reliability, and scalability.

This section will explore common T-SQL anti-patterns, explain why they are problematic, and provide recommended alternatives.

The "`SELECT *`" Anti-Pattern

Problem: Using `SELECT *` retrieves all columns, including the unnecessary ones, which:

- **Problem**: Using `SELECT *` retrieves all columns, including unnecessary ones, which:

  - Increases I/O and memory usage.
  - Breaks applications if schema changes (for example, new columns appear).
  - Prevents query optimization, since the engine cannot prune unneeded columns.
- **Example**:

```
SELECT * FROM Orders;
```

- **Preferred Approach**: Explicitly select only the required columns.

```
SELECT OrderID, CustomerID, OrderDate
FROM Orders;
```

Cursors for Row-by-Row Processing

Cursors loop row by row, which is inefficient compared to set-based operations. They cause locking overhead, and consume tempdb resources.

- **Problem**:
  - Cursors loop row by row, which is inefficient compared to set-based operations.
  - They cause locking overhead and consume tempdb resources.
- **Bad Example:**

```
DECLARE cur CURSOR FOR
SELECT CustomerID FROM Customers;
```

- **Preferred Approach**:

  Replace with set-based operations or window functions:

```
UPDATE Customers
SET CreditLimit = CreditLimit * 1.1
WHERE Region = 'West';
```

Scalar Functions in SELECT or WHERE

Using scalar functions in queries can severely degrade performance and limit the query optimizer's ability to parallelize work.

- **Problem**:
  - Scalar UDFs force row-by-row execution.
  - They prevent the optimizer from parallelizing queries.
- **Example**:

```
SELECT CustomerID
FROM Customers
WHERE dbo.fn_GetRegion(CustomerID) = 'West';
```

- **Preferred Approach**:

  Inline table-valued functions or **JOIN**s:

```
SELECT c.CustomerID
FROM Customers c
JOIN Regions r ON c.RegionID = r.RegionID
WHERE r.Name = 'West';
```

Overuse of Triggers

Triggers can hide business logic, and create unexpected behavior, making code harder to maintain and debug.

- **Problem**:
  - Hidden business logic leads to unpredictability.
  - Recursive triggers create maintenance nightmares.
  - Performance issues when large updates fire triggers unnecessarily.
- **Preferred Approach**:
  - Use stored procedures or explicit constraints.
  - Keep triggers small, transparent, and documented, if unavoidable.

Improper Index Usage

Efficient indexing is crucial for query performance; improper index design can lead to slow queries and high maintenance overhead.

- **Common Mistakes**:
  - Missing Indexes: Leading to full table scans.
  - Too Many Indexes: Slows down inserts/updates.
  - Non-SARGable Predicates (for example, `WHERE YEAR(OrderDate) = 2025`).
- **Preferred Approach**:
  - Use the Database Engine Tuning Advisor or DMVs to analyze index usage.
  - Design covering indexes for critical queries.
  - Rewrite predicates to be SARGable:
  - ```
    -- Bad
    WHERE YEAR(OrderDate) = 2025;
    ```
  - ```
    -- Good
    WHERE OrderDate >= '2025-01-01' AND OrderDate < '2026-01-01';
    ```

Hard-Coded Values

Embedding literal values directly in SQL queries reduces flexibility, and increases maintenance overhead.

- **Problem**:
  - Leads to rigid, unmaintainable SQL code.
  - Causes duplication when business logic changes.
- **Preferred Approach**:
  - Store values in configuration tables or parameters.
  - Use variables in stored procedures.

Design for Portability and Cloud Readiness

Modern database development requires not only high performance and maintainability but also portability across environments and readiness for cloud deployment. Portability ensures that your database can migrate between development, staging, and production environments — or even between on-premises SQL Server and cloud platforms like Azure SQL Database, AWS RDS, or Google Cloud SQL — without major rewrites. Cloud readiness ensures that the database can leverage cloud-native features such as elasticity, security, and automated management.

This section explores best practices for designing databases that are environment-agnostic, maintainable, and optimized for cloud deployment.

Avoiding Platform-Specific Features

Relying on proprietary SQL Server features can limit portability, and complicate future migrations.

- **Problem**: Using SQL Server-only features (for example, certain T-SQL system functions, SQLCLR, or proprietary partitioning) can prevent migration to other platforms.
- **Recommended Approach**:
    - Favor ANSI-standard SQL for queries and schema.
    - Isolate platform-specific logic in stored procedures or service layers.
    - Document all platform dependencies clearly for migration planning.

Parameterization and Environment Configuration

Configuring environment-specific settings in a flexible way ensures that your SQL code is portable and maintainable across development, test, and production environments.

- **Problem**: Hard-coded server names, file paths, or database references hinder portability.
- **Recommended Approach**:
    - Use variables, parameters, or configuration tables to handle environment-specific settings.
    - Use environment-specific connection strings stored in configuration files or secrets managers.
    - **Example**:

```
DECLARE @TargetDB NVARCHAR(100) = (SELECT Value FROM Config WHERE Name = 
'TargetDB');
EXEC('USE ' + @TargetDB + '; SELECT COUNT(*) FROM Customers;');
```

Schema Versioning and Migrations

Maintaining a controlled and versioned approach to database schema changes ensures consistency, portability, and safe deployment across environments.

- **Problem**: Direct updates to production schema complicate portability and versioning.
- **Recommended Approach**:
    - Implement schema versioning using tools like Flyway, Liquibase, or SSDT.
    - Use migration scripts instead of ad-hoc DDL changes.
    - Maintain environment-specific branches in source control to synchronize changes across dev, test, and production.

Use of Compatible Data Types

Choosing widely supported and standard data types ensures portability, consistent behavior, and easier cloud migration.

- **Problem**: Platform-specific data types (for example, `MONEY`, `SMALLDATETIME`, `SQL_VARIANT`) may not exist or behave differently in the cloud.
- **Recommended Approach**:
  - Use standard and widely supported data types like `DECIMAL`, `DATETIME2`, `NVARCHAR`.
  - Avoid relying on implementation-specific behaviors (for example, string padding).
  - Consider cloud scaling requirements — for example, prefer `INT/BIGINT` over `NUMERIC` for large-scale datasets.

Avoid Tightly Coupled Dependencies

Minimizing tight dependencies between databases and applications improves flexibility, maintainability, and cloud portability.

- **Problem**: Hard dependencies between databases, services, or external applications reduce flexibility and portability.
- **Recommended Approach**:
  - Use abstraction layers via views, APIs, or stored procedures.
  - Decouple data access logic from business logic wherever possible.
  - Apply microservice-friendly database design, if planning for cloud-native architectures.

Leveraging Cloud-Native Features

Designing databases to take full advantage of cloud-native capabilities ensures scalability, reliability, and reduced operational overhead.

- **Elastic Scaling**: Design tables and indexes with sharding, partitioning, or horizontal scaling in mind to handle growth in cloud environments.
- **Automatic Backups and Geo-Replication:** Ensure that the schema supports cloud backup policies and disaster recovery options.
- **Serverless or PaaS Considerations:** Avoid designs that assume control over storage or server-level settings, as cloud services handle these automatically.

Conclusion

This chapter consolidates the knowledge gained throughout the book into a comprehensive set of best practices. You learned how to write clean, efficient, and maintainable T-SQL code, make performance-oriented design decisions, and enforce security and auditing standards.

The chapter also covered architectural principles, transaction and concurrency management, as well as modern development workflows including CI/CD integration. By following these practices, you are equipped to build robust, scalable, and maintainable database solutions that adhere to industry standards.

To conclude, as this is the final chapter, readers are now well-prepared to apply all the skills, techniques, and strategies from previous chapters in real-world SQL Server environments, combining optimization, security, automation, and modern development approaches for long-term success.

Index

B

E

J

K

L

M

N

O

P

Q